Fraud Analytics in Action

Abdelrahim Al Aqqad

Fraud Analytics in Action

Data Science and Machine Learning Techniques for Detecting Fraud in the Digital Age

palgrave
macmillan

Abdelrahim Al Aqqad
Doha, Qatar

ISBN 978-3-032-16022-5 ISBN 978-3-032-16023-2 (eBook)
https://doi.org/10.1007/978-3-032-16023-2

This Palgrave Macmillan imprint is published by the registered company Springer Nature Switzerland AG
The registered company address is: Gewerbestrasse 11, 6330 Cham, Switzerland

Competing Interests The author has no competing interests to declare that are relevant to the content of this manuscript.

Contents

List of Figures

Understanding Fraud: Numbers, Definitions, and the Fraud Triangle

Different Types of Fraud and Their Impact

Fraud Analytics and Its Importance

The Fraud Management Cycle with Key Components of Fraud Analytics

Techniques and Approaches in Fraud Analytics

Data Preparation Techniques

Feature Engineering

Advanced Feature Engineering Techniques for Fraud Analytics

Handling Imbalanced Data Sets

Unsupervised Learning Techniques

Clustering for Fraud Detection

Regression in Fraud Detection

Classification Techniques in Supervised Learning

Fraud Detection Excellence—A Deep Exploration of Model Metrics, Optimization, and Governance

Fraud and Social Network Analysis

Social Network Analysis Practical Examples

Fraudulent Patterns: Unveiling Deception Through Text Analysis and Topic Modeling

List of Tables

Feature Engineering

Advanced Feature Engineering Techniques for Fraud Analytics

Handling Imbalanced Data Sets

Unsupervised Learning Techniques

Classification Techniques in Supervised Learning

PART I

Introduction to Fraud

Fraud costs the global economy trillions of dollars annually—and the scale, speed, and sophistication of fraudulent schemes continue to grow. Tackling it effectively requires more than intuition or experience; it demands a structured understanding of what fraud is, how it operates, and what analytical tools are available to detect and prevent it. Part I builds that foundation across five chapters. Chapter 1 opens with the fundamentals—definitions, global statistics, and the Fraud Triangle, the enduring model that explains fraud through pressure, opportunity, and rationalisation. Chapter 2 broadens the view, mapping the many forms fraud takes—from financial statement manipulation and insurance fraud to payment card crime and cyber-enabled schemes—and examining their economic and reputational consequences. Chapter 3 introduces fraud analytics as a discipline, making the case for why data-driven approaches have become essential in modern fraud management. Chapter 4 places those approaches within the Fraud Management Cycle, tracing the full arc from prevention and detection through to investigation and response. Chapter 5 completes Part I with a survey of the core analytical methods available to practitioners—rule-based systems, machine learning, deep learning, hybrid approaches, and specialised techniques including anomaly detection, social network analysis, and text analytics—along with a discussion of model interpretability and the ethical responsibilities that accompany AI-driven fraud detection. By the end of Part I, you will have the conceptual grounding and methodological vocabulary needed to engage with the practical data engineering, modelling, and application work that follows in Parts II, III, IV, and V.

CHAPTER 1

Understanding Fraud: Numbers, Definitions, and the Fraud Triangle

This chapter lays the groundwork for understanding and counteracting fraud. It introduces the nature of fraud, explains why it occurs, and highlights the conditions that enable it to persist. With this foundation, the reader will be better prepared to explore the concepts and applications of fraud analytics later in this book.

Fraud is a pervasive problem that wreaks havoc across individual, business, and governmental realms. This chapter commences by offering a broad picture of fraud, highlighting its prevalence from grassroots to federal levels. The most commonly reported forms of fraud are examined, as well as the sectors perceived as most vulnerable. The statistics presented underline the urgent need for proficient fraud analytics.

Fraud can manifest in numerous forms, from identity theft and insurance fraud to credit card and online fraud. This chapter introduces the broader fraud landscape and clarifies the often-misunderstood distinctions between fraud, abuse, and waste. More detailed discussion of specific fraud types is provided in the following chapter.

A crucial part of understanding fraud is the *Fraud Triangle*, a model that elucidates the three elements necessary for fraud to occur: opportunity, pressure, and rationalization. The reader will learn how fraudsters exploit these elements and how their manipulation sets the stage for fraudulent activities. Strategies for mitigating the risk of fraud by eliminating conditions that encourage fraudulent behaviors are also explored.

A. Al Aqqad, *Fraud Analytics in Action*
https://doi.org/10.1007/978-3-032-16023-2_1

Fraud in Numbers and Fraud Analytics

The vast scope of fraud stretches across numerous industries and regions. Looking at the numbers clarifies the sheer magnitude of the fraud issue and underlines the vital role of effective fraud analytics in tackling it.

Fraud continues to have a significant impact on the global economy, affecting various industries. According to the latest Association of Certified Fraud Examiners[1] (ACFE) Report to the Nations (2024), organizations worldwide lose approximately 5% of their annual revenues to fraud. This percentage translates into staggering global losses of nearly $5 trillion annually, highlighting the need for robust fraud prevention and detection strategies.

Furthermore, data from *the Nilson Report*[2] indicate that global payment card fraud losses reached approximately $33.83 billion in 2023. Looking ahead, Nilson Report-related coverage indicates that global card payment fraud losses are projected to reach approximately $403.88 billion cumulatively over the next ten years. These numbers emphasize the growing urgency for more effective fraud detection mechanisms, especially as financial transactions increasingly move into the digital space.

Regulatory evidence[3] further supports this trajectory. According to the Federal Trade Commission's Consumer Sentinel Network data, U.S. consumers reported over $12.5 billion in fraud losses in 2024, a 25% increase from 2023. The FTC received roughly 2.6 million fraud reports in 2024, including substantial losses from investment scams, imposter scams, and other online fraud categories. Overall fraud and identity theft complaints numbered in the millions, with identity theft accounting for more than 1.1 million reports for the year. These figures illustrate the scale and growing economic impact of fraud on consumers and underscore the critical role of advanced fraud analytics in mitigating escalating risks.

[1] Association of Certified Fraud Examiners. *Occupational Fraud 2024: Report to the Nations* (ACFE, 2024). Estimates indicate that typical organizations lose about 5% of revenue annually to fraud.

[2] The Nilson Report. *Annual Fraud Statistics* (The Nilson Report, 2025). Global payment card fraud losses reached approximately $33.83 billion in 2023, with industry projections indicating continued large-scale growth.

[3] Federal Trade Commission. (2025). *Consumer Sentinel Network Data Book 2024.*

Through the understanding of fraud in numbers, organizations can better prepare themselves to thwart and detect fraudulent conduct. This comprehension is enhanced by examining pertinent metrics, such as the one illustrated in Fig. 1.1, which provides a visual insight into the correlation between the duration of a fraudulent act and the corresponding financial damage.

Fighting fraud is a challenging task because it evolves. Organizations must constantly update their fraud prevention and detection systems because fraudsters adapt to new technologies and methods. For example, following the COVID-19 outbreak, scammers began targeting healthcare businesses, online scams, and government programs such as unemployment assistance.

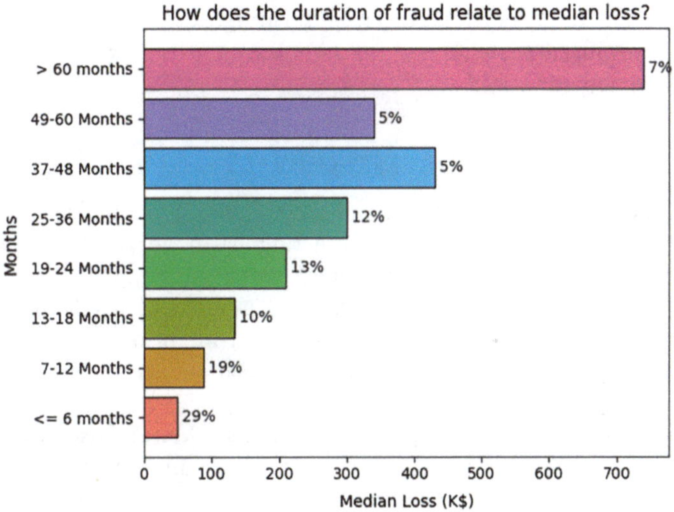

Fig. 1.1 Relationship between fraud duration and median loss. Short-duration fraud cases (six months or less) represent the highest proportion of incidents (29%) but carry the lowest median losses. In contrast, long-duration cases exceeding 60 months account for only 7% of cases yet result in the highest median losses, reaching approximately $740K. This inverse relationship demonstrates that financial impact is strongly driven by how long fraud remains undetected. From a governance perspective, fraud duration serves as a proxy indicator of control effectiveness, underscoring the importance of early detection strategies and continuous monitoring to minimize financial damage.

> NOTE
>
> This is where fraud analytics come into play. Organizations need to utilize advanced analytics and machine learning approaches to identify and thwart fraudulent behavior effectively. This entails sifting through enormous data sets for trends and abnormalities that could suggest fraudulent activity using statistical techniques and data analytics. An essential component of fraud analytics is developing models and strategies that can be used to predict and prevent future fraud.

> TIP
>
> Businesses should adopt a proactive approach to fraud prevention and detection, rather than merely responding to problems as they occur. Thus, fraud prevention techniques must be updated as fraud tendencies evolve. Keeping up with fraud trends and investing in effective fraud prevention solutions can help firms protect their assets, reputation, and risk of fraud.

Fraud is a threat to the global economy. Understanding numbers can help combat fraud, but it's not enough on its own. Organizations must leverage advanced analytics and machine learning to prevent and identify fraudulent activities.

Defining Fraud

Fraud, as a concept, entails intentional deception or misrepresentation with the aim of personal gain or inflicting harm on another person or organization. According to a definition provided by Oxford[4] in 2015, fraud is 'Wrongful or criminal deception intended to result in financial or personal gain. This means that fraud is an intentional act of trickery with the purpose of gaining dishonest financial or other advantages over others.

Extending this conceptual understanding, Van Vlasselaer, Bravo, Caelen, and colleagues[5] characterize fraud as an "uncommon, well-considered, imperceptibly concealed, time-evolving, and often carefully organized crime that manifests in various types and forms." This description appears in their study *APATE: A Novel Approach for Automated*

[4] Oxford Dictionaries. (2015). *Fraud*. Oxford University Press.

[5] Van Vlasselaer, V., Bravo, C., Caelen, O., Eliassi-Rad, T., Akoglu, L., Snoeck, M., & Baesens, B. (2015). *APATE: A novel approach for automated credit card transaction fraud detection using network-based extensions*. **Decision Support Systems, 75**, 38–48. https://doi.org/10.1016/j.dss.2015.04.013

Credit Card Transaction Fraud Detection Using Network-Based Extensions, published in *Decision Support Systems* (2015). Their definition highlights the adaptive, covert, and structured nature of fraud, underscoring why traditional rule-based detection methods are often insufficient. The following section examines each of these defining characteristics in greater detail.

Uncommon

Since fraud occurs less frequently than typical transactions or activities, detecting and learning from previous examples proves difficult. The limited examples available for developing robust fraud detection systems emphasize the importance of advanced analytical tools to identify patterns in the data.

Imperceptibly Concealed

Fraudsters often attempt to blend in with their environment by mimicking normal behavior, making their detection reliant on identifying subtle deviations from expected patterns.

Well-Considered and Intentional

Fraudsters usually design intricate fraud schemes ahead of time and adapt their tactics in response to changes in detection mechanisms. This necessitates organizations remaining alert and adaptive in their fraud prevention strategies.

Time-Evolving

Fraudsters' tactics evolve in tandem with advancements in fraud detection technologies, resulting in a perpetual cat-and-mouse game. Detection systems must be dynamic and frequently updated to adapt to emerging risks and changing fraud trends.

Carefully Organized

Fraudsters often collaborate in groups, making it essential to analyze the relationships between them. Investigating connections between individuals and organizations can reveal valuable information about fraud networks.

Fraud is a complex issue that manifests in various ways, often inflicting financial or personal harm on unsuspecting individuals or organizations. It is crucial to distinguish between fraud, waste, and abuse. Fraud entails intentional deception, whereas waste refers to inefficiency or wasteful spending, and abuse involves the improper or personal use of resources or finances.

Organizations must have strong internal controls and risk management systems to combat well-organized fraud. This may entail doing routine evaluations of the risk of fraud, training staff members in fraud prevention and detection methods, and implementing cutting-edge fraud detection tools like artificial intelligence and machine learning. Fraud detection also requires strong internal and external cooperation and information exchange with law enforcement entities.

Utilizing strong governance, data analysis, machine learning, and fostering a culture of collaboration and information sharing, organizations can proactively and adaptively respond to emerging fraud tactics. These robust measures aid in the detection and prevention of different types of fraud, ultimately reducing financial losses and offering protection to both businesses and their consumers. This book promises to delve into each of these aspects in more detail, providing practical guidance on how to effectively address and combat the ever-evolving landscape of fraud.

The Fraud Triangle

The Fraud Triangle illustrates the necessary conditions for fraud to occur: opportunity, rationalization, and pressure. This model, established by criminologist Dr. Donald Cressey, includes the psychological aspects that could lead to fraud. A visual representation of this concept is provided in Fig. 1.2.

The Fraud Triangle says that for fraud to occur, all three of these conditions must be met. Organizations can combat fraud by identifying and resolving these components.

Fig. 1.2 Fraud Triangle as conceptualized by Dr. Donald Cressey. This figure illustrates the Fraud Triangle model, which explains fraudulent behavior through the interaction of three core elements: pressure (motivation to commit fraud), opportunity (the ability and means to carry out fraud), and rationalization (justification of dishonest behavior). Adapted from the Fraud Triangle model developed by Dr. Donald R. Cressey

The Fraud Triangle serves as a crucial model, shedding light on the psychological elements that may potentially drive individuals to indulge in fraudulent actions. Proactively addressing the opportunity, rationalization, and pressure components enables organizations to preempt and spot instances of fraud while promoting an environment rooted in ethics and honesty. A comprehensive approach to fraud prevention not only lessens an organization's susceptibility to fraud but also safeguards its assets and reputation.

The rest of this section provides some examples of how fraudsters exploit the three elements of the Fraud Triangle and some strategies for mitigating the risk of fraud by removing opportunities.

Opportunity

Opportunity is the first element of the Fraud Triangle referring to the conditions that make it possible for fraud to occur. Opportunity often arises when internal controls and supervision are weak, or when an individual has access to sensitive information, assets, or funds. When there is no opportunity for fraud, it is much less likely to occur.

Fraudsters can exploit opportunities to commit fraud in many ways, such as the following:

- Taking advantage of a lack of internal controls or oversight
- Exploiting weaknesses in systems or processes
- Using their position of authority or access to sensitive information to commit fraud

To mitigate the risk of fraud by removing opportunities, organizations can implement strong internal controls, including these:

- Segregating duties to ensure that no one individual has too much control or access
- Conducting regular audits to identify potential areas of weakness or risk Implementing security measures to protect sensitive information and financial resources.

Rationalization

Rationalization is the second leg of the fraud triangle. This refers to a person's ability to explain or defend dishonest behavior. This may comprise convincing oneself that the behavior is necessary or justified, or blaming other factors for their acts.

Fraudsters can rationalize their behavior in a variety of ways, including the following:

- Justifying their actions as necessary for personal or financial reasons
- Blaming external factors for their actions
- Convincing themselves that their behavior is not really fraud or is justified in some way

To mitigate the risk of fraud by removing rationalization, organizations can do the following:

- Promote a culture of honesty and ethics, including developing a code of conduct and providing regular training on ethical behavior
- Encourage employees to report any suspicious activity or behavior

Conduct regular performance reviews and feedback sessions to ensure that employees are meeting ethical standards and expectations.

Pressure

Pressure is the third leg of the fraud triangle. This refers to the pressures that a person may feel from the outside or the inside that led to dishonest behavior. This might include both financial and non-financial demands, such as a need for prestige or recognition, as well as financial pressures such as debt or gambling.

Fraudsters may feel pressured to engage in fraudulent activities due to various reasons:

- Financial pressures, such as debt or gambling
- Non-financial pressures, such as the desire for status or recognition
- Personal circumstances, such as family or health problems

To mitigate the risk of fraud by removing pressure, organizations can do the following:

- Provide support to employees who may be experiencing financial or personal pressures, such as offering financial counseling or mental health services
- Encourage employees to take breaks and practice self-care to reduce stress and avoid burnout
- Monitor employee behavior for signs of excessive stress or pressure, and intervene when necessary to provide support or assistance

There are a variety of methods that fraudsters might make use of the Fraud Triangle's elements. Organizations can devise strategies for reducing the risk of fraud by removing opportunities, causes, and pressures that might motivate fraudulent behavior by studying how fraudsters use these elements. Strong internal controls, the promotion of an honest and ethical culture, and assistance to staff can all help organizations lower their risk of falling victim to fraud and protect their assets and reputation.

The expanding world of digital and financial transactions has led to the development of models and frameworks to understand and analyze the risks of fraud. The Fraud Pentagon adds two more dimensions—Arrogance and Competence—to the existing elements of Incentives/Pressures, Opportunities, and Attitudes/Rationalizations. These five elements provide insights into the motivations, opportunities, rationalizations, and skills that individuals may possess to engage in fraudulent activities. The newly introduced elements are described as:

- *Arrogance:* This term reflects a certain sense of superiority, entitlement, or even greed present in potential fraudsters. It characterizes an attitude where individuals might consider themselves above the anti-fraud measures and rules, leading them to discount ethical standards and making them more likely to commit fraudulent acts.
- *Competence:* This aspect relates to the knowledge, skills, and abilities that an individual possesses to orchestrate and execute fraudulent schemes effectively. It encompasses several factors such as the ability to gain access to assets, people, or systems; the ability to override controls; the skill to conceal wrongdoings; and the ability to manipulate social situations through rationalization, persuasion, lies, or coercion. A high level of competence not only enables the perpetrators to carry out fraud more effectively, but it also diminishes the likelihood of their fraudulent activities being detected.

With the rise of digital assets such as cryptocurrencies, nonfungible tokens (NFTs), decentralized finance (DeFi), and decentralized autonomous organizations (DAOs), new types of financial and regulatory risks have emerged. To navigate these challenges, the Fraud and Anti-Money Laundering Landscape (FRAML) model has been introduced. FRAML builds upon the Fraud Pentagon by integrating a "what-based" triangle of fraud action involving the Act (the fraudulent activity), Concealment (hiding the activity), and Conversion (benefiting from the fraud).

Both the Fraud Pentagon and FRAML highlight the importance of anti-fraud measures in preventing and mitigating fraud. These measures include implementing strong internal controls, segregation of duties, monitoring mechanisms, and knowing your customer (KYC) procedures, which prevent doing business with potentially malicious actors.

Regulators emphasize that the monitoring and evaluation of compliance programs should be data-driven and continuous. Regular feedback from various sources such as internal and external audits, investigations, and employee surveys is critical to ensuring that these programs evolve and remain risk based.

By understanding the factors contributing to fraud through models like the Fraud Pentagon and FRAML, and by implementing comprehensive risk assessments and robust anti-fraud measures, organizations can better navigate the challenges posed by both traditional financial transactions and the new digital asset ecosystem. This comprehensive approach allows organizations to detect, manage, and mitigate the risks associated with fraudulent activities (Fig. 1.3).

Summary

This chapter introduced the complex world of fraud, discussing its many definitions, global implications, and psychological drivers. The main paradigm discussed was the fraud triangle, which identifies opportunity, justification, and pressure as primary triggers for fraudulent behavior. The importance of understanding these aspects of fraud to effectively identify, prevent, and combat them is emphasized.

In Chapter 2 you will learn about financial statement fraud, embezzlement, and Ponzi schemes. You'll explore the motives, defenses, and tactics of scammers. A detailed look at a common type of fraud, credit card fraud, with a special focus on IP manipulation, is also on the agenda. All of this is intended to enrich your understanding and enhance your ability to detect and prevent fraud. Chapter 2 awaits you with more helpful discussion.

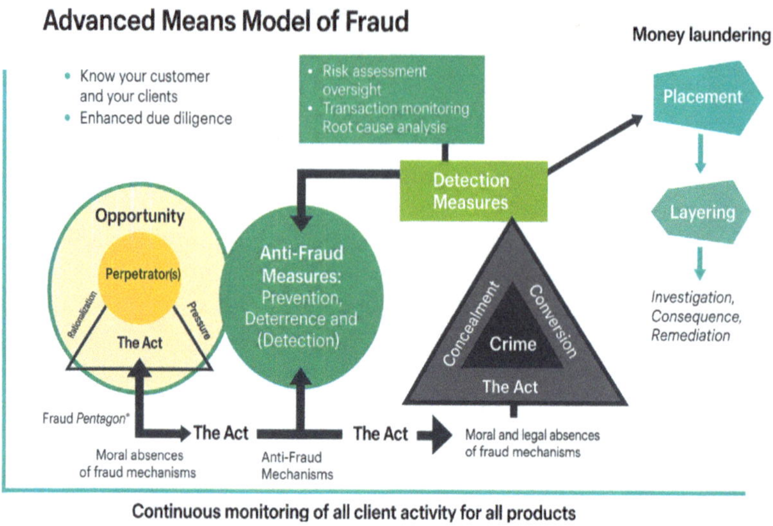

Fig. 1.3 Advanced meta-model of the fraud and anti-money laundering (AML) landscape. This figure presents an integrated fraud and AML framework linking perpetrator drivers, anti-fraud controls, and crime outcomes, aligned with the money laundering stages of placement, layering, and integration. The model synthesizes key elements from established fraud risk assessment lifecycles and publicly available AML and fraud risk frameworks to illustrate the interconnected nature of financial crime prevention and response. Adapted from Baker Tilly, White House Framework on Digital Assets, available at: https://www.bakertilly.com/insights/white-house-framework-on-digital-assets

CHAPTER 2

Different Types of Fraud and Their Impact

This chapter examines different types of fraud and their impact across financial, organizational, and digital environments. It introduces major fraud categories and explains how fraudulent activities differ in their methods, objectives, and consequences. The chapter then explores the growing rise of digital fraud, including identity theft, phishing, account takeover, payment fraud, and synthetic identity fraud, as well as the technologies used to combat these threats. In addition, it analyzes the traits, tactics, and behavioral patterns of fraudsters, showing how understanding offender behavior can improve fraud detection and prevention. To provide a more practical perspective, the chapter also presents fraudster archetypes, including opportunists, insiders, organized fraud actors, colluders, and cybercriminals. These profiles help explain how fraud is carried out in real settings and why different fraud risks require different countermeasures. Overall, this chapter provides a practical foundation for understanding how fraud operates, how it evolves in digital environments, and how organizations can strengthen their defenses through stronger controls, analytics, and fraud awareness.

A. Al Aqqad, *Fraud Analytics in Action*
https://doi.org/10.1007/978-3-032-16023-2_2

Types of Fraud

In the intricate realm of fraud, deceptive activities manifest in a multitude of forms. These activities differ significantly in their methods, objectives, and the victims they target. Table 2.1 classifies a range of such instances into common types of fraud, providing a clearer snapshot of the broad spectrum of fraudulent behavior.

Table 2.1 Types of fraud, definitions, and examples

Type of Fraud	Definition	Examples
Financial fraud	This encompasses a broad range of activities, all centered around deceitful tactics intended to result in financial gain	Securities fraud, embezzlement, and accounting fraud
Identity theft	This form of fraud involves stealing someone else's personal information and using it for illegal activities.	Obtaining credit, goods, services, or to commit another crime.
Insurance fraud	This involves false claims or exaggerated losses reported to insurance companies to gain larger settlements. It can also involve insurers who defraud customers by denying legitimate claims.	This type of fraud can be categorized into two types: *Hard Fraud:* This kind of fraud surfaces when someone invents a loss, injury, or damage to benefit from an insurance payout. It's typically a well-thought-out, intentional act. *Soft Fraud:* This type of fraud comes into play when someone inflates an existing insurance claim, maybe by overstating the degree of damage or inflating the worth of stolen items. It's more frequently encountered and often viewed as less severe, but it's important to remember it's still a fraudulent act. *Examples*: A restaurant owner, struggling with finances, intentionally sets their restaurant on fire. They then file an insurance claim, falsely stating that the fire was an accident to collect insurance money. This act is an example of hard insurance fraud. In contrast, if the owner had a legitimate fire but exaggerated the extent of the damage to get a larger insurance payout, it would be an instance of soft insurance fraud.
Corruption	This type of fraud typically involves a person in a position of power who performs illegal actions for personal gain	Bribery, embezzlement, and kickbacks are common forms of corruption
Credit card fraud	This occurs when an individual uses another person's credit card information to make unauthorized transactions	This can happen through a variety of ways, including card theft, skimming, or phishing

The Rise of Digital Fraud

In recent years, the rapid shift to digital and online transactions has made fraud more common and harder to catch. The boom in e-commerce, online banking, and digital payment systems has given fraudsters numerous new opportunities to exploit weaknesses in these platforms. Digital fraud now includes many dangerous activities, such as identity theft, phishing, account takeover (ATO), payment fraud, and synthetic identity fraud.

Cybercriminals are becoming more sophisticated, using advanced techniques like hacking, malware, and social engineering to stay maintain an advantage over detection systems. The COVID-19 pandemic sped up this change, as more businesses and people relied on online platforms for their financial transactions, giving fraudsters further opportunities to exploit vulnerabilities.

Some of the most common types of digital fraud are:

- *Identity Theft:* Using someone's personal information without permission to commit fraud.
- Phishing Attacks: Tricking people into giving away sensitive information, like passwords and credit card numbers, by pretending to be a trusted source.
- *Account Takeover (ATO):* Breaking into someone's account without permission, often through stolen passwords or clever tricks.
- *Payment Fraud:* Making fake transactions using stolen credit cards or manipulating payment systems.
- *Synthetic Identity Fraud:* Creating a fake identity by mixing real and fake information to open fraudulent accounts.

Emerging Solutions for Digital Fraud

To combat the rise of digital fraud, advanced technologies like Artificial Intelligence (AI), Machine Learning (ML), and Blockchain are stepping up as powerful tools. These technologies are helping to detect and stop fraud more effectively as they keep up with the evolving tricks of cybercriminals.

Technologies to Combat Digital Fraud

1. *Artificial Intelligence (AI) and Machine Learning (ML):* AI and ML are crucial for fraud detection, analyzing vast datasets to identify suspicious activities. These technologies monitor transactions in real-time, flagging deviations from normal patterns. ML models continuously learn from past and evolving fraud trends, improving accuracy over time.

For example, financial institutions use AI to detect unusual account behavior and potential account takeovers. ML algorithms adapt quickly to new threats, reducing false positives and enhancing detection.

Case Study: Capital One Data Breach (2019) A major breach exposed over 100 million records due to a vulnerability in cloud infrastructure. AI-driven monitoring could have detected unusual access patterns sooner, potentially preventing the attack.

Reflection Exercise:

- How can your organization use AI and ML for fraud detection?
- What additional data sources could enhance anomaly detection?

2. *Blockchain Technology:* Blockchain is a secure, decentralized ledger that prevents data tampering. It's effective in combating fraud, such as synthetic identity fraud and money laundering, by ensuring transaction records are immutable and transparent.

Case Study: Equifax Data Breach (2017) The Equifax breach exposed personal data of 147 million people due to unpatched vulnerabilities. Using blockchain could have safeguarded this data by making it tamper-proof and harder to exploit.

Reflection Exercise:

- Could blockchain improve your organization's data security?
- Which processes would benefit from blockchain's transparency and immutability?

3. *Biometric Verification:* Biometric authentication, such as fingerprint scans and facial recognition, offers stronger security compared to traditional passwords. Biometric data is harder to replicate, making it effective against fraud.

Case Study: Biometric Failure in Retail Fraud A major retail chain faced high false-positive rates with a facial recognition system, mistakenly flagging legitimate customers. This highlights the need for accurate implementation and integration with other security measures.

Reflection Exercise:

- How could biometric authentication enhance security in your organization?
- What challenges might arise when adopting biometric technologies?

4. *Multi-Factor Authentication (MFA):* MFA requires multiple verification steps, like a password and a fingerprint, making it harder for fraudsters to gain access. It's widely used to reduce the risk of account takeovers.

Case Study: *Dropbox Data Breach (2012)* Hackers accessed Dropbox files using stolen credentials. In response, Dropbox introduced two-factor authentication, which greatly improved security.

Reflection Exercise:

- Is MFA implemented for all sensitive accounts in your organization?
- Which MFA solutions could be easily integrated into your existing systems?

5. *Tokenization:* Tokenization replaces sensitive data, like credit card numbers, with unique tokens, making the original data inaccessible during transactions. Even if intercepted, tokens are useless without the secure tokenization system.

Case Study: Target Data Breach (2013) Attackers stole credit card information from over 40 million customers. Tokenization could have rendered this data unusable, preventing the attackers from exploiting the stolen details.

Reflection Exercise:

- How can tokenization improve your organization's data security?
- Which sensitive data would benefit most from tokenization?

6. *Behavioral Analytics:* Behavioral analytics monitors how users interact with systems, such as typing speed and mouse movements, to detect unusual patterns. These insights can help prevent fraud by flagging suspicious behavior even when correct login credentials are used.

Case Study: PayPal's Behavioral Analytics PayPal uses behavioral analytics to identify account takeover attempts. By detecting changes in user behavior, they can prevent fraud in real-time.

Reflection Exercise:

- What user behaviors could your organization track to spot fraud early?
- How could behavioral analytics complement your current fraud detection strategies?

Traits of Fraudsters

Recognizing fraudster traits is vital in the fight against fraud. Identifying these characteristics helps organizations anticipate and manage potential risks, protecting both their financial stability and reputation.

Commonly, fraudsters display certain personality traits that hint at their fraudulent tendencies. Greed, entitlement, and overconfidence are common. These people often cheat to obtain their ambitions. These traits provide organizations with key insights that can aid in fraud prevention and detection.

Moreover, fraudsters are known to rationalize their actions, even when aware of their wrongfulness. They may operate outside the boundaries of societal norms and exploit vulnerabilities in internal systems for their benefit. Certain behavioral patterns such as high-pressure sales tactics, unusual work habits, or secrecy can also serve as clues to potential fraud.

Several situational circumstances might increase the risk of fraud, including weak internal controls, pressure to meet targets, personal financial problems, and access to substantial assets or sensitive information. While not all individuals with these traits or circumstances engage in fraud, understanding these can assist organizations in detecting potential risks and preventing fraudulent actions.

You'll also want to pay attention to additional red flags such as unusual work schedules, reluctance to share responsibilities, unexplained wealth, large unaccounted-for loans or credit lines, resistance to providing information to superiors or auditors, missing financial documentation, resistance to internal controls, and a history of ethical infractions.

Through understanding and recognizing these behaviors and traits, you can improve your organization's ability to detect potential fraud and mitigate its impact.

It's important to note that not all fraudsters or people with the traits I have mentioned commit fraud. However, understanding these traits might help organizations spot fraud risks and prevent it. **See** Fig. 2.1.

- **Impersonation Techniques**

Fraudsters often impersonate legitimate individuals through tactics like account takeovers, synthetic identity creation, and social engineering. Their goal is to gain unauthorized access to sensitive systems or financial

Fig. 2.1 Overview of six key fraudster tactics. Impersonation techniques involve posing as legitimate users through account takeovers and synthetic identity creation. Deceptive techniques include phishing, spoofing, and deepfakes. Social engineering exploits human psychology to extract confidential information. Dark web activity leverages anonymity for illicit marketplaces and fraud networks. Fraud rings involve coordinated groups evading detection through simulated legitimate behaviour. Volatility refers to sudden behavioural changes—such as transaction spikes or unusual login patterns—that signal potential fraud

resources. These techniques exploit authentication loopholes, and businesses must counter them through tools like identity verification, anomaly detection, and continuous monitoring of user behavior.

- **Deceptive Techniques**

Deception is at the core of many fraudulent schemes. Techniques like phishing, spoofing, deepfakes, or Trojan horses are used to mislead victims and gain illicit access. Fraud detection models must adapt quickly to detect new deception patterns using behavioral analytics, biometric security, link analysis, and natural language processing (NLP).

- **Social Engineering**

This technique manipulates human psychology to bypass technical safeguards. Fraudsters may coerce individuals into revealing confidential information or performing actions they wouldn't normally do—like transferring money or sharing credentials. Social engineering detection requires combining social network analysis, machine learning, and anomaly detection to track behavioral shifts or relationship-based manipulation.

- **Dark Web Activity**

The Dark Web hosts illicit marketplaces, fake identities, and financial-fraud networks. Fraudsters exploit its anonymity to coordinate attacks, sell stolen data, or launder money. Despite its hidden nature, machine learning and blockchain analytics can help uncover patterns and connections associated with dark web–linked fraud.

- **Fraud Rings**

Fraud rings involve coordinated groups working together to commit fraud. These groups often simulate legitimate behavior to avoid detection, but tools like graph analytics, predictive modeling, and data visualization can help uncover ring structures, shared attributes, and transaction anomalies—especially in areas like insurance, telecom, or online retail fraud.

- **Volatility**

Volatile behavior is often a red flag for fraud. Sudden changes in transaction frequency, login times, or user activity may signal fraudulent behavior or account compromise. Machine learning models trained to detect behavioral shifts or unusual activity patterns can generate real-time alerts for further investigation.

Fraudster Archetypes

This section breaks down the various groups of fraudsters based on their motivations, features, and behavior, also known as *fraudster archetypes*. Understanding these archetypes can aid in the identification of possible fraud threats as well as the development of effective fraud prevention and detection measures Fig. 2.2.

The Opportunist

Opportunists act when opportunity knocks. With little planning, they exploit gaps in systems or processes for personal gain. Subtypes include:

- *Amateur Fraudster:* Uses basic, low-tech methods (e.g., check tampering or card theft).
- Cookie-cutter Fraudster: The Mass Deceiver: Leverages bulk strategies like phishing kits or fake ads.

Fig. 2.2 Illustration titled "The Opportunist" depicting three types of fraudsters. On the left, an "Amateur Fraudster" holds a bank card and credit card, described as using simple deception and low-tech methods. In the center, a "Cookie-Cutter Fraudster" wears sunglasses and a hoodie, holding a card labeled "BUY" with a megaphone icon, described as utilizing pre-packaged strategies and mass marketing tactics. On the right, a "Gig Economy Fraudster" is shown with a laptop and ID card, described as creating multiple accounts with fake identities Fig. 2.3

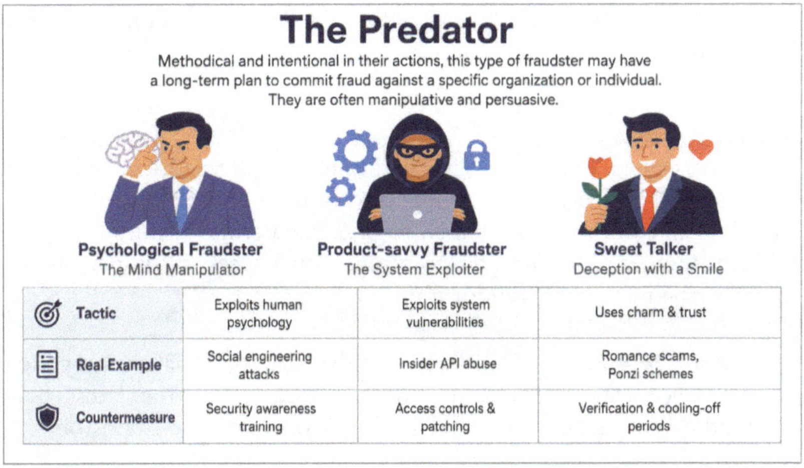

Fig. 2.3 The Predator fraudster archetype and its three subtypes. The Psychological Fraudster (The Mind Manipulator) exploits human psychology through social engineering; countermeasure: security awareness training. The Product-savvy Fraudster (The System Exploiter) targets system vulnerabilities using insider knowledge; countermeasure: access controls and patching. The Sweet Talker (Deception with a Smile) uses charm and trust in schemes such as romance scams and Ponzi schemes; countermeasure: verification and cooling-off periods.

- Gig Economy Fraudster: The On-demand Scammer: Exploits platforms using fake identities and ghost services.

The Predator

Predators are calculated and manipulative. They often target specific organizations over time. Subtypes include:

- *Psychological Fraudster:* The Mind Manipulator: Skilled manipulators who exploit human behavior.
- *Product-savvy Fraudster:* The System Exploiter: Exploits service or product vulnerabilities with insider knowledge. Exploiting gaps or weaknesses in the product and gaining access to sensitive information.

- *The Sweet Talker:* Deception with a Smile: Uses charm and social engineering (e.g., romance scams, Ponzi schemes).

Organized Crime Fraudster

Organized Crime Fraudster: The Syndicate Swindler: Organized Crime Fraudsters are individuals or groups involved in complex, sophisticated fraudulent operations, often linked to organized crime syndicates.

The Impostor: The Art of Deception: Gains access by impersonating trusted individuals (e.g., vendor fraud).

- *Countermeasures:* Multi-factor authentication, data encryption, employee training, and staying informed about the latest fraud methods are among the effective ways to thwart the Impostor.

The Authority Scammer: Deception by Power: Fakes government or law enforcement roles. Examples include:

- Government officials: Scammers impersonate officials from the IRS or other government institutions, demanding tax payments or threatening legal action.
- Law enforcement impersonation: Fraudsters act as law enforcement officers, warning of an arrest warrant or other legal issues and demanding payment to avoid consequences.
- Utility company impersonation: Scammers pretend to be utility company employees, threatening to cut off services unless immediate payment is made.
- Tech support impersonation: Fraudsters pretend to be tech support representatives from companies like Microsoft or Apple, claiming the victim's computer is infected and offering to fix it for a fee.
- Charity fraud: Scammers impersonate charity representatives to solicit donations, using high-pressure tactics to get people to donate, and the money may not go to the intended cause.

The Con Artist: The Charismatic Deceiver: Con Artists are fraudsters who use deception and charm to mislead victims into parting with their money or personal information. They often have captivating personalities and are proficient at earning trust Fig. 2.4.

Fig. 2.4 Organized crime fraudster archetypes: The Syndicate Swindler. Three profiles are shown—The Con Artist (charm and deception; countermeasure: due diligence checks), The Authority Scammer (fake authority and power; countermeasure: call-back verification), and The Impostor (impersonation of trusted individuals; countermeasure: multi-factor authentication and identity verification)

The Insider

This type of fraudster is an employee or a trusted member of an organization who uses their position to commit fraud. They are intimately familiar with the organization's operations and may be able to bypass controls or manipulate records Fig. 2.5.

- The *Inside Man:* The Betrayer Within: Leverages position and knowledge (e.g., Fastow at Enron).
- *Countermeasures*: Rigorous internal controls, continuous monitoring, and periodic audits are key strategies to counter Inside Men. Famous examples include:

- *The* Grifter*:* The Emotional Manipulators: Exploits emotions and relationships (e.g., Madoff, Abagnale).

The Cybercriminal

This type of fraudster utilizes technology to commit fraud. They usually gain access to confidential information or systems through phishing scams, malware, or other tactics. They are often difficult to track down and may operate from other countries.

- *The* Techno-*Wizard:* Digital Illusionists: Techno-Wizards are fraudsters with high expertise in cybersecurity, computer programming, or other technical fields. They use these skills to exploit digital vulnerabilities and execute their fraudulent acts.
- *Countermeasures:* Identifying weaknesses proactively, strengthening cybersecurity defenses, educating employees, cooperating with law enforcement, and sharing information with other companies are effective strategies against Techno-Wizards Fig. 2.6.
- Bot Generator: The Automated Trickster: Bot Generators are software experts who create and run automated bots, which can be used for various malicious activities like fraud, spamming, and social media manipulation
- Tech-savvy Fraudster or The Technologist: The Digital Deceiver: Tech-Savvy Fraudsters leverage their expertise in technology to exploit vulnerabilities in computer systems or networks, create false identities, and steal sensitive data or money.

The Colluder

This type of fraudster collaborates with others to commit fraud. They may collude with other employees, vendors, or customers to bypass controls or steal assets .

- The *Colluder:* The Unseen Alliance: Colluders are fraudsters who conspire with others, often from within the target company, to commit fraud. They make detection difficult due to the conspiracy between two or more individuals.

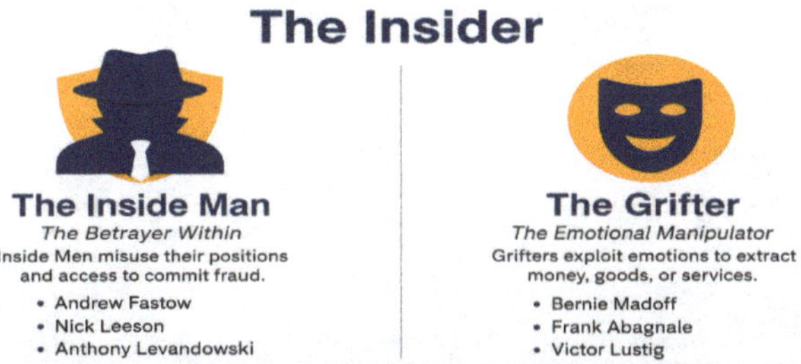

	The Inside Man	The Grifter
Tactic	Misuses position and access	Exploits emotions and relationships
Real Examples	Andrew Fastow, Nick Leeson, Anthony Levandowski	Bernie Madoff, Frank Abagnale, Victor Lustig
Countermeasure	Rigorous internal controls & periodic audits	Due diligence & relationship verification

Fig. 2.5 The Insider fraudster archetype with two subtypes. The Inside Man (The Betrayer Within) misuses organisational access to commit fraud, with notable examples including Andrew Fastow, Anthony Levandowski, and Nick Leeson. The Grifter (The Emotional Manipulators) exploits personal relationships and emotions, with examples including Bernie Madoff, Frank Abagnale, and Victor Lustig

- *Countermeasures:* Implementing strong internal controls, conducting regular audits, and fostering an open and accountable culture are key to combating collusion Fig. 2.7.

Credit Card Fraud

Credit card fraud generally falls into two broad categories: application fraud and behavioral fraud.

Application fraud occurs at the point of card issuance. In these cases, fraudsters rely on forged, synthetic, or stolen personal information to apply for new credit cards. Their objective is to pass identity checks, obtain approval, and quickly exploit the account before detection mechanisms are triggered. This form of fraud is primarily driven by weaknesses in onboarding and identity verification processes.

Behavioral fraud, by contrast, takes place after a card has been legitimately issued. The most prevalent example is card-not-present (CNP) fraud, where stolen card credentials are used to conduct online or remote

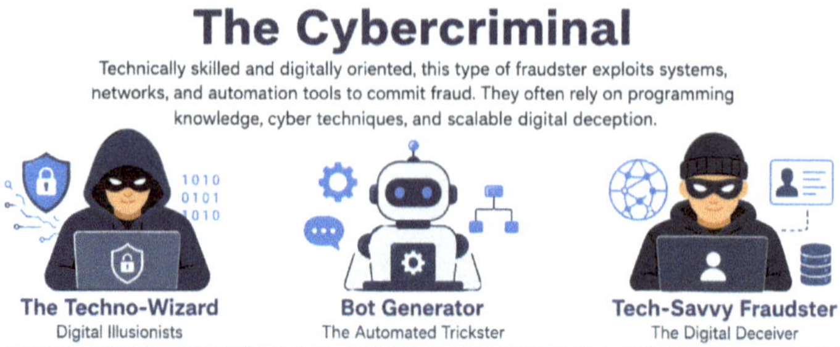

	The Techno-Wizard	Bot Generator	Tech-Savvy Fraudster
Tactic	Exploits digital vulnerabilities using cybersecurity & programming expertise	Creates automated bots for fraud, spamming & social media manipulation	Exploits network vulnerabilities to steal data and create false identities
Real Example	Nation-state hackers, APT groups	Credential stuffing attacks, fake account farms	Synthetic identity fraud, data theft networks
Countermeasure	Proactive vulnerability testing & cybersecurity training	CAPTCHA systems & bot detection tools	Multi-factor authentication & network monitoring

Fig. 2.6 The Cybercriminal fraudster archetype and its three subtypes. The Techno-Wizard (Digital Illusionists) exploits technical expertise to attack digital systems; countermeasure: proactive vulnerability testing and cybersecurity training. The Bot Generator (The Automated Trickster) deploys automated bots for fraud and manipulation; countermeasure: CAPTCHA and bot detection tools. The Tech-Savvy Fraudster (The Digital Deceiver) exploits network vulnerabilities to steal data and create false identities; countermeasure: multi-factor authentication and network monitoring

transactions without the physical card. These credentials are typically obtained through data breaches, phishing campaigns, or malware. In practice, CNP fraud often follows recognizable behavioral patterns, such as small test transactions followed by larger purchases, rapid sequences of online transactions, or attempts to exhaust available credit limits. These patterns make CNP fraud particularly suitable for detection using machine learning models that monitor transaction behavior in real time.

Over time, CNP fraud has become the dominant form of credit card fraud. As consumer activity increasingly shifts toward digital and remote channels, fraud has followed the same trajectory. Industry data consistently shows that CNP fraud now accounts for the majority of global

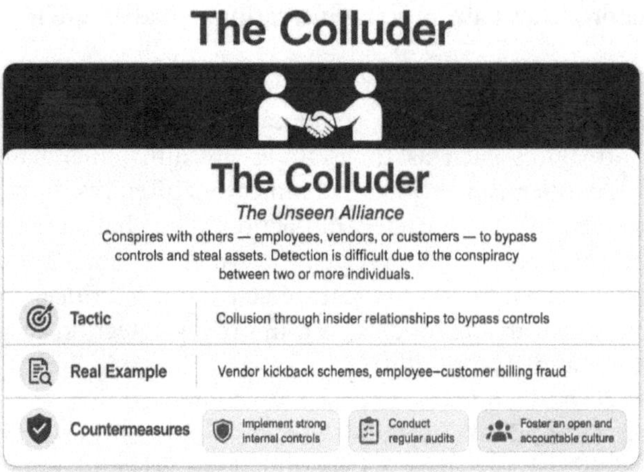

Fig. 2.7 The Colluder fraudster archetype: The Unseen Alliance. Colluders conspire with insiders — including employees, vendors, or customers — to bypass controls and commit fraud, making detection difficult. Key countermeasures include implementing strong internal controls, conducting regular audits, and fostering an open and accountable organisational culture

payment card fraud losses,[1] with little indication that this trend will reverse. This evolution has significant implications across the payment ecosystem, affecting card issuers, merchants, payment processors, and consumers.

A major structural factor behind this shift is the widespread adoption of EMV (Europay, MasterCard, and Visa) chip technology. Since its rollout began in 2015, EMV has substantially reduced fraud at physical points of sale. However, rather than eliminating fraud altogether, it displaced criminal activity toward online and remote environments,[2] where authentication controls are inherently weaker. As a result, traditional rule-based

[1] The Nilson Report. *Annual Fraud Statistics*. Industry data consistently indicates that card-not-present fraud accounts for the majority of global payment card fraud losses.

[2] EMVCo; Federal Reserve. *EMV Migration and Fraud Trends*. Following the introduction of EMV chip technology beginning in 2015, card-present fraud declined significantly, while fraud activity increasingly shifted toward card-not-present transactions.

detection approaches have become increasingly inadequate for addressing CNP fraud.

Modern fraud detection systems therefore rely on the analysis of rich transaction-level data. Each credit card transaction typically includes dozens of attributes such as timestamps, amounts, merchant information, issuer identifiers, and contextual indicators often resulting in datasets containing 70 to 80 variables per transaction. The challenge lies not only in collecting this data, but in determining which variables are most informative. This process, known as feature selection, is critical for building effective machine learning models, as it improves detection accuracy while reducing noise and false positives.

Both supervised and unsupervised machine learning models play a central role in credit card fraud detection. Supervised models learn from historical, labeled data to identify known fraud patterns, while unsupervised models focus on detecting unusual or emerging behaviors without relying on predefined labels. Together, these approaches enable fraud detection systems to adapt to both established and evolving fraud schemes.

Readers seeking a deeper discussion of feature selection methods and advanced data preparation techniques are referred to *Chapter* 7 and 8 *Feature Engineering and Advanced Techniques for Fraud Analytics in Part II of this boo*k.

Unmasking E-Commerce Fraudsters: A Glimpse into Impersonation and Deception

A fraudster aims to impersonate a credit card owner and make a purchase on an e-commerce retailer's website, taking steps to avoid detection. They use a clean device, matching device settings, IP provider, geolocation, and browsing habits to the cardholder's profile. They choose a target retailer that aligns with the victim's purchase history and ensure the stolen card hasn't been used before on the retailer's system.

The fraudster carefully provides the cardholder's name, billing/shipping address, email address, and phone number, making sure the details closely resemble the victim's information. In some cases, they may need to avoid providing additional personally identifiable information (PII). Once all necessary details are given, the fraudster completes the order, hoping to successfully purchase the stolen goods.

Detecting Credit Card Fraud

IP fraud identification is one of several important components in the complicated challenge of detecting credit card fraud. First, though, let's define *IP address.*

Each node in a network that makes use of the Internet Protocol (IP) has its own distinct numerical label known as an IP address. Its primary purpose is to both identify the host or network interface and to pinpoint the host within the network.

With a clearer understanding of IP addresses, we can now delve into the ways this tool is utilized to combat fraud:

1. *Profiling Mismatches*: This involves assessing the organization to which an IP is registered. If the IP is discovered in a context that doesn't align with the expected activities of the registered organization, it could signal that the IP is being used as a proxy for fraudulent operations.
2. *Geolocation/Profiling Mismatches*: This entails comparing the geolocation of an IP address with the stated location or profile of the cardholder. However, caution should be exercised with geolocation data, as it isn't always accurate or dependable.
3. *Repeat Offender IPs*: While connecting repeat offenses to specific IP addresses can be insightful, it's important to remember that IP addresses can represent numerous individuals and IP reputation lists aren't always reliable.
4. *Use of Public WiFi Networks*: Fraudsters may sometimes use public WiFi networks to hide their identities, although this tactic appears to be less popular nowadays.

Once potentially rogue IPs have been identified, manual research methods such as "traceroute checks" can be employed. For clarification, a traceroute check is a network diagnostic tool used to track the pathway a data packet takes from one device to another, effectively providing a mapped journey of the packet. Should the traced route not align with the expected journey, it might indicate obfuscation. However, more extensive investigation and consideration of other data points are necessary to conclude whether the transaction is legitimate or fraudulent.

Machine learning models can also be a highly valuable resource for analyzing fraud data. They have the capability to highlight anomalous user behaviors requiring further examination. These algorithms train to spot fraud, lowering false positives and negatives and improving accuracy. “In the book, Parts 3 and 4 dive into the intricacies of unsupervised and supervised learning methods as they pertain to fraud detection. These sections provide readers with a comprehensive understanding of how these machine learning techniques can be effectively employed to identify and prevent fraudulent activities. The book offers practical insights, case studies, and real-world examples to illustrate the application of these methods in various fraud detection scenarios.

Credit card fraud detection requires a multifaceted approach. Manual investigation, IP fraud detection, and machine learning models help organizations defend themselves and their customers from emerging fraud strategies. Technology will make internet purchasing safer.

Preventing Stolen Credit Card Fraud

To combat credit card fraud, it’s crucial to impart knowledge to *end-users* about best practices like constructing secure passwords and dodging phishing emails. Implementing multi-factor authentication and single-use passwords for online transactions provide an additional layer of security, deterring unauthorized access.

The application of real-time analytics can significantly aid in promptly spotting irregular transaction trends and recurrent IP usage, which are potential red flags for fraudulent activities. Additionally, it’s key to cultivate a cooperative network with other businesses and law enforcement agencies, sharing data that could help identify potential fraudsters.

Parts 3 and 4 dive deeper into how advanced fraud detection tools can be utilized to scrutinize various aspects such as user behavior and transaction data, offering early insight into fraudulent behavior.

Finally, maintaining the security of your online platforms is paramount—adopting encryption and conducting frequent security updates are vital measures to keep your platforms safeguarded from potential threats.

Summary

This chapter covered a range of fraud types, extending from financial statement misrepresentations to cyber fraud. It underscored the importance of understanding these frauds to effectively prevent and detect them. This chapter also focused on the people behind fraudulent operations, shedding light on their typical traits and tactics. It emphasized the utility of behavioral analytics and machine learning in fraud detection, suggesting that these modern technologies are crucial in the battle against increasingly sophisticated fraudsters.

Different types of fraudsters, their motivations, and modus operandi were discussed. Insight into these personalities is essential in developing an effective fraud prevention strategy. The chapter also explained credit card fraud, particularly application and behavioral fraud. It pointed out the role machine learning plays in detecting fraud patterns and discussed the growing issue of Card Not Present (CNP) fraud due to the introduction of EMV chips.

The chapter ended with an exploration of email analysis and IP fraud identification in the context of credit card fraud. Customer education, real-time transaction monitoring, and improved fraud detection systems were stressed.

Chapter 3 introduces the domain of fraud analytics. This technology detects fraud using accounting, data science, and computer science. You'll learn about fraud analytics' history, present, and future in business. You'll see why organizations should invest in fraud analytics to prevent and identify fraud. Chapter 3 also discusses the evaluation of fraud prevention strategies, offering insights on how businesses can measure the effectiveness of their fraud analytics efforts. This knowledge will help you understand the critical role of fraud analytics in countering illegal activities.

Further Reading

Association of Certified Fraud Examiners. Occupational Fraud 2024: A Report to the Nations (ACFE, 2024).

Federal Trade Commission. Consumer Sentinel Network Data Book 2024 (FTC, 2025).

Federal Bureau of Investigation, Internet Crime Complaint Center. 2024 IC3 Annual Report (FBI, 2024).

Federal Trade Commission. What To Know About Identity Theft (FTC Consumer Advice, n.d.).

National Institute of Standards and Technology. Digital Identity Guidelines: Authentication and Lifecycle Management (NIST SP 800-63B) (NIST, 2020). https://doi.org/10.6028/NIST.SP.800-63b

PayPal Developer. Graph Usage in Combating ATO Fraud Risk (PayPal Developer, 2023).

PayPal. Fraud Detection Data Analytics (PayPal Business Resource Center, 2025).

PCI Security Standards Council. Tokenization Product Security Guidelines (PCI SSC, 2015).

U.S. Securities and Exchange Commission. SEC Charges Bernard L. Madoff for Multi-Billion Dollar Ponzi Scheme (SEC Press Release 2008–293, 2008).

U.S. Department of Justice. Former Enron Chief Financial Officer Andrew S. Fastow Charged with Fraud, Money Laundering and Conspiracy (DOJ, 2002).

CHAPTER 3

Fraud Analytics and Its Importance

Today's fast-paced business world prioritizes fraud prevention. Companies seek better fraud detection and prevention methods. ***Fraud analytics***, a powerful tool that mines data for trends and anomalies that may signal fraud, is a game-changer.

A fascinating blend of accounting, data science, and computer science, fraud analytics unites experts from these varied disciplines. These professionals can help companies stand guard against fraud by identifying potential red flags. They do this using the latest and most effective analytical techniques and technologies.

This chapter is your guide through the intricate landscape of fraud analytics. The chapter delves into its rich history, offers a clear definition, and underscores its crucial role in the contemporary corporate world. You'll explore why businesses should embrace fraud analytics, focusing particularly on its role in fraud prevention and detection.

Toward the end, you'll see a comprehensive review of fraud prevention measures and find out insights on how businesses can gauge the effectiveness of their fraud analytics strategies. By the end, you'll understand how fraud analytics protects businesses and prevents fraud. Let's start!

A. Al Aqqad, *Fraud Analytics in Action*
https://doi.org/10.1007/978-3-032-16023-2_3

History of Fraud Analytics

In the early days, back in the 1970s, the concept of fraud analytics was a lot simpler and a lot more hands-on. Can you imagine credit card companies trawling through transactions manually to spot odd spending patterns? That was the humble beginnings of fraud analytics, an approach soon adopted by the insurance and banking sectors too.

In the 1990s, things got exciting. Along came e-commerce with its dizzying array of online transactions, opening up new playgrounds for fraudsters. But technology was ready to rise to the challenge. We saw the grand entrance of artificial intelligence and machine learning into the fraud detection arena, marking a significant shift in the fight against fraud.

Today, fraud analytics taps into a treasure trove of data: transactional, device, biometric, and even social media data. With every swipe, click, or tweet, valuable information is gathered, helping to stay one step ahead of fraudsters. And as the digital landscape evolves with new developments like mobile payments, cryptocurrencies, big data analytics, and cloud computing, fraud analytics adapts and grows, proving its crucial role in our increasingly digital lives.

Definition of Fraud Analytics

The term *fraud analytics* might seem modern, but its roots reach way back. Born out of the necessity to protect businesses from financial and reputational damage, this field has come a long way. Initially, the focus was more on *fraud detection*, aiming to spot fraudulent activities after they had taken place. But as we entered the age of digital transactions, the concept evolved to become fraud analytics, marking a proactive approach, leveraging data mining, machine learning, and statistical analysis to predict and prevent fraudulent activities. Fraud analytics, a burgeoning field of technology and analytics, is playing an increasingly significant role in business operations worldwide. Distinguished academics and practitioners have approached the field from different angles, but they all concur on its core characteristics and purposes.

Fraud analytics encompasses advanced tools and methods employed to identify, prevent, and potentially investigate fraudulent activity. The process involves diving deep into massive volumes of structured and unstructured data, such as financial transactions, customer behavior, and operational data, to fish out irregularities or anomalies. Once detected, these inconsistencies can offer businesses valuable insights to act upon, preventing massive losses and legal issues. Chapter 5 goes deeper into this intriguing aspect of data analytics, guiding you through its intricate landscape.

Thanks to machine learning algorithms, it's possible to anticipate or predict fraudulent behavior. This was emphasized by Ahmed Abbasi from the University of Virginia, Conan C. Albrecht from Brigham Young University, Anthony Vance from Temple University, and J. Eric W. Hansen from Polytechnic Institute of New York University in their paper "MetaFraud: A Meta-Learning Framework For Detecting Financial Fraud," published in MIS Quarterly in 2012. They highlighted that these algorithms, which learn and improve over time, work on a variety of datasets to identify potential fraudulent patterns. This strengthens businesses against future threats.

But what's truly fantastic about fraud analytics is its adaptability. As fraudsters develop new tricks, fraud analytics evolves too. It's like a guardian, constantly learning, adapting, and improving to protect organizations. It's not just about detecting or even predicting fraud; it's about preventing it, which is why it's so valuable to organizations across different sectors.

Fraud analytics is a philosophy, not a tool. It's about staying ahead, defending businesses, and making the digital world safer. This book explores these aspects in great detail, revealing how this potent blend of technology and analytics is redefining the way businesses tackle the menace of fraud.

Importance of Fraud Analytics

Fraud analytics is instrumental for businesses in safeguarding their financial assets and maintaining their reputations. Here are several specific ways this is accomplished:

- The first line of defense in this field is *proactive threat recognition*. Learning from past patterns and behaviors, fraud analytics empowers businesses to spot potentially fraudulent activities before they occur. It's a bit like a detective who can predict a crime before it happens.

- Secondly, fraud analytics is all about *financial protection*. It acts as a safeguard for organizations, shielding them from the severe financial impacts that fraudulent activities could cause. Think of it as a financial bodyguard that keeps your assets safe.
- The *reputation safeguarding* aspect shouldn't be overlooked either. Fraud can lead to a significant loss of trust among customers, partners, and stakeholders. Fraud analytics helps maintain that trust by ensuring that operations run in a way that upholds ethical standards. It's akin to a reputation manager who ensures that the business's public image remains untarnished.
- Lastly, when it comes to *compliance assurance*, especially in heavily regulated sectors like healthcare and finance, fraud analytics is indispensable. It's a handy tool that helps firms adhere to all the regulations, preventing them from facing hefty penalties and legal actions.

Effective fraud management, driven by sophisticated fraud analytics, paves the way for enhanced customer trust and loyalty—both of which are crucial for any business's long-term success. Fraud management is not just about dealing with fraudulent activities; it's about creating an environment that promotes trust and reliability.

Why Organization Should Invest in Fraud Analytics

Fraud is a growing and persistent problem in today's fast-paced digital environment. For this reason, investment in fraud analytics has become crucial for organizations.

Crafty fraudsters are always concocting new schemes to trick and take advantage of the system. Luckily, fraud analytics and its groundbreaking tech and methods can give organizations the upper hand. And consider the digital transformation sweeping across industries—a tidal wave of online transactions and data that unfortunately makes organizations more vulnerable to fraud. In this risky environment, fraud analytics steps up as a strong defensive line, armed with the tools and strategies to detect and put a stop to fraud attempts.

There is an undeniable financial benefit of implementing fraud analytics. Deploying these solutions can lead to big cost savings. By cutting down on financial losses from fraud and reducing the need for manual detective work, it helps organizations run a tight ship, efficiently allocating resources and trimming down operational costs.

And don't forget the competitive advantage that comes with advanced fraud analytics solutions. It's like an organizational superpower. Demonstrating a steadfast commitment to security and ethical business practices, businesses can gain the trust of customers and partners, laying the foundation for growth and success.

Key Characteristics of Successful Fraud Analytics Models

For a fraud detection model to be effective, it should possess the following attributes:

- *Statistical accuracy:* The model should have high precision in detecting fraudulent activities.
- *Interpretability:* Stakeholders should be able to understand the model's process and outcomes.
- *Regulatory compliance:* The model should abide by all relevant laws and regulations, particularly around privacy.
- *Economic impact:* The model should offer a good return on investment and have an affordable total cost of ownership.
- *Integration with expert-based approaches:* Data-driven models can often benefit from being complemented by traditional expert-based fraud detection methods.

Challenges of Fraud Detection Models

Building a successful fraud detection model comes with its share of difficulties:

- *Data imbalance:* In many contexts, the instances of legitimate activities vastly outnumber fraudulent cases, making it challenging to train a model that can accurately detect fraud.
- *Operational efficiency:* Depending on the application, the model might need to make decisions within a very short timeframe.
- *False positives:* Incorrectly flagging legitimate activities as fraudulent could potentially lead to customer dissatisfaction and lost business.

Imbalanced Data and the Confusion Matrix

Imbalanced data refers to a situation where the number of observations belonging to one class is significantly lower than those belonging to the other classes. In fraud detection, this usually means there are far fewer fraudulent cases than legitimate ones. Example 1 shows some code to visualize imbalanced data as a pie chart, and Fig. 3.1 shows the output.

Example 1. Visualize the Imbalanced Data as a Pie Chart

```
import pandas as pd  # Importing the pandas library to work with data in
tables
import matplotlib.pyplot as plt  # Importing matplotlib for creating
visualizations

# Read the data from a CSV file and store it in a table called
'transfers_df'
transfers_df = pd.read_csv('transfers.csv')

# Count the number of fraud and non-fraud cases, and calculate their
percentage
fraud_label_counts =
transfers_df['fraud_flag'].value_counts(normalize=True)

# Create labels for the pie chart with each label showing the category and
its percentage
labels = [f'{label} {round(percentage * 100, 2)}%' for label, percentage
in fraud_label_counts.items()]

# Define the colors for the different parts of the pie chart
colors = ['blue', 'red']

# Set the size of the chart
plt.figure(figsize=(10, 6))  # Make the chart 10 inches wide and 6 inches
high

# Create the pie chart using the data, labels, and colors
plt.pie(fraud_label_counts, labels=labels, colors=colors,
autopct='%1.1f%%')
# 'autopct' shows the percentage on each slice of the pie chart

# Add a title to the chart
plt.title('Distribution of Fraud Cases')  # Set a clear title

# Display the chart
plt.show()  # Show the pie chart
```

The Confusion Matrix (Fig. 3.2) is an instrumental tool in evaluating the performance of a classification model. It portrays the number of true positives, true negatives, false positives, and false negatives, enabling a calculation of the model's accuracy. However, for imbalanced datasets, frequently encountered in fraud detection, conventional metrics such as accuracy are often less informative. In such contexts, it's essential to utilize metrics like precision, recall, and the F1 score for a more exhaustive evaluation of a model's performance.

Precision refers to the fraction of correctly identified positive instances—is especially important when false positives carry high costs. In contrast, *recall*—the fraction of all actual positive instances that are accurately identified—becomes critical when the cost of missing a positive instance is substantial. The F1 score, calculated as the harmonic mean of precision and recall, is useful in scenarios where both types of errors are of equal importance.

For example, businesses dealing with fraud detection often have to balance precision and recall due to their unique consequences. A company may prioritize precision to prevent fraudulent transactions, but this could lead to an increase in false negatives. Accordingly, businesses must weigh the costs associated with false negatives and false positives to make an informed choice.

Beyond these metrics, considerations like explainability, transparency, and fairness are vital for model selection:

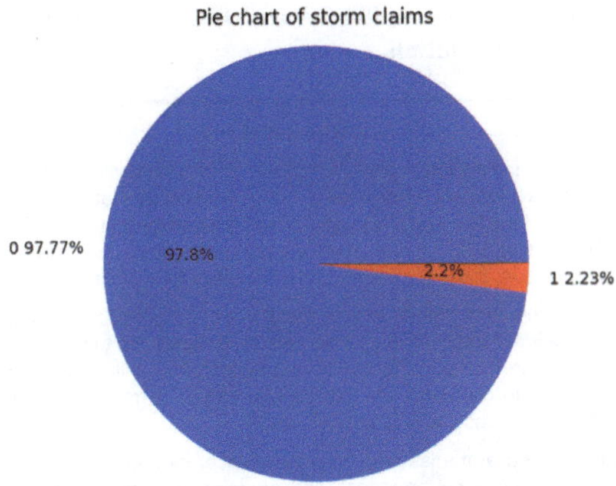

Fig. 3.1 Pie Chart of Fraud Case Distribution: This figure presents a pie chart titled "Pie Chart of Fraud Case Distribution," visualizing the proportion of fraud and non-fraud cases in the dataset. The chart consists of two segments: a large blue segment, labeled "0," representing non-fraud cases at 97.8%, and a smaller red segment, labeled "1," representing fraud cases at 2.2%. This visualization highlights the significant imbalance between fraud and non-fraud cases

- Explainability is key when the decision-making process must be conveyed to stakeholders, such as regulators and customers.
- Transparency is crucial for auditing, ensuring the model operates as anticipated.
- Fairness is critical to confirm that the model's outcomes are devoid of unintentional bias, potentially impacting certain groups disproportionately.

In summary, dealing with imbalanced datasets, particularly in fraud detection, necessitates careful consideration of several facets. These include the selection of relevant performance metrics that encapsulate the balance between different types of errors and broader aspects like explainability, transparency, and fairness.

The economic implications of handling imbalanced datasets, especially in fraud detection, are significant. The total cost due to fraud typically represents the sum of all fraudulent amounts. Failing to detect these fraudulent activities can lead to substantial financial losses for an organization, underscoring the importance of precision, recall, and other evaluation metrics in model selection and performance assessment. Refer to Chapter 11 for more details.

Summary

This chapter mapped out the evolution and significance of fraud analytics in the modern business landscape, tracing its transformation from humble origins to the intricate applications of artificial intelligence (AI) and machine learning (ML) seen today. The focus remained on the vital role fraud analytics plays in protecting financial resources, ensuring regulatory compliance, and preserving an organization's reputation, thus underscoring the necessity for such investments.

The chapter dissected the components of successful fraud analytics models and the challenges encountered during their assembly. You saw how these models need to strike a delicate balance between precision, interpretability, compliance, and economic viability. Furthermore, they must be specifically designed to overcome the unique challenges of fraud detection, such as data imbalance, operational efficiency, and false positives.

Finally, the chapter looked at the issue of data imbalance, introduced tools like the confusion matrix for evaluating model performance, and underscored the financial implications of overlooking fraud. This exploration established the importance of fraud analytics not just as a detection tool, but also as a key part of fraud prevention, equipping organizations with the knowledge to stay ahead in the fight against fraud.

Chapter 4 examines the cyclical nature of fraud management. It explores its key stages, including detection, investigation, remediation, and prevention, and demonstrates how these stages are interconnected and require ongoing monitoring and enhancement for effective fraud management. This progression will not only deepen your understanding of fraud analytics but will also provide you with the necessary tools for effective and efficient fraud detection and prevention. The journey to gain knowledge, step by step, continues.

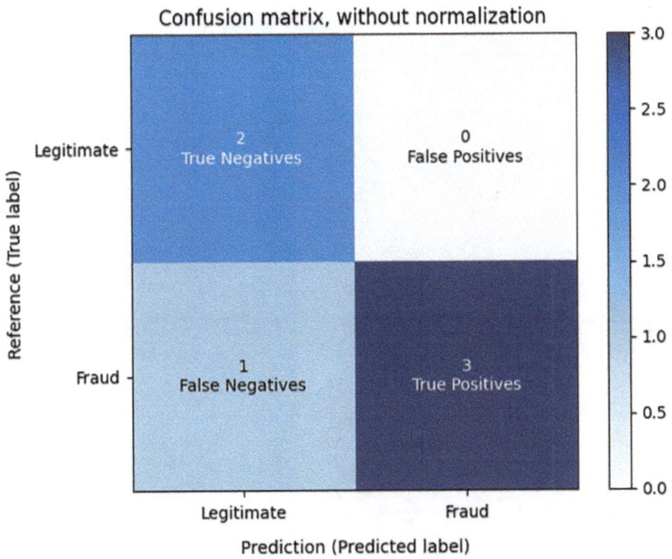

Fig. 3.2 Confusion Matrix for Classification Model: This figure illustrates a confusion matrix for a binary classification model without normalization. The matrix provides a visual representation of model performance, showing the counts of true positives, true negatives, false positives, and false negatives. The top-left quadrant indicates 2 true negatives (Legitimate predicted as Legitimate), the top-right quadrant shows 0 false positives (Fraud predicted as Legitimate), the bottom left quadrant highlights 1 false negative (Legitimate predicted as Fraud), and the bottom right quadrant displays 3 true positives (Fraud predicted as Fraud). A color gradient bar to the right ranges from light to dark blue, representing values from 0 to 3, corresponding to the intensity of prediction counts

CHAPTER 4

The Fraud Management Cycle with Key Components of Fraud Analytics

Today, fraud management is a proactive and continuous effort, far more than just a reactive task. This chapter explores the concept of the *Fraud Management Cycle*. It presents a seamless interplay of detection, investigation, resolution, and prevention stages, illustrating the relentless monitoring and enhancements required for efficient fraud management.

The chapter also takes a strategic, data-driven look at fraud analytics, showing how a blend of high-quality data, advanced models, and skilled personnel empowers organizations to counter fraudulent activities effectively. It emphasizes the need for clear objectives, comprehensive data integration, stringent data security, compliance, and continuous model evaluation to maintain the effectiveness and reliability of fraud analytics.

You'll also find discussions about essential *key performance indicators* (KPIs) and challenges in fraud analytics. These serve as guides in measuring the effectiveness of fraud analytics and pinpointing areas needing improvement. By the end of this chapter, you'll gain a comprehensive understanding of the Fraud Management Cycle and the core components of fraud analytics. This knowledge will equip you to devise and implement successful strategies for fraud detection, prevention, and management.

Now, let's investigate the intricate web of fraud management and analytics.

A. Al Aqqad, *Fraud Analytics in Action*
https://doi.org/10.1007/978-3-032-16023-2_4

Understanding the Fraud Management Cycle

The Fraud Management Cycle is a concept used by businesses to control and reduce the risk of fraud. It is divided into five crucial stages:

- Prevention
- Detection
- Investigation
- Resolution
- Reporting

Each stage plays a significant role in the effective management of fraud within a business context. Figure 4.1 depicts the relations of the five stages of this cycle, showing how each stage interacts and overlaps with the others to create a complete and continuous cycle of fraud management.

Fig. 4.1 Fraud Management Lifecycle: Flow chart illustrating the Fraud Management Lifecycle. Central text reads "Fraud Management Lifecycle." The cycle includes five stages: Prevention, Investigation, Detection, Resolution, and Reporting, each represented by a circular icon with relevant symbols. Arrows connect the stages in a clockwise direction, indicating a continuous process

Prevention

Fraud *prevention*, an integral part of the Fraud Management Cycle, demands an ongoing commitment from organizations to protect their financial and reputational assets. The first crucial step involves regular assessments of systems, processes, and organizational culture to identify potential weak spots that fraudsters might exploit.

Upon identifying vulnerabilities, organizations need to promptly establish safeguards. Physical security measures such as access controls, surveillance systems, and secure storage help prevent unauthorized access to crucial assets and locations. Additionally, cultivating an environment that values honesty and integrity is key. Organizations can achieve this through frequent training sessions, clear communication, a code of conduct, and a reporting system that enables employees to share suspicious behaviors without fear of retribution.

Regular *risk assessments* form another crucial preventive measure. Such evaluations identify areas particularly susceptible to fraud and assess the potential financial or reputational impact. Robust *internal controls* can be deployed alongside these assessments, with measures such as role segregation, monitoring financial transactions, two-factor authentication, and regular audits significantly fortifying an organization's defenses.

Thorough *background checks* during the recruitment process screen potential employees and third parties for any history of fraudulent or criminal activity. Simultaneously, it's essential to empower the workforce with knowledge about fraud red flags, ethical behavior, and integrity through awareness training. Doing so allows for the quick spotting and reporting of suspicious activities.

Data analytics and machine learning (ML) have become indispensable tools for fraud prevention. Analysis of large datasets can detect patterns, monitor employee behavior, predict potential fraud, and highlight areas requiring tighter control.

To foster an open and accountable culture, establishing a clear code of conduct and a mechanism for reporting fraud is crucial. These initiatives encourage an atmosphere where ethics are valued, and misconduct is swiftly addressed.

> TIP
>
> Fraud prevention is a continuous cycle of evaluation, strategy refinement, and action. By identifying vulnerabilities, implementing protective measures, and fostering an ethical culture consistently, organizations can deter fraud, protect assets, and stave off financial losses and reputational damage.

Detection

The detection phase serves as a pivotal element of the Fraud Management Cycle, warranting stringent focus due to its capacity to preempt substantial issues through the early identification of prospective fraud. To fortify their defense against fraudulent activities, organizations can instigate several detection protocols. Regular financial audits, comprising meticulous examination of financial records, transactions, assets, and employee access logs, can bring to light inconsistencies or suspicious maneuvers. The deployment of fraud detection software further enhances this process, enabling an advanced analysis of data to pinpoint anomalies and thus aid in the unearthing of potential fraud. This might encompass monitoring mechanisms for bank transactions, social media activity, or other relevant data sources.

Organizations can also establish a conducive environment for fraud reporting, encouraging employees to disclose any suspicious behavior via a dedicated hotline or other reporting avenues. This participative vigilance significantly bolsters the identification and prevention of fraudulent activities. Monitoring social media activity forms another pivotal strategy, enabling organizations to identify potential threats, gather critical intelligence, and proactively curb fraud. Scrutinizing large volumes of data, such as financial records or employee activity, allows for the discernment of patterns and aberrations that might signal fraudulent activity.

> TIP
>
> Being a crucial line of defense, the detection phase facilitates the uncovering of suspected fraud and enables the organization to trigger appropriate measures to contain further damage. By maintaining persistent surveillance of financial transactions and data, utilizing cutting-edge fraud detection tools, offering anonymous reporting pathways, and conducting regular internal audits, organizations can proficiently detect and address fraudulent undertakings.

Investigation

The investigation phase plays a distinctive role in maintaining objectivity and ensuring appropriate resolution of fraud cases. It unfolds in six crucial steps, each contributing to a comprehensive understanding of the alleged fraudulent activity:

- *Defining the scope:* The first step is to detail the suspected fraudulent activities and identify the individuals involved in the investigation.

This provides a clear framework for the subsequent stages of the process.

- *Assembling the team:* The next step is to put together a competent team of experts, often including internal auditors, forensic accountants, and legal professionals. This team is tasked with conducting the investigation.
- *Conducting interviews:* The team is responsible for interviewing employees and vendors suspected of fraud, aiming to collect necessary information through professional, unbiased discussions.
- *Securing and maintaining evidence:* Parallel to conducting interviews, it is crucial to secure and preserve relevant documents such as bank records and emails. This step ensures the integrity and authenticity of the evidence, laying the groundwork for its subsequent analysis.
- *Analyzing the evidence:* The collected evidence is then reviewed to assess the extent of the fraud and identify the perpetrators. Utilization of forensic accounting and data analysis can help uncover financial trends and inconsistencies, strengthening the case.
- *Reporting:* The team writes a report about the fraud, the suspects, and the evidence after the investigation. Top management and legal counsel should evaluate this material to identify the next steps.

TIP

The investigation's findings should prompt the organization to address any control weaknesses or inefficiencies that might have enabled the fraud. Remedial measures could range from implementing new internal controls, organizing staff training, to modifying company policies. By conducting such thorough investigations, organizations can showcase their commitment to ethics and transparency, ultimately building trust among stakeholders and preventing future instances of fraud.

Resolution

In the resolution or remediation phase, organizations address the root causes of fraud and implement measures to prevent its recurrence. This phase requires a series of critical actions and can be seen as the stage that strengthens the organization's defenses against fraudulent activities.

Initially, corrective measures must be put in place to address identified weaknesses in internal controls and procedures. This could involve adjusting policies or adopting new methods to tighten security. Subsequently, prosecuting those responsible for fraud is a crucial step that sends a resounding message to all members of the organization: fraudulent activities will not be tolerated.

In tandem with these actions, transparency is key in maintaining the trust of stakeholders. Organizations should keep stakeholders informed about the steps taken to rectify the situation and prevent future fraud. Transparency extends to the ongoing evaluation of results where organizations regularly audit and review internal controls and procedures to assure their effectiveness in preventing fraud.

In addition to these direct responses, upgrading fraud prevention systems can greatly improve resilience against fraud. By incorporating new technologies and data analytics techniques, organizations can detect anomalies and potential fraud, further fortifying their defenses.

Integral to all these efforts is fostering an ethical and transparent culture within the organization. This involves consistently communicating and enforcing the organization's values and code of conduct, promoting a speak-up culture where employees feel safe to report suspicious behavior, and offering regular fraud awareness training. These actions can strengthen the organization's ethical fabric and help deter fraud.

TIP

The resolution phase is, thus, a critical point in the Fraud Management Cycle that helps organizations address and rectify the root causes of fraud while laying down a roadmap to prevent future occurrences. With proactive fraud reduction measures, organizations can avert financial losses, foster stakeholder trust, and cultivate a culture that values ethical behavior and transparency.

Reporting

The reporting stage requires organizations to articulate fraud incidences succinctly and accurately to minimize financial losses, shield reputation, and uphold their commitment to ethics and transparency. This phase necessitates a careful approach in handling the gathered information about the fraud incident and making it accessible to the right entities.

Writing a comprehensive report is the initial step where organizations document the alleged fraud, including details about the involved individuals and gathered evidence. It's vital for this report to undergo legal scrutiny to ensure all aspects are in line with legal standards and maintain the organization's reputation.

Subsequently, the organization needs to engage stakeholders by informing top management, regulators, and law enforcement about the incidence of fraud. This open communication underscores the organization's commitment to ethics and transparency, thereby fostering stakeholder trust. In addition to reporting, organizations can assist law enforcement by providing evidence, testifying in court, or aiding in the identification of other fraudsters. This collaborative approach helps fortify the broader fight against fraud and underscores the company's commitment to justice.

Evaluating the effectiveness of stakeholder and regulatory reporting is a crucial aspect of this phase. Organizations can use methods such as stakeholder surveys or interviews to verify the report's comprehensiveness, legal compliance, and its reception among stakeholders.

TIP

The reporting *phase* allows organizations to mitigate financial and reputational damage resulting from fraud incidents, while concurrently showcasing their commitment to ethics and transparency. Through prompt and transparent reporting of fraud, organizations can cultivate trust, prevent the recurrence of such incidents, and fulfill their legal obligations. Regular evaluation of reporting processes ensures the legal adequacy of the reports, thus keeping the organization compliant and bolstering its credibility in the eyes of stakeholders.

Other Factors

In addition to the five main phases of the Fraud Management Cycle, organizations need to incorporate other crucial elements for effective fraud prevention and management, notably evaluation and improvement, as well as interdepartmental communication and collaboration.

After traversing the five phases, organizations must commit to the regular examination and assessment of their fraud prevention and detection systems. This helps identify any potential weaknesses or vulnerabilities that may have been missed initially or have evolved over time. Various methods such as risk assessments, internal control testing, and employee training reviews can help ensure these systems are robust and reliable. Based on the outcomes of these evaluations, companies can refine and enhance their fraud prevention and detection techniques, leading to reduced fraud risk.

Furthermore, open communication and teamwork among different departments and stakeholders are vital. Fraud is often a multifaceted issue involving various departments and individuals within an organization. Hence, ensuring that all relevant parties are actively communicating and cooperating is crucial in identifying, managing, and preventing fraudulent activities. Organizations should establish clear communication channels, define roles and responsibilities, and foster a culture of transparency and accountability. By promoting ethical behavior and personal responsibility among employees, organizations can fortify their defenses against fraud (Fig. 4.3).

Key Components of Fraud Analytics

Fraud analytics' effectiveness hinges on the triumvirate of data, models, and people (DMP), as shown in Fig. 4.2, each playing a pivotal role in the process.

- *Data:* Acts as the critical cornerstone of fraud analytics, with the collection and analysis of high-quality, accurate information from various sources forming its backbone. Effective scrutiny of this data can unearth patterns and red flags indicative of fraudulent activities, providing the basis for preventive action.
- *Models:* These comprise the algorithms and statistical models used for fraud identification and prevention, constitute the second element. Careful data preparation paves the way for the creation of flexible, scalable fraud detection models, a crucial cog in the fraud analytics machine.
- *People:* These include a variety of skilled professionals such as fraud analysts, auditors, data analysts, and IT experts. Their specialized skills and expertise are instrumental in successfully executing and monitoring fraud analytics programs. The clear delineation of their roles and responsibilities ensures efficient functioning and maximizes the utility of data and models.

Prior to implementing a fraud analytics program, understanding the organizational context is crucial, necessitating clear goal setting, key fraud risk identification, comprehension of regulatory requirements, and clear definition of the program's scope. Fraud analytics leverages descriptive,

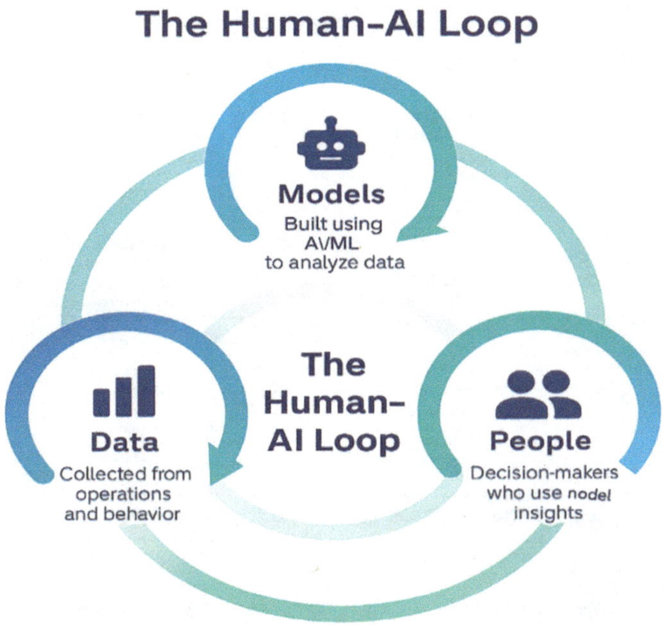

Fig. 4.2 Key components of fraud analytics: Flow chart titled "The Human-AI Loop" illustrating a cyclical process. At the top, "Models" are built using AI/ML to analyze data. On the left, "Data" is collected from operations and behavior. On the right, "People" are decision-makers who use model insights. Arrows connect these elements, forming a loop, emphasizing the continuous interaction between data, models, and people.

predictive, and prescriptive analytics for identifying trends, making future predictions, and recommending prevention strategies, respectively. Efficient alert and reporting processes facilitate communication of fraud concerns, with data visualization tools and reports enhancing their comprehensibility.

> WARNING
>
> In the realm of fraud analytics, data privacy and security are paramount. Compliance with data protection regulations such as GDPR and CCPA is mandatory, calling for the implementation of robust access controls, encryption methods, and routine data privacy and security training for all team members. These stringent security standards must also extend to any third-party vendors granted access to sensitive data.

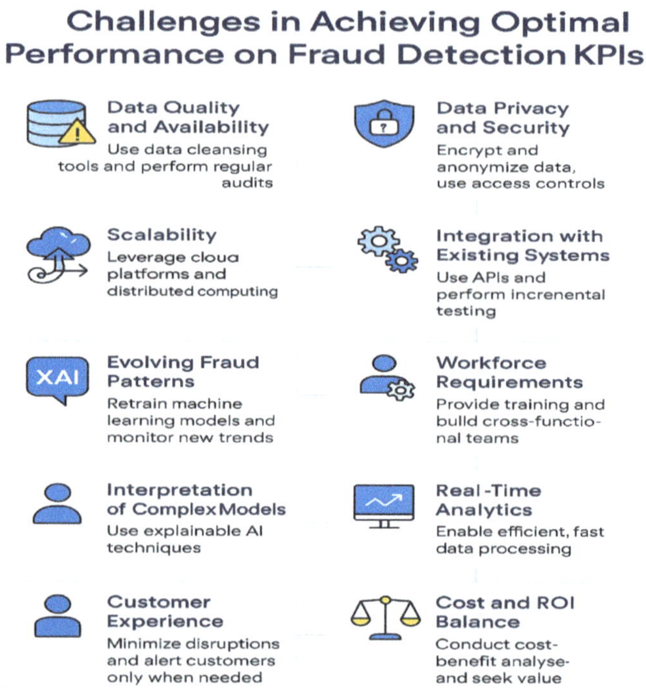

Fig. 4.3 This flowchart summarizes ten key barriers to effective fraud detection performance, including data quality, privacy, scalability, system integration, evolving fraud trends, workforce readiness, model interpretability, real-time analytics, customer experience, and cost-benefit balance. Each area is visually represented with an icon to highlight critical operational and strategic considerations

The final stage in the process entails model evaluation and validation to ensure the accuracy and reliability of the fraud detection system. Regular review and testing of these models using performance metrics such as precision, recall, F1 score, and AUC-ROC, help fine-tune the system and enhance its fraud detection capabilities.

A strategic, data-driven approach to fraud analytics, with a strong emphasis on data privacy and security, allows organizations to effectively detect and preempt fraud, protecting their reputation and financial resources while fostering a culture of transparency and accountability.

Fraud Analytics KPIs and Challenges

KPIs and associated challenges are integral in optimizing and maintaining the effectiveness of fraud detection and prevention systems. These KPIs are listed in Table 4.1. Fraud analytics KPIs include detection rate, false positives and negatives, investigation efficiency, customer satisfaction, financial impact, adaptability, and staff training. Each of these indicators provides organizations with a mechanism for evaluating their fraud prevention systems and tracking progress.

Challenges in Achieving Optimal Performance on Fraud Detection KPIs

Organizations face several challenges when striving to meet key performance indicators (KPIs) for effective fraud detection. Below are some major barriers and practical tips to overcome them:

1. *Data Quality and Availability:* High-quality, accurate data is crucial. Poor data quality can lead to unreliable results and a higher risk of fraud going undetected.
   - Tip: Use data cleansing tools and perform regular audits to ensure data consistency and integrity.
   - Tools: *Talend*, *Trifacta*, *OpenRefine*—these tools help with data cleaning, preparation, and transformation.
2. Scalability: As data volumes increase, the system must efficiently handle larger loads.
   - Tip: Use cloud-based platforms and distributed computing to scale up as needed, ensuring smooth performance.
   - Tools: Amazon Web Services (AWS), Google Cloud Platform (GCP), Apache Hadoop—these platforms support scalable data processing.

Table 4.1 Fraud analytics KPIs

KPI	Description
Detection rate	The rate at which fraud is detected by the system. A higher rate is indicative of an efficient fraud detection system.
False positives and negatives	A false positive refers to a situation where legitimate transactions are incorrectly flagged as fraudulent, leading to customer dissatisfaction and unnecessary investigations. On the other hand, a false negative refers to a fraudulent transaction slipping through the detection system unnoticed, leading to financial losses. The goal is to minimize both.
Investigation efficiency	The speed and effectiveness of investigations conducted after potential fraud is detected. Faster, more efficient investigations can limit the impact of fraud.
Customer satisfaction	An effective fraud prevention system should operate without inconveniencing customers. Thus, maintaining high customer satisfaction is key.
Financial impact	The cost of implementing and maintaining the fraud detection system should be justified by the savings from preventing fraud. Regular cost-benefit evaluations can assist in assessing this.
Adaptability	The ability of the system to evolve and adapt to new fraud patterns.
Staff training	Employees need to be adequately trained to use and manage the fraud prevention system.

3. Evolving fraud patterns: Fraudsters constantly change their tactics to evade detection.
   - Tip: Use machine learning models that learn continuously and retrain regularly with updated data. Monitor new trends proactively.
   - Tools: TensorFlow, H2O.ai, AutoML—these frameworks allow for continuous learning and model retraining.
4. Interpretation of complex models: Machine learning models can be hard to explain, especially to non-technical stakeholders.
   - Tip: Use explainable AI (XAI) techniques to make model decisions clearer.

- Tools: LIME (Local Interpretable Model-agnostic Explanations), SHAP (SHapley Additive exPlanations)—these are popular XAI tools that help explain machine learning model outputs by providing insight into feature importance and local explanations.

Other tools include:

- Anchor: Provides precise feature explanations.
- ELI5: Explains model decisions and visualizes important features.
- InterpretML: A toolkit from Microsoft with various model explanation options.
- What-If Tool (WIT): Google's tool to explore model predictions.
- AIX360 (AI Explainability 360): IBM's toolkit for a wide range of interpretability techniques.

5. *Customer experience:* Fraud detection should not negatively impact the user experience.
   - Tip: Implement systems that operate in the background with minimal disruptions. Alert customers only when necessary.
   - *Tools: Sift, Kount, Signifyd*—fraud detection platforms that integrate into customer systems without interrupting the user experience.
6. Data privacy and security: Compliance with regulations like GDPR and CCPA is essential. Any breach can have severe consequences.
   - Tip: Use strong encryption, anonymization, and access controls. Conduct regular security audits to ensure compliance.
   - Tools: IBM Guardium, Vormetric Data Security Platform, Symantec Data Loss Prevention (DLP)—these tools focus on data privacy and security, ensuring compliance with regulations like GDPR and CCPA.
7. Integration with existing systems: New solutions must work seamlessly with current systems.
   - Tip: Use APIs and integration platforms for smooth data flow. Perform incremental testing to avoid disruptions.

   - Tools: MuleSoft, Zapier, Dell Boomi—integration platforms that can bridge different systems and enable seamless data flow.

8. Workforce requirements: A skilled team is essential to manage and run fraud detection systems effectively.
   - Tip: Offer training programs and certifications. Create cross-functional teams with a mix of data scientists, IT professionals, and fraud experts.
   - Tools: Coursera, Udemy, edX—these platforms offer training courses and certifications for data analytics, machine learning, and fraud detection.
9. Real-time analytics: Detecting fraud in real time requires efficient and fast data processing.
   - Tip: Invest in high-performance analytics platforms and use optimized algorithms to ensure speed and accuracy.
   - Tools: Apache Kafka, Azure Stream Analytics, Google BigQuery—these platforms support real-time data processing and analytics.
10. Cost and ROI balance: The cost of fraud detection systems should be justified by the savings they provide.
    - Tip: Conduct cost-benefit analyses regularly to measure ROI. Choose scalable and cost-effective solutions.
    - Tools: Tableau, Power BI, Looker—these tools can be used to track ROI and create data visualizations to support decision-making.

Summary

This chapter explored the Fraud Management Cycle, studying the stages of detection, investigation, remediation, and prevention. You saw how each stage interplays to form an ongoing cycle of fraud management. You also discovered key components of fraud analytics such as the importance of quality data, advanced models, skilled personnel, clear objectives, data security, and continuous model evaluation. The role of key performance indicators (KPIs) in measuring fraud analytics' effectiveness was another focal point. This chapter equipped you with essential knowledge to devise effective strategies for fraud detection, prevention, and management.

In Chapter 5, the focus will shift to the techniques and methodologies used in fraud analytics. Starting with traditional rule-based methods, you will learn about the increasingly popular data-driven approaches. You'll gain insights into expert-based systems and explore the depths of machine learning techniques like supervised, unsupervised, and deep learning.
The potential of a hybrid approach, which combines the strengths of expert-based and data-driven methods, will also be discussed. Finally, you'll learn about specific fraud analytics techniques such as anomaly detection, social network analysis, data visualization, and text analytics.

CHAPTER 5

Techniques and Approaches in Fraud Analytics

This chapter provides a structured overview of the key approaches and techniques used in fraud analytics. It begins with conventional rule-based, expert-driven methods—well-established frameworks that leverage the domain knowledge and experience of fraud investigators to identify known fraud patterns. The discussion then extends to data-driven methodologies, which have gained prominence with advances in computing and machine learning (ML). These approaches offer organizations a broader and more adaptive toolkit for detecting both known and emerging forms of fraud. Where appropriate, the chapter also examines hybrid approaches that combine the strengths of expert-based and data-driven methods, resulting in more robust and comprehensive fraud detection frameworks. The chapter concludes with an exploration of specialized fraud analytics techniques, including anomaly detection, social network analysis, data visualization, text analytics, and the application of artificial intelligence (AI) in identifying fraudulent patterns and behaviors.

Starting with expert-based systems, this investigation of fraud analytics moves. You will closely examine these rule-based systems that primarily rely on fraud investigators' experienced judgment and domain expertise. These professionals highlight any hazards that might pass under the algorithmic radar using their thorough awareness of fraud trends. From there, we go to data-driven methods, negotiating the field of ML under the direction of supervised and unsupervised learning and deep learning.

A. Al Aqqad, *Fraud Analytics in Action*
https://doi.org/10.1007/978-3-032-16023-2_5

These methods uncover known and new fraud patterns, allowing the study of the fundamental core of data.

The issue then becomes: why use just one strategy when both have advantages? Combining the data-crunching ability of data-driven approaches with the knowledge of expert-based approaches results in a hybrid approach. This symbiotic mix can produce more complete and strong fraud detection systems.

The chapter ends with an illuminating discussion of particular fraud analytics methods. You'll find techniques including text analytics, social network analysis, data visualization, and anomaly identification. Moreover, you will show how the forefront of artificial intelligence (AI) may be used to expose trends and anomalies suggesting fraud.

With companies utilizing expert-based and data-driven techniques, fraud analytics—the data analysis process used to identify and stop fraudulent behavior—is becoming more critical. Expert-based approaches use fraud analysts' experience and domain knowledge to build strategies based on identified patterns employing rules and heuristics, utilizing which possible fraud risks are found. Although these methods are easy to use and maintain, their limited capacity to identify developing fraud trends requires constant updates.

As digitalization and data availability advance, data-driven methodologies and ML-based methods—such as supervised, unsupervised, and social network analysis—are increasingly appealing. These techniques demand advanced analytical methods and high-quality data, yet they are more successful in spotting known and developing fraud trends.

Section A: Approaches in Fraud Analytics

Expert-Based Approaches

The expert-driven, or rule-based, method of fraud detection relies on the experience and intuition of fraud experts. This traditional approach involves creating systems made up of simple IF-THEN rules that highlight known fraud patterns. When these rules are applied, the system flags suspicious activities, like a large transaction from a high-risk area soon after an account is created.

For example, a rule might be:

> If an account is created in one country and used to make a large transaction in a high-risk region within 24 hours, flag it as suspicious.

Another example:

> If an account is created in China and a ride request is made in New York shortly after, flag the transaction for investigation.

Building an Expert-Based Rule Engine:

1. *Gathering Domain Expertise:* Start by collecting insights from fraud experts who understand common scams and patterns.
2. *Identifying Fraud Indicators:* Pinpoint key signs of fraud, called red flags, which will serve as the basis for your rules. These could include unusual transaction amounts or geographic mismatches.
3. *Creating Business Rules:* Use these indicators to set up rules, from simple ones like "transaction amount over a certain threshold" to more complex, multi-condition rules. Be careful not to create too many, as this could lead to false alarms.
4. *Continuous Enhancement:* Fraudsters adapt, so regularly review and update your rules based on new trends and insights.

Rule-Based Fraud Detection: A Practical Example from Uber
An illustrative case of rule-based fraud detection comes from Uber, which regularly encounters fraudulent riders using stolen credit cards. Fraudulent activities often follow identifiable patterns or structures, making them suitable for rule-based detection. See Fig. 5.1.

Uber uses rule-based systems to tackle common fraud schemes, such as riders using stolen credit cards. These systems analyze account behavior and flag discrepancies, like:

- *Geographical Inconsistency:* Accounts created in one region but used in places like New York or London.
- *Account Creation Patterns:* Multiple accounts made in quick succession using random email addresses.
- *Payment Method Red Flags:* The same credit card being used across multiple accounts. (See Fig. 5.2)

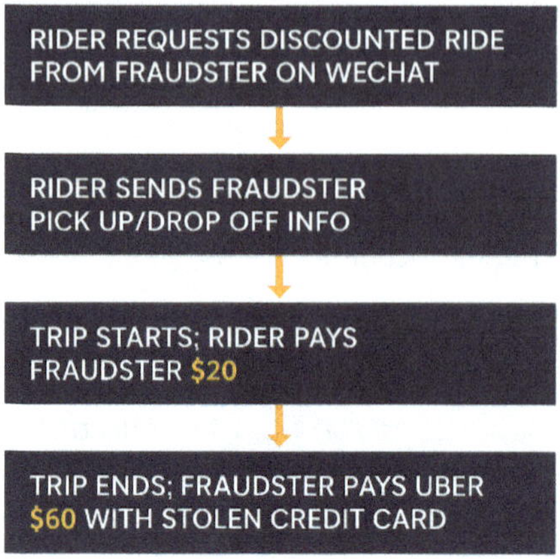

Fig. 5.1 Flowchart of a Fraudulent Ride Scheme: This figure illustrates the process of a fraudulent ride scheme. The flowchart begins with the rider requesting a discounted ride from a fraudster on WeChat. Next, the rider sends the fraudster the pickup and drop-off information. The trip starts, and the rider pays the fraudster $20. Finally, the trip ends, and the fraudster pays Uber $60 using a stolen credit card. Arrows indicate the sequence of actions, highlighting the steps involved in this scheme

Challenges in Uber's Rule-Based Fraud Detection: While Uber's rule-based systems offer effective detection, they face several challenges:

- *Adaptive Fraudsters:* Fraudsters keep changing tactics, like switching to IP addresses in new regions.
- *Manual Rule Creation:* Analysts have to continually create and adjust rules, which takes time.
- *Ongoing Adaptation:* Both Uber and fraudsters are in a continuous race to outsmart each other.

TIP
Rule-based systems are easy to understand and implement but become less effective as fraud tactics evolve. Companies like Uber often combine these systems with machine learning for a stronger defense.

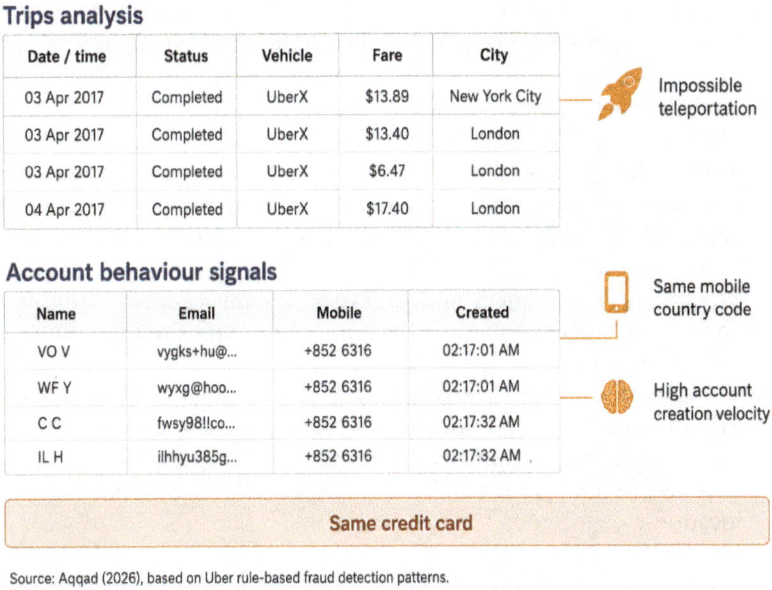

Date / time	Status	Vehicle	Fare	City
03 Apr 2017	Completed	UberX	$13.89	New York City
03 Apr 2017	Completed	UberX	$13.40	London
03 Apr 2017	Completed	UberX	$6.47	London
04 Apr 2017	Completed	UberX	$17.40	London

Name	Email	Mobile	Created
VO V	vygks+hu@...	+852 6316	02:17:01 AM
WF Y	wyxg@hoo...	+852 6316	02:17:01 AM
C C	fwsy98!!co...	+852 6316	02:17:32 AM
IL H	ilhhyu385g...	+852 6316	02:17:32 AM

Fig. 5.2 Suspicious Activity in a Ride-Sharing App: This figure presents two tables illustrating suspicious patterns in a ride-sharing app. The first table, labeled "Trips," displays four completed UberX rides on April 3, 2017, with fares and locations in New York City and London. Annotations highlight "impossible 'teleportation'"between cities. The second table, "Clients Related by Payment Profile," lists five accounts linked by the same credit card, featuring gibberish names, identical mobile country codes, and rapid account creation times. Annotations emphasize "same mobile country code" and "high account creation velocity," signaling potential fraudulent activity

Example: Applications across Different Sectors

Expert-based detection systems can be adapted for different sectors. Examples include:

- *Insurance claims:* Aside from the fire incident claims example already mentioned, these systems can help identify suspicious activities in insurance claims, such as repeated claims from the same person or entity, unusual surge in claim amounts, or claims filed immediately after a policy was taken.

- *Banking transactions:* Expert systems can flag unusual banking activities, like sudden large withdrawals, multiple failed login attempts, or transactions originating from locations that the account holder doesn't usually operate from.
- *Online retail:* Potential fraud in online retail can be detected by looking for patterns like high numbers of returns from the same customer, multiple orders of the same item shipped to different addresses, or orders with rushed delivery followed by immediate cancellation.
- *Healthcare:* In the medical field, expert systems can help spot insurance fraud, such as patients frequently changing providers, duplicate billing, or overutilization of services.
- *Telecommunications:* The systems can flag unusual call patterns that may indicate SIM card cloning or other fraudulent activities, such as an unusually high number of calls made in a short period, repeated calls to premium-rate numbers, or calls made to or from high-risk locations.

Examples of fraud detection rules that can be derived from these policies and deviations:

- If multiple advance payments are made for the same claim, flag it as suspicious.
- If a settlement is paid without approval, flag it.
- If the same person proposes and approves a settlement, flag it.
- If a claim is altered after being granted, flag it.
- If a previously rejected claim is later processed, flag it.

Implementing an expert-based system can significantly aid in detecting potential fraud cases and mitigating associated risks. However, for the system to remain effective, it needs to be subject to regular monitoring, enhancements, and updates.

Advantages and Challenges of Expert-Based Approaches

Advantages

- Straightforward and transparent for analysts.
- Utilizes the knowledge of experts to identify known fraud patterns.

Challenges

- Struggles to catch new or changing fraud tactics.
- Rules need constant updates to stay effective.
- Analysts must regularly craft and revise rules to keep up with fraud trends.

> TIP
>
> While expert-based systems are foundational, they should be combined with advanced methods like machine learning to stay effective against evolving threats.

Data-Driven Approaches

Data-driven or statistically based fraud detection techniques are becoming more and more popular as the limits of expert-based fraud detection systems show themselves. Three primary causes of this change are as follows:

- *Precision*: Data-driven approaches sift enormous volumes of information in search of latent fraud trends. In jobs like credit scoring and client attrition prediction, they beat conventional methods in maximizing detection efficiency and reducing false positives.
- *Operational efficiency*: Automated systems rapidly evaluate vast data to provide real-time decision-making needs in credit card transactions and customs inspections.
- *Cost efficiency*: Data-driven systems improve return on investment (ROI) by lowering the labor-intensive requirements for creating and operating expert-based systems.

Growing public, governmental, and commercial interest also supports this change, driving more research and financing in fraud detection technologies.

Methods in Data-Driven Fraud Detection

Supervised learning trains models on labeled data—e.g., *fraud or non-fraud—so that they may forecast results for new, unprocessed transactions.*

- *Case Study: JPMorgan Chase analyzes past transaction data using supervised machine learning. This strategy has greatly raised detection rates by spotting unexpected trends and behaviors that conventional approaches sometimes overlook.*

To find anomalies, unsupervised learning finds latent patterns in unlabeled data, such as clustering-like behaviors.

- *Mastercard monitors millions of daily transactions using anomaly detection, identifying anomalies deviating from consumer behavior. This approach successfully identifies newly developing fraud forms devoid of specific labeling.*

Deep learning is a specialized subset of machine learning in which complicated patterns in big datasets are found by means of numerous layers within neural networks. This is very helpful for jobs like spotting advanced fraud schemes.

- *These techniques demand high-quality data and advanced analytics yet are better at spotting new and existing fraud tendencies. Chapters in Parts III, IV, and V go more deeply.*

Important Considerations for Application

1. *Data cleaning and preparation: Reliable models depend on accurate models, which depend on clean, consistent data. This covers variable transformations for analysis, addressing outliers, and missing value removal (see Table* 5.1*).*

2. *Feature engineering*: Create new variables that capture meaningful patterns to improve model precision. For example, aggregating transaction frequencies or creating customer risk scores can enhance prediction accuracy.

Table 5.1 Missing values in the dataset

Feature	NaN Count	Question Mark Count
months_as_customer	0	0
age	0	0
collision_type	0	178
property_damage	0	360
police_report_available	0	343

3. *Addressing imbalanced datasets:* Fraudulent transactions are often vastly outnumbered by legitimate ones. Techniques like random oversampling, under-sampling, and SMOTE help balance datasets for better model performance (see Fig. 5.3).

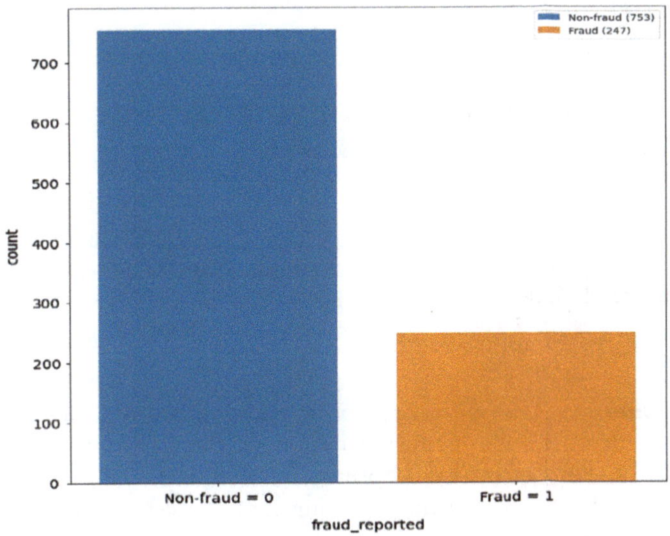

Fig. 5.3 Checking imbalanced dataset: Comparison of Non-Fraud and Fraud Cases: This figure displays a bar chart comparing the count of non-fraud and fraud cases. The blue bar represents 753 non-fraud cases, while the orange bar represents 247 fraud cases. The chart emphasizes the higher occurrence of non-fraud cases compared to fraud cases, providing an overview of the dataset's class distribution

Table 5.2 Comparison of model results (Precision, Recall, F1-score, AUC)

Model	Precision	Recall	F1-Score	AUC
XG-Boost Classifier	0.849	0.850	0.849	0.89
Logistic Regression	0.886	0.873	0.877	0.910
Support Vector Machine	0.892	0.880	0.883	0.911
Random Forest	0.754	0.777	0.742	0.893
Naive Bayes	0.775	0.703	0.721	0.781
LGBMClassifier	0.844	0.846	0.845	0.877

4. *Model validation and evaluation:* Fraud detection models must perform well in real-world scenarios. Evaluation metrics like precision, recall, F1-score, and AUC-ROC (see Table 5.2) assess the trade-off between false positives and missed fraud cases. Cross-validation methods, like k-fold validation, ensure consistent performance. Chapter 18 provides further details. (See Fig. 5.4)

The Evolution of Fraud Detection: Traditional Methods to ML-Based Systems

Fraud detection has evolved significantly, starting with traditional methods like reputation lists and device fingerprinting. While foundational, these approaches are increasingly insufficient against rapidly evolving fraud tactics.

Challenges of Traditional Methods

- *Reputation Lists:* Effective for identifying known fraudsters but become obsolete as fraudsters frequently change identities.
- *Device Fingerprinting:* Captures device-specific information, but fraudsters can bypass this by using new devices or clearing digital footprints.

As fraud tactics become more sophisticated, traditional methods alone cannot keep up. To address this, organizations are adopting hybrid approaches that combine traditional rule-based systems with machine learning (ML) models.

```
Classification Report:
              precision    recall  f1-score   support

           0       0.96      0.88      0.92       224
           1       0.71      0.89      0.79        76

    accuracy                           0.88       300
   macro avg       0.83      0.88      0.85       300
weighted avg       0.90      0.88      0.88       300
```

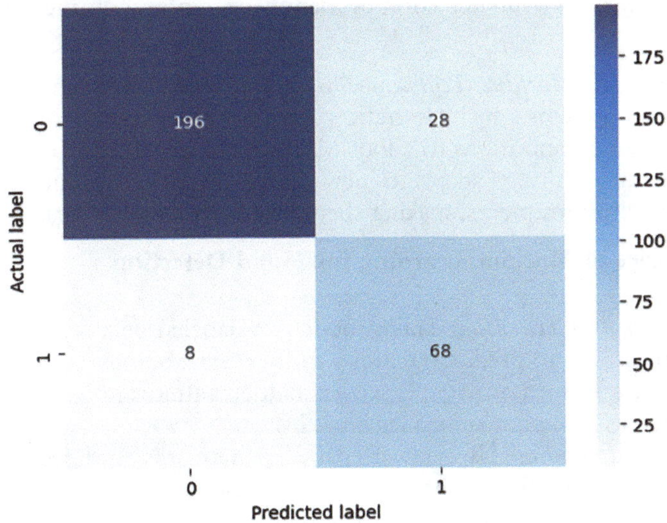

Fig. 5.4 Classification Report and Confusion Matrix for a Binary Model: This figure presents the classification report and confusion matrix for a binary classification model. The classification report outlines key metrics for two classes (0 and 1): Class 0 achieves a precision of 0.96, recall of 0.88, and f1-score of 0.92 with 224 samples, while Class 1 attains a precision of 0.71, recall of 0.89, and f1-score of 0.79 with 76 samples. The overall model accuracy is 0.88. The confusion matrix details true negatives (196), true positives (68), false positives (28), and false negatives (8). A color gradient in the matrix visualizes the frequency of predictions, with darker shades representing higher values

Bridging Traditional and Machine Learning Methods

A hybrid approach integrates the strengths of rule-based systems with the adaptability of machine learning. Rule-based systems excel at detecting known fraud patterns, while ML models uncover new and evolving threats. This combination offers a balanced, comprehensive fraud detection framework.

Example: Uber initially relied on rule-based detection but later integrated machine learning to adapt to emerging fraud tactics. The hybrid model improved fraud detection by identifying subtle anomalies that rules missed.

Transition to Machine Learning-Based Approaches: The limitations of rule-based systems—such as static rules and labor-intensive updates—have driven organizations to adopt ML-based systems. Machine learning models automatically adapt to new fraud patterns without requiring manual rule adjustments, making them more efficient and scalable.

Categories of Machine Learning for Fraud Detection

- *Supervised Learning:* Trains models on labeled data (e.g., fraud vs. non-fraud) to predict outcomes for new transactions.
- *Unsupervised Learning:* Discovers hidden patterns in unlabeled data, such as grouping anomalies into clusters.
- *Deep Learning:* Uses advanced neural networks to detect complex and evolving fraud schemes in large datasets.

Advantages of ML-Based Systems

- *Flexibility:* Capable of detecting both known and unknown fraud patterns.
- *Adaptability:* Models improve with exposure to new data.
- *Scalability:* Handles large transaction volumes efficiently.

Example: Mastercard uses anomaly detection (unsupervised learning) to monitor millions of daily transactions, uncovering fraud without requiring predefined labels.

By transitioning to ML-based approaches, organizations can better address the dynamic nature of fraud, staying ahead of increasingly sophisticated fraudsters.

Model Interpretability: Understanding "Black Box" Systems

While ML-based systems excel at detecting fraud, their complexity often makes them "black boxes," where the decision-making process is unclear. Ensuring interpretability is critical for trust, compliance, and actionable insights (Fig. 5.5). This section dives into various XAI techniques, illuminating their significance in uncovering fraudulent activities.

The terms *black box* and *glass box* refer to the transparency and understandability of algorithms:

- *Black-box models:* These models are complex, and their internal workings are not easily understood. They can make highly accurate predictions, but it's challenging to decipher how they reach their conclusions. This opacity can be problematic in fields where interpretability is critical, such as healthcare or finance. Examples include deep learning models like neural networks and ensemble methods like gradient boosting machines.
- *Glass box models:* These models are transparent, and their decision-making processes are easily interpretable. Even though they might sometimes trade-off some predictive power, their transparency can

Fig. 5.5 Model Explanation with Feature Contributions: This figure illustrates a machine learning model with an output of 0.4 and a base rate of 0.1. The model's prediction is influenced by four features: 'incident_severity' (+0.4), 'total_claim_amount' (−0.3), 'months_as_customer' (−0.3), and 'insured_hobbies' (−0.3). An arrow labeled "Explanation" points to a detailed breakdown of feature contributions, showing how each factor impacts the final output

be more suitable for applications requiring clear explanations. Examples include linear regression, logistic regression, and simpler decision trees.

The black-box issue has come to light because, with the increasing use of complex models in critical decision-making processes, there's a rising demand for transparency and accountability. Misunderstood or mistrusted decisions made by black-box models can lead to undesired outcomes and societal pushback.

- *Model-specific approaches:* These methods are tailor-made for a specific type of model. Examples include feature importance for tree-based models or coefficients for linear models.
- *Model-agnostic approaches:* These methods can be applied irrespective of the model's inner workings. Tools like SHAP and LIME are examples.

Explainable AI (XAI): Model Interpretability

Techniques like LIME (Local Interpretable Model-agnostic Explanations) and SHAP (SHapley Additive Explanations) shed light on how ML models make predictions, making their decisions more transparent and actionable. (see Chapter 16 for a real-world example involving insurance claims) further details.

LIME: Localized Interpretability
LIME explains individual predictions by approximating complex models with simpler ones (e.g., linear models) in specific regions of the data. Figure 5.6 illustrates.

Practical Implementation:

- Train a model (e.g., random forest) on transaction data.
- Use LIME to explain why specific transactions were flagged as fraudulent.
- Example: LIME reveals that a high transaction amount combined with an unusual location triggered a fraud alert.

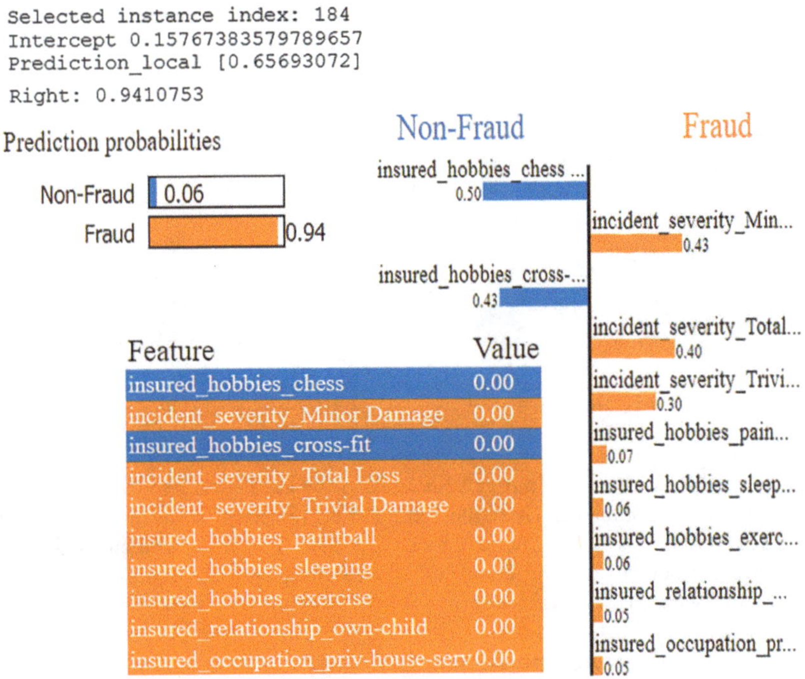

Fig. 5.6 LIME-Based Prediction Analysis for Insurance Fraud Detection: This figure demonstrates a LIME-based prediction analysis for insurance fraud detection. The model predicts a 6% probability of non-fraud and a 94% probability of fraud. A bar chart highlights the contributions of key features to each prediction. Fraud predictions are strongly influenced by factors like "incident severity" and "insured hobbies" such as paintball and exercise. Conversely, non-fraud predictions are associated with hobbies like chess and cross-fit. This analysis underscores how LIME explains feature-level contributions, enhancing interpretability in determining fraud likelihood

SHAP

SHAP (Shapley additive explanations) is a technique that provides a unified measure of feature importance by attributing an importance value to each feature in a prediction. The underlying concept aims to fairly distribute the "contribution" of each feature to the prediction (see Fig. 5.7).

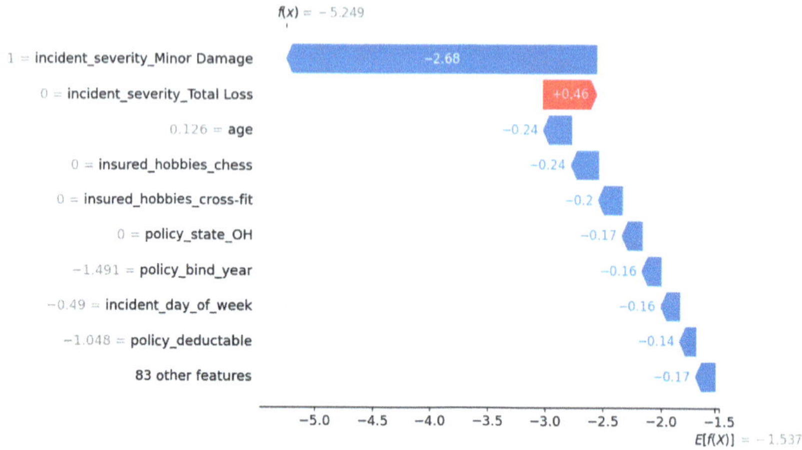

Fig. 5.7 SHAP Feature Impact Visualization for Prediction Model: This figure presents a horizontal bar chart illustrating the impact of various features on a prediction model's output, which totals −5.249. The most influential feature is "incident_severity_Minor Damage," contributing −2.68. Positive contributions are seen in "incident_severity_Total Loss" with +0.46. Other notable features include "insured_hobbies_chess" and "insured_hobbies_cross-fit," each contributing −0.24, and "policy_state_OH" at −0.2. Features like "policy_bind_year," "incident_day_of_week," and "policy_deductable" show smaller negative impacts. The chart summarizes the cumulative effect of 83 other features, with the model's expected output value at −1.537. This visualization highlights SHAP's ability to quantify and rank feature contributions, aiding in model interpretation

SHAP uses Shapley values from cooperative game theory to assign importance scores to features, offering a unified measure of feature contribution.

Practical Implementation:

- Train an ensemble model (e.g., XGBoost) on transaction data.
- Use SHAP to compute feature contributions for fraud predictions.
- Example: SHAP shows that "transaction time" and "transaction amount" were the most influential factors in detecting fraud.

Comparing LIME and SHAP

LIME and SHAP are both essential tools that help in the explanation of machine learning models. However, they are applied differently, and their outcomes vary as well. These techniques assist in understanding the decision-making process of complex models, contributing to XAI.

Consider a fraud detection system that examines credit card transactions and predicts potential frauds. In this context, both LIME and SHAP can be employed to interpret the model's decisions.

With LIME, you could create a simpler, surrogate model, which operates similarly to the complex model but uses fewer features. This model could reveal that higher transaction amounts are more likely to be fraudulent, providing a simplified perspective of the model's decision-making process.

By contrast, SHAP utilizes a mathematical approach to calculate a feature importance score for each attribute involved in the model's prediction. For instance, SHAP might indicate that transactions occurring at specific times of the day carry higher chances of being fraudulent, irrespective of the transaction amount.

The choice between LIME and SHAP depends on the specific requirements. LIME provides a quicker overview of the most impactful factors in a model's predictions. It is particularly useful when you need a swift understanding of the model, such as when deciding whether to approve a transaction.

SHAP, on the other hand, delivers a more detailed and holistic view. It is beneficial when you need a thorough understanding of the model's decision-making process, for instance, when analyzing fraud patterns over time.

> TIP
>
> Organizations can use LIME for quick instance-based explanations and SHAP for broader insights into model behavior.

Other Tools

While LIME and SHAP are widely used, additional tools like partial dependence plots (PDPs), individual conditional expectation (ICE) plots, decision tree surrogates, and counterfactual explanations provide valuable insights into machine learning models. These tools offer different perspectives, enabling a more holistic understanding of complex systems.

- *Partial Dependence Plots (PDPs)*: PDPs visualize the average effect of one or two features on a model's predictions, helping identify relationships between features and outcomes.
  In fraud detection, a PDP can show how the transaction amount affects the likelihood of fraud. For example, it might reveal specific thresholds where fraud predictions increase significantly.
  PDPs provide a global view of feature importance, making them useful for understanding overarching trends in the data.
- *Individual Conditional Expectation (ICE) Plots:* ICE plots, a granular version of PDPs, illustrate how individual data points respond to feature changes.
  An ICE plot in fraud detection could reveal how a particular transaction's fraud prediction changes with the transaction amount, showing variability across individual transactions.
  ICE plots highlight heterogeneity in model responses, offering deeper insights into specific predictions.

Both PDPs and ICE plots are invaluable tools for interpreting ML models. Although they may not provide as detailed an attribution as LIME or SHAP, they offer a different perspective, focusing on the average and individual effects of features, respectively. These tools, together with LIME and SHAP, can provide a holistic view of a model's decision-making process, facilitating transparency and trust in machine learning systems.

> NOTE
>
> For more information on PDPs and ICE plots, consider checking out the Interpretable Machine Learning Book, the chapter on PDP and ICE, and the Python library for PDPs and ICE plots.

Decision Tree Surrogate

This technique involves the creation of an interpretable model, such as a *decision tree*, that approximates the decisions made by a more complex, black-box model. The interpretable model acts as a surrogate, providing insights into the complex model's decision-making process.

For example, consider a complex neural network designed to predict customer churn. A decision tree surrogate model could be trained to emulate this neural network's predictions. The decision tree might identify that customers with less than a year of subscription and who made

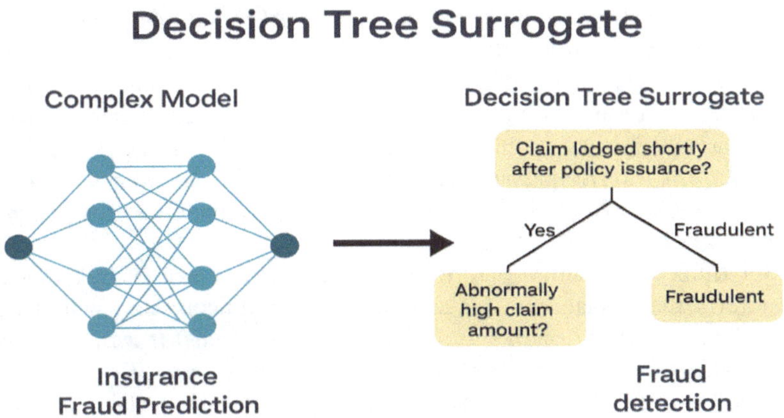

Fig. 5.8 Decision Tree Surrogate: This diagram illustrates how a complex insurance fraud prediction model can be approximated using a decision tree surrogate. The left side represents a black-box model with complex internal logic. By applying a decision tree surrogate, the model's decisions become interpretable. The simplified tree asks questions such as "Was the claim lodged shortly after policy issuance?" or "Is the claim amount abnormally high?"—leading to classifications such as "Fraudulent." This approach enhances transparency and supports explainable AI in fraud analytics

fewer than three purchases in the last month are most likely to churn. This decision tree then becomes a comprehensible explanation of the complex neural network model.

Applying a similar process in a fraud detection scenario, suppose you have a sophisticated machine learning model predicting insurance claim fraud. A decision tree surrogate could be used to mirror the original model's predictions. It might highlight those claims with certain characteristics, such as being lodged shortly after policy issuance or involving abnormally high claim amounts, are most likely to be fraudulent. This surrogate model thus aids in understanding the complex model's decisions, shedding light on the pivotal factors for fraud detection (Fig. 5.8).

Counterfactual Explanations

This method involves providing explanations for a model's prediction by indicating minimal changes in the input features that would result in a different prediction. To illustrate, imagine an AI model rejecting a credit application. A counterfactual explanation here could be: *The application would have been approved if the applicant's annual income was $5000 higher.* A healthcare AI algorithm may forecast a patient's diabetes risk. Counterfactual explanation for a high-risk patient: *The patient would have been deemed low risk if their weight was 20 pounds lower and their daily sugar intake was 10 grams less.* This shows how little patient status changes might alter the result.

Or think about an AI algorithm predicting insurance claim fraud. A counterfactual explanation for a potentially fraudulent claim would be: *The claim would have been classified as non-fraudulent if it was submitted 60 days after the policy issuance instead of 2 days, and if the claimed amount was $1000 lower.* This statement explains how claim features can change the forecast, helping investigators understand the model's decision-making process (Fig. 5.9).

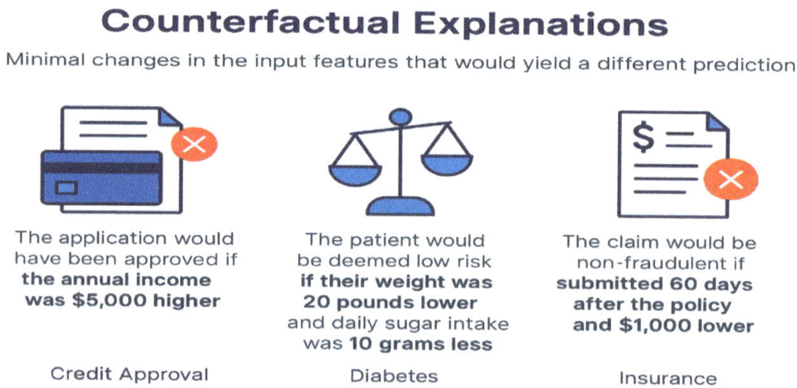

Fig. 5.9 Counterfactual Explanations: This flowchart illustrates how counterfactual explanations offer insight into model decisions by presenting small, actionable changes that would alter a prediction. The first scenario, Credit Approval, explains that approval would be granted if the applicant's income were $5000 higher. In the second, Diabetes Risk, the model would predict low risk if the individual's weight was 20 pounds lower and daily sugar intake reduced by 10 grams. The third, Insurance Fraud, shows that a claim would be classified as non-fraudulent if it were submitted 60 days after policy issuance and the claim amount was $1000 lower. These examples emphasize the interpretability and transparency benefits of counterfactual reasoning in decision-making systems

These techniques enable better understanding and trust in the models, by providing interpretability and explainability.

Best Practices for Model Deployment and Monitoring: Transitioning fraud detection models into production requires careful planning and continuous monitoring to ensure effectiveness in real-world scenarios. Key considerations include:

1. Model Deployment and Monitoring
    - Ensure seamless integration with existing systems.
    - Monitor for performance degradation due to data drift or shifts in fraud patterns.
2. Collaboration and Communication
    - Foster collaboration between domain experts, data scientists, and IT teams.
    - Establish clear communication channels to enhance understanding and application.
3. Training and Education
    - Regularly train stakeholders on fraud analytics principles and best practices.
    - Keep teams updated on new tools and developments in the field.
4. Data Privacy and Security
    - Adhere to regulations like GDPR and CCPA to protect sensitive data.
    - Implement encryption, access controls, and anonymization techniques to safeguard information.

Ethical Considerations in AI

Ethical considerations go beyond addressing bias, and include aspects like fairness, transparency, accountability, and privacy. These issues can manifest in various ways in AI systems and have significant societal impacts if not appropriately managed. In particular, AI systems can inadvertently perpetuate or even amplify discrimination if careful considerations are not made:

1. *Fairness*: AI models are typically trained on historical data. If this data contains discriminatory practices, the model could learn and replicate these biases. To ensure fairness, it's critical to perform an audit of the training data and model predictions to identify any potential discriminatory bias. If detected, techniques such as fairness through unawareness, individual or group fairness, or counterfactual fairness can be employed.
2. *Transparency*: Being transparent about how a model makes predictions is crucial for users to understand and trust its decisions. Tools like LIME, SHAP, PDPs, and ICE plots can help with transparency by providing interpretable explanations for model predictions. In addition, it's important to be transparent about the limitations of a model and the potential for errors in its predictions.
3. *Accountability*: It's vital to establish mechanisms that hold AI systems and their creators accountable for their outcomes. This includes creating thorough documentation of how the model was developed and tested, the data it was trained on, its performance metrics, and any known limitations. It also involves establishing procedures for handling errors, updating the model, and redressing harm that might arise from its decisions.
4. *Privacy*: AI models, especially those in sensitive fields like healthcare or finance, often require access to personal information. It's essential to ensure this data is handled in a secure and private manner, complying with data protection regulations like GDPR. Techniques like differential privacy can help protect individual's information while still allowing the model to learn from the data.

AI ethics is an active area of research. For additional resources, refer to AI Ethics Guidelines provided by organizations like IEEE and ISO.

SIDEBAR

Transparency in the U.S. vs. the European Union

Efforts to ensure transparency and accountability in AI differ across regions, with key developments highlighted below:

The U.S. Approach

5. *Algorithmic Accountability Act:* Proposed legislation mandating impact assessments for high-risk AI systems, focusing on fairness and transparency. Although not yet enacted, it represents growing attention to AI ethics.
6. *State-Level Laws:* California's CCPA empowers residents to understand data collection practices, indirectly promoting transparency.
7. *Sector-Specific Guidelines:* Finance and healthcare sectors have regulations addressing algorithmic fairness.
8. *Federal Trade Commission (FTC):* The FTC monitors companies deploying biased AI under deceptive or unfair practices guidelines.

The European Union's GDPR

4. *Right to Explanation:* Individuals have the right to understand how algorithmic decisions are made, particularly for significant decisions.
5. *Deep Learning:* GDPR emphasizes transparency but allows the use of complex algorithms like neural networks if explanations are provided.
6. *Cross-Border Cooperation:* Recent proposals aim to streamline GDPR enforcement across EU Member States.

SIDEBAR

The Future of XAI and More

Explainable AI tools like LIME and SHAP are foundational for interpreting ML models, particularly in high-stakes areas like fraud detection. However, as fraud detection systems grow more complex and real-time responses become critical, XAI faces new challenges and opportunities:

Emerging Trends

1. *Real-Time Interpretability:* Parallelizing computations and leveraging gradient boosting frameworks like LightGBM can improve the efficiency of interpretability techniques.
2. *Hybrid Models:* Combining the speed of LIME with the depth of SHAP could offer tailored explanations for different use cases.
3. *User-Centric Interfaces:* Future XAI tools will prioritize actionable, user-friendly explanations, improving decision-making.
4. *Regulatory Alignment:* Standards for XAI will evolve, with tools like LIME and SHAP potentially becoming benchmarks for compliance.

Ethical Considerations in XAI: XAI tools also help detect and mitigate bias, ensuring fairness and ethical AI practices.

Challenges in Model Interpretation

While interpretability is crucial, it comes with certain trade-offs:

1. *Accuracy* vs. *Interpretability:* Simplified models (e.g., decision trees) may sacrifice accuracy compared to complex ones (e.g., deep neural networks).
2. *Simplified Insights:* Interpretable insights must be taken with caution; they provide a simplified view of the model's decision process.
3. *Consistency Across Tools*: Different tools can yield slightly different explanations, requiring careful interpretation.

CAUTION

Fraud detection is inherently dynamic. Fraudsters continually evolve their tactics, exploiting system weaknesses. To stay ahead, organizations must invest in adaptive fraud detection systems, combining advanced tools with robust monitoring and regular updates.

Ethical considerations are integral to developing responsible AI systems. By addressing fairness, transparency, accountability, and privacy, organizations can create trustworthy and effective fraud detection systems. Leveraging tools like LIME, SHAP, PDPs, and ICE plots, coupled with compliance to evolving regulations, ensures AI systems not only meet operational goals but also uphold ethical standards.

Hybrid Approach: Combining Expert Knowledge with Machine Learning

In today's fraud detection landscape, hybrid approaches—blending expert-based rule systems with machine learning models—have become indispensable. While rule-based systems excel at capturing known fraud patterns, machine learning models adapt to emerging threats, making the combination of the two a powerful strategy.

A hybrid approach leverages the strengths of both methodologies:

- *Rule-Based Systems:* These provide an initial layer of detection, relying on predefined rules crafted by fraud experts.
- *Machine Learning Models:* These analyze complex patterns and identify novel fraud tactics, complementing the limitations of static rules.

By integrating human expertise with data-driven algorithms, organizations can create scalable, flexible, and adaptive fraud detection systems that address both existing and emerging risks.

Advantages:

- Combines the precision of rule-based detection with the adaptability of machine learning.
- Effectively detects both traditional and evolving fraud patterns.
- Reduces false positives, minimizing disruption for legitimate users.

Challenges:

- More complex to implement and maintain than standalone systems.
- Requires ongoing collaboration between domain experts and data scientists.
- Necessitates regular updates to address emerging threats.

Real-World Applications of Hybrid Approaches

To better understand the benefits of hybrid fraud detection, here are some real-world examples:

1. *Case Study: PayPal's Hybrid System:* PayPal, a global leader in online payments, processes millions of transactions daily. To maintain user trust, it employs a hybrid approach that combines rule-based systems with machine learning models. Rule-based systems help capture known fraud patterns, such as sudden high-value transactions from unusual locations. In contrast, machine learning models analyze large-scale transaction data, detecting new or nuanced fraud patterns that predefined rules may miss. This approach allows PayPal to minimize false positives, reducing unnecessary disruptions for legitimate users. The machine learning models also adapt over time, learning from new data to improve fraud detection continuously.
2. *Case Study: JP Morgan Chase's Credit Card Fraud Detection:* JP Morgan Chase uses a hybrid fraud detection system where rule-based algorithms identify common fraud patterns, such as abnormal spending behavior, while machine learning models analyze historical

data to detect subtler fraud types. By combining rule-based systems with machine learning models, JP Morgan Chase successfully detects both traditional and emerging fraud tactics. This reduces the time taken to respond to fraudulent activities while improving overall accuracy.

3. *Case Study: Microsoft Azure's Fraud Detection Framework:* Microsoft Azure employs a hybrid fraud detection system that layers machine learning models on top of a rule-based framework. The rule-based system handles routine fraud detection, while machine learning models monitor transaction data for emerging fraud patterns that might not conform to pre-established rules. The combination of rule-based and machine learning approaches allows Azure to adapt quickly to new fraud strategies, continuously updating its models to detect the latest threats.

The most effective fraud detection systems are tailored to the organization's specific needs, data availability, and resources. A hybrid approach offers a balanced solution, integrating the advantages of both expert-driven and data-driven methodologies.

Key Takeaway: Regular updates, collaboration, and stakeholder education are essential for sustaining the effectiveness of hybrid systems.

Section B: Fraud Analytics Techniques

Fraud analytics combines data mining, machine learning (ML), and statistical analysis to uncover patterns and irregularities that signal potentially fraudulent activities. By analyzing diverse data sources—such as financial transactions, operational logs, and user behavior—organizations can detect and prevent fraud proactively.

Anomaly Detection

Anomaly detection identifies unexpected patterns in data that deviate from normal behavior, often signaling potential fraud. This approach is particularly effective for uncovering novel or previously unidentified fraudulent behaviors. Statistical models (e.g., Gaussian distribution), clustering algorithms, decision trees, and random forests form the foundation of anomaly detection.

Case Study: Stripe: Stripe, a global payment processor, employs anomaly detection to prevent fraud in real-time. For example, its ML models flag sudden transaction spikes or unusual user locations, enabling swift intervention while minimizing disruption for legitimate customers.

Data Visualization

Data visualization transforms complex data into visual formats like graphs and charts, enabling analysts to identify trends and outliers indicative of fraud. For instance:

- *Heatmaps:* Highlight transaction density in high-risk areas.
- *Time-series plots*: Show spending patterns that may indicate fraudulent behavior. Data visualization simplifies the interpretation of complex datasets, making it an indispensable tool in fraud analytics.

Machine Learning-Based Approaches for Fraud Detection

Machine learning (ML) has transformed fraud detection by enabling models to learn from past behaviours and recognise new patterns of fraudulent activity. By analysing historical data, ML systems adapt to changing fraud trends and help organisations pre-empt emerging threats, continuously refining their understanding of transaction data and customer behaviour. The ML techniques most commonly used in fraud analytics fall into three broad categories:

- *Supervised learning:* Supervised Learning uses labeled data to train models, allowing them to predict fraud by learning from past patterns. *Example*: Decision trees and random forests classify transactions as fraudulent or legitimate.
- *Unsupervised learning:* Discovers hidden patterns in unlabeled data, helping identify new fraud schemes. *Example*: Clustering methods like K-means group similar transactions for anomaly detection.
- *Deep learning:* Uses neural networks to analyze complex fraud patterns, though resource intensive.

Steps in Machine Learning (ML)-Based Approaches for Fraud Detection:

1. *Understanding What is Normal:* ML models train on historical transaction data to define "normal" behavior. Features such as transaction frequency, monetary values, and user behavior provide context for identifying anomalies. *Example*: A sudden series of high-value transactions could indicate fraud, but the context—such as the user's past spending patterns—determines whether the activity is genuinely suspicious (Figs. 5.10 and 5.11).
2. *Finding Anomalies:* E-commerce is a prime target for fraud due to the ease of opening new accounts or accessing existing ones. The ML model detects unusual activities that deviate from the norm, such as unusual spending patterns, rapid account changes, or logins from suspicious locations (Fig. 5.12).

Behavioral analytics further refines these detections by grouping users with similar patterns, creating tailored fraud baselines (Fig. 5.13).

For example, when a customer makes a purchase, the transaction's characteristics are analyzed and compared to those of other buyers within the same segment. Recognizing that late night shoppers or frequent

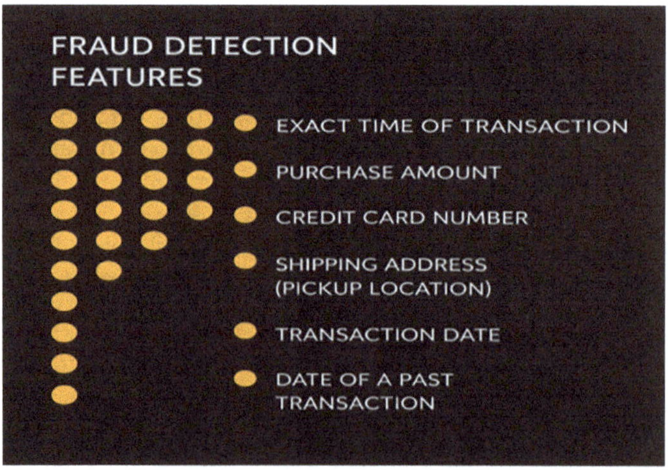

Fig. 5.10 Key Features Used in Machine Learning Models for Fraud Detection: This figure illustrates essential transaction attributes, such as time, amount, credit card details, and historical data, that are analyzed by machine learning models to define "normal" behavior and detect anomalies

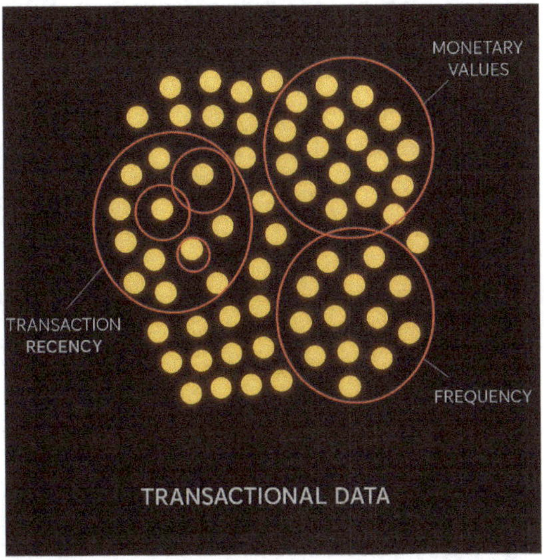

Fig. 5.11 Categorizing Transaction Features for Fraud Detection: This figure represents a clustering of data points categorized into "Transaction Recency," "Monetary Values," and "Frequency," highlighting key areas of analysis for machine learning models in detecting anomalies and patterns indicative of fraudulent behavior

travelers may have varied purchasing behaviors that are not necessarily indicative of fraud is crucial (Fig. 5.14).

The system calculates a fraud score based on the predictive power of all features. Low scores approve purchases, while high scores flag transactions as suspicious (Fig. 5.15).

3. *Eliminating Mistakes:* Advanced fraud detection systems are highly effective but still face challenges like false positives or negatives. Advanced fraud detection systems are effective in 99% of cases, but the remaining 1% are errors, either false positives or false negatives. False positives occur when legitimate transactions are incorrectly flagged as fraudulent, leading to customer dissatisfaction. False negatives represent actual fraudulent transactions that are not detected by the system, posing a significant risk to financial integrity (Fig. 5.16).

Deep neural networks significantly enhance detection accuracy, learning from complex datasets and reducing errors.

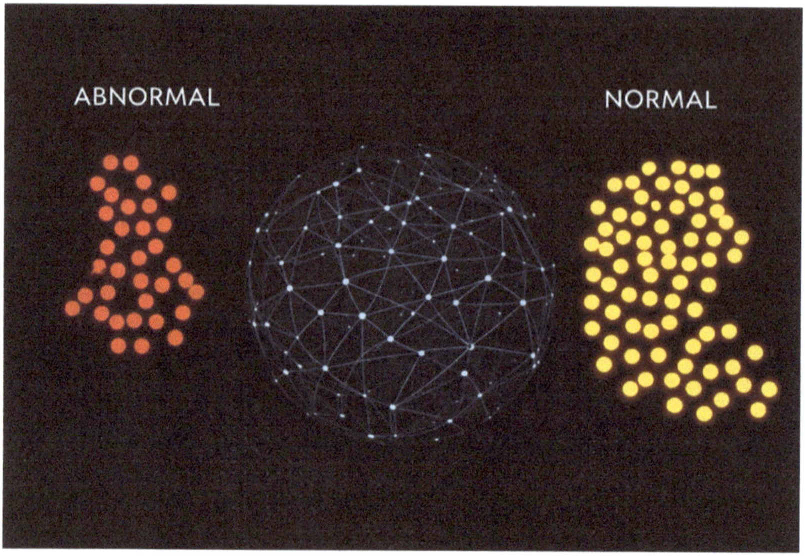

Fig. 5.12 Comparing Normal and Abnormal Data Patterns in Fraud Detection: This figure contrasts irregular, abnormal data patterns (red dots) with densely clustered normal patterns (yellow dots). The central network of interconnected nodes illustrates the complexity of data relationships analyzed by machine learning models to detect potential fraud. This distinction between normal and abnormal behavior underpins the network-based analysis shown in Fig. 5.13

TIP
Leveraging AI and ML technologies in fraud detection enhances the ability to stay ahead of fraudsters, ensuring the protection of financial operations and customer trust.

Artificial Neural Networks (ANN): Artificial Neural Networks (ANN) are computational models inspired by the human brain, containing over ~86 billion neurons that communicate through electrical and chemical signals. ANNs mimic this biological process using mathematical models to recognize patterns and make decisions (Fig. 5.17).

How Neural Networks Learn: Similar to human learning, ANNs adjust based on experience. They are trained on historical data to recognize patterns, adjusting internal parameters (weights) based on feedback from each data exposure to improve their accuracy over time (Fig. 5.18).

Fig. 5.13 Network-Based Behavioral Analysis for Fraud Detection: This figure illustrates a digital network sphere surrounded by groups representing user behavior clusters. The orange figures within each group highlight unique or anomalous behaviors detected by machine learning models, aiding in fraud identification

Structure of Neural Networks

- *Neurons:* The basic units of ANNs process input signals and produce output signals. Each neuron processes inputs using a weighted sum and passes the result through an activation function.
- *Layers:*
  - *Input Layer:* Receives the initial data.
  - *Hidden Layers:* Intermediate layers where neurons process inputs.
  - *Output Layer:* Produces the final prediction or decision.

Training Process: Neural networks use a two-step process for learning:

1. *Forward Propagation:* Inputs pass through the layers, where neurons process and transform them, ultimately producing an output.
2. *Backward Propagation:* The output is compared to the actual result to calculate an error. This error is propagated back through

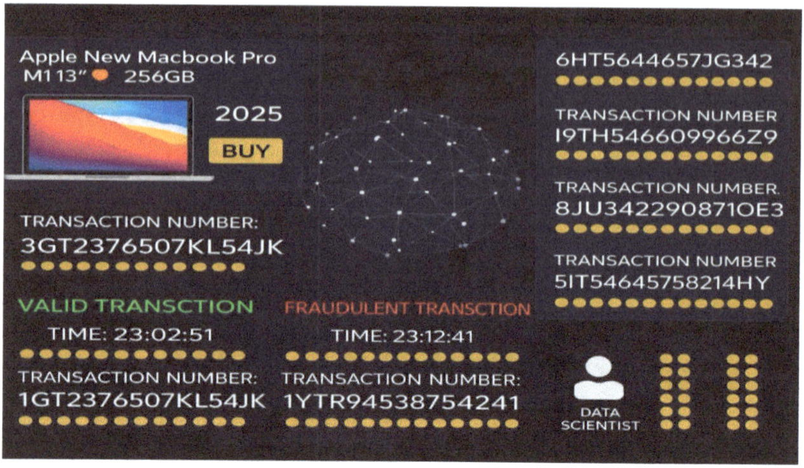

Fig. 5.14 Identifying Fraudulent Transactions Through Behavioral Analysis: This figure compares a valid transaction with a fraudulent one, showcasing details such as transaction IDs, timestamps, and associated purchase data (e.g., an Apple MacBook Pro promotion). The network graphic symbolizes the use of machine learning to analyze transaction behaviors and detect anomalies in real-time

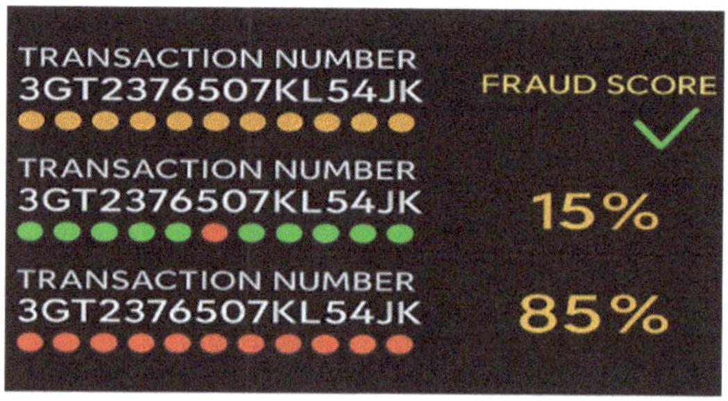

Fig. 5.15 Fraud Scoring System for Transaction Risk Assessment: This figure illustrates a fraud scoring system applied to transactions. Scores range from neutral (beige, no specific percentage) to low risk (15%, green dots with a check mark) and high risk (85%, red dots with a cross). The network-like background emphasizes the interconnected analysis performed by machine learning models to evaluate transaction risks

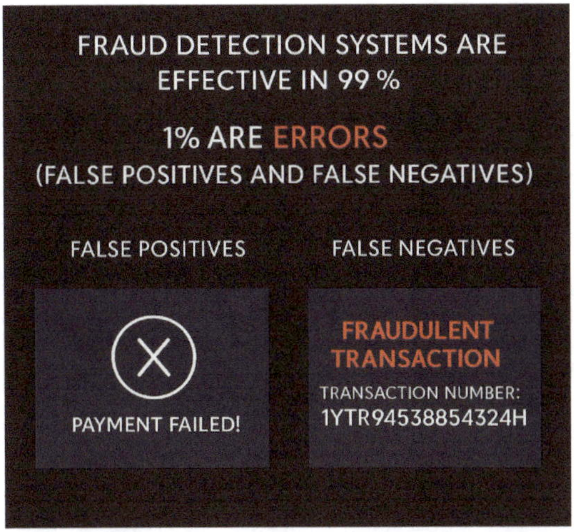

Fig. 5.16 Error Types in Fraud Detection Systems: This figure highlights the 99% effectiveness of fraud detection systems alongside the 1% error rate. It depicts a false positive with a "Payment Failed!" message (cross symbol) and a false negative with a flagged "Fraudulent Transaction" (transaction ID: 1YTR94538854324H). The red text emphasizes these error types, underscoring the challenges in achieving flawless fraud detection

the network to adjust the weights, reducing the error in future predictions.

Activation Functions: Functions like ReLU (Rectified Linear Unit), Sigmoid, and Tanh introduce non-linearity into the model, allowing it to learn complex patterns.

Applications: ANNs are used in a variety of applications, including:

- *Image and Speech Recognition:* Identifying objects or transcribing spoken words.
- *Fraud Detection:* Analyzing transaction patterns to identify fraudulent activities.
- *Medical Diagnosis:* Assisting in diagnosing diseases by analyzing medical data.

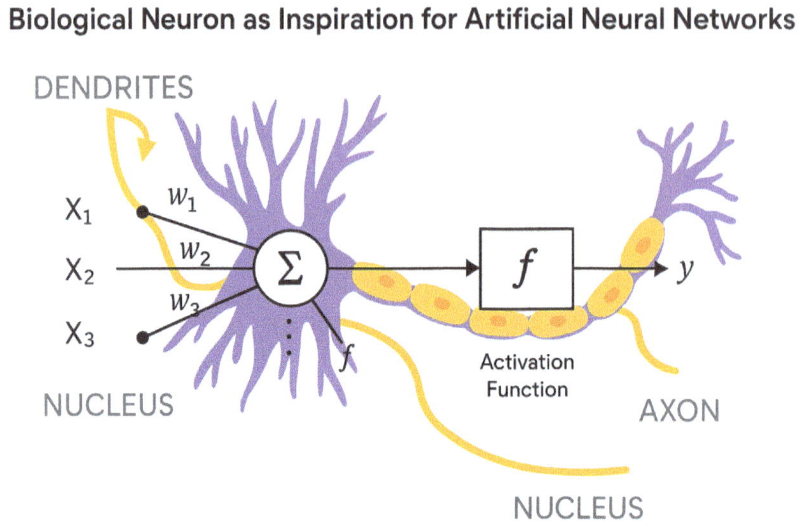

Fig. 5.17 Biological neuron as inspiration for artificial neural networks. This schematic illustrates how artificial neurons in machine learning are conceptually inspired by the structure and function of biological neurons. In biological neural systems, dendrites receive signals from many inputs, which are integrated in the cell body and transmitted via the axon; artificial neurons similarly aggregate weighted inputs, apply an activation function, and produce an output. This analogy underlies the design of modern artificial neural networks used in pattern recognition and predictive modeling. Adapted from https://en.wikipedia.org/wiki/Neural_network_(machine_learning)

Advantages and Challenges of ANNs

- *Advantages:* ANNs learn from experience, improving their performance with more data. They handle complex patterns and understand intricate relationships in data.
- *Challenges:* The "black box" nature of ANNs makes them difficult to interpret, and they require large amounts of high-quality data for optimal performance.

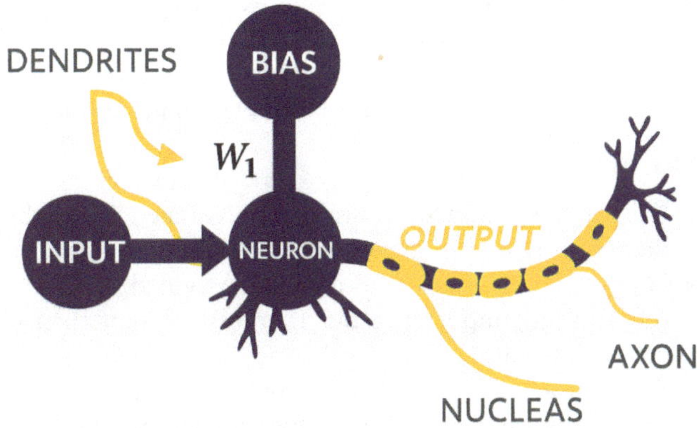

Fig. 5.18 Simplified Artificial Neuron Model: This diagram illustrates the structure of an artificial neuron in a neural network. It shows how input signals, combined with a bias and weighted by W1, are processed through a neuron and transmitted via the axon to produce an output. Key components include dendrites, neuron, bias, axon, and nucleus, mimicking biological neural processing

TIP

Artificial neural networks are powerful tools inspired by the human brain. They learn from data, adjust based on feedback, and are capable of recognizing complex patterns, making them essential for various advanced applications.

ANN are designed to recognize patterns and learn from data, making them an essential tool for fraud detection, especially in scenarios like detecting anomalies in credit card transactions.

One common use case is fraud detection in financial systems.

Example: Detecting Fraud in Credit Card Transactions.

In this scenario, the goal is to identify potential fraud in credit card transactions by analyzing two main factors: the transaction amount and the time of the transaction.

1. Inputs Defined:

- Transaction Amount: Large transactions may be flagged as suspicious depending on typical account activity.
- Time of Transaction: Transactions during unusual hours, such as late at night or early morning, may indicate fraud.

2. Model Weights and Bias:

- Weight_1 (Transaction Amount): Assigned a weight of 0.5, highlighting its significant role in detecting fraud.
- Weight_2 (Time of Transaction): Assigned a weight of 0.3, reflecting its importance but to a lesser extent than the transaction amount.
- Bias: Set at −0.2 to adjust the decision threshold, making the system slightly more conservative in flagging fraud.

3. Mathematical Model:

The neuron formula used to calculate the output is:
Output = (Input_1 × Weight_1) + (Input_2 × Weight_2) + Bias
Example Calculation: For a $500 transaction at 2 AM:
Output = (500 × 0.5) + (2 × 0.3)–0.2 = 250.4

4. Decision-Making Criteria:

- Fraud Alert Threshold: Transactions yielding an output above 250 are considered potentially fraudulent.
- Action: In this case, the transaction would be flagged for further review.

This model provides a quick assessment of transactions based on crucial fraud indicators, and its outputs can contribute to more complex evaluations in larger neural networks that consider other factors like merchant type or geographical location.

In summary, the system uses the transaction amount and time to generate a fraud score. If the score exceeds a certain threshold, the transaction is flagged for review. This efficient initial screening allows transactions to be analyzed quickly, with more complex models handling subsequent layers of analysis if necessary.

Further Integration in Fraud Detection: Neural networks can integrate individual neuron outputs with other data points to determine actions such as transaction approval, customer alert, or blocking. The input layer receives data such as transaction details and customer information, while hidden layers analyze complex patterns and interactions between data points. Finally, the output layer delivers a prediction on the transaction's legitimacy. Using *supervised learning, the* network learns from labeled data, distinguishing between fraudulent and legitimate transactions, and adjusts based on feedback to reduce errors over time.

Neural Networks and Deep Neural Networks: Application in Fraud Detection.

Real-World Implementation:

Neural networks are trained to detect anomalies and patterns indicative of fraud by comparing new transactions against learned behaviors. Over time, the network's ability to identify subtle signs of fraud improves, reducing false positives and enhancing detection precision. These systems are particularly useful in complex fraud scenarios where patterns are not easily discernible by simpler machine learning methods. Deep neural networks (DNNs) are employed for their capacity to identify hidden patterns in large volumes of data (Fig. 5.19).

Pros:

- Complex Relationship Modeling: Neural networks can model non-linear and complex relationships, making them highly effective in detecting sophisticated fraud patterns.
- Handling Large Datasets: They can efficiently process and analyze large volumes of data.
- Improved Accuracy: As they learn from more data, neural networks continually improve their detection accuracy.

Cons:

- Computing Resources: Neural networks require substantial computing power and large datasets to train effectively.
- Complexity and Time: Setting up and fine-tuning these networks is complex and time-consuming.
- Black-Box Nature: Neural networks often act as "black boxes," where the decision-making process is not easily interpretable or transparent.

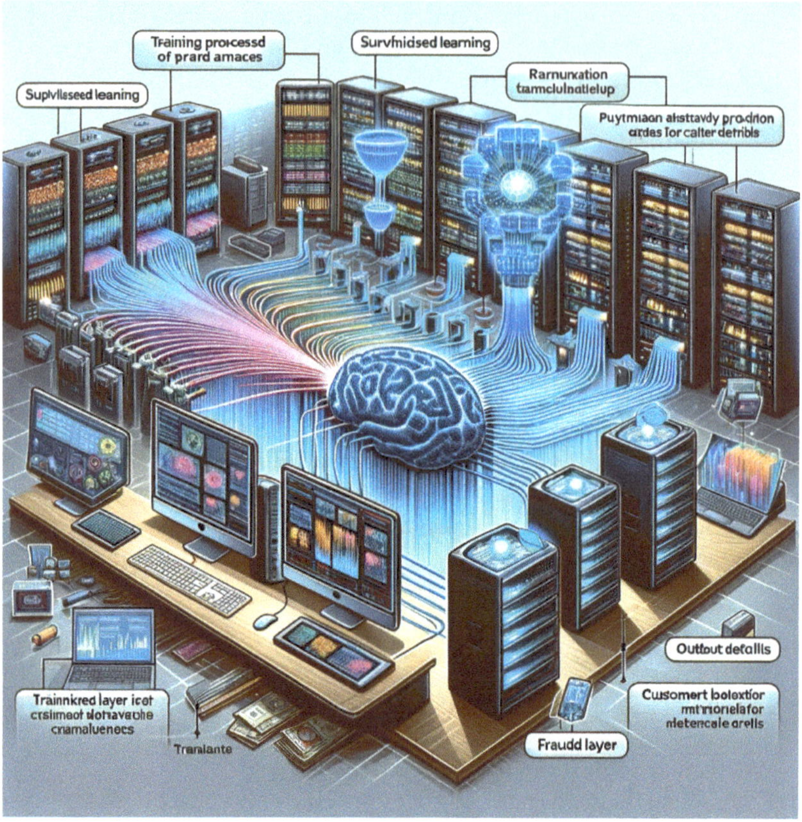

Fig. 5.19 AI-Driven Data Processing in Fraud Detection Systems: This figure represents a futuristic data center where artificial intelligence and machine learning are central to fraud detection. A glowing brain symbolizes the AI core, connected to servers labeled with functions such as "Supervised Learning," "Training Processed," and "Fraud Layer." Colorful data streams illustrate the dynamic flow and integration of information between the AI system and the servers

Neural Networks and Deep Neural Networks: Structure & Function

Neural networks are inspired by the neurons in the human brain. They excel at identifying non-linear relationships in data, using multiple processing layers. Neural networks typically include 1–2 hidden layers that transform input data to make decisions. Deep neural networks (DNNs), on the other hand, have significantly more layers, enabling them to analyze complex patterns and offer precise results by deeply analyzing the data through multiple transformations.

However, deep neural networks require substantial computing power and more time to process data due to their complexity (Fig. 5.20).

Deep Neural Networks: As the complexity of fraud patterns increases, deep neural networks (DNNs) are often implemented for their capacity to handle large volumes of data and recognize intricate fraud patterns. These models learn from massive datasets and can capture subtle deviations in behavior that might otherwise go unnoticed. See Fig. 5.21.

Scenario: Fraud Detection in Credit Card Transactions using DNNs.

Consider RetailBank, which handles millions of credit card transactions daily. With vast numbers of legitimate transactions mixed with potential fraud, the bank requires a highly efficient and accurate fraud detection system. RetailBank implements a deep neural network (DNN) to enhance its fraud detection capabilities due to the model's ability to learn complex patterns and process large data volumes.

Step-by-Step Implementation of Deep Neural Networks:

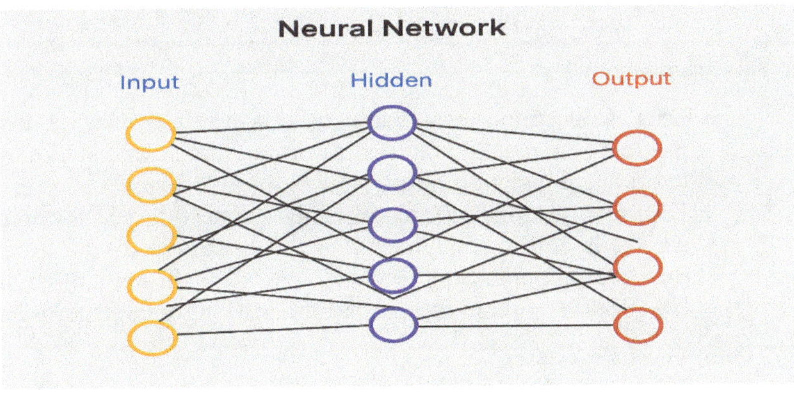

Fig. 5.20 Structure of a Neural Network with Three Layers: Diagram of a neural network with three layers: input, hidden, and output. The input layer has five orange nodes, the hidden layer has five purple nodes, and the output layer has four red nodes. Black lines connect nodes between layers, illustrating the flow of information. Labels indicate each layer's function

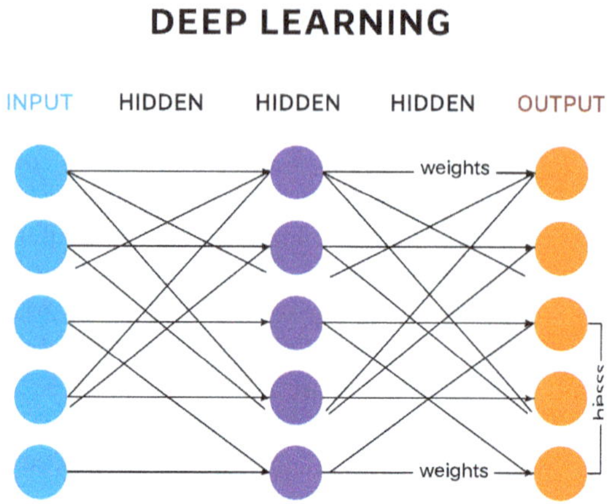

Fig. 5.21 Deep Learning Neural Network Structure: Diagram of a deep learning neural network. It consists of four layers: an input layer with blue nodes, three hidden layers with purple nodes, and an output layer with orange nodes. Arrows indicate connections between nodes, labeled as "weights" and "biases." The structure illustrates the flow of information from input to output through the hidden layers

1. Learning from Data
   - Data Collection: RetailBank collects various data points, including transaction amounts, times, merchant categories, locations, transaction history, and behavioral factors.
   - Feature Learning: Instead of manually selecting key features, the DNN automatically identifies the most predictive features for detecting fraud. It processes raw data through multiple layers, learning more complex representations of fraud patterns.
2. Non-linear Processing
   - Model Training: The DNN identifies non-linear relationships within the data. For example, it might discover that a combination of high transaction amounts late at night, from a new device, and from a foreign country is predictive of fraud.
   - Pattern Recognition: The model recognizes complex patterns, such as unusual transaction sequences that deviate from a

customer's typical behavior, which are often too subtle for traditional models to detect.

3. Volume and Variety of Data

   - Integration of Diverse Data Sources: RetailBank integrates data from transaction records, customer profiles, customer service interactions, and even social media behaviors to form a comprehensive view of each customer.
   - Analysis of Big Data: The DNN processes large volumes of data in real-time, allowing it to analyze thousands of transactions and identify potential fraud in environments with high transaction volumes.

Example Transaction Analysis:

- Transaction Details: A customer, Hazem, makes a $300 purchase at an electronics store at 2 am, followed by an immediate attempt to buy a high-value item from a rarely visited online luxury goods store.
- DNN Analysis: The DNN evaluates the transactions based on:
  - The time of the transaction (late night).
  - The rapid succession of high-value purchases.
  - Deviation from Hazem's typical purchasing behavior.
  - Use of an unregistered device.

Outcome: The system flags the transactions as suspicious based on the combination of learned factors. RetailBank either blocks the transactions pending further investigation or triggers an alert for manual review.

Combining Models: Building Robust Ensembles: Combining models in an ensemble approach enhances fraud detection accuracy and efficiency. The process begins with initial filtering, where simpler models like logistic regression quickly sift through data, identifying clear cases of legitimate and suspicious transactions. Suspicious cases are then processed through a sophisticated ensemble of models, including SVM (Support Vector Machines), Random Forests, and Neural Networks. Each model processes the transaction independently and provides input. A final decision is made based on a majority vote or a weighted decision system that considers the confidence level of each model's output.

PayPal's Approach: One real-world example of using ensemble methods is PayPal. PayPal employs a tiered model where initial assessments are conducted using simpler models. Transactions flagged as suspicious undergo further scrutiny by an ensemble of models that includes linear models, neural networks, and deep learning techniques. This multi-layered approach allows for high accuracy in fraud detection while maintaining efficiency, ensuring that legitimate transactions are not unnecessarily blocked and fraudulent ones are caught with greater precision.

Industry Applications and Successes: Despite the historical dominance of rule-based systems in fraud detection, leading financial institutions are increasingly adopting machine learning (ML) technologies to combat fraud effectively. Below are examples of real-world applications and successes:

- MasterCard Case Study: MasterCard uses machine learning and artificial intelligence (AI) to track variables such as transaction size, location, and time, providing real-time assessments of transactions. This initiative has significantly reduced the number of false declines in merchant payments, addressing the estimated $118 billion lost annually due to such declines.
- Feedzai's Findings: Feedzai, a company specializing in AI-based risk management, claims that finely tuned ML solutions can detect up to 95% of all fraud, which significantly reduces the cost associated with manual reconciliations. Currently, 25% of fraud-related expenditures are attributed to these manual processes.
- Capgemini's Research: According to Capgemini, systems that integrate machine learning and analytics can reduce fraud investigation times by up to 70% and improve detection accuracy by 90%. This has a direct impact on operational efficiency and financial risk management for institutions implementing these solutions.

TIP

Integrating machine learning into fraud detection systems allows institutions to enhance their ability to identify fraudulent activities quickly and accurately, thereby protecting their operations and maintaining customer trust.

Key Aspects of Implementing ML in Fraud Prevention: Implementing machine learning (ML) in fraud prevention involves navigating several key considerations to ensure effectiveness, adaptability, and alignment with business objectives:

1. *Accuracy* vs. *Explainability*: The trade-off between accuracy and interpretability is crucial. While highly accurate models provide robust predictions, explainability fosters trust and enables actionable insights.
   - Example: Random forest models offer a balance, being interpretable while maintaining high accuracy. Figure 5.22 illustrates the relationship between model accuracy and interpretability, emphasizing that the best model aligns with your specific fraud prevention goals.

Feedback loop: A robust feedback loop allows teams to refine data labeling and enhance model iterations continuously. This is essential for adapting to evolving fraud patterns and maintaining model relevance.

Classification vs. *clustering:* Fraud detection often combines:

Fig. 5.22 Trade-Off Between Model Interpretability and Prediction Accuracy: This scatter plot highlights the balance between prediction accuracy and model interpretability. Complex models like neural networks and XGBoost offer higher accuracy but lower transparency, while simpler models such as decision trees and clustering are easier to interpret but generally less accurate

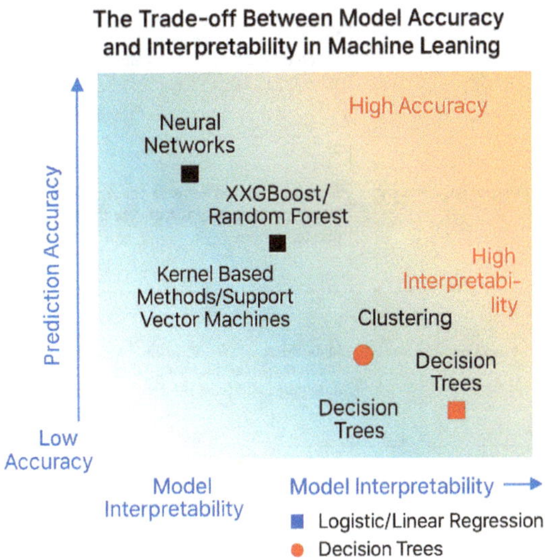

- *Classification:* Supervised learning methods to predict fraudulent vs. non-fraudulent cases.
- *Clustering:* Unsupervised learning methods to uncover hidden patterns in data. Table 3 highlights the differences, showing how these methods complement each other in comprehensive fraud detection systems.

A comprehensive fraud detection system can combine these methods. Table 5.3 shows this interaction. This table shows each method's unique benefits and capabilities, making fraud detection evident.

Table 5.3 Characteristics of classification versus clustering models

Parameter	Classification	Clustering
Type	Primarily used in supervised learning scenarios	Primarily used in unsupervised learning scenarios
Basic premise	Involves classifying input instances based on predefined class labels	Groups instances together based on their inherent similarity; no predefined class labels are required
Dataset requirements	Requires labeled datasets for training and testing to validate the created model	Does not require labeled datasets for training or testing as there are no predefined classes
Complexity	Generally, it is more complex due to the necessity of handling labeled data and validation process	Typically, less complex as it does not involve training or validation on labeled data
Example algorithms	Logistic regression, naive Bayes, decision trees, support vector machines	K-means clustering, fuzzy C-means clustering, Gaussian (expectation-maximization) clustering, DBSCAN

Precision vs. *recall:* Fraud detection systems must balance:

- *Precision:* Minimizing false positives (fewer legitimate transactions flagged).
- *Recall:* Maximizing fraud detection coverage.

The optimal balance depends on organizational goals, including financial stability and customer experience priorities.

Key performance indicators (KPIs): Establish clear KPIs to measure model success, such as precision, recall, and false-positive rates. Regular manual reviews of training and validation datasets can help identify areas for improvement.

Adaptability: Fraud patterns evolve rapidly, requiring models to adapt dynamically.

- *Example:* During the COVID-19 pandemic, adaptive models outperformed static ones by identifying novel fraud patterns. Ensure models are fine-tuned regularly to maintain effectiveness.

Collaboration: Encourage collaboration between:

- *Data scientists:* Experts in technical model development.
- *Fraud analysts:* Professionals with domain expertise to provide critical context and insights.

Continuous Improvement: Fraud tactics continually change, necessitating ongoing evaluation and updates to models. Leverage feedback from fraud analysts to refine predictions and stay ahead of emerging threats.

Creating a successful ML-based fraud prevention system requires balancing accuracy with interpretability, integrating classification and clustering methods, and fostering adaptability through feedback loops and continuous improvement. By focusing on these aspects, businesses can develop robust, scalable, and adaptive fraud detection systems that evolve alongside emerging threats.

Social Network Analysis (SNA)

Social network analysis (SNA) investigates the interactions and relationships between entities like individuals or organizations to detect and preempt fraudulent activities. SNA delves into the relationships and interactions between entities, such as individuals or organizations. Its primary function is to detect potentially fraudulent activities and enable preventative measures by analyzing the dynamics within the network. This technique uncovers hidden linkages and behavioral patterns within networks, which helps in unearthing complex fraudulent schemes. Graph theory and network science form the basis of SNA, aiding in the representation and analysis of social structures and relationships. Social network analysis aids in fraud detection by identifying the following:

- Collaborative fraudulent activities involving multiple entities, as seen in insurance claims or financial transactions.
- Money laundering networks characterized by complex transactions designed to mask the source of illicit funds.
- Unusual relationships that might suggest identity theft.

Case Study: eBay: eBay uses social network analysis to detect organized fraud rings. Fraudsters often collaborate in groups, creating networks of accounts that work together to appear legitimate. eBay's network analysis maps out relationships between users based on transaction patterns and reviews, allowing it to identify and stop coordinated fraud efforts before they spread.

While SNA offers a comprehensive view of relationships, its implementation can be challenging due to computational demands and privacy concerns.

Text Analytics

The practice of analyzing unstructured text data to discover potential fraud trends or signs is known as text analytics. *Text analytics* refers to the process of extracting meaningful information from unstructured text data, which can be used to identify potential fraud trends or signs. Text analytics assists organizations in uncovering insights and patterns from sources such as emails, customer reviews, and social media that may not be visible from structured data. Text analytics tools for fraud detection include natural language processing, sentiment analysis, and entity recognition.

Case Study: Wells Fargo: Wells Fargo uses text analytics to analyze unstructured data such as emails, customer support logs, and chat messages. By applying natural language processing (NLP), the bank identifies fraud-related keywords and communication patterns that might indicate insider fraud or attempts at collusion. This proactive approach helps the bank spot potential fraud that wouldn't be captured by traditional data analysis methods.

Artificial Intelligence (AI)

Building intelligent machines that can learn and solve problems like humans does is the goal of artificial intelligence research. Automatic data processing, pattern recognition, and intelligent inference are all ways in which AI may improve fraud analytics. Machine learning and text analytics are only two examples of how artificial intelligence can be utilized to enhance the efficacy of fraud detection.

Summary

This chapter explored a range of key techniques that form the foundation of fraud analytics. We began with anomaly detection, which identifies irregular patterns or outliers that may indicate fraudulent activity. We then examined social network analysis (SNA), showing how relationships and connections can uncover complex, organized fraud schemes. You also saw how data visualization transforms complex information into clear insights, and how machine learning (ML) enhances both detection and prediction of fraud.

Supervised, unsupervised, and deep learning approaches were each discussed in terms of their applications, strengths, and challenges. Together, these analytical techniques demonstrate how data science can expose, understand, and prevent fraudulent behavior from multiple angles.

With this foundation, you are now prepared to enter the next stage of your journey—data preparation for fraud analytics, where raw information becomes structured, reliable, and ready for advanced modeling.

PART II

Data Preparation for Fraud Analytics

Welcome to Part II, where we focus on preparing and refining data for effective fraud detection and prevention.

This part will equip you with the skills to build strong, high-performing fraud detection models—models that protect both organizations and their customers. We begin with Chapter 6—Foundations of Data Preparation, which covers data collection from multiple sources, along with data-wrangling techniques for cleaning, reshaping, and consolidating information into reliable datasets.

Next, Chapters 7 and 8 dive into feature engineering—first introducing the core concepts of feature selection and creation, then advancing into sophisticated methods such as feature transformation, dimensionality reduction, and interaction features tailored for fraud analytics.

Finally, Chapter 9—Handling Imbalanced Data Sets addresses one of the most common challenges in fraud modeling: unequal class distributions. You'll learn practical strategies and algorithms to correct these imbalances and evaluate models more effectively.

Across these chapters, you'll gain a hands-on understanding of how strong data foundations and thoughtful feature design transform raw information into insight—laying the groundwork for powerful, reliable fraud detection systems.

CHAPTER 6

Data Preparation Techniques

In fraud detection, data preparation is the compass that guides us through the maze of anomalies, ensuring every piece of information is primed for discovery.

Data preparation holds a critical position in the data analytics process. It transforms raw data into a format suitable for further analysis, significantly affecting the outcome of any analytics project. This chapter unveils various aspects essential to data preparation, including handling outliers, managing missing values, integrating, sampling, and discretizing data.

In the era of big data, unique challenges have emerged. One of the most prominent is the assurance of the quality and accuracy of the data utilized in decision-making and analytics. This necessity has given birth to a set of techniques called *data preparation*.

The chapter first tackles the ubiquitous issue of missing values in data, which can notably distort the analysis and potentially lead to misleading conclusions. It presents various techniques for managing these missing values, such as deletion and imputation, assessing the strengths and drawbacks of each approach.

The spotlight then shifts to *outliers*. These are data points that significantly deviate from other observations, which could disrupt an accurate analysis. These anomalies might result from data entry errors, measurement inaccuracies, or genuinely extreme observations. Identifying and

A. Al Aqqad, *Fraud Analytics in Action*
https://doi.org/10.1007/978-3-032-16023-2_6

handling these outliers ensures that they don't distort statistical measures and predictive modeling.

I'll investigate the different methods for spotting and managing outliers, including treating incorrect observations as missing values, truncation, capping, and winsorizing. Real-life examples illustrate the application of each method, providing a thorough treatment of when and how to utilize these techniques.

The chapter talks about *data integration*, a process that combines data from diverse sources into a cohesive, unified dataset. This is followed by exploring data sampling, which selects a subset from a larger dataset, simplifying data handling and hastening data processing.

Finally, the discussion explores the concept of *data discretization*. This procedure entails transforming quantitative data into qualitative data and is frequently employed as a preliminary step for diverse machine learning algorithms.

This chapter teaches the basics of data preparation, its applications, and its ramifications. Data analysts can improve data quality and reliability by mastering these strategies.

The key steps in the fraud data analysis process include data wrangling, exploratory data analysis (EDA), and feature engineering. These aid in comprehending, organizing, and putting the data in a modeling and analysis-ready state.

Data wrangling (also called *data cleaning*) is the process of translating and mapping raw data into a more acceptable format for analysis. Dealing with missing values, contradictions, duplicates, and errors in the data is a part of data wrangling. Data wrangling can be done in a variety of ways, including:

- Removing or filling in missing values
- Converting data types
- Removing duplicate records
- Fixing inconsistencies and errors in data
- Handling outliers

Data wrangling is important because it contributes to data quality improvement, which increases the accuracy and efficiency of the succeeding processes of data analysis, including data pre-treatment. Although *data wrangling* and *data preprocessing* are closely related, data preprocessing usually concentrates on getting the cleaned data ready specifically for use in machine learning algorithms and models, whereas data wrangling is a more general process of guaranteeing data quality and consistency.

Handling Missing Values

In the world of fraud analytics, a well-prepared dataset is the foundation upon which trust is built.

Missing value management is a necessary component of data cleansing and preparation for fraud data analytics. Missing values in data can lead to biased and erroneous conclusions and poor judgment. Missing values may occur due to a variety of factors, including inaccurate data entry, system errors, or user errors.

For instance, missing values can frequently arise when detecting credit card fraud using transaction data for a variety of reasons, such as non-applicability, concealed information, or merging mistakes (Table 6.1). There are various methods for handling missing values, including replacing, deleting, imputing, predicting, or keeping the missing values. (By the way, *NAN* is a nudge from Python, meaning *not a number*.)

Deletion

The simplest solution is *deletion*; however, this can lead to the loss of important data. Deletion is among the most popular techniques employed to handle missing values in a dataset. As you might expect, it entails

Table 6.1 Missing values

ID	Age	Income	Marital Status	Credit Bureau Score	Fraud
1	32	3,500	NAN	770	No
2	39	2,400	Divorced	NAN	Yes
3	25	1,700	Married	NAN	No
4	65	2,800	Widowed	680	Yes
5	60	2,900	Single	NAN	No
6	48	NAN	NAN	NAN	Yes
7	31	2,000	Divorced	NAN	No
8	38	2,300	Married	520	No
9	43	NAN	Single	NAN	No
10	57	3,100	Single	NAN	Yes

deleting from the dataset the observations or variables that have missing values. Two categories of deletion techniques exist: *listwise deletion* and *pairwise deletion*.

Listwise deletion, is deleting any observation that has one or more missing values, is also known as *complete case analysis*. This approach is straightforward and easy to use, but it may result in a large loss of data, particularly if the dataset contains a lot of missing values. If the missing values are *missing completely at random* (MCAR), then the fact that the data points are missing has nothing to do with the observed or unobserved data. If the data are not MCAR, then using listwise deletion can introduce bias into the analysis.

Pairwise deletion, also known as *available case analysis*, involves analyzing only the observations that contain data for the variables being analyzed. In other words, pairwise deletion only removes the missing values for a specific variable and keeps the observations for the remaining variables. This method allows for more data to be used in the analysis compared to listwise deletion, but it can also result in biased estimates if the missing values are not MCAR.

Advantages of the deletion method include the following:

- Easy to implement.
- Does not involve any imputation techniques or assumptions about how the data is distributed.
- Retains the structure of the dataset and avoids the need for imputing values.

Disadvantages of the deletion method include the following:

- Can lead to a significant loss of data, especially if the dataset contains a large number of missing values.
- Can introduce bias into the analysis if the missing values are not MCAR.
- Can lessen sample representativeness if the missing values are not MCAR.

Deletion processes are simple, but if the missing values are not MCAR, they can lose a lot of data and skew the study. Thus, it's vital to thoroughly examine the analysis's potential influence of missing values and choose the proper technique based on the research's context and goals.

Imputation

Imputation substitutes missing data with estimates based on statistical metrics like the mean, median, or mode. It is another widely used method to handle missing numbers. Imputation techniques include single, multiple, and k-nearest neighbor imputation, among others.

Imputation is the process of managing missing values by guessing or "filling in" the gaps in the data. Imputation can lessen the bias that might result from deleting observations with missing values while also preserving the size and structure of the dataset. There are a couple of techniques for impute missing values:

- *Mean/Mode imputation:* This includes filling in the gaps using the available data for that variable's mean (for continuous variables) or mode (for categorical variables), respectively. Although mean/mode imputation is straightforward and simple to use, it makes the assumption that missing values are completely random (MCAR) and can lead to biased estimates if the data is not MCAR.
- *Regression imputation:* This involves estimating missing values based on the relationship between the variable with missing values and other variables in the dataset. Essentially, it treats the variable with missing data as the dependent variable in a regression equation and uses the remaining variables to predict what the missing value might have been. This method uses data set interrelationships to estimate missing values more accurately. However, it assumes a statistical model that may add bias if it does not precisely reflect variable connections.
- *Predictive imputation: Predictive imputation* uses statistical models to estimate missing values based on available data.
- *Model selection:* Options include linear regression, logistic regression, decision trees, k-Nearest Neighbors, and deep learning.
- *Split and predict:* Train a model on complete data and predict missing values on incomplete data.

- *Iterative imputation:* Methods like MICE repetitively impute missing data using regression models.

Benefits include:

- Integrates data from other variables
- Handles systematic missingness.

Disadvantages include:

- Overfitting
- Relationship assumptions and computational complexity
- Numerous imputations

Other Imputation Methods

While the previously mentioned imputation methods, such as Mean/Mode, Regression, and Predictive imputation, primarily rely on statistical models and the inherent relationships within the dataset to estimate missing values, there are other techniques that utilize different strategies. These methods are often more specialized and can be particularly useful in specific scenarios, such as time series data or when considering the spatial or sequential nature of the data. Here's a breakdown:

- *Last observation carried forward* (LOCF): In sequential or time series data, the LOCF approach fills missing values with the last observed value.
- *Next observation carried backward* (NOCB): replaces missing values with the next available observation after the missing point.
- *Interpolation:* approximates missing values by averaging nearby data points, commonly used in time series data.
- In *extrapolation*, data points outside the observed range are estimated using trends or patterns in available data, generally at the start or conclusion of a time series.
- *K-Nearest Neighbors Imputation: KNN imputation* imputes missing values by averaging or mode of the *k* most similar instances based on distance measurements.

- *Numerous imputation*: Creates numerous datasets by imputing missing values differently, reflecting uncertainty, and averages findings for analysis.

> TIP
>
> Before choosing a course of action for handling missing values, it is crucial to statistically assess whether the missing data is related to the target variable or not. Imputation techniques may be secure to apply if the missing data is unrelated to the target variable. But it is preferable to utilize the retain technique and classify the missing data into a new category if it is connected to the target variable. This can help to preserve the crucial information that the missing data offers while still enabling accurate analysis.

One of the most important steps in cleaning and getting data ready for fraud data analytics is ***managing missing values***. Each method for handling missing values has pros and cons. It's vital to carefully analyze your alternatives and pick the ideal one if you want precise and reliable results. It's also important to account for missing values, data duplication, discrepancies, and outliers to provide clean data for analysis.

When dealing with missing values in fraud data analytics, it's important to do all of the following:

1. Determine the values that are missing and why they are missing.
2. Determine whether or not the missing data is connected to the desired variable.
3. Think about the benefits and drawbacks of each technique, such as deletion, imputation, and prediction, for handling missing values.
4. Consider all of your options carefully before choosing the best course of action.
5. Think about other poor data quality issues such as outliers, discrepancies, and duplicate data.

Following these steps can ensure that the data is cleaned and prepared for analysis and that the analysis results are accurate and reliable.

Based on the type of data and situation, multiple approaches to addressing missing values could be used for Table 6.2. Here are some potential tactics:

- *Measuring the mean, median, and mode:* This method uses the mean, median, or mode of the dataset to fill in missing values. For example, in Table 6.2, the average age of the other participants could be used to fill in the missing age value for ID 7. The median income of the other participants might replace the missing income for ID 6.
- *The dataset's last/next observed value:* This approach involves using either the preceding or succeeding observed value to fill in missing data. In Table 6.2, ID 6's age could be used for ID 7's missing age since ID 6 is the last observed age. Similarly, ID 5's income could replace ID 9's missing income, as ID 5 is the last observed income.
- *Drop missing values (deletion):* This method involves removing any rows or columns with missing values. In Table 6.2, IDs 7 and 9, which have missing values, could be removed.
- *Expert knowledge:* To fill in the gaps, this technique uses expert knowledge or domain competence. For instance, if we know that PhDs earn more money, we could replace ID 9's income value with one higher than the median income value of other people with bachelor's degrees but lower than the median income value of other PhDs. This technique leverages domain expertise to fill in missing values. For instance, knowing that individuals with PhDs typically have higher incomes, ID 9's lost revenue could be set at a value higher than the median for those with bachelor's degrees but lower than the median for Ph.D. holders.

These are a few potential methods for dealing with the missing values in this instance. The specifics of the problem's context and the make-up of the lost data will influence the strategy choice.

Example: Using Mean Imputation in Python to Handle Missing Values

The following code takes the mean of the available values to impute the missing values in the *Age* column:

The preceding code will fill in the missing values in the *Age* column with the mean age of the available values (in this case, the mean age is 27.5). See Table 6.3.

As you can see in Table 6.4, the missing values in the *age* column have been filled with the mean age value (27.5 in this example).

Table 6.2 Handling missing values

ID	Age	Gender	Education	Income
1	24	M	Bachelor	45,000
2	38	F	Master's	72,000
3	29	F	PhD	63,000
4	32	M	PhD	80,000
5	41	F	Bachelor	54,000
6	25	M	High	NAN
7	NAN	F	Master's	59,000
8	33	M	High	73,000
9	42	F	Bachelor	NAN
10	37	M	Master's	67,000

Table 6.3 Original data frame

	Name	Age
0	John	25.0
1	Alice	Nan
2	Bob	30.0
3	Cathy	Nan

Table 6.4 Data frame after mean imputation

	Name	Age
0	John	25.0
1	Alice	27.5
2	Bob	30.0
3	Cathy	27.5

Example: Using Regression Imputation to Handle Missing Values

Table 6.5 shows a data set with details on credit card transactions, including the transaction amount, the account holder's age, and the balance. The *Account Balance* column in particular lacks some data. Based

Table 6.5 Missing values before using regression imputation technique

Transaction Amount	Age	Account Balance
1,000	35	2,000
500	42	1,500
200	27	NaN
800	56	3,000
1,200	38	NaN
600	29	1,000
900	45	NaN
1,500	31	500
400	50	1,200

on the correlation between the account balance and the other variables, you can apply regression imputation to approximate the missing values.

First, find the variables related to the missing data. This example assumes the missing variable is the account balance. Transaction quantity and accountholder age may be factors.

The missing values can then be estimated by constructing a regression model with these variables. To create this model, use the account balance as the dependent variable, with the transaction amount and age acting as the independent variables. This model will then be employed to predict the missing values in the account balance.

Imagine, for example, that you set up a linear regression model with the account balance as the response variable and the transaction amount and age as predictors. The resulting model could have the following equation:

Account Balance = 500 + 10 * Transaction Amount – 50 * Age

This model can be used to predict the missing values in the *Account Balance* column. For instance, you can substitute the values for the transaction amount (200) and age (27) into the equation to predict the account balance for the third row:

Account Balance: 500 + 10 * 200 – 50 * 27

Account Balance: 500 + 2000 – 1350

Table 6.6 The dataset after implementing the regression imputation technique

Transaction Amount	Age	Account Balance
1,000	35	2,000
500	42	1,500
200	27	1,150
800	56	3,000
1,200	38	1,900
600	29	1,000
900	45	2,350
1,500	31	500
400	50	1,200

Account Balance: 1150

This process can be replicated for any other missing values in the dataset. In this way, you can make informed estimates of missing data based on existing, related information. Table 6.6 shows the table after doing this.

Based on the correlation between the transaction amount, age, and account balance variables, we have estimated the missing values for the account balance column using regression imputation. As a result, we can use the entire dataset for additional research and fraud detection.

The following code performs regression imputation in Python using the Pandas and scikit-learn libraries:

```
import pandas as pd
import numpy as np
from sklearn.linear_model import LinearRegression

# Create the dataset
data = {'Transaction Amount': [1000, 500, 200, 800, 1200, 600, 900, 1500, 400],
        'Age': [35, 42, 27, 56, 38, 29, 45, 31, 50],
        'Account Balance': [2000, 1500, np.nan, 3000, np.nan, 1000, np.nan, 500, 1200]}
df = pd.DataFrame(data)

# Separate the data into two DataFrames: one with complete data and one with missing account balances
complete_data = df.dropna()
missing_indices = df['Account Balance'].isna()  # Get the boolean indices of missing data

# Fit a linear regression model using the complete data
X_complete = complete_data[['Transaction Amount', 'Age']]
y_complete = complete_data['Account Balance']
reg = LinearRegression().fit(X_complete, y_complete)

# Predict the missing account balances using the regression model
X_missing = df.loc[missing_indices, ['Transaction Amount', 'Age']]
df.loc[missing_indices, 'Account Balance'] = reg.predict(X_missing)

# Display the imputed dataset
print("Imputed Dataset:")
print(df)
```

Imputed Dataset:

Transaction	*Amount*	*Age*	*Account Balance*
0	1000	35	2000.00
1	500	42	1500.00
2	200	27	568.55

(continued)

(continued)

Transaction	*Amount*	*Age*	*Account Balance*
3	800	56	3000.00
4	1200	38	1482.63
5	600	29	1000.00
6	900	45	1829.89
7	1500	31	500.00
8	400	50	1200.00

Detecting and Handling Outliers

Outliers in data are like the whispers of deceit, often overlooked but crucial to unearthing the truth.

Extreme observations that are considerably different from the majority of the population are known as *outliers*. *Valid* observations and *invalid* observations are the two categories of outliers. Extreme values that accurately reflect true though outlying data, such as a CEO's exorbitant salary, are considered valid observations. Extreme or illogical figures, such as a person's age being 300, are examples of invalid observations.

Why are outliers important?

- *Impact on mean and standard deviation:* Outliers can significantly impact the mean and standard deviation of a dataset. This can be problematic, as many statistical tests and machine learning models rely on these measures.
- *Skewness*: Outliers can skew the distribution of data, leading to incorrect analyses.
- *Impact on machine learning models*: Outliers can adversely affect the performance of machine learning models. Some models, like linear regression, are particularly sensitive to outliers.

Outliers can manifest in different dimensions of data. *Univariate* outliers are outliers that appear in one variable or feature. *Multivariate* outliers appear when considering combinations of variables, even if the individual variables do not contain outliers, and they can be detected using a variety of graphical tools and statistical techniques.

Some common methods for detecting outliers include the following:

Fig. 6.1 Histogram of data

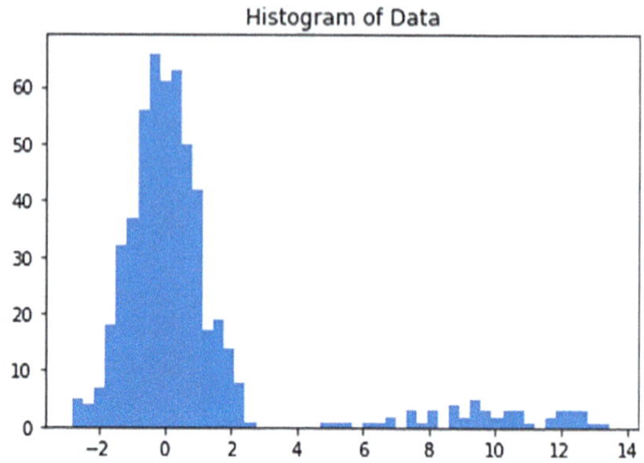

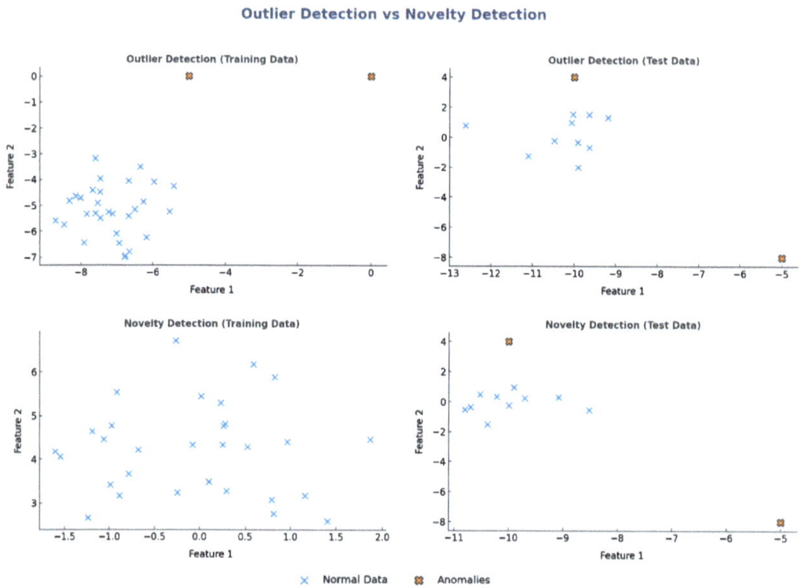

Fig. 6.2 Outlier detection versus novelty detection using machine learning.

- *Visual inspection*: This entails visualizing the data and visually scanning for any potentially outlying extreme numbers. Examples of visual analysis tools include *histograms* (Fig. 6.1), *box plots, scatter-plots, and heatmaps*.

Always start with a visual inspection of your data. Graphical tools like histograms, box plots, and scatter plots give a quick sense of the distribution of data and potential outliers.

- *Statistical methods:* These methods employ arithmetic to discover outliers. The Z-score, which measures how many standard deviations a data point is from the mean, is one such method. Outliers are observations with a Z-score greater than a preset level. Another method to identify data outliers is using the interquartile range (IQR). Outlier observations are those outside the first or third quartiles by 1.5 times the IQR.
- While visual inspection is a good starting point, statistical methods provide a more objective way to identify outliers. The Z-score and IQR are popular methods, but always remember to consider the nature of your data and the implications of labeling a data point as an outlier.
- Context matters: always consider the context of your data. For instance, a salary of $1 million might be an outlier for a dataset of school teachers but not for CEOs of Fortune 500 companies.
- *Machine learning methods:* Outliers can also be found using ML algorithms like k-means clustering, principal component analysis (PCA), and support vector machines (SVM). These techniques are especially effective at locating multivariate outliers. A machine learning technique called *outlier detection* looks for data points that deviate from the majority using an unsupervised approach. In the realm of machine learning, we often discuss two related but distinct concepts: outlier detection and novelty detection (refer to Fig. 6.2).

These are powerful tools, especially for high-dimensional data. However, they often require a deeper understanding of the underlying algorithms and may be computationally intensive.

- *Novelty detection:* This refers to the identification of new or different data points when provided with a dataset that is considered to be *clean* (that is, free from outliers). In this context, the model is trained

on a dataset without outliers and is then used to detect any new points that deviate from this training set.
- *Outlier detection:* Outlier detection pertains to the identification of anomalous data points within a dataset that might already contain outliers. This process essentially aims to detect data points that significantly deviate from the majority or expected behavior of the data.

This figure contrasts outlier detection and novelty detection by illustrating how models behave when applied to training data versus unseen test data. In outlier detection, anomalies may be present within the training set and are identified relative to the overall data distribution. In contrast, novelty detection assumes that training data consist only of normal observations, and anomalies are detected only when new, previously unseen data points deviate from learned patterns. This distinction is particularly important in fraud detection, where models must be carefully selected based on whether anomalous behavior is expected during training or emerges only in production environments

Adapted from: A. Müller, Outlier Detection, Applied Machine Learning https://amueller.github.io/aml/03-unsupervised-learning/03-outlier-detection.html

- *Motivation*: The practical applications of outlier and novelty identification include fraud detection, network failure detection, intrusion detection in networks, engineering fault detection, and locating noteworthy or pertinent material. Outliers are typically thought to diverge from the norm in specific ways.

> TIP
>
> These unsupervised methods have various applications, including fraud detection, network failure detection, intrusion detection, defect detection, and news or intelligence analysis. The primary goals are to modify the data distribution $p(X)$ and identify data points that defy the model. The data point is an outlier if $p(X) > 0$. Since the dataset may already contain outliers, modeling $p(X)$ robustly is crucial for outlier detection.

There are several outlier detection methods under machine learning:

- *Elliptic envelope:* Outlier detection involves fitting a Gaussian distribution to data and identifying outliers. This technique seeks a trustworthy mean and covariance matrix approximation to recover the genuine covariance matrix while accepting some outliers in the training sample. The elliptic envelope finds a robust covariance matrix with the lowest determinant that covers a large percentage of the data. Most outlier identification methods require the predicted number of outliers and generate a covariance matrix to include the remaining data points while minimizing the determinant. This method identifies outlier data points which differ significantly from the mean by a preset number of standard deviations.
- *Kernel density estimation (KDE):* A non-parametric density model that approximates each data point with a Gaussian blob. However, because it is unsupervised, choosing the kernel bandwidth is necessary and can be difficult. KDE can be sluggish and struggle in environments with many dimensions.
- *One class SVM:* Similar to KDE, this just chooses support vectors while covering the data using Gaussian kernels. The kernel bandwidth must be changed, and the *nu* option must be used to specify the outlier ratio (contamination). As there is no probability model to use for cross-validation, adjusting the gamma parameter is challenging.
- *Isolation forests:* This is a non-parametric approach that doesn't call for parameter adjustment. To separate out data points, the idea is to construct numerous, entirely arbitrary trees and quantify their path lengths. To assess whether a point is an inlier or an outlier, you use normalized path length scores. The contamination rate must be specified, but the procedure is reasonably straightforward and effective.

Overall, each method has advantages and disadvantages, and the best one to use depends on the particular dataset and application.

Outlier and novelty detection are the most important unsupervised methods for finding outliers. These methods can detect fraud, network difficulties, and other real-life anomalies. However, their efficacy depends on assumptions about data distribution and outlier classification, and the tasks usually need to be better defined.

Example: Outlier Detection Using Z-Score

Table 6.7 shows a dataset with information on a company's employees' pay. The columns in the dataset are *Employee ID*, *Department*, and *Salary*. The dataset contains a few outlier values that significantly differ from the majority of values in the dataset. To ensure the accuracy of our analysis, it's crucial to identify and manage these outliers.

To locate outliers in this dataset, use the Z-score or IQR. The Z-score can identify values more than three standard deviations from the mean:

- Z-score=(x-mean)/standard deviation
- Outliers are values with a Z-score of 3 or −3.

We can calculate the Z-score for each salary value in the dataset to pinpoint the outliers. Table 6.7 illustrates that the mean salary is $40,000 and the standard deviation is $20,000, presenting the Z-scores for each salary value.

From Table 6.8, it's evident that the salaries of workers 005 and 008 are considerably higher than all other workers in the dataset. Their Z-scores, *3.0* and *2.5* respectively, indicate their status as outliers.

This is one example of employing outlier identification to handle dataset outliers. Other methods, such as the IQR, can be used to identify and respond to outliers.

Table 6.7 Dataset with some outliers

Employee ID	Department	Salary
001	Sales	35,000
002	Marketing	45,000
003	HR	25,000
004	Sales	37,000
005	Marketing	100,000
006	HR	27,000
007	Sales	38,000
008	Marketing	90,000
009	HR	28,000
010	Sales	39,000

Example: Outlier Detection Using IQR

Table 6.9 The following dataset represents the heights of 10 people in centimeters.

To detect outliers using the IQR method, we first calculate the IQR as follows:

- Sort the dataset in ascending order:
- Height: [110, 155, 157, 160, 170, 175, 180, 185, 190, 250]

Table 6.8 Outlier detection using the Z-score method

Employee ID	Department	Salary	Z-score
001	Sales	35,000	-0.5
002	Marketing	45,000	0.5
003	HR	25,000	-1.5
004	Sales	37,000	0
005	Marketing	100,000	3.0
006	HR	27,000	-1.0
007	Sales	38,000	0.1
008	Marketing	90,000	2.5
009	HR	28,000	-0.9
010	Sales	39,000	0.2

Table 6.9 Heights of 10 people in centimeters

Transaction	Amount	Age	Account Balance
0	1000	35	2000.00
1	500	42	1500.00
2	200	27	568.55
3	800	56	3000.00
4	1200	38	1482.63
5	600	29	1000.00
6	900	45	1829.89
7	1500	31	500.00
8	400	50	1200.00

- Calculate the 25th percentile, the first quartile (Q1). The dataset has 10 values; hence, Q1 is the 2.5th value: *Q1=(155+157)/2=156.*
- Calculate the 75th percentile, the third quartile (Q3). Q3 is the 7.5th value: *Q3=(180+185)/2=182.5.*
- Calculate the IQR, which is Q3 minus Q1: *IQR=26.5.*
- Calculate outlier lower and upper boundaries using the formula: *lower bound=156−(1.5x 26.5), upper bound=182.5+(1.5x 26.5).* Hence, 116.25 and 222.25 are the lower and upper bounds, respectively.

As you know, outliers are values outside the lower and upper boundaries. 110 and 250 are outliers because they fall outside the bottom and upper boundaries, respectively.

These outliers can be removed from the dataset or replaced with the nearest non-outlier values. For instance, we can alter 250 to 190 and 110 to 155. The final dataset:

Height: [160, 175, 157, 180, 185, 155, 190, 155, 170, 190]

As you can see, now the dataset is free of outliers and ready for further analysis.

Outlier Treatment

Treatment comes next when outliers have been located. Whether or not an observation is an outlier depends on its validity. One method is to treat incorrect observations as missing values. These numbers can be eliminated from the dataset or swapped for the data's mean, median, or mode. Another strategy is to correct or impute the values. For instance, if a figure for 300 years is false, it can be updated with a more accurate number using the data at hand.

> TIP
>
> Once you've identified outliers, you need to decide how to handle them. This decision should be based on the nature of the outlier (valid vs. invalid) and the potential impact on your analysis.

Truncation, *capping*, and *winsorizing* are popular methods for valid observations.

- *Truncation*: This includes eliminating extreme values above a predetermined limit.
- *Capping*: Setting a cap on the highest or lowest value a word can take.
- *Winsorizing*: Like capping, winsorizing replaces extreme values with the closest non-outlying value rather than imposing a limit on the highest or minimum value.

Outlier discovery and treatment are crucial phases in data analytics. Outliers can be found using various techniques, and their handling depends on whether or not they represent genuine or invalid observations. The individual situation and the analyst's discretion determine the method to choose. It's also crucial to evaluate the effects of outlier treatment on the analysis and record the causes.

Studying income distribution within a company can be skewed by the exceptionally high salaries of executives and senior managers. To address this, we can use truncation or capping. *Truncation* involves removing all salaries above a certain threshold from the dataset, whereas *capping* means setting a maximum limit to the salaries, with any amount above that adjusted to the cap. For instance, truncating at $75,000 would exclude all salaries above this, whereas capping at this amount would adjust any higher salaries down to $75,000.

In a testing scenario where scores range from 0 to 100, extremely low results by a minority of students can significantly skew the overall interpretation of the test results. These scores may be legitimate, for example, from students who did not prepare or who have learning challenges. *Winsorizing* is a technique that can be applied to address this issue. It involves replacing extreme values with the nearest non-outlier value. For instance, if we choose to winsorize the scores at the 5th percentile, any scores below this would be replaced with the value at the 5th percentile, and similarly, scores above the 95th percentile would be replaced with the 95th percentile value. This reduces the impact of extreme scores on the overall interpretation of the data.

Example: Outlier Treatment Using Truncation

Imagine a scenario in which a bank investigates credit card transaction data for signs of fraud. Each purchase is documented in a database along with the corresponding ID, date, sum, and client id. They find some

Table 6.10 Dataset before truncation

Transaction ID	Transaction Date	Transaction Amount	Customer ID
1	2022-01-01	100	1234
2	2022-01-02	250	5678
3	2022-01-03	5,000	9101
4	2022-01-04	150	1234
5	2022-01-05	3,000	5678
6	2022-01-06	7,500	9101

Table 6.11 Dataset after truncation

Transaction ID	Transaction Date	Transaction Amount	Customer ID
1	2022-01-01	100	1234
2	2022-01-02	250	5678
4	2022-01-04	150	1234

transactions with extremely high transaction amounts that could possibly be fraudulent during the data analysis process. They chose to solve this by removing these transactions from the dataset using outlier treatment techniques.

Truncation is one method they employ, where they put a limit on the largest transaction amount and eliminate any transactions that exceed it. They chose to set the threshold at three times the transaction amount variable's standard deviation. Table 6.10 shows a dataset before truncation.

Transactions 3, 5, and 6 in Table 6.11 were eliminated from the dataset because their transaction amounts exceeded the cap established by the bank using the truncation procedure. This makes it easier to identify and prevent fraud by reducing the impact of possibly fraudulent transactions in the dataset.

Example: Outlier Treatment Using Winsorizing

Assume a bank is investigating John's transactional data to look for any indications of fraud. The financial institution observes that John's average transaction value is $500, but a few transactions had values of $10,000,

$15,000, and $20,000 instead. These transactions have the potential to be anomalies that point to fraud. See Table 6.12.

The bank can manage these extreme values using winsorizing, which involves substituting exceedingly high or low values with less extreme ones, thus minimizing their impact on data analysis. In this case, the bank can retain the overall distribution of transaction amounts while substituting outlier values with others that are more aligned with the mean transaction amount. This makes the data more representative and accurate for further analysis.

1. Calculate the mean and standard deviation of the transaction data:

Mean transaction amount = (500 + 400 + 10,000 + 15,000 + 500 + 20,000 + 600 + 700)/8 = $4900.
Standard deviation = $7351.98

2. Set the upper and lower bounds for the winsorizing technique. For example, the bank may choose to replace values that are more than two standard deviations from the mean:

Upper bound = $4900 + 2 * $7351.98 = $19,604.
Lower bound = $4900 – 2 * $7351.98 = –$9804 (set to $0)

3. Replace the outlier values with the upper or lower bound as appropriate.

Table 6.12 How winsorizing can be applied to John's transaction data

Transaction ID	Transaction Amount
1	500
2	400
3	10,000
4	15,000
5	500
6	20,000
7	600
8	700

Table 6.13 How winsorizing can be applied to John's transaction data

Transaction ID	Transaction Amount
1	500
2	400
3	4,900
4	4,900
5	500
6	4,900
7	600
8	700

From the winsorizing procedure presented in Table 6.13, we observe that the outlier transaction values of $10,000, $15,000, and $20,000 have been effectively replaced with the mean value of $4900. This value is much closer to the mean transaction amount, thereby preserving the central tendency of John's transaction data. As a result of this adjustment, the bank can undertake a more accurate and comprehensive examination of John's transaction patterns, thereby enhancing its ability to detect any potentially fraudulent activities that might have been obscured by these abnormally high transaction values.

WARNING

Replacing outliers with mean/median or other imputation methods can introduce bias. Always consider the implications of your outlier treatment method.

· *False positives:* Always be wary of false positives. Just because a data point is far from the mean doesn't necessarily mean it's an error or an outlier.

· *Data loss*: Removing outliers can lead to loss of information. Always weigh the pros and cons before deciding to remove an outl ier.

Assumptions: Many statistical methods for outlier detection make certain assumptions about the distribution of data. Ensure these assumptions hold before applying these methods.

Data Integration

Data integration is a vital process in data wrangling that involves merging data from multiple sources into a singular dataset. Key methodologies used to address data inconsistency and duplication include record linkage and entity resolution. These processes ensure the creation of a reliable dataset for future analysis.

- *Record linkage:* This process involves identifying and associating records from various data sources that relate to the same entity. Attributes like names, addresses, and unique identifiers are compared using methods such as deterministic and probabilistic linkage. Fraud data analysts often use record linkage to consolidate client data from different sources into a single dataset.
- *Entity resolution:* This is a process similar to record linkage, but it focuses on identifying and linking related records within the same data source. It involves locating duplicate records in a dataset, merging them into one, and updating the dataset.

Record linkage and entity resolution techniques improve data quality by minimizing duplication and inconsistencies. These methods automate the process of merging relevant records, saving time and resources, and leading to a reliable integrated dataset suitable for analysis and decision-making.

Example: Vertical Data Integration Using Two Tables

Consider the customer information data in Table 6.14 and the purchase information shown in Tables 6.15.

In this example, the two tables are vertically integrated by combining them into one table (Table 6.16), based on the shared *Customer ID* column.

We can now view the customer's purchase history and demographic data in one table by vertically integrating these two tables. This can give a

Table 6.14 Customer Information

Customer ID	Name	Age	Gender	Phone Number
101	John	25	Male	555-1234
102	Mary	32	Female	555-5678
103	Tom	40	Male	555-9876
104	Sarah	28	Female	555-2345

Table 6.15 Purchase information

Customer ID	Date	Product	Price
101	2021-01-05	Shoes	50
101	2021-02-10	Shirt	30
102	2021-01-15	Jacket	80
103	2021-01-30	Shoes	60
104	2021-02-14	Hat	20

Table 6.16 Integrated customer and purchase information

Customer ID	Name	Age	Gender	Phone Number	Date	Product	Price
101	John	25	Male	555-1234	2021-01-05	Shoes	50
101	John	25	Male	555-1234	2021-02-10	Shirt	30
102	Mary	32	Female	555-5678	2021-01-15	Jacket	80
103	Tom	40	Male	555-9876	2021-01-30	Shoes	60
104	Sarah	28	Female	555-2345	2021-02-14	Hat	20

more complete picture of the customer's behavior and make analysis and decision-making more fruitful.

Data Sampling

Data sampling is a method used in data analytics to select a subset of data for examination, which is especially useful in fraud analytics when analyzing large volumes of data is impractical or time-consuming. Techniques include the following:

- *Simple random sampling:* Each data point has an equal chance of being chosen, helping to maintain accuracy while analyzing a manageable amount of data.
- *Stratified sampling:* Data is divided into subgroups (strata) based on specific features, and a random sample is chosen from each, ensuring each subgroup is represented, improving the precision of estimates for the whole population.

- *Cluster sampling:* The population is divided into clusters based on factors like location or demographics, and the entire population of each chosen cluster is included in the sample, reducing sampling costs but potentially leading to greater variability in the sample.
- *Systematic sampling:* Samples are selected at regular intervals from the population. It's an efficient technique but may be biased if the population exhibits a recurring pattern.
- *Stop or go sampling:* A subset of transactions is chosen for further investigation based on specific criteria, such as transaction size or client history. Transactions are then scored based on the likelihood of fraud.
- *Convenience and snowball sampling:* These non-probability methods involve selecting the most readily available participants.
- *Quota sampling:* Participants are chosen according to preset quotas to ensure the sample is representative of the entire organization.

The sampling method used depends on the objectives of the fraud analysis and the features of the dataset. Careful validation of the sampling technique and the results obtained from the sample is necessary to ensure representative results.

Data Discretization

Discretizing data involves transforming continuous data into distinct categories or *bins*. In fields like data mining and machine learning, it's a common practice to morph continuous variables into categorical ones to better serve as features in various models.

Here are three methods for data discretization:

- *Uniform-width binning:* This approach carves up the data range into equal-sized bins or intervals. For instance, if we choose to create five bins within a range of 20 (0–20, 20–40, 40–60, 60–80, 80–100), each bin covers a span of 20 units. Data values are then placed into their respective bins. However, this simple method might falter when dealing with data distributions that are not evenly spread.
- *Equal frequency binning:* This technique ensures each bin contains approximately the same number of data points, even though the actual bin widths may differ. For example, if we're dealing with a

dataset of 100 points that needs to be divided into 5 bins, each bin will hold 20 points. This method, though a tad more complex than uniform-width binning, is usually better suited for uneven data distributions.

- *K-means clustering:* This is a machine learning method that groups data into a predetermined number of clusters based on the similarity between data points. Each cluster then serves as a bin.

Some practical applications of data discretization:

- *Grouping by age:* Customers can be discretized into age groups like 18–24, 25–34, 35–44, 45–54, 55–64, and 65+.
- *Temperature grouping:* Temperature data can be discretized into *cold*, *cool*, *warm*, and *hot* categories.
- *Income grouping:* Employee income data can be grouped into *Less than* $30,000, $30,000–$50,000, $50,000–$75,000, $75,000–$100,000, and *More than $100,000.*
- *Rating classification:* Movie and product ratings might be *poor*, *fair*, *good*, *very good*, and *excellent*.

WARNING

Discretization can make data easier to handle and comprehend, but if done inappropriately, it can lead to data loss or mistakes. The data type and analysis purpose should determine the discretization technique and bin size to minimize negative effects on results.

Summary

In this chapter, you explored the foundations of data preparation—an essential stage in any fraud analytics workflow. You learned how to manage missing values and outliers, along with different treatment methods and their respective advantages and limitations.

You also examined key techniques such as data integration, sampling, and discretization, which transform raw, messy information into well-structured, analysis-ready datasets. Mastering these preparation techniques allows you to enhance both the quality and reliability of your data, directly improving the accuracy and credibility of downstream models.

As you move into Chapter 7–Feature Engineering, you'll take the next step in the analytical pipeline: learning how to convert cleaned data into meaningful predictive features. You'll discover how to select, extract, and construct variables that reveal fraud patterns, increase model interpretability, and boost performance. Together, these skills bridge the gap between raw data and intelligent fraud detection models.

CHAPTER 7

Feature Engineering

Feature engineering is the alchemy of data science—it turns raw data into gold. This chapter dives into the essence of *feature engineering*, a crucial process that enhances the performance of machine learning models, particularly in fraud analytics. Feature engineering involves creating new features or modifying existing ones to extract more meaningful information from data, thus boosting its usefulness for model development.

The chapter introduces various techniques of feature engineering, including *feature selection, feature extraction, one-hot encoding, feature scaling, and feature creation.*

The performance of AI/ML models must be improved by proper *feature engineering*. It assists in extracting the dataset's most pertinent and important characteristics, deleting superfluous or pointless features, and adding new features that can be helpful for the model.

In fraud analytics, the creation of a set of features with the ability to precisely capture the traits of fraudulent transactions and function for analysis is the aim of feature engineering. Fraud analysts can increase the precision and efficacy of their fraud detection algorithms and more precisely pinpoint fraudulent practices by carefully choosing and developing features.

By emphasizing key data points and deleting outliers or unneeded information, feature engineering can assist fraud data analysts in spotting fraudulent transactions. The data can also be enhanced with domain

A. Al Aqqad, *Fraud Analytics in Action*
https://doi.org/10.1007/978-3-032-16023-2_7

knowledge and skills to produce fresh features that the model might find useful.

The art of adding new features that weren't in the original dataset is known as *feature engineering*. In order to capture complex interactions between variables, it entails choosing the most pertinent features, transforming existing features into new ones, and combining existing features. The ability to discern between honest and dishonest transactions can be achieved through feature engineering. Feature engineering is a critical step in the data preprocessing stage of fraud analytics since it can help increase the precision and efficacy of fraud detection algorithms.

Because feature engineering is essential for creating effective machine learning models, data analysts spend about 80% of their time doing it. Model training and hyperparameter optimization take up the remaining 20% of the time.

For feature engineering in fraud analytics, a number of strategies can be used, including:

- Feature selection
- Feature extraction
- Feature scaling
- Feature creation

WARNING

The possibility of overfitting, which can happen when the features are too unique to the training data and do not generalize well to fresh data, is a crucial factor to take into account while developing features. Use a balanced approach to feature engineering and test the performance of the features on both the training and testing data in order to prevent overfitting.

The possibility of overfitting, which can happen when the features are too unique to the training data and do not generalize well to fresh data, is a crucial factor to take into account while developing features. Use a balanced approach to feature engineering and test the performance of the features on both the training and testing data in order to prevent overfitting.

Chapter 15 "Fraud Detection Excellence—A Deep Exploration of Model Metrics, Optimization, and Governance" talks more about overfitting and strategies to mitigate it, specifically in the section "Model Optimization."

Feature Selection

Feature selection is a crucial step in the machine learning pipeline. It involves selecting the most relevant features (or attributes) from the original set of features in the dataset. The primary goal is to remove redundant or irrelevant features that don't contribute or that might even decrease the predictive performance of the model.

> TIP
>
> Always prioritize feature selection before model training for optimal results.

Benefits of feature selection include the following:

1. *Improves model performance:* Removing irrelevant features allows models to focus on features that truly matter, leading to improved accuracy.
2. *Reduces overfitting:* Less redundant data means less chance of making decisions based on noise.
3. *Speeds up training:* Fewer data points reduce the algorithm's complexity and training time.
4. *Provides better understanding:* Important features can give insight into the dataset and the underlying processes that generated it.

Methods of feature selection include the following:

1. *Statistical tests:* Measure the correlation or association of each feature with the target variable. Common methods include:
   - Pearson correlation coefficient
   - Mutual information
   - Chi-Squared test

2. *Feature importance ranking:* Many machine learning models, such as *random forest (RF)*, inherently rank features based on their importance. Random forest, for instance, provides an importance score for each feature, indicating its relevance in making accurate predictions.
3. *Ensemble boosting methods:* Boosting algorithms like XGBoost and LightGBM also offer feature importance scores. These models build multiple decision trees during training and rank features based on how frequently a feature is used to split the data and how much it improves the model's performance.
4. *Model-based selection:* Uses machine learning algorithms to evaluate the importance of features. Among these methods, recursive feature elimination stands out.

    - *Recursive feature elimination (RFE):* This is a feature selection method that fits a model and removes the weakest feature (or features) until the specified number of features is reached. RFE aims to select features by recursively considering smaller and smaller sets of features.
    - *Recursive feature elimination with cross-validation (RFECV):* This is an extension of RFE that uses cross-validation to determine the optimal number of features. RFECV provides an automatic selection approach, ensuring that only the most influential features are retained, optimizing model performance.

5. *Wrapper methods:* These methods evaluate multiple models with different subsets of input features and select those features that result in the best-performing model. Examples include forward selection, backward elimination, and recursive feature elimination.
6. *Embedded methods:* Algorithms that have built-in feature selection methods. For instance, LASSO regression performs feature selection by shrinking less important features' coefficients to zero.

Here's an example of feature selection: Consider a dataset of credit card transactions with attributes like transaction amount, date, merchant category, card type, card issuer, and whether the transaction was fraudulent. You can identify the most influential features for predicting fraudulent transactions using methods like *RFE, RFECV*, or even feature importance scores from models like Random Forest, *XGBoost, or LightGBM*. Features like "*transaction amount*" or "*merchant category*" might be more significant than "transaction date." Employing these methods ensures the retention of only the most relevant features, optimizing the model's predictive power.

Note: Feature importance ranking and model-based selection are covered in depth in *Part 4 under* Chapter 15, *which provides further details on the real-world scenario*. Feature selection is critical to building a robust machine learning model. Whether using statistical tests or model-based methods or leveraging the inherent feature ranking capabilities of models like Random Forest, *XGBoost, or LightGBM*, the goal is to enhance the model's performance and provide insights into the data's features.

WARNING

Always validate the selected features using a separate validation set to ensure they genuinely improve model performance.

Always validate the selected features using a separate validation set to ensure they genuinely improve model performance.

Feature Extraction

Feature extraction is a pivotal step in the machine learning pipeline, transforming raw data into a reduced set of meaningful, relevant features. By leveraging mathematical or statistical techniques, the most significant characteristics of the data are extracted, making it more amenable for machine learning algorithms.

TIP

Feature extraction is especially useful when dealing with high-dimensional data.

In the realm of fraud analytics and detection, *feature extraction* is a cornerstone, unveiling hidden patterns indicative of suspicious activities. Methods such as *scaling* and *normalization* are vital for adjusting data to a standard scale and enhancing the performance of many algorithms that thrive when features are on a similar scale. *Binning*, which transforms continuous data like transaction amounts into discrete categories, aids in identifying unusual transaction ranges that might hint at fraud.

One-hot encoding is very important for categorical data that is often used to find fraud, like transaction types or merchant categories. It turns these categories into binary variables that algorithms can easily understand. *Dimensionality (Dimensionality refers to the number of columns or features in your dataset.) reduction* uses methods like principal component analysis (PCA) and singular value decomposition (SVD) to break down large amounts of transactional data into their most important parts and draw attention to any unusual patterns.

Finding the most important independent components is what *independent component analysis* (ICA) does. This makes it perfect for datasets where fraud is not the norm. With the surge of online transactions, *text analytics*, which leverages natural language processing, becomes crucial in gleaning insights from unstructured text, like reviews, potentially flagging fraudulent merchants or products.

The combined effect of variables, revealed through interaction terms, can sometimes be more indicative of fraud than individual variables. Furthermore, *temporal features*, such as the intervals between transactions or odd-hour transactions, are paramount, often serving as red flags in fraud detection scenarios.

Examples of feature extraction include the following:

- *Variable transformation:* Creating new variables by combining or altering existing ones can offer deeper insights. For instance, computing ratios, differences, or percentages can provide a comparative perspective on the data.
- *Encoding categorical variables:* Techniques like one-hot encoding or target encoding transform categorical data into a format more suitable for machine learning algorithms. *Discussed in detail below.*
- *Temporal features:* In scenarios like fraud detection, temporal aspects like the time since the last transaction can be revealing.
- *Device and IP analysis*: Features related to the device used for transactions, such as device type, browser, or IP address, can help in identifying suspicious activities. Multiple transactions from different accounts but from the same device or IP can be a red flag.
- *Social network analysis*: In cases of collusion fraud, where multiple entities work together to commit fraud, analyzing the network of

transactions can reveal patterns of suspicious behavior. Part 5 of this book dives deep into social network analysis for fraud detection.

- *Text analysis*: If you have textual data like transaction descriptions, use text analytics techniques to extract features. Suspicious keywords or patterns in the description can be indicative of fraud. Part 6 of this book dives deep into textual data in fraud analysis.

One-Hot Encoding

Think of one-hot encoding as a nifty tool that makes your categorical data ready for machine learning. It's like a translator, converting categorical values into a binary language of 0s and 1s that machine learning algorithms can understand.

In a dataset (Fig. 7.1) the "*color*" column contains green, yellow, and red. To use this data in a machine learning model, turn these color labels into integers. That's precisely where one-hot encoding comes to the rescue.

This process, as it can be seen in Fig. 7.1, would give birth to three new columns: "*red*," "*green*," *and* "*yellow*." The new column corresponding to a row's color value now displays a 1 while the other columns become

COLOR
RED
YELLOW
GREEN
YELLOW
YELLOW

RED	YELLOW	GREEN
1	0	0
0	1	0
0	0	1
0	1	0
0	1	0

Fig. 7.1 One-hot encoding example: This figure demonstrates the one-hot encoding process, converting a categorical column of color values into binary columns. Each unique value—RED, YELLOW, and GREEN—is represented by a separate column with a 1 indicating presence and 0 otherwise. One-hot encoding is essential for preparing categorical variables for machine learning algorithms that require numerical input

0. For instance, if a row's color is red, the red column gets a 1, but the green and yellow columns become 0.

The magic of one-hot encoding lies in two key advantages:

- *Makes categorical data ready for machine learning (ML):* Converting data into a binary format that algorithms can understand.
- *Prevents assumptions*: Avoids establishing a numerical relationship among categories.

However, you might wonder: Why not just replace the categories with simple integer values? Here's the twist: machine learning models, at their core, are mathematical entities. So, if you start replacing categories with integers, you unintentionally establish a numerical relationship among categories, which can lead to confusion.

Imagine you assign numbers to colors, as shown in Fig. 7.2. This would wrongly suggest that green is greater than yellow and yellow is greater than red, which doesn't align with the reality of these being distinct, non-hierarchical categories.

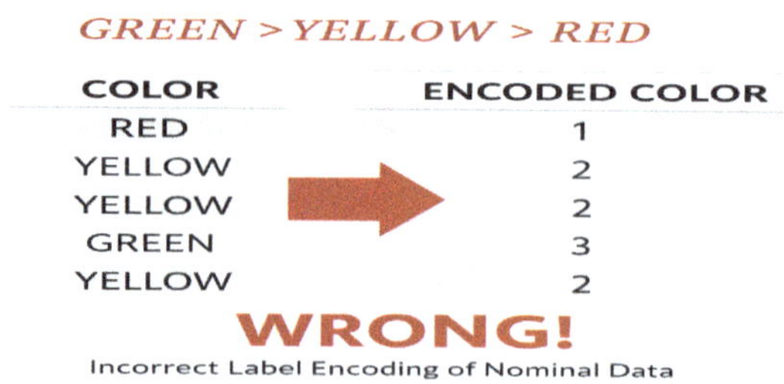

Fig. 7.2 Incorrect Label Encoding of Nominal Data: This figure highlights a common mistake in encoding categorical variables—applying label encoding to nominal data. The "COLOR" column (a nominal feature) is numerically encoded as 1, 2, 3, which incorrectly implies an ordinal relationship (GREEN > YELLOW > RED). Such encoding can mislead machine learning models into assuming a hierarchy that does not exist. One-hot encoding is the recommended approach in such cases

> WARNING
>
> One-hot encoding can significantly increase the dimensionality of your data. *Dimensionality* refers to the number of columns (or features) in your dataset. With one-hot encoding, each unique value in the original column gets its own new column. For instance, if a column has 10 unique values, one-hot encoding will result in 10 new columns. This increase might not be suitable for all algorithms, especially those sensitive to the "curse of dimensionality."

One-hot encoding can significantly increase the dimensionality of your data. *Dimensionality* refers to the number of columns (or features) in your dataset. With one-hot encoding, each unique value in the original column gets its own new column. For instance, if a column has 10 unique values, one-hot encoding will result in 10 new columns. This increase might not be suitable for all algorithms, especially those sensitive to the "curse of dimensionality."

While one-hot encoding is incredibly useful, it's not perfect. It can lead to a dramatic increase in the number of columns, which can raise computational costs and risk overfitting. Also, if your categorical variable has a lot of unique values, one-hot encoding can end up creating a sparse dataset filled with 0s, which requires careful handling in machine learning algorithms.

In essence, despite some drawbacks, one-hot encoding remains a powerful technique for preparing categorical variables for machine learning tasks. It's a great tool to have in your data science toolkit.

Here's an example of one-hot encoding: Consider a dataset of credit card transactions; in Table 7.1 each row represents a single transaction and contains details like the transaction amount, the name of the retailer, and the date of the transaction. The transaction category (the *Category* column), which identifies whether the transaction was for a cash advance, a balance transfer, a purchase of goods or services, or some other category, is a crucial component.

We can utilize one-hot encoding to produce a binary feature for each potential category in order to employ this categorical feature in a fraud detection model. For instance, if there are four categories (*A, B, C,* and *D*), you can construct four new features called "*Category_A*," "*Category_B*," "*Category_C*," *and* "*Category_D*," where each feature is binary (0 or 1) and indicates if the transaction belongs to that category.

Table 7.1 One-hot encoding: what the original dataset might look like

Transaction_ID	*Amount*	*Merchant_Name*	*Transaction_Date*	*Category*
1	100	Amazon	2022 January 1	Goods
2	50	Starbucks	2022 January 2	Services
3	200	Wells Fargo	2022 January 3	Cash
4	75	Target	2022 January 4	Goods
5	150	Chase	2022 January 5	Transfer

To perform one-hot encoding on the *Category* feature, you first create four new features as just described. Table 7.2 shows the dataset after one-hot encoding.

These new binary attributes can now be used as inputs for our fraud detection model. As a result, the model can treat each category as an independent feature with a different weight, enabling it to better capture patterns and correlations in the data. Without one-hot encoding, the *category* feature would be viewed as a single categorical feature without any intrinsic meaning or order, which may make it less effective at identifying fraud.

TIP

Feature extraction is more than just a data preprocessing step; it's an art that involves creating new, more informative variables from the existing ones. Whether it's through PCA, text analytics, or simply creating interaction terms, the goal is to provide the machine learning model with the most relevant and meaningful input features, optimizing its predictive power.

Feature extraction is more than just a data preprocessing step; it's an art that involves creating new, more informative variables from the existing ones. Whether it's through PCA, text analytics, or simply creating interaction terms, the goal is to provide the machine learning model with the most relevant and meaningful input features, optimizing its predictive power.

Feature Scaling

The feature scaling technique is used in feature engineering to transform variables into a different scale or format. *Feature scaling* is the process of converting different variables to a common scale. When distinct variables have different scales or units of measurement, this is especially helpful.

Table 7.2 One-hot encoding: a dataset after one-hot encoding

Transaction_ID	*Amount*	*Merchant_ Name*	*Transaction_ Date*	*Category*	*Category_ Goods*	*Category_ Services*	*Category_ Cash*	*Category_ Transfer*
1	100	Amazon	2022 January 1	Goods	1	0	0	0
2	50	Starbucks	2022 January 2	Services	0	1	0	0
3	200	Wells Fargo	2022 January 3	Cash	0	0	1	0
4	75	Target	2022 January 4	Goods	1	0	0	0
5	150	Chase	2022 January 5	Transfer	0	0	0	1

Normalization and *standardization* are the two methods of feature scaling that are most frequently utilized. Rescaling the variables into a specific range, usually between 0 and 1, is the process of normalization. When the range of values for various variables fluctuates greatly, this is helpful. During standardization, the variables are changed to have a mean of 0 and a standard deviation of 1. This is helpful when comparing variables with various units of measurement.

TIP

Feature scaling is essential when working with algorithms that rely on the magnitude or distance of data points, such as k-means clustering or gradient descent-based algorithms. It ensures that each feature contributes equally to the model's performance.

Feature scaling is essential when working with algorithms that rely on the magnitude or distance of data points, such as k-means clustering or gradient descent-based algorithms. It ensures that each feature contributes equally to the model's performance.

Not all forms of data and analysis may benefit from normalization. In some circumstances, it might be preferable to employ different methods, like binning or logarithmic transformation. The exact data and analytic objectives will determine the normalization method to use.

Transforming the variables into a more usable format for analysis through feature scaling is a key strategy in feature engineering. The technique chosen will depend on the particular requirements of the analysis, how the data is distributed, and the properties of the variables. Before using feature scaling, it is crucial to carefully consider how it will affect the data because it could significantly alter the outcomes of the analysis.

WARNING

Before applying feature scaling, ensure that you understand the nature of your data. For instance, if you have categorical data encoded as numbers, scaling might not be appropriate. Also, remember to scale the new data in the same way as the training data before making predictions.

Before applying feature scaling, ensure that you understand the nature of your data. For instance, if you have categorical data encoded as numbers, scaling might not be appropriate. Also, remember to scale the new data in the same way as the training data before making predictions.

Normalization

Think of ***normalization*** as a balancing act. It's like adjusting the scales so that each number in your data set has a fair chance to show its impact, usually within the 0 and 1 range. This technique shines when you have variables in your dataset that vary greatly in range. Without normalization, your data can tilt heavily toward the variable with the larger scale, introducing bias and skewing your results. But with normalization, each variable gets a fair shot, making your subsequent analysis or modeling more trustworthy.

There are a few different ways to do this balancing act, one of which is ***min–max scaling***. It's basically a mathematical trick that changes your variables to 0 and 1. Divide each variable value by its range, subtracting the minimum value. Voila! The lowest value becomes 0, the greatest becomes 1, and every other value moves in between.

There's another trick in the normalization toolkit called Z-score normalization, or standardization. This method is a bit like the fairy godmother from "Cinderella." It transforms your data so it has a mean of 0 and a standard deviation of 1. The fairy godmother waves her wand (or, in our case, you subtract the mean from each value and divide by the standard deviation), and suddenly each value in the dataset is expressed as the number of standard deviations it is away from the mean.

Before we dive into the details of normalization, let's take a look at a code example that demonstrates how to normalize data using the MinMaxScaler from the scikit-learn library:

```
from sklearn.preprocessing import MinMaxScaler

scaler = MinMaxScaler()
normalized_data = scaler.fit_transform(data)
print(normalized_data)
```

Now, let's discuss the underlying formula (Fig. 7.3) used in the normalization process. The formula for normalization is as follows:

$$\text{Normalized Value} = (\text{Value} - \text{Minimum Value})/(\text{Maximum Value} - \text{Minimum Value})$$

This formula ensures that the data values are scaled between 0 and 1.

Fig. 7.3 Normalization formula

$$x' = \frac{x - \min(x)}{\max(x) - min(x)}$$

TIP

Use normalization when your data has features with different ranges and you want to bring them to a common scale, typically [0,1]. It's especially useful for algorithms that compute distances between data points, like k-NN.

Use normalization when your data has features with different ranges and you want to bring them to a common scale, typically [0,1]. It's especially useful for algorithms that compute distances between data points, like k-NN.

To make things a bit more concrete, let's imagine you have a dataset with features like employment and interest rates (see Tables 7.3 and 7.4). Without normalization, the grandness of employment values could dwarf interest rates, creating a skewed bias in any machine learning model trained on the data. It's a bit like trying to hear a flute solo in the middle of a heavy metal concert. By turning the volume down on employment and up on interest rates, feature scaling brings these variables into balance (Fig. 7.4), allowing each feature to shine without being overshadowed.

Table 7.3 Original dataset before normalization

	Interest rates	*Employment*	*S&P 500 price*
0	1.943859	55.413571	2206.680582
1	2.258229	59.546305	2486.474488
2	2.215863	57.414687	2405.868337
3	1.97796	49.908353	2140.434475
4	2.437723	52.035492	2411.27663
5	2.143637	56.060598	2187.344909
6	2.148647	51.513208	2263.049249
7	2.176184	53.475909	2281.496374
8	2.125352	63.993396	2355.163011
9	2.225682	56.993396	2326.330337
10	1.814469	55.36178	2078.553895
11	2.281897	58.484752	2337.504507
12	2.426738	55.709328	2485.774097

Table 7.4 Descriptive statistics of the original dataset

Feature	*Count*	*Mean*	*Std*	*Min*	*25%*	*50%*	*75%*	*Max*
Interest rates	1000	2.2	0.24	1.5	2.04	2.2	2.36	3
Employment	1000	56.25	4.86	40	53.03	56.16	59.42	70
S&P 500 price	1000	2320	193	1800	2190	2312.44	2456.76	3000

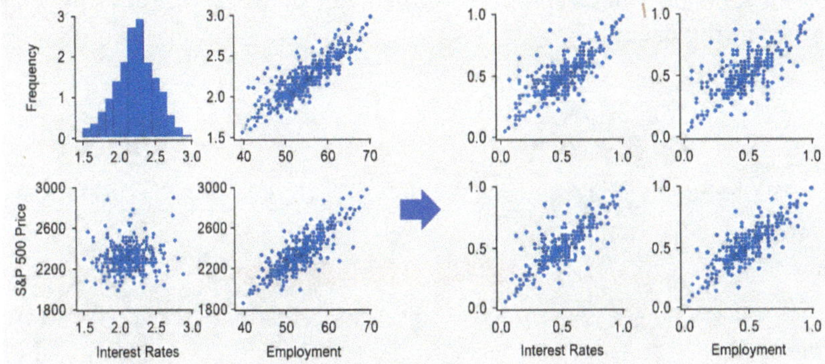

Original data

	Interest Rates	Employment	S&P 500 Price
count	1000	1000	1000
mean	2.20	56.25	2320.00
std	0.24	4.86	193.00
min	1.50	40.00	1800.00
25%	2.04	53.03	2190.00
50%	2.20	56.16	2312.44
75%	2.36	59.42	2456.76
max	3.00	70.00	3000.00

Normalized data

	Interest Rates	Employment	S&P 500 Price
count	1000	1000	1000
mean	0.47	0.54	0.43
std	0.16	0.16	0.16
min	0.00	0.00	0.00
25%	0.36	0.43	0.33
50%	0.47	0.54	0.43
75%	0.57	0.65	0.55
max	1.00	1.00	1.00

Fig. 7.4 Data normalization impact on distributions and summary statistics: This figure compares raw versus normalized data for three variables—Interest Rates, Employment, and S&P 500 Price. The top panel shows pairplots before and after normalization, where original distributions differ in scale while normalized data is scaled between 0 and 1. The bottom panel presents corresponding descriptive statistics, emphasizing changes in min–max values post-normalization. This highlights the effect of normalization on comparability and machine learning readiness

So, normalization, through techniques such as min–max scaling or standardization, is like the conductor of our data orchestra. It fine-tunes the scale and format of variables, ensuring that every feature gets a fair shot to contribute. In doing so, it not only reduces bias and enhances data processing, but it also boosts the performance of machine learning models. Like a well-conducted orchestra, a well-normalized dataset can deliver a harmonious, balanced, and impactful performance. Figure 7.5 shows how normalization works.

This table provides a summary of the main statistical measures for each feature in the dataset.

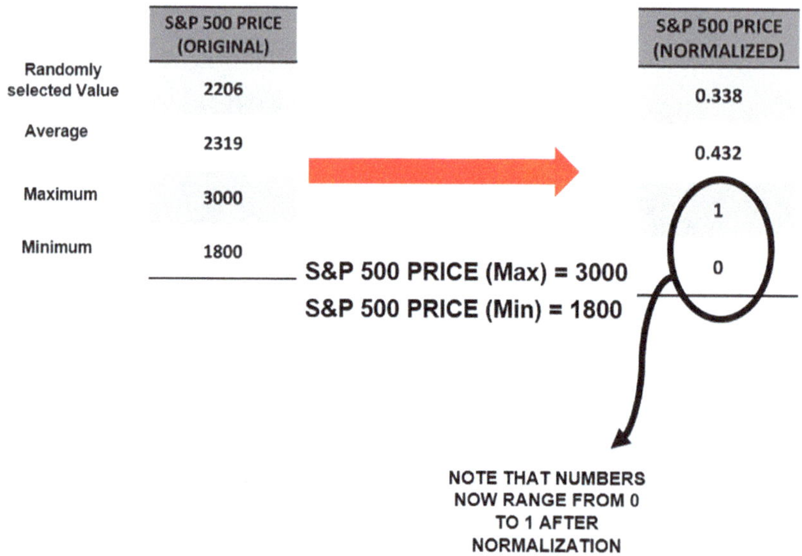

Fig. 7.5 How normalization works—Min–Max Normalization: Transforming Raw Values to a Standardized Scale: This figure demonstrates the process of min–max normalization using the S&P 500 Price variable. The left side shows the original values, ranging from 1800 (min) to 3000 (max), with a randomly selected value of 2206. The right side shows the corresponding normalized values scaled between 0 and 1. A red arrow highlights the transformation step, while the annotation emphasizes that normalization allows for direct comparison across features on a common scale—critical for improving model performance in machine learning

Figure 7.5 visualizes the normalization process. Let's break down the potential components of the figure:

1. *Original data*: The figure starts by showing a dataset (S&P 500 Price (Original)) with features that have different scales. For instance, features range from 1800 to 3000.
2. *Transformation*: The next part of the figure demonstrates the process of normalization. As seen in the graphical representations showing how data points are adjusted to fit a new scale.
3. *Normalized data*: Finally, the figure displays the dataset after normalization. All features will now be on a similar scale, making it easier to compare them directly.

The main advantage of normalization is that it brings all variables to the same scale, allowing algorithms to treat them equally in terms of importance. This can lead to better performance and more accurate models.

WARNING

When normalizing, ensure you save the minimum and maximum values from your training set. You'll need them to normalize new data in the future. Avoid applying normalization blindly; as mentioned, it might not be suitable for all datasets or algorithms.

When normalizing, ensure you save the minimum and maximum values from your training set. You'll need them to normalize new data in the future. Avoid applying normalization blindly; as mentioned, it might not be suitable for all datasets or algorithms.

Here's an example of Z-score normalization under data normalization: suppose you have a dataset of the heights of a group of people in centimeters (Table 7.5).

Table 7.5 Heights dataset

Height (cm)
170, 175, 160, 165, 180, 155

> TIP
>
> Z-score normalization is beneficial when you want to compare data that doesn't come from a standard normal distribution. It can help in reducing the influence of outliers.

Z-score normalization is beneficial when you want to compare data that doesn't come from a standard normal distribution. It can help in reducing the influence of outliers.

To normalize this data using Z-score normalization, you would follow these steps:

1. Calculate the mean and standard deviation of the data:
   - Mean = (170 + 175 + 160 + 165 + 180 + 155)/6 = 167.5
   - Standard deviation = sqrt((170 – 167.5)^2 + (175 – 167.5)^2 + (160 – 167.5)^2 + (165 – 167.5)^2 + (180 – 167.5)^2 + (155 – 167.5)^2)/6) = 9.35
2. For each height in the dataset, calculate its Z-score: see Table 7.6.

3. The normalized dataset using Z-score normalization would look like Table 7.7.

You can see that the heights in the dataset are now on a similar scale, with a mean of 0 and a standard deviation of 1, which makes it easier to analyze and model the data.

Table 7.6 Z-score calculation

Height (cm)	*Z-Score*
170	(170 – 167.5)/9.35 = 0.27
175	(175 – 167.5)/9.35 = 0.80
160	(160 – 167.5)/9.35 =- 0.80
165	(165 – 167.5)/9.35 =- 0.27
180	(180 – 167.5)/9.35 = 1.34
155	(155 – 167.5)/9.35 = - 1.34

Table 7.7 Normalized dataset after using Z-score normalization

Height (cm)	*Z-Score*
170	0.27
175	0.80
160	−0.80
165	−0.27
180	1.34
155	−1.34

WARNING

After standardizing, your data will have a mean of 0 and a standard deviation of 1. However, this doesn't mean the data follows a normal distribution. Always check the distribution of your data before and after standardization.

After standardizing, your data will have a mean of 0 and a standard deviation of 1. However, this doesn't mean the data follows a normal distribution. Always check the distribution of your data before and after standardization.

Decimal scaling normalization is an additional technique for normalizing data. According to a predetermined scaling factor, each value's decimal point is shifted to the left or right in this manner. This approach lessens the influence of outliers while maintaining the data's rank order.

TIP

Decimal scaling is a quick way to reduce the influence of large numbers in your dataset. It's especially useful when dealing with financial data or other datasets with large numbers.

Decimal scaling is a quick way to reduce the influence of large numbers in your dataset. It's especially useful when dealing with financial data or other datasets with large numbers.

For example, consider the dataset of salaries in Table 7.8.

To normalize this dataset, we can use decimal scaling. One way to choose a scaling factor is to consider the highest value in the dataset. In this case, the highest salary is 150,000. To bring this value close to 1, we can choose a scaling factor of 1000, which means moving the decimal point three places to the left. This is because $10^3 = 1000$, and dividing by this factor will shift the decimal three places.

Table 7.8 Salaries dataset

Employee	*Salary*
A	55,000
B	75,000
C	90,000
D	120,000
E	150,000

Table 7.9 Dataset after decimal scaling normalization

Employee	*Salary*
A	55
B	75
C	90
D	120
E	150

The resulting normalized dataset, after applying the scaling factor of 1000, is shown in Table 7.9.

Now the salary values are all between 0 and 200, and the rank order of the data is preserved. This dataset can be used for further analysis or modeling.

WARNING

When using decimal scaling, ensure that you document the scaling factor used. You'll need it to reverse the scaling or to scale new data points in the future.

When using decimal scaling, ensure that you document the scaling factor used. You'll need it to reverse the scaling or to scale new data points in the future.

Standardization

Standardization (see Fig. 7.6) is conducted to transform the data to have a mean of zero and a standard deviation of 1. Standardization is also known as Z-score normalization, in which properties will have the behavior of a standard distribution.

$$z = \frac{x - \overline{x}}{\sigma}$$

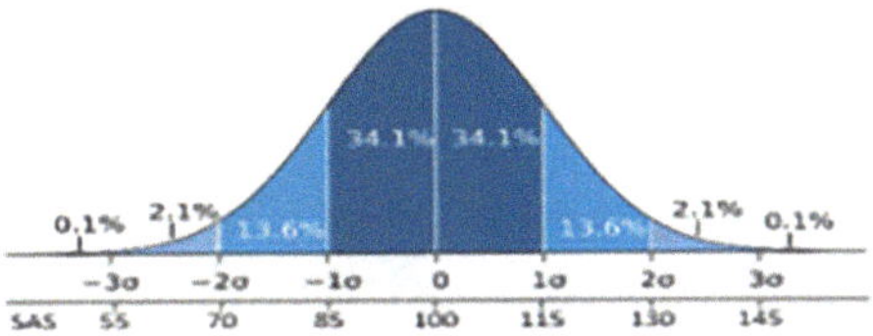

Fig. 7.6 Standardization Formula. Adapted from: Wikimedia Commons, Wechsler https://commons.wikimedia.org/wiki/File:Wechsler.svg

> TIP
>
> Standardization is your go-to method when you want to transform your data to have properties of a standard normal distribution. It's especially useful for algorithms that assume data is centered around zero.

Standardization is your go-to method when you want to transform your data to have properties of a standard normal distribution. It's especially useful for algorithms that assume data is centered around zero.

Before we dive into the details of standardization, let's take a look at a code example that demonstrates how to standardize data using the StandardScaler from the scikit-learn library:

```
from sklearn.preprocessing import StandardScaler
scaler = StandardScaler()
standardized_data = scaler.fit_transform(data)
print(standardized_data)
```

Now, let's discuss the underlying formula (Fig. 7.7) used in the standardization process. The formula for standardization is as follows:

$$\text{Standardized Value} = (\text{Value} - \text{Mean}) / \text{ Standard Deviation}$$

This formula ensures that the data values have a mean of 0 and a standard deviation of 1, making the data centered around zero and ensuring that all features have the same spread.

> WARNING
>
> As with normalization, when you standardize your training data, make sure you save (document somewhere) the mean and standard deviation. You'll need them to standardize new data in the future.

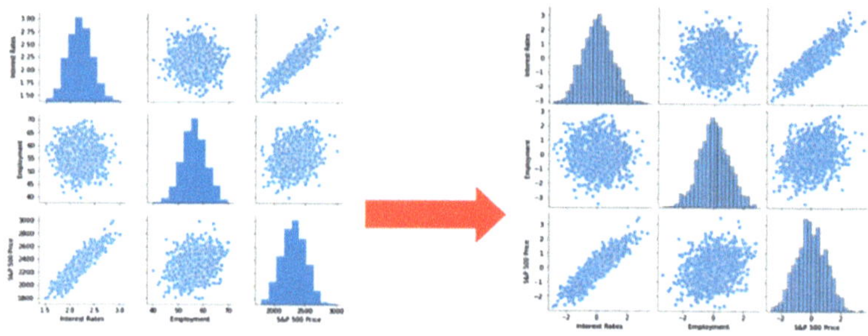

	Interest Rates	Employment	S&P 500 Price
count	1000.00	1000.00	1000.00
mean	2.20	56.25	2320.00
std	0.24	4.86	193.85
min	1.50	40.00	1800.00
25%	2.04	53.03	2190.45
50%	2.20	56.16	2312.44
75%	2.36	59.42	2455.76
max	3.00	70.00	3000.00

	Interest Rates	Employment	S&P 500 Price
count	1000.00	1000.00	1000.00
mean	0.00	0.00	-0.00
std	1.00	1.00	1.00
min	-2.88	-3.34	-2.68
25%	-0.66	-0.66	-0.67
50%	0.01	-0.02	-0.04
75%	0.68	0.65	0.70
max	3.33	2.83	3.51

Fig. 7.7 Standardization of Data Using Z-Score Transformation: This figure compares raw versus standardized data for three variables: Interest Rates, Employment, and S&P 500 Price. The top row shows pairplots before and after standardization, where the original data varies in scale and distribution, while the standardized version centers all variables around a mean of 0 with a standard deviation of 1. The tables below highlight summary statistics pre- and post-standardization, with red highlights marking changes in percentiles and maximum values. This transformation ensures that all features contribute equally to distance-based algorithms such as k-NN and clustering

As with normalization, when you standardize your training data, make sure you save (document somewhere) the mean and standard deviation. You'll need them to standardize new data in the future.

Figure 7.8 visualizes the standardization process. Let's break down the potential components of the figure:

- *Original data:* The figure starts by showing a dataset (e.g., "S&P 500 Price (Original)") with features that have different means and standard deviations. For instance, one feature might have a mean of

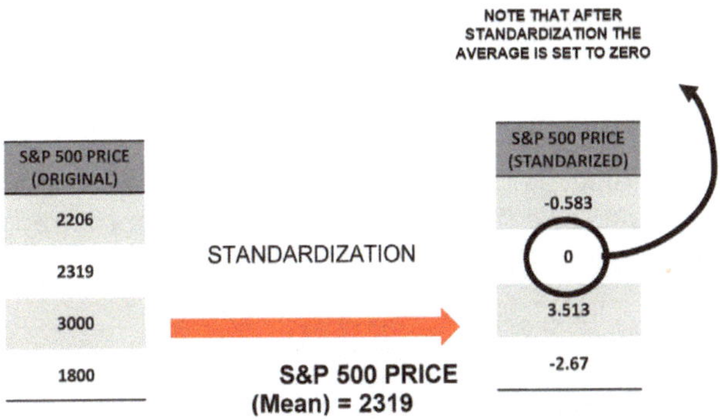

Fig. 7.8 How standardization works: This figure illustrates the process of Z-score standardization applied to the S&P 500 Price. The left side shows the original values, including the mean (2319), minimum (1800), and maximum (3000). The right side presents the standardized values, where the mean becomes 0, and other values are re-expressed in terms of standard deviations from the mean. The red arrow and annotation emphasize that standardization centers the data, enabling fair comparison across features in statistical modeling and machine learning

2000 and a standard deviation of 50, while another might have a mean of 100 and a standard deviation of 5.

- *Transformation:* The next part of the figure demonstrates the process of standardization. Graphical representations show how data points are adjusted to have a mean of 0 and a standard deviation of 1.
- *Standardized data:* Finally, the figure displays the dataset after standardization. All features now have a mean of 0 and a standard deviation of 1, making them centered around zero and ensuring that they have the same spread.

The main advantage of standardization, as seen in Fig. 7.8 is that it ensures that features have the same scale in terms of mean and variance. This is particularly important for algorithms that rely on distances or gradients, as it ensures that all features contribute equally to the model's performance.

Always remember the following:

- A normalized dataset will always have a range from 0 to 1.

- A standardized dataset will always have a mean of 0 and a standard deviation of 1, but can have any upper and lower values.

When deciding between normalization and standardization, consider the algorithm you're using. For instance, algorithms that rely on distances between data points, like SVM or k-NN, might benefit more from standardization.

> WARNING
>
> Don't mix up the terms! Remember, normalization typically scales data to a range of [0,1], while standardization shifts the distribution to have a mean of 0 and a standard deviation of 1. Ensure you're using the right technique for your specific needs.

Don't mix up the terms! Remember, normalization typically scales data to a range of [0,1], while standardization shifts the distribution to have a mean of 0 and a standard deviation of 1. Ensure you're using the right technique for your specific needs.

Deciding Between Standardization and Normalization

Both standardization and normalization are scaling techniques used in machine learning to transform features to a similar scale. However, they serve different purposes and are used in different scenarios.

Standardization has the following characteristics:

- Standardization (often called z-score normalization) transforms data to have a mean of zero and a standard deviation of one.
- It's beneficial for algorithms that assume input features to have a Gaussian distribution, such as k-nearest neighbors and artificial neural networks.
- Standardization allows data analysts to compare numbers with different scales or units of measurement.
- It can reduce the impact of outliers, though it's more sensitive to them than normalization. Outliers can affect the mean and standard deviation, thus influencing the standardized results.
- In fraud analytics, standardization is applied to financial data like revenue and transaction amounts. Anomalies can be detected by

observing transaction amounts that deviate significantly (in terms of standard deviations) from the mean.
- Standardization is frequently applied to methods like principal component analysis (PCA) and linear discriminant analysis (LDA) that presume a zero-centered distribution.

Normalization has the following characteristics:

- Normalization scales features to lie between a given minimum and maximum value, often between 0 and 1.
- It's useful when the relative values or proportions of data are more important than the absolute values.
- Algorithms that use distance-based metrics, such as clustering or k-nearest neighbors, frequently employ normalization.
- Normalization is frequently used with algorithms that do not assume any particular distribution in the input variables.
- Normalization reduces the influence of outliers in the data.

Here's my advice on when to use which:

- Any algorithm that computes gradients, such as optimization algorithms, benefits from scaling. This includes regression algorithms (both linear and logistic) and artificial neural networks.
- Variable scales for each feature can lead to different step sizes in gradient descent, making it harder to converge to the optimal solution.
- While tree-based algorithms like decision trees, random forests, and XGBoost don't inherently require scaling, distance-based algorithms like K-Means Clustering and SVMs can benefit from it.

Let's dive into an example to showcase how feature engineering can enhance fraud detection in financial transactions. Imagine you're sifting through credit card transactions, trying to pinpoint fraudulent ones. A handy method in this situation is to create a new variable—say, the ratio of a specific transaction value to the average transaction amount of a customer.

Consider a customer who has made three transactions of $100, $200, and $50, respectively. In this case, the total transaction amount is $350, averaging around (350$/3) = $116.67 per transaction. Now, to calculate the ratio for each transaction:

- *Transaction 1 ratio:* $100/$116.67 = 0.857
- *Transaction 2 ratio:* $200/$116.67 = 1.714
- *Transaction 3 ratio:* $50/$116.67 = 0.429

These ratios, now considered new variables, can be a crucial addition to your analysis. Any transaction where the ratio *veers significantly from 1* could indicate potential fraud. A high ratio suggests unusually large transactions, whereas a lower ratio could denote remarkably small transactions.

Additionally, you could innovate with feature engineering by calculating the percent difference between transaction amounts and average amounts or fabricating new variables based on the transaction's timing. These variations help in identifying unusual patterns, which may be a signal of fraud.

Fig. 7.9 show how these new variables (amount ratio and amount percentage difference) relate to fraud labels. A transaction that substantially deviates from the norm could be fraudulent, and using these variables as features in a machine learning model could boost fraud detection.

Interpretation and Recommendations: Based on the box plots in Fig. 7.9, when analyzed alongside fraud labels, fraudulent transactions demonstrate a noticeably broader spread, suggesting they deviate significantly from typical transaction patterns. Additionally, fraudulent transactions often exhibit:

- A higher median amount ratio than genuine transactions, indicating that fraud tends to involve larger sums relative to the customer's historical average.
- A greater percentage difference from the average transaction amount, reinforcing the pattern that frauds often stand out due to unusually large values.

These patterns reveal important behavioral distinctions between legitimate and fraudulent activity.

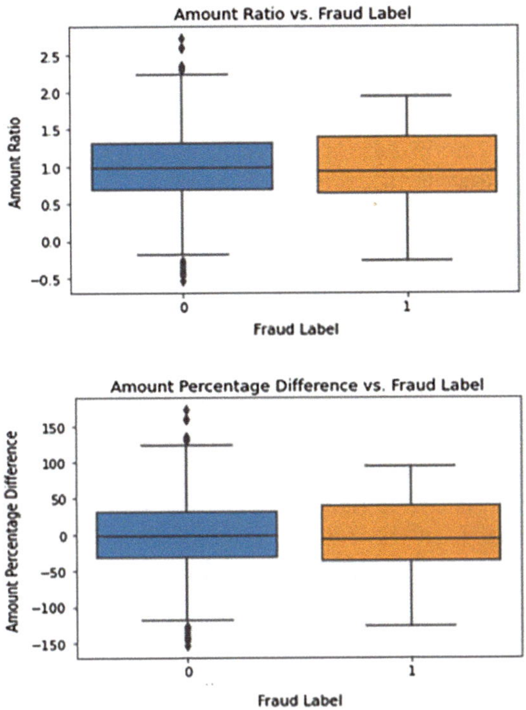

Fig. 7.9 "Amount Ratio vs. Fraud Label" and "Amount Percentage Difference vs. Fraud Label": These boxplots compare the distribution of S&P 500 Price data before (left) and after (right) Z-score standardization. The original scale shows a wider range and the presence of multiple outliers. After standardization, the data is centered around a mean of zero with reduced scale variation, allowing for better comparison across features and improving performance in models sensitive to magnitude, such as distance-based algorithms.

Based on these observations, actionable recommendations for modeling:

- Incorporate *amount ratio* and *amount percentage difference* into your fraud detection model. These variables could improve the model's efficiency by tracking the relative variations between a specific transaction and the customer's average amount.

- Be on the lookout for transactions with exceptionally high or low values for the amount ratio and amount percentage difference. Such transactions, which deviate from the customer's regular spending habits, might hint at potential fraud.
- Consider additional feature engineering techniques, such as creating variables based on the transaction's timing. These could further help in identifying fraudulent patterns.
- Regularly update and retrain your fraud detection model to keep up with new fraudulent trends and patterns.

Example of interaction terms by multiplying two or more variables together

Interaction terms are derived features created by multiplying two or more original features together. They are used to capture the combined effect of those features on the target variable, which might not be evident when those features are used individually.

As an illustration of developing interaction terms using feature engineering to detect fraud in e-commerce transactions, consider multiplying the distance between the shipping address and the billing address by the transaction amount. When the shipping location is far from the billing address but the transaction amount is substantial, this can be a red flag for suspicious transactions that might be fraudulent.

Let's use an e-commerce transaction dataset as an example. This dataset comprises the transaction amount, billing address, shipping address, and the separation between the two addresses. By multiplying the transaction amount with the shipping distance, you can produce a new variable named "shipping distance x transaction amount," as shown in Table 7.10.

By generating this additional variable, you can identify transactions where the product is being transported to a location distant from the billing address, yet the transaction amount is significant. Such patterns may indicate potential fraud. This variable can then be incorporated as a feature in a machine learning model to assist in identifying potentially fraudulent transactions.

Multiplying *Transaction Amount* by *Shipping Distance* reveals that a new variable called *Shipping Distance* × *Transaction Amount* has been introduced to the dataset. A machine learning algorithm can then utilize this variable to identify possibly fraudulent transactions.

Table 7.10 How the shipping distance × transaction amount variable could be added to the dataset

Transaction ID	*Transaction amount*	*Billing address*	*Shipping address*	*Shipping distance*	*Shipping distance × transaction amount*
1	100	New York	Los Angeles	2500	250,000
2	50	Boston	New York	200	10,000
3	500	San Francisco	Chicago	2500	1,250,000
4	200	Miami	Miami	0	0
5	300	Chicago	Houston	900	270,000

Feature Creation

Feature creation is an essential component of the fraud detection pipeline. When you create new features from existing data, you can uncover hidden patterns and relationships indicative of fraudulent activities, thereby enhancing the dataset's utility for machine learning algorithms designed to detect such anomalies.

> TIP
>
> Always keep an eye out for new patterns and trends in fraudulent activities. Regularly updating and refining features can help in adapting to evolving fraud techniques.

Always keep an eye out for new patterns and trends in fraudulent activities. Regularly updating and refining features can help in adapting to evolving fraud techniques.

Here are some techniques for feature creation for fraud analytics:

- *Polynomial features:* In the realm of fraud detection, polynomial features can help capture intricate patterns. For instance, if we consider features like transaction amount (a) and frequency of transactions (b), we can generate new features like a^2, b^2, and a × b. These can be instrumental in identifying non-linear patterns that might indicate sophisticated fraud schemes.

- *Interaction terms:* Creating interaction features can highlight suspicious combinations. For instance, the interaction between *transaction amount* and *time of transaction* might pinpoint large transactions happening at unusual hours, a potential sign of fraud.
- *Text analytics:* Fraud often manifests in textual data, such as transaction descriptions or customer feedback. Techniques include:
- *Keyword extraction:* Identifying recurring words or phrases in transaction notes that might be linked to suspicious activities.
- *Sentiment analysis:* Analyzing transaction descriptions to discern negative or unusual sentiments that could indicate fraudulent intent.
- *Topic modeling:* Extracting prevalent themes from transaction notes to identify recurring patterns of potential fraud.
- *Temporal features:* Fraudulent activities may exhibit specific temporal patterns. By dissecting timestamps, we can identify transactions occurring at odd times or on unusual days, which might be indicative of fraud.
- *Aggregated features:* For datasets with multiple transactions per user, aggregated features like *average transaction amount in the last month* or *number of high-value transactions in the last week* can be insightful in detecting anomalies.
- *Domain-specific features:* In the context of fraud detection, features like *number of transactions from high-risk locations* or *frequency of transactions just below the reporting threshold* can be pivotal.

WARNING

Although feature creation can provide valuable insights, it's essential to avoid overfitting when using it. Too many features, especially if they're not relevant, can make the model overly complex and less generalizable.

Although feature creation can provide valuable insights, it's essential to avoid overfitting when using it. Too many features, especially if they're not relevant, can make the model overly complex and less generalizable.

Feature creation in fraud analytics is a blend of art and science. It requires domain expertise, intuition, and a deep understanding of fraudulent behaviors. When executed correctly, it can significantly boost the performance of fraud detection models, providing them with the nuanced signals needed to identify even the most sophisticated fraud schemes.

However, it's crucial to ensure that the created features are relevant and don't introduce noise or redundancy. In fraud detection, the quality of input features can make the difference between catching a fraudulent transaction and letting it slip through. Investing time in feature creation is, therefore, crucial for the effectiveness and robustness of fraud detection systems.

Summary

This chapter went deep into the intricacies of feature engineering, emphasizing its pivotal role in molding raw data into a structured format that's more amenable to machine learning algorithms, particularly in the fraud detection domain. The chapter unraveled many techniques, such as feature selection, one-hot encoding, feature scaling, feature extraction, and dimensionality reduction. Each design was explored, showcasing its potential to amplify the efficacy of fraud detection models.

Chapter 8 builds on this foundation, emphasizing the importance of time analysis in fraud detection. The spotlight is on the creation and significance of RFM (recency, frequency, and monetary) features, which are robust indicators of transactional patterns. Beyond RFM, the chapter introduces advanced techniques like time-based aggregations, interaction features, and anomaly detection features, all aimed at enriching the dataset. The synergy between data wrangling, exploratory data analysis (EDA), and feature engineering is also highlighted, emphasizing their collective contribution to the preparation and enhancement of data, ultimately leading to more robust and reliable machine learning models tailored for fraud detection.

CHAPTER 8

Advanced Feature Engineering Techniques for Fraud Analytics

Detecting fraud is an art; feature engineering is the brush that paints clarity on the canvas of analytics. In the vast ocean of data, feature engineering is the lighthouse guiding us to the shores of genuine insights. This chapter discusses the intricate realm of *feature engineering*, emphasizing its paramount significance in fraud data analytics. Transforming raw data into meaningful and actionable insights is pivotal for achieving enhanced predictive accuracy and model interpretability. Given the nature of fraud detection, temporal attributes frequently serve as crucial determinants, making timestamp analysis an indispensable asset in identifying irregular patterns.

The chapter explores the formulation of RFM (recency, frequency, and monetary) features and introduces advanced concepts and techniques such as *time-based aggregations*, *interaction features*, and *anomaly detection* mechanisms. Such methodologies enrich the data repository and amplify the efficacy of fraud detection models. Toward the end of the chapter, you'll dive into the foundational aspects of data wrangling, exploratory data analysis (EDA), and feature engineering. These elements synergistically aid in comprehending, refining, and using preparing data, setting the stage for developing resilient and trustworthy machine learning architectures.

A. Al Aqqad, *Fraud Analytics in Action*
https://doi.org/10.1007/978-3-032-16023-2_8

The quality and relevance of features play a pivotal role in the effectiveness of predictive models in the realm of fraud analytics. Featurization, therefore, becomes a cornerstone process in building robust fraud detection systems.

Featurization is the art and science of transforming raw data into meaningful features that bolster the efficacy of machine learning algorithms. Understanding customers' spending patterns improves standard data points like the transaction amount, authentication method, and beneficiary's country in the context of detecting credit card fraud. Incorporating insights into how customers typically spend allows the model's predictive capability to be significantly improved. Additional features that consider aspects such as time, recent events, frequency, and monetary patterns further refine the model's accuracy:

- *Time-based features*: These might include hours of the day, days of the week, or months of the year and can illuminate customer spending patterns at different times. Trends revealed by these temporal features can help detect suspicious activities occurring outside of a customer's typical transactional hours.
- *Recency features*: These measure the time elapsed since the last transaction or activity. A sudden increase in recency could indicate an unusual change in customer behavior or signal potential fraud.
- *Frequency features*: These encapsulate the number of transactions or activities over a specific time period. The analysis of frequency patterns can identify atypical spikes or drops in transactional activity, potentially flagging fraudulent behaviors.
- *Monetary features*: As the name suggests, these represent the transaction amount or spending patterns of the customer. Metrics derived from this feature, such as the average, minimum/maximum, most recent value, or trends, can help detect anomalies in spending habits.

Integrating these new features with traditional ones leads to a more comprehensive set of variables that can be fed into machine learning models. As a result, these models can more effectively distinguish between legitimate and fraudulent transactions by identifying critical characteristics.

Featurization should aim to generate as many relevant features as possible. This enables the machine learning model to recognize complex patterns and correlations between variables that might not be readily apparent when using a limited set of features.

> WARNING
>
> Adding *too* many features, though, can introduce noise or multicollinearity. *Multicollinearity* refers to a situation in which two or more features in a dataset are highly correlated, making it difficult for the model to distinguish between their individual effects. This can potentially adversely affect the performance model. Therefore, striking a balance between adding relevant features and managing potential issues like multicollinearity is essential.

Implementing these techniques during the featurization process enables the development of a robust set of features, enhancing the overall performance of machine learning models in identifying fraudulent transactions. This, in turn, results in more effective fraud detection systems, offering improved protection for customers and financial institutions from the harmful effects of fraud.

Time Features

In fraud detection, incorporating time-related features is paramount. These features not only provide insights into temporal patterns of transactions but also highlight anomalies that might indicate fraudulent activities. However, the cyclical nature of time data presents unique challenges, especially when accounting for periodic behavior.

The Von Mises Distribution Approach

One sophisticated method to handle time data is to model timestamps using the Von Mises distribution. This distribution is named after Richard Von Mises, an Austrian mathematician known for his contributions across various fields, including statistics and probability theory. The von Mises distribution is essentially a probability distribution tailored for variables that exhibit normal distribution characteristics but are wrapped around a circle, making it ideal for time data.

Leveraging the von Mises distribution can extract features that offer a more nuanced representation of the temporal aspect of events. For instance, the confidence interval-based indicator: This potent feature is a binary indicator that determines if a particular timestamp falls within a specified confidence interval. To derive this feature, do the following:

1. Estimate the parameters of the von Mises distribution using a collection of timestamps corresponding to transactions executed by a specific customer.
2. Compute the likelihood or density for each timestamp.
3. Establish a confidence interval with a predetermined probability.
4. Identify which timestamps reside inside or outside this interval.

Timestamps that lie outside the confidence interval can be *red flags*. Their deviation from the expected periodic behavior might suggest potential fraudulent activities.

Example: Detecting Anomalous Transaction Times with the Confidence Interval-Based Indicator

Imagine a bank that has observed that a particular customer, Mr. Smith, usually makes transactions between 9 a.m. and 11 a.m. and from 4 p.m. to 6 p.m. The bank wants to use this pattern to detect any anomalous transaction times that might indicate potential fraud.

To detect such anomalies, you first need to estimate parameters. In this case, the bank collects a set of timestamps over a month corresponding to Mr. Smith's transactions. Using this data, they estimate the parameters (mean angle and concentration) of the von Mises distribution. Let's assume the mean angle indicates peak transaction times around 10 a.m. and around 5 p.m.

After estimating parameters, the next step is computing likelihood. For each timestamp in the dataset, the bank computes the likelihood, or *density*, using the von Mises distribution. This gives a probability value for each timestamp, indicating how "typical" that transaction time is for Mr. Smith.

Once the likelihood is computed, the bank proceeds to establish a confidence interval. They decide to set a confidence interval of 95%. This means they want to capture the range of times in which 95% of

Mr. Smith's transactions occur. Based on the von Mises distribution, they determine this interval to be from 8:45 a.m. to 11:15 a.m. and 3:45 p.m. to 6:15 p.m.

Finally, the bank focuses on identifying anomalies. Any transaction timestamp that falls outside these intervals is flagged. For instance, if there's a transaction by Mr. Smith at 2 a.m., that would be outside the confidence interval and would thus be flagged as anomalous.

Using the confidence interval-based indicators lets the bank keep an eye on Mr. Smith's transactions and send him alerts or take other steps to stop them if they happen at odd times, which improves security and stops fraud.

> TIP
>
> Incorporating time-based features into fraud detection algorithms significantly bolsters an organization's capability to pinpoint and thwart fraudulent transactions. Understanding and analyzing temporal patterns and deviations allows businesses to proactively identify risks and take preventive measures, ensuring the security and trust of their customers.

Example: Using Time Features for Fraud Detection in Online Banking

An online banking platform has noticed an increasing number of fraudulent transactions in recent months. The company wants to identify patterns in the transaction data that could help detect potential fraud and enhance the security of their platform.

Here are their objectives:

- Explore transaction time distributions.
- Visualize transaction activity using a circular histogram.
- Detect anomalies using circular statistics via the von Mises distribution.

The dataset consists of transaction timestamps (in hours) for a sample of online banking transactions. The timestamps represent the time of day when the transactions occurred.

Lab access: I invite you to embark on this analytical journey and explore the intricacies of online bank transactions. To start your exploration, click here for lab access and dive into the lab.

Analysis: To gain a comprehensive understanding of the transaction timestamp data, you'll first need to load it and then create a circular histogram to visualize the distribution of transaction times. By calculating the arithmetic mean and periodic mean of the timestamps, you can identify central tendencies in the transaction times. Further insights can be drawn by estimating parameters such as mu (the periodic mean) and kappa (the concentration) from the von Mises distribution. With these parameters in hand, you can calculate a confidence interval and overlay it on the circular histogram, which will help in identifying the range of expected transaction times. Finally, it's crucial to determine and highlight potentially fraudulent transactions, especially those that fall outside the confidence interval, on the histogram. This process will provide a clearer picture of the data and any anomalies present.

Below are the coding steps for fraud detection in online banking transactions.

First, let us start with importing libraries and generate sample data:

```
# Step 1: Import required libraries
import pandas as pd
import numpy as np
import matplotlib.pyplot as plt
from scipy.stats import vonmises
import seaborn as sns

# Step 2: Simulate sample data for transaction timestamps (in hours)
np.random.seed(42)  # Ensure reproducibility
timestamps = np.random.uniform(0, 24, 1000)  # Generate 1000 random
timestamps from 0 to 24 hours

# Step 3: Create DataFrame
df = pd.DataFrame({'timestamps': timestamps})
```

The sample data is shown in Table 8.1. To ensure reproducibility, a random seed is established. Following this, 1000 random timestamps, ranging between 0 and 24 hours, are produced using a uniform distribution. These timestamps are subsequently transformed into a DataFrame to facilitate easier handling.

Next, let's plot a circular histogram. Figure 8.1 shows the results:

Table 8.1 Plotting circular histogram and computing basic statistics

	Timestamps
0	8.988963
1	22.817143
2	17.567855
3	14.367804
4	3.744447

```
# Step 4: Plot Circular Histogram
plt.figure(figsize=(8, 8))
ax = plt.subplot(111, projection='polar')

# Convert hour-based timestamps to degrees (multiply by 15 to map 0-24 to
0-360)
n, _, _ = ax.hist(np.radians(df['timestamps'] * 15), bins=48,
color='dodgerblue', alpha=0.75)

# Polar chart adjustments
ax.set_theta_zero_location('N')        # Set 0 at the top
ax.set_theta_direction(-1)             # Clockwise
ax.set_rlabel_position(90)             # Radial labels at 90°
ax.set_title("Figure 1. Circular Histogram of Transaction Timestamps",
va='bottom')
plt.show()

# Step 5: Basic stats
print(f"Total transactions: {len(df)}")
print(f"Mean timestamp: {df['timestamps'].mean():.2f} hours")
print(f"Mode timestamp: {df['timestamps'].mode().iloc[0]:.2f} hours")
print(f"Max bin count: {n.max()}")
print(f"Min bin count: {n.min()}")
```

In Fig. 8.1, a circular histogram (often referred to as a *rose plot*) is used to visualize the distribution of transaction timestamps. This visualization method is especially effective for cyclical data, such as time. The histogram is segmented into 48 bins, and the data points are represented in a blue shade with 75% opacity. Regarding the theta configuration of the plot, North (N) is set to 0 degrees, and the plotting direction is clockwise, as indicated by −1. This configuration is typical for time data, where 0 degrees would align with midnight and the data progresses in a clockwise manner.

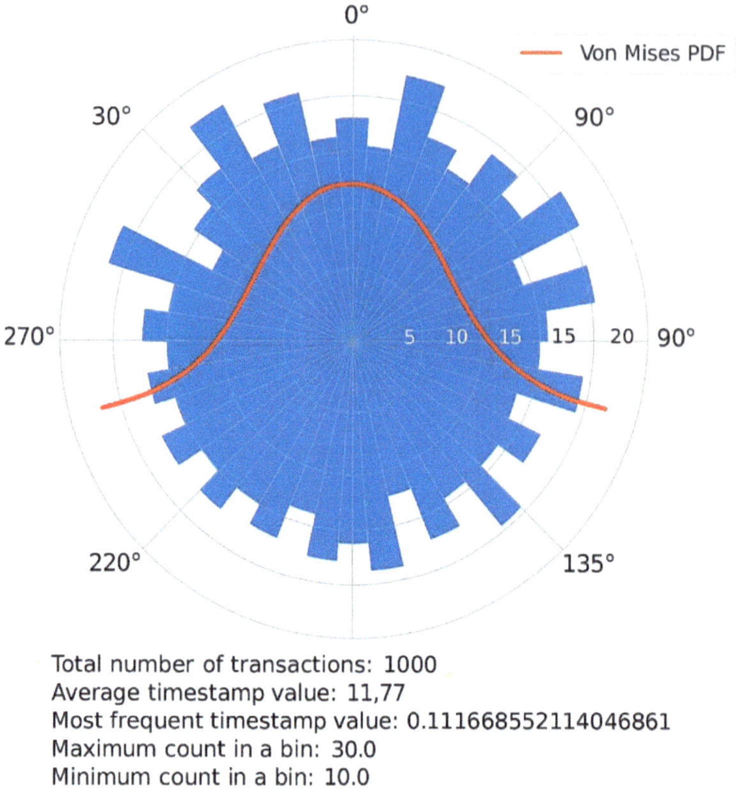

Fig. 8.1 Circular Histogram of Transaction Timestamps: This figure visualizes the distribution of 1000 online banking transactions based on the hour of day they occurred, using a circular histogram. Each bin represents a 30-minute interval, mapped onto a 360° polar coordinate system. The chart reveals temporal patterns in transaction behavior, aiding in the identification of high-activity periods. This visualization is particularly useful in fraud detection for spotting time-based anomalies, such as transactions occurring at atypical hours

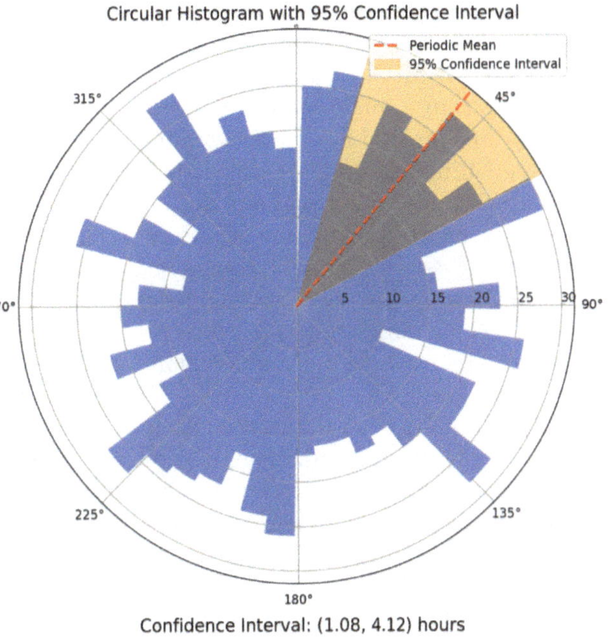

Fig. 8.2 Circular Histogram with 95% Confidence Interval: This figure displays a circular histogram of transaction timestamps, with a red dashed line indicating the periodic mean and a shaded wedge representing the 95% confidence interval derived from the von Mises distribution. Transactions falling outside this interval may indicate anomalous or potentially fraudulent activity. This visualization bridges exploratory and statistical analysis, making it a valuable tool in time-based fraud detection

Considering the total transactions, there are a total of 1000 transactions in the dataset df. The average timestamp value of the transactions is 11.77. This value represents hours and fractions of an hour in a 24-hour format. (To clarify, *11:77* is not a standard time notation. Instead, the 0.77 represents 77% of an hour, which is approximately 46 minutes. Thus, the average transaction time is around 11:46 am). Delving into the most frequent timestamp, the most frequently occurring timestamp value is 0.11116855211046861. This value, when converted to hours, is approximately 0.11 hours after midnight, or around 12:07 a.m.

Regarding ***histogram bin counts***, the maximum number of transactions in a single bin (or time interval) of the histogram is 30, indicating that the busiest time interval has 30 transactions. Conversely, the minimum number of transactions in a single bin of the histogram is 10, indicating that the least busy time interval has 10 transactions.

From the potential implications, we can deduce that the distribution of transactions is not uniform throughout the day. Sometime intervals have three times as many transactions as others. The most frequent timestamp value being shortly after midnight might suggest a regular event or process occurring just after midnight, leading to transactions. Additionally, the average timestamp value being around mid-morning might indicate a general trend of more transactions occurring during the morning hours.

Next, you will compute both the arithmetic mean and the periodic (circular) mean of the transaction timestamps. While the arithmetic mean gives the standard average, it fails to account for the cyclical nature of time (e.g., 23:59 is very close to 00:01). Hence, you also calculate the periodic mean using trigonometric functions. Then you will estimate the mean resultant length (r) and the kappa parameter of the von Mises distribution to measure data concentration. A higher kappa indicates that timestamps are tightly clustered around the circular mean.

```
# Calculate the arithmetic mean of timestamps
arithmetic_mean = df['timestamps'].mean()

# Step 1: Convert timestamps (in hours) to radians (0-360 degrees mapped
to 0-2π)
angles = np.radians(df['timestamps'] * 15)  # 15° per hour

# Step 2: Compute sine and cosine components
sin_sum = np.sum(np.sin(angles))
cos_sum = np.sum(np.cos(angles))

# Step 3: Compute resultant length (r) and circular mean angle (theta)
r = np.sqrt(sin_sum**2 + cos_sum**2) / len(df)
theta = np.arctan2(sin_sum, cos_sum)

# Step 4: Convert theta to periodic mean in hour scale (0-24)
periodic_mean = np.degrees(theta) / 15
if periodic_mean < 0:
    periodic_mean += 24  # Ensure result is within 0-24 hour range

# Step 5: Estimate von Mises concentration parameter (kappa)
kappa = r * len(df)
mu = periodic_mean  # Circular mean

# Output results
arithmetic_mean, periodic_mean, mu, kappa
```

For this simulation, the arithmetic mean of transaction times is approximately 11.77 hours. The periodic mean is around 2.60 hours, reflecting the circular center of mass on the 24-hour clock. The kappa value, approximately 24.85, is derived from multiplying the mean resultant length by the sample size. Since the simulated data follows a uniform distribution, this value does not indicate true directional concentration but rather reflects the sample size effect. In practice, with real-world transaction data that exhibits genuine temporal patterns, this parameter would provide a more meaningful measure of how tightly transactions cluster around the periodic mean.

Now it's time to calculate the confidence interval using the von Mises distribution. The *confidence interval* offers a range where the true periodic mean is anticipated to reside with a specified confidence level, which is 95% in this scenario. Subsequently, the circular histogram is visualized once more, emphasizing both the periodic mean and its associated confidence interval. The next bit of code shows how to calculate the confidence interval, and Fig. 8.2 shows the results:

```
from scipy.stats import vonmises

# Step 1: Set confidence level (95%)
alpha = 0.05
z = vonmises.ppf(1 - alpha / 2, kappa)  # Quantile for the CI

# Step 2: Compute confidence interval around mu (in hours)
conf_interval = (mu - np.degrees(z) / 15, mu + np.degrees(z) / 15)

# Step 3: Adjust for circular wrap-around (keep values within 0-24 hours)
if conf_interval[0] < 0:
    conf_interval = (conf_interval[0] + 24, conf_interval[1])
if conf_interval[1] > 24:
    conf_interval = (conf_interval[0], conf_interval[1] - 24)

# Step 4: Plot histogram with CI
plt.figure(figsize=(8, 8))
ax = plt.subplot(111, projection='polar')

# Circular histogram
ax.hist(np.radians(df['timestamps'] * 15), bins=48, color='royalblue',
alpha=0.7)

# Periodic mean line
ax.axvline(np.radians(mu * 15), color='red', linestyle='dashed',
linewidth=2, label='Periodic Mean')

# Confidence interval (shaded)
ax.axvspan(np.radians(conf_interval[0] * 15),
           np.radians(conf_interval[1] * 15),
           color='orange', alpha=0.3, label='95% Confidence Interval')

# Polar plot styling
ax.set_theta_zero_location('N')
ax.set_theta_direction(-1)
ax.set_rlabel_position(90)
ax.set_title("Figure 2. Circular Histogram with 95% Confidence
Interval", va='bottom')
ax.legend(loc='upper right')
plt.show()

# Output the actual interval
conf_interval
```

The next step is to identify suspicious transactions. Transactions that fall outside the confidence interval are deemed suspicious, operating on the premise that legitimate transactions typically adhere to a specific pattern. Any significant deviation from this pattern could indicate potential fraud. To visualize this, a new circular histogram is created that differentiates between normal and suspicious transactions. Following this, the details of the suspicious transactions are presented for further scrutiny.

The following code aims to visualize the distribution of transaction timestamps, calculate the periodic mean and its confidence interval, and identify transactions that fall outside this interval as potentially suspicious. Figure 8.3 shows the results:

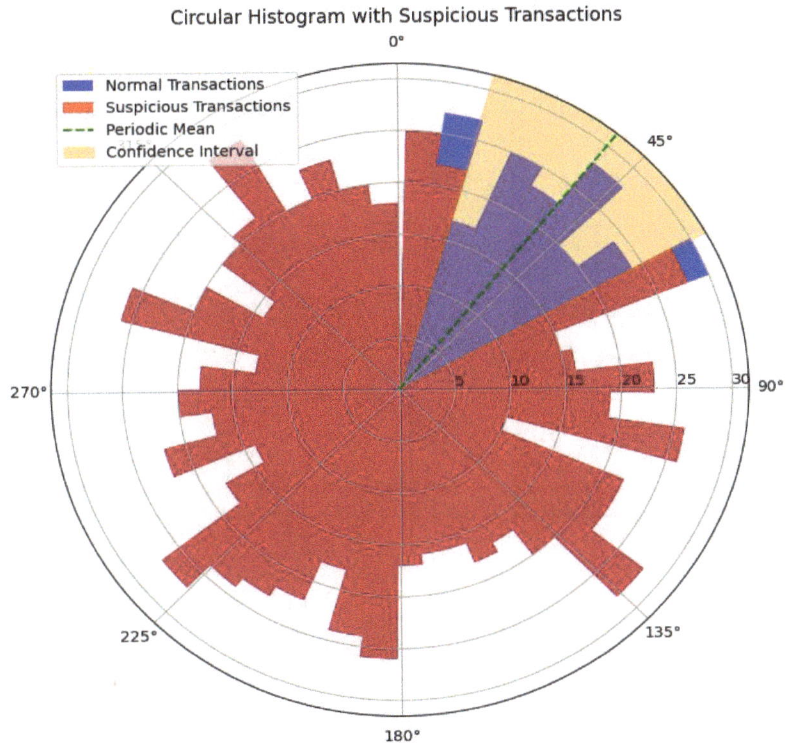

Fig. 8.3 Circular Histogram with Suspicious Transactions: This figure highlights suspicious transactions based on their deviation from the expected transaction time pattern. Normal transactions appear in blue, while red bars indicate outliers that fall outside the 95% confidence interval. The periodic mean (dashed green line) and the confidence region (orange wedge) help contextualize expected behavior. This visual technique supports early fraud detection by identifying anomalies in transactional timing

```
# Step 1: Identify potentially suspicious transactions outside the
confidence interval
suspicious_transactions = df[
    (df['timestamps'] < conf_interval[0]) | (df['timestamps'] >
conf_interval[1])
]

# Step 2: Plot circular histogram with normal vs. suspicious transactions
plt.figure(figsize=(8, 8))
ax = plt.subplot(111, projection='polar')

# Plot normal transactions
ax.hist(np.radians(df['timestamps'] * 15), bins=48, color='steelblue',
alpha=0.7, label='Normal Transactions')

# Overlay suspicious transactions
ax.hist(np.radians(suspicious_transactions['timestamps'] * 15), bins=48,
color='crimson', alpha=0.7, label='Suspicious Transactions')

# Periodic mean line
ax.axvline(np.radians(mu * 15), color='green', linestyle='dashed',
linewidth=2, label='Periodic Mean')

# 95% confidence interval wedge
ax.axvspan(np.radians(conf_interval[0] * 15), np.radians(conf_interval[1]
* 15), color='orange', alpha=0.3, label='Confidence Interval')

# Format polar chart
ax.set_theta_zero_location('N')
ax.set_theta_direction(-1)
ax.set_rlabel_position(90)
ax.set_title("Figure 3. Circular Histogram with Suspicious
Transactions", va='bottom')
ax.legend(loc='upper right')

plt.show()

# Step 3: Output suspicious transactions
suspicious_transactions
```

After implementing the code, the data in Table 8.2 will be generated. The data in Table 8.2 reveals that, from the entire set of transactions in the dataset df, 856 are flagged as suspicious.

Interpretation of Results and Analytical Insights: After executing the code, several meaningful insights emerge from both the visual and tabular outputs. The primary purpose of the procedure is to identify suspicious transactions based on deviations in their timestamps. Specifically, transactions falling outside the 95% confidence interval around the periodic mean are flagged as potentially suspicious.

Visual Analysis (Fig. 8.3).

Table 8.2 Suspicious transaction

	timestamps
0	8.988963
1	22.817143
2	17.567855
3	14.367804
7	20.788227
...	...
993	14.165536
994	8.663374
996	22.015526
998	22.805696
999	10.704139

856 rows × 1 columns

The circular histogram (or rose plot) provides a highly intuitive visualization of transaction activity across the 24-hour cycle—a critical capability for time-based fraud analytics. In this figure:

- Normal transactions are shown in blue.
- Suspicious transactions, which lie outside the confidence interval, appear in red.
- The periodic mean (μ) is indicated by a green dashed line, centered within the time range of highest activity.
- The 95% confidence interval is shaded in orange, visually delineating the expected range of legitimate behavior.

The polar plot is oriented such that 0° (North) corresponds to midnight, and time flows clockwise, reflecting natural human interpretation of time progression.

Quantitative Summary (Table 8.2)

According to the results:

- 856 out of 1000 transactions have been classified as suspicious.

- These transactions occur outside the confidence interval, which spans from approximately 1:05 AM to 4:07 AM based on the von Mises distribution parameters estimated from the data.

This high volume of flagged transactions suggests a significant deviation from the core behavioral pattern inferred from the von Mises distribution.

Implications and Interpretive Considerations: The detection of such a large number of outliers raises important considerations:

- Model sensitivity: The confidence interval may be too narrow, leading to over-flagging. Adjusting the confidence threshold (e.g., using a 99% interval) could provide a more balanced assessment.
- True anomalies: The flagged transactions may genuinely reflect atypical behavior, possibly tied to fraud or irregular user activity.
- Contextual influences: Spikes in late night or early morning activity could be driven by seasonal events, promotions, or regional user behavior, requiring contextual data for deeper validation.

This analysis demonstrates the power of combining circular statistics, polar visualization, and anomaly detection for uncovering potential fraud in online banking systems. However, while the statistical model provides valuable leads, human review and contextual analysis remain essential to interpreting the flagged behaviors accurately.

Recency Features

In data analytics, the temporal dimension is crucial, especially when the goal is to detect anomalies or potentially fraudulent activities. This brings us to the concept of *recency features*, which provide a lens into the time that has passed since a specific event or transaction took place.

At its core, recency measures the time gap between two similar events. To illustrate, consider Alice making two transactions using the same authentication method. The time interval between these two transactions is what we term recency. A recency value that's close to 1 suggests that two similar events happened in quick succession. A recency value that's closer to 0 indicates a significant time lapse between two similar events. When applied to fraud detection, an extremely low or even zero recency can raise alarms, hinting at unusual or potentially fraudulent activities.

The formal definition of recency is quite mathematical. It's defined as the exponential of negative gamma multiplied by t, where t denotes the time interval between two similar events. The gamma parameter, which users can define, dictates the rate at which recency decreases as the time gap grows. A common practice is to adjust gamma so that the recency value reaches 0.01 after a span of 180 days. This sets gamma to –log(0.01)/180.

When it comes to implementation in Python, you can design a function, perhaps named recency_fun, to calculate the recency for each event. If an event is a first-time occurrence, its recency is set to zero. However, if it has happened before, the time difference between the two instances is utilized to determine the recency. Once a suitable gamma value is chosen, the data can be organized by a specific identifier, such as account_name. Following this, the recency feature can be integrated using the groupby and apply functions.

The significance in fraud detection of recency cannot be overstated. When paired with other metrics like frequency and timestamps, recency can significantly enhance a model's predictive capabilities. It's especially powerful in the domain of fraud analytics. Here, patterns like a sudden surge of transactions within a brief period can signal potential fraud. By meticulously scrutinizing recency data, fraud analysts can identify such patterns and subject them to more in-depth analysis.

Here's a practical illustration: consider Hakeem, a bank customer with a typical transaction pattern of one weekly credit card transaction, primarily at grocery stores and gas stations, averaging around $100. However, in the last two days, there have been a spate of transactions, including high-value purchases at electronics and jewelry stores. These transactions not only deviate from Hakeem's usual spending habits but also exhibit high recency. Such anomalies would prompt the bank's fraud detection system to flag these transactions as potentially fraudulent, leading to immediate actions like contacting Hakeem or temporarily blocking his credit card (Fig. 8.4).

TIP

Recency is a potent tool in the arsenal of fraud detection. By tracking the time elapsed since the last transaction and juxtaposing it against an individual's typical transaction behavior, businesses can swiftly spot and counteract suspicious activities. This proactive approach not only safeguards the customers' interests but also fortifies the financial infrastructure against potential threats.

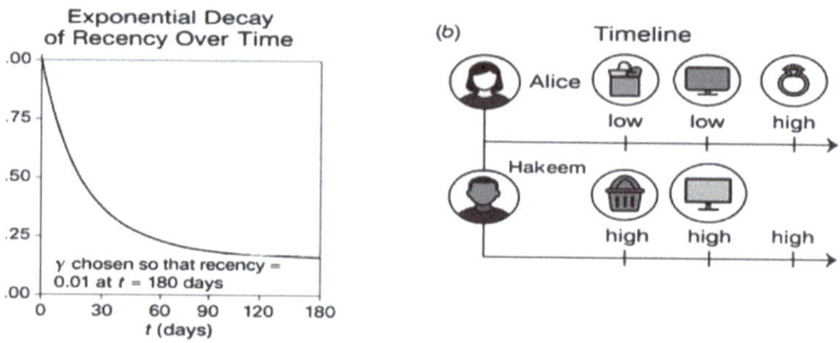

Fig. 8.4 Visualization of Recency in Fraud Detection: *This figure illustrates how recency is calculated using an exponential decay function, where recent transactions yield higher recency scores. A second panel compares two customers: one with regular transaction intervals and one with an abnormal burst of activity, demonstrating how recency can be used to flag potentially fraudulent behavior when combined with transaction context*

Frequency Features

Frequency features play a paramount role in the domain of fraud data analytics. They capture the *recurrence* or *rate* of specific events within a defined time span and are invaluable tools for detecting irregular patterns that may hint at fraudulent activities.

Among the key components of frequency features, we find that *temporal counts* depict the accumulation of events across distinct time windows. Examples include *daily, weekly,* or *monthly* tallies of suspicious login endeavors or observing the frequency of high-value transactions within a brief period, which might be red flags for activities like credit card testing or account takeover attempts.

> WARNING
>
> Watch out for temporal sensitivity. Frequency features are sensitive to the time span considered. For instance, daily frequency counts might show a different pattern than monthly counts do. Choosing the appropriate time frame for analysis is essential.

Payment method specificity zeroes in on the repetition of transactions based on the selected payment avenue. A sudden surge in transactions via a particular payment method, say wire transfers, could be a harbinger of a compromised technique or an ongoing fraud stratagem.

Merchant or *category* analysis concentrates on transactions associated with a specific vendor or those categorized under a particular bracket. An abrupt rise in dealings with a hitherto unfamiliar merchant might be suggestive of a merchant-centric fraud scheme.

> TIP
>
> To enhance the predictive power, combine frequency features with other types of features, such as monetary values, geolocation, and user behavior patterns.

Identifying Anomalies

Let's move on to identifying anomalies with frequency features: by meticulously scrutinizing these features, fraud analysts are equipped to spot deviations from normative patterns. Consider a scenario where a user who usually indulges in one high-ticket purchase monthly suddenly embarks on a spree of such acquisitions weekly. This could be indicative of an account takeover. Such frequency aberrations often serve as harbingers of potential fraudulent conduct, warranting immediate probes.

Lastly, working with features that work well together shows that frequency features are strong indicators on their own, but they work even better when combined with other data aspects. For example, putting frequency data next to geolocation data can help find card-not-present fraud, especially if transactions happen a lot from different places in a short amount of time. In a similar vein, melding frequency features with user behavior analytics can provide a comprehensive snapshot of a user's engagements, thereby simplifying the task of identifying anomalies (Fig. 8.5).

> TIP
>
> Use advanced anomaly detection techniques to identify unusual spikes or drops in frequency, which might be indicative of fraud.

This figure illustrates temporal frequency patterns and payment channel-specific transaction surges. The left panel shows how weekly transaction volume anomalies can indicate account takeovers. The right panel highlights suspicious spikes in wire transfer usage and sudden merchant concentration. Combined with behavioral and location-based features, frequency metrics offer powerful insight into potential fraud schemes.

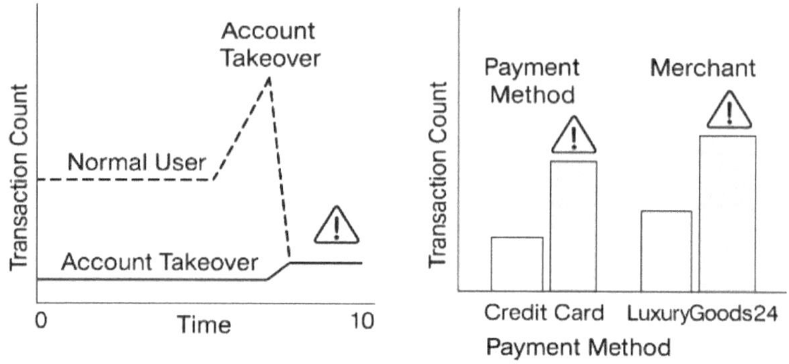

Fig. 8.5 Visualizing Frequency-Based Anomalies in Fraud Detection

Example: Generating Frequency Feature for Multiple Accounts

In fraud detection, understanding the frequency of specific events, such as the use of a particular payment channel, can be instrumental in identifying unusual activities. A frequency feature can help track how often a particular event has occurred in the past, providing valuable insights into user behavior patterns.

The objectives of this analysis are as follows:

- To load and explore the transactional dataset.
- To generate a statistical summary and obtain dataset information.
- To visualize any missing values in the dataset.
- To create a frequency feature from the categorical feature "channel_cd" and understand its significance in the context of the dataset.

The trans dataset consists of transactions executed by Helen and David. Your task is to generate a freq_channel frequency feature grounded on the same channel_cd column as in the previous exercise. You can access this lab at **Github**.

Here is the procedure:

1. Segregate the data based on account_name.
2. Use groupby and cumcount() to calculate the frequency of each channel for each user.

3. Visualize and interpret the results, especially for any fraud indicators.

To achieve this in Python, use the groupby function to segregate data by account_name, and cumcount to compute the frequency of channel_cd usage per account. Display features using DataFrame indexing (see Table 8.3).

This Python script reads transaction data from a CSV file, calculates a new feature called freq_channel for each account, and prints out the result. See Table 8.3.

```
#Import pandas as pd
import pandas as pd

#Read the CSV file into a DataFrame
trans_df = pd.read_csv('trans.csv')

#Generate statistical summary
trans_df.describe()


#Now plot the heatmap with missing values represented as
'np.nan'sns.heatmap(trans_df.isnull(), yticklabels=False, cbar=False,
cmap="Blues")

#Create the 'freq_channel' column
trans_df['freq_channel'] = trans_df.groupby(['account_name',
'channel_cd']).cumcount()

# Print the specified columns of the DataFrame
print(trans_df[['account_name', 'channel_cd', 'freq_channel',
'fraud_flag']])
```

Table 8.3 showcases the newly created feature, freq_channel, which represents the frequency of each channel_cd usage for multiple accounts. This feature helps in tracking the number of times a specific channel has been used by an account holder. For instance, if David uses CH07 three times, the freq_channel for CH07 under David's account will show values 0, 1, and 2 in sequential transactions. This feature can be instrumental in identifying patterns or anomalies in transaction behaviors.

> TIP
>
> Instead of analyzing frequency features for the entire user base, consider *segmenting* users based on certain criteria (for example, new vs. returning users, high-value vs. low-value users) and analyzing frequency features within each segment.

Table 8.3 Newly created freq_channel feature for multiple accounts

	account_name	channel_cd	freq_channel	fraud_flag
0	David	CH07	0	0
1	Helen	CH04	0	0
2	David	CH07	1	0
3	David	CH06	0	0
4	Helen	CH07	0	0
5	David	CH06	1	0
6	Helen	CH04	1	0
7	David	CH07	0	0
8	Helen	CH01	0	0
9	David	CH02	0	0
10	David	CH06	0	0
11	Helen	CH03	0	0
12	Helen	CH04	3	0
13	Helen	CH04	3	0
14	Helen	CH04	3	0
15	David	CH07	3	0
16	David	CH07	3	0
17	David	CH07	5	0
18	Helen	CH01	1	0
19	Helen	CH04	5	0
20	David	CH02	1	0
21	Helen	CH04	6	0
22	Helen	CH04	7	0
23	David	CH07	6	0
24	Helen	CH04	8	0
25	David	CH06	3	0
26	Helen	CH04	9	0
27	Helen	CH04	10	0
28	Helen	CH04	11	0
29	David	CH02	0	0
30	Helen	CH04	12	0
31	Helen	CH01	0	0
32	Helen	CH01	3	0
33	David	CH07	7	0
34	Helen	CH04	13	0
35	Helen	CH04	14	0
36	David	CH06	3	0
37	Helen	CH04	15	0
38	David	CH05	0	1
39	Helen	CH05	0	1

From the given transaction data in Table 8.3. You can make a few observations:

1. *Multiple accounts:* This dataset involves transactions made by two individuals, David and Helen. The frequency of their transaction channels, channel_cd, is tracked separately for each person.
2. *Channel preferences*: Both David and Helen seem to have preferred transaction channels. For David, it's CH07, and for Helen, it's CH04. These preferences are reflected by the higher frequency counts for these channels.
3. *Less common channels*: Channels like CH01, CH02, CH03, and CH06 are less commonly used by both individuals. This could indicate that these channels are used for specific types of transactions or are used under certain circumstances.
4. *Fraudulent activities*: Both David and Helen have a fraud flag raised when channel CH05 is used for the first time. This could indicate that this channel was used fraudulently or that transactions using this channel tend to be suspicious.
5. *Usefulness of frequency feature*: The freq_channel feature effectively tracks the frequency of channel usage for each account. It can help in detecting any anomalies in behavior, such as a sudden change in the frequently used channel or the introduction of a new channel, and can be a vital tool for fraud detection algorithms (Fig. 8.6).

This figure illustrates how the freq_channel feature tracks the number of times each channel is used by individual account holders. The plot highlights David's repeated use of CH07 and Helen's preference for CH04. Both users exhibit fraud flags upon first use of CH05, marked as anomalous events. Such frequency patterns offer strong indicators for behavioral shifts and potential fraud detection.

> TIP
>
> Instead of using static thresholds (such as flagging all transactions above a certain frequency), consider using *dynamic thresholds*, which adjust based on recent trends or seasonality.

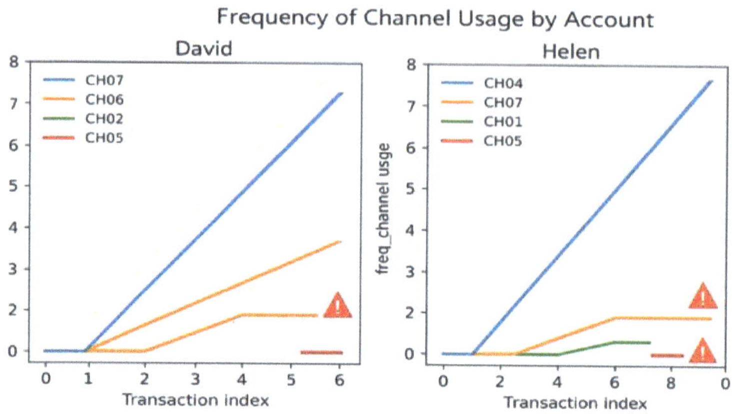

Fig. 8.6 Frequency of channel usage by account

Monetary Features

Monetary features are crucial in the realm of fraud detection and analytics. These features, which capture the value or amount associated with specific events, are essential tools for identifying unusual patterns that may suggest fraudulent activities.

Key Components

Key components of monetary features include the following:

1. *Transaction amounts:* These represent the value of transactions within specific events. For instance:
   (a) Large, round-number transactions could indicate money laundering attempts.
   (b) Small transactions followed by a large withdrawal could suggest credit card testing or account takeover attempts.
2. *Payment method amounts:* This dimension focuses on the total value of transactions based on the chosen payment medium. An unusual spike in the total value of transactions using a specific payment

method, like wire transfers, might indicate a compromised method or a fraud scheme in play.

3. *Merchant or category amounts:* Here, the emphasis is on the total value of transactions linked to a particular vendor or those that belong to a specific category. A sudden increase in transaction amounts with a previously unknown merchant could be a sign of a merchant fraud scheme.

Examining monetary features meticulously, fraud analysts can identify anomalies by pinpointing deviations from established patterns. For example, a user who typically makes small purchases but suddenly starts making large, round-number purchases could be involved in money laundering. Such anomalies in transaction amounts often signal potential fraudulent behavior and necessitate immediate investigation.

Although monetary features are potent standalone indicators, their true potential is realized when combined with other data elements. For instance, correlating transaction amounts with geolocation can help detect large transactions made from unusual locations. Similarly, combining monetary features with user behavior analytics can provide a holistic view of a user's spending habits, making it easier to spot outliers (Fig. 8.7).

This figure illustrates three types of monetary anomalies: (A) a sharp deviation in individual transaction amounts, often linked to laundering or stolen cards; (B) a sudden spike in total payment amounts via a specific

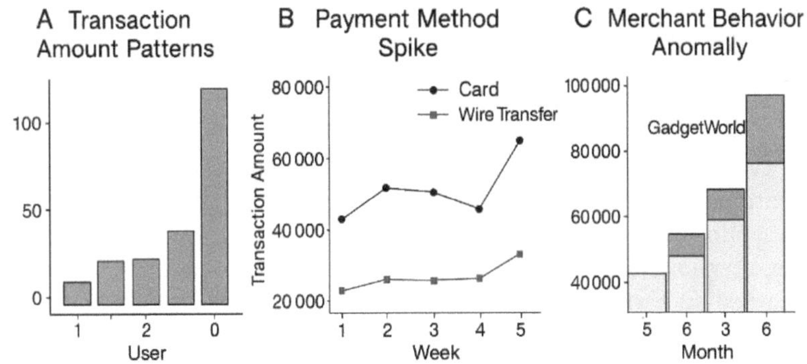

Fig. 8.7 Visualizing Monetary Feature Anomalies in Fraud Detection

method, indicating method compromise; and (C) abnormal growth in transaction amounts linked to a newly registered merchant, suggesting merchant-based fraud schemes. These features, especially when paired with behavioral and geolocation insights, can enhance the precision of fraud analytics.

Example: Detecting Fraudulent Activities in an Online Retail Store

Imagine an online retail store, ShopEase, that offers a wide range of products, from electronics to clothing. The store has a loyal customer base, and most transactions are routine. However, ShopEase wants to enhance its fraud detection system by focusing on monetary features.

Transaction amounts can reveal suspicious activities. For instance, ShopEase might observe a transaction of $10,000 for 50 identical high-end smartphones on a typical day. The precise round number and bulk purchase could indicate a money laundering attempt or a purchase using stolen credit card details. Another example could be when a new customer makes several small purchases totaling $50 over a week and then suddenly buys a high-end laptop for $5000. This suggests that the small transactions might have been tests to see if a stolen card works, followed by a significant fraudulent transaction.

Payment method amounts can also be telling. If ShopEase sees a 300% increase in transactions made via wire transfers in a particular week, it could mean that the wire transfer details of some customers have been compromised or that there's a new fraud scheme targeting this payment method.

Merchant or category amounts offer another layer of insight. ShopEase, which collaborates with various third-party merchants, might notice a surge in transactions linked to a new merchant, "GadgetWorld," added just a week ago. This could indicate a merchant fraud scheme where the merchant processes fake orders to siphon off money.

Identifying anomalies is crucial. For example, a regular customer, Emma, who typically buys books and household items, might suddenly purchase ten luxury watches totaling $20,000. Such a deviation from their usual spending pattern suggests a potential account takeover or misuse.

Collaboration with complementary features can further enhance fraud detection. Geolocation correlation can be instrumental. If ShopEase detects a $3000 transaction for electronics from Eastern Europe, but the delivery address is in the US and the customer's previous transactions have always been from the US, it's a clear discrepancy and should throw a red flag.

Finally, user behavior analytics can provide deeper insights. By analyzing Emma's browsing behavior, ShopEase might find that she had no browsing history related to watches before her luxury watch purchase, strengthening the suspicion that her account might have been compromised (Fig. 8.8).

This multi-panel figure visualizes suspicious patterns in monetary features that are indicative of fraud in online retail settings. The left-most panel shows a spike in transaction amount with a bulk purchase of 50 identical smartphones—suggestive of a possible money laundering attempt. The center panel highlights a new customer making several small purchases followed by a sudden high-value laptop transaction, indicating possible card testing behavior. The right panel displays a sudden surge in wire transfer usage, potentially signaling a compromised payment method. These illustrations underscore how anomalies in transaction amount, timing, and payment method can help flag high-risk behaviors in fraud detection systems.

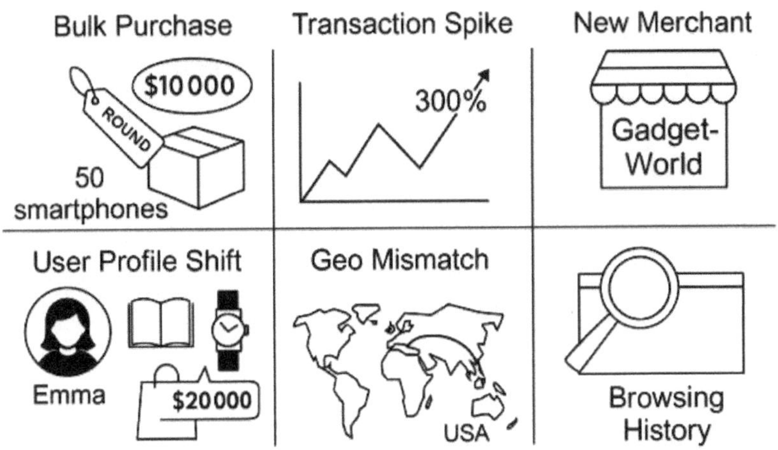

Fig. 8.8 Monetary Anomalies in Retail Transactions

Summary

At their core, Chapters 7 and 8 provide an exhaustive overview of feature engineering and advanced feature engineering methods in fraud analytics. These chapters pave the way for addressing imbalanced datasets in Chapter 9.

In this chapter, the spotlight was on the pivotal role of time analysis in fraud detection. We went deeply into the creation and significance of RFM features, which encapsulate transactional data's *recency*, *frequency*, and *monetary* aspects.

The chapter sheds light on crafting RFM features, which stand as strong indicators of transactional patterns and play a crucial role in spotting potential fraud. In addition to RFM, the chapter looked at advanced methods to enrich the dataset. This included time-based aggregations that show patterns over time, interaction features that show how different parts of the data affect each other, and anomaly detection features that are good at finding outliers or strange data points. Highlighting the intricate web of various data processes, the chapter stressed the harmony between data wrangling, exploratory data analysis (EDA), and feature engineering. At the same time, these steps clean, probe, and expand the data, making it possible for powerful machine learning models designed to find fraud.

The next chapter addresses the problem of imbalanced datasets in machine learning, a common issue where one class greatly outnumbers the other. This situation can lead to biased models that favor the majority class, which is not ideal when the minority class is the one of interest.

Chapter 9 will explore why standard accuracy metrics may not work well for imbalanced data and will introduce other metrics such as *precision, recall, F1-score*, and the *area under the ROC curve (AUC-ROC).*

It will also guide you through different techniques for handling imbalanced datasets. This includes resampling strategies and more advanced methods such as cost-sensitive learning and ensemble methods. Examples and case studies will be provided to illustrate how these techniques can be applied effectively. By the end of the next chapter, you'll be equipped to handle the challenges of imbalanced data and design better, more balanced machine learning models.

CHAPTER 9

Handling Imbalanced Data Sets

Balancing data is not just a technical necessity; it's an art that ensures every voice, no matter how faint, is heard. In the world of data, attaining perfect balance often proves elusive. Datasets mirror the complexity and disparities of the real-world phenomena they capture, and this is particularly evident in the case of imbalanced datasets. This skewed representation challenges machine learning algorithms, especially in binary classification situations where one class significantly outnumbers the other. This chapter unpacks class disparity, its origins, and potential solutions.

In machine learning, the term "class" refers to a category or group that a particular data point belongs to based on some defined features. For example, in a dataset of email messages, the classes might be *spam* or *not spam*. In many machine learning scenarios, the less frequent or minority class is often the target of prediction. Examples of this include identifying fraudulent transactions in a predominantly legitimate transaction dataset, diagnosing a rare disease within a large healthy population, or pinpointing instances of customer churn in a mostly loyal customer base. However, traditional machine learning models may develop a bias toward the more common or majority class when trained on datasets that have a significant imbalance between classes. This imbalance can impede the model's ability to accurately detect and predict instances of the minority class, which is often the focus of the analysis.

A. Al Aqqad, *Fraud Analytics in Action*
https://doi.org/10.1007/978-3-032-16023-2_9

This chapter unravels the concept of imbalanced datasets and their impact on model performance. It explains why conventional accuracy metrics might fall short as performance measures in such scenarios and introduces more suitable metrics like precision, recall, F1-score, and the area under the ROC curve (AUC-ROC).

Moreover, this chapter offers a comprehensive examination of various techniques for managing imbalanced datasets. You'll navigate through multiple methods, from simple resampling strategies like random over-sampling and under-sampling to more intricate approaches such as cost-sensitive learning, ensemble methods, transfer learning, and hybrid methods. Each of these techniques comes with its own unique advantages and trade-offs.

This chapter also includes practical examples and case studies showcasing the effective application of these techniques in handling imbalanced datasets.

By the chapter's end, you'll have a firm grasp of the challenges of imbalanced datasets and the best strategies for dealing with them. This knowledge empowers you to design robust and unbiased machine learning models, even when the data skews toward one class. Let's begin this journey toward attaining balance in imbalanced data.

Strategies to Tackle Class Imbalance: Enhancing Fraud Detection in Machine Learning

Class imbalance is a common challenge in machine learning, where one class significantly outnumbers the other in the training dataset. This unequal representation can lead to biased models toward the majority class, often failing to accurately predict the minority class, which is typically the primary focus of the analysis.

In the context of fraud analytics, this issue is particularly pronounced. Fraudulent transactions are typically rare, constituting a small fraction (a minority class) of total transactions. As a result, models might excel at identifying legitimate transactions but struggle to detect fraudulent ones.

The repercussions of class imbalances in machine learning models encompass the following:

- *Bias toward the majority class*: Such models might display high accuracy for the majority class but suffer from low recall or sensitivity for the minority class.
- *Challenges in distinguishing the minority class*: The distinct patterns of the minority class can be overshadowed by the dominant majority class, making it challenging for the model to recognize them.
- *Elevated false positives*: An imbalanced dataset can escalate the rate of false positives, leading to unnecessary investigations and potentially increasing operational costs.

Addressing this imbalance is crucial for the success of machine learning models. *Balancing* the dataset prior to model construction is vital to improving the detection of the minority class, such as fraudulent transactions. Various strategies and techniques exist to counteract the effects of class imbalance, ensuring models are unbiased and effective.

One of the primary strategies to tackle this challenge is *resampling*. Within this approach, there are two main techniques. The first is *random under-sampling,* where some instances of the majority class are removed to balance the class distribution. While straightforward, this method has the downside of potentially discarding crucial information. The second is *random oversampling*, where instances of the minority class are either duplicated or synthetically created using methods like SMOTE (the synthetic minority over-sampling technique) or ADASYN (Adaptive Synthetic Sampling). This helps increase the minority class's representation but can sometimes lead to overfitting.

Another strategy is *cost-sensitive learning*. Here, different misclassification costs are assigned to different classes. By doing so, the classifier is nudged to be more attentive to the minority class, as the penalty for misclassifying it is higher.

Ensemble methods have also proven effective against imbalanced datasets. Techniques like *bagging* involve training multiple base classifiers on varied data subsets and amalgamating their predictions through mechanisms like majority voting. On the other hand, *boosting* trains classifiers sequentially, with each new classifier focusing more on instances that its predecessors misclassified.

Transfer learning is a newer approach where models pre-trained on a different but related task are fine-tuned for the specific imbalanced dataset. This leverages the knowledge gained from the initial task to aid the current one.

When evaluating models trained on imbalanced data, it's crucial to use *evaluation metrics* that offer a comprehensive view of the model's capabilities. Metrics such as precision, recall, F1-score, and AUC-ROC are less influenced by class imbalance and can provide insights into the model's true performance.

Here's a brief overview of these metrics in the context of fraud detection:

- *Precision* measures the proportion of transactions that were correctly identified as fraudulent out of all those that were predicted to be fraudulent by the model. It answers the question, "Of all the transactions flagged as fraudulent by the model, how many were actually fraudulent?" High precision is important in fraud detection to avoid the costs associated with false alarms, such as customer dissatisfaction and unnecessary investigations.
- *Recall,* also known as sensitivity, measures the proportion of actual positive cases (in this context, fraudulent transactions) that were correctly identified by the predictive model. It is calculated as the number of true positives divided by the sum of true positives and false negatives. In other words, it answers the question: "Of all the transactions that are actually fraudulent, how many did the system correctly detect?" High recall in fraud detection is crucial because failing to identify a fraudulent transaction can have significant financial implications.
- *F1-score* combines precision and recall into a single metric by taking their harmonic mean. Given the critical nature of fraud detection, where both failing to catch fraud (false negatives) and mislabeling legitimate transactions as fraudulent (false positives) can have serious consequences, the F1-score provides a balance between precision and recall. It is particularly useful when there is a significant class imbalance between fraudulent and non-fraudulent transactions.
- *AUC-ROC* (area under the receiver operating characteristic curve) evaluates the model's ability to distinguish between classes—in this case, between genuine and fraudulent transactions. An AUC-ROC value of 1 indicates perfect discrimination, meaning the model can flawlessly differentiate between genuine and fraudulent transactions. Conversely, a value of 0.5 suggests that the model's performance is

no better than random chance. In fraud detection, a high AUC-ROC value is desirable as it indicates the model is effective at flagging fraudulent transactions while minimizing false positives.

For a deeper understanding and exploration of these metrics in fraud detection, see Chapter 15 "Fraud Detection Excellence—A Deep Exploration of Model Metrics, Optimization, and Governance", where these concepts are discussed in detail.

Data augmentation is another technique that involves creating new instances of the minority class by applying slight transformations, like rotations or zooms, to the existing data. This not only increases the representation of the minority class but also introduces variability.

Hybrid methods combine the strengths of multiple techniques. For instance, one might undersample the majority class while oversampling the minority class, aiming for a dataset that is both balanced and rich in information.

Lastly, the *Adjust posterior probability estimates* (APPE) method tweaks the posterior probabilities of the minority class, aiming to reduce any inherent model bias.

In fraud detection, where datasets are often heavily imbalanced, with fraudulent transactions being the minority, these techniques are invaluable. Properly addressing dataset imbalances ensures that the model doesn't just naively classify most transactions as non-fraudulent. Instead, it becomes adept at spotting subtle patterns and indicators of fraudulent activity. Using appropriate metrics for evaluation further ensures that the model's performance is gauged accurately, leading to reliable and trustworthy fraud detection systems.

Random Under-Sampling

Random under-sampling is a technique utilized in fraud analytics to counteract the issue of imbalanced data, where the number of legitimate transactions vastly surpasses that of fraudulent ones. The method works by selectively reducing the number of legitimate transactions, thus creating a more balanced dataset to enhance the performance of machine learning algorithms in detecting fraud. It accomplishes this by randomly selecting a subset from the majority class, that is, legitimate transactions, and eliminating these entries until a balanced ratio between both classes is achieved.

Despite its simplicity and ease of implementation, random under-sampling has a key drawback: the potential for valuable information loss from the excluded majority class data. This loss can become a significant issue, especially for datasets with an extremely low count of fraudulent transactions.

To mitigate these limitations, synthetic data augmentation techniques like SMOTE and ADASYN have been developed. These methods create synthetic instances of fraudulent transactions, thereby augmenting the minority class without losing critical information intrinsic to the majority class.

While random under-sampling can improve the performance of fraud detection models on imbalanced datasets, its inherent risk of information loss must not be overlooked. Synthetic oversampling methods like SMOTE and ADASYN offer more balanced and information-preserving alternatives. Therefore, selecting the most suitable technique should be conducted case-by-case, carefully evaluating the specific dataset and the model's requirements.

Example: Random under-Sampling

Imagine a dataset containing 100,000 credit card transactions, as depicted in Table 9.1. Within these, 1000 transactions are fraudulent, making up just 1% of the entire dataset. The remaining transactions are legitimate, creating a significant imbalance that can bias a fraud detection model toward predicting transactions as non-fraudulent.

Table 9.1 represents the imbalanced dataset before applying random under-sampling, where most transactions are non-fraudulent.

To address this imbalance, random under-sampling is applied to create a dataset with an equal number of fraudulent and legitimate transactions. For example, alongside the 1000 fraudulent transactions, 1000 legitimate transactions are randomly selected to form a new, balanced dataset of 2000 transactions in total.

Table 9.2 shows an excerpt from the dataset after applying random under-sampling. It now contains an equal number of fraudulent and non-fraudulent transactions, exemplifying a balanced dataset for model training.

With a balanced dataset, as illustrated in Table 9.2, a machine learning model can be effectively trained to identify fraudulent transactions without the bias introduced by an imbalanced dataset.

Table 9.1 Original imbalanced dataset before applying random under-sampling

Transaction ID	Transaction Amount	Transaction Time	Fraudulent
1	100.00	2022-01-01 01:00:00	0
...	...	...	...
100000	500.00	2022-12-31 23:59:59	0

Note Only a selection of transactions is displayed, not the full set of 100,000

Table 9.2 Dataset post random under-sampling

Transaction ID	Transaction Amount	Transaction Time	Fraudulent
1	100.00	2022-01-01 01:00:00	0
...	...	...	...
100000	500.00	2022-12-31 23:59:59	1

Note This is a representative sample from the balanced dataset, not a complete listing of all 2000 transactions

WARNING

Random under-sampling, by its nature, omits certain legitimate transactions, potentially leading to the loss of valuable insights. It's imperative to weigh the benefits of a balanced dataset against potential information loss when employing random under-sampling in fraud analytics.

Random Oversampling

Random oversampling is a pivotal technique in the machine learning toolbox, designed to address class imbalances by augmenting minority class observations. In essence, it seeks to bolster the representation of the minority class, thereby rectifying skewed distributions. When applied to fraud detection, this technique can amplify the presence of rare fraudulent transactions, forging a more harmonious dataset.

At its core, random oversampling duplicates specific observations, such as instances of fraud, to craft a training sample where both fraudulent and legitimate transactions are equally represented. However, it's crucial to highlight that many studies indicate a preference for under-sampling over oversampling in terms of producing superior classifiers. It's imperative that any sampling strategy, be it over or under, is exclusively executed on the training data. The sanctity of the test data must be preserved to ensure a sober assessment of the model's prowess.

Identifying the ideal class distribution for sampling often requires an iterative, experimental approach. You can find the best balance by building models on different class distributions and testing their work on a separate validation set using metrics like the area under the curve (AUC). While industry practices often gravitate toward an 80:20 split between non-fraudulent and fraudulent transactions, the ideal balance can be dataset-specific and demands careful consideration.

Random oversampling shines especially in scenarios where the minority class is sparsely populated, making it challenging to extract meaningful patterns. By amplifying these rare instances, the technique provides the model with a richer tapestry to learn from. However, this approach has pitfalls. Overfitting, where the model becomes excessively tailored to the training data, and potential biases in predictions are genuine concerns. To counteract these, it's paramount to employ rigorous cross-validation and assess the model on data it hasn't seen before. Moreover, advanced methods such as the synthetic minority oversampling technique

(SMOTE) provide an alternative by creating new synthetic instances for the minority class instead of just copying existing data.

The Kaggle Credit Card Fraud Dataset

The Kaggle credit card fraud dataset, available at Kaggle Credit Card Fraud Dataset, encapsulates approximately 300,000 transactions made by European credit card holders over two days in September 2013. Each transaction is labeled either as fraudulent or legitimate. The data has 28 anonymous numerical variables (V1–V28), a time variable that shows how many seconds passed between each transaction and the first transaction in the dataset, the amount of each transaction, and a class variable that shows what kind of transaction it was.

From this dataset, a subset of 24,600 observations is extracted, comprising 24,108 legitimate transactions and 492 fraudulent ones. Given that only 2% of the transactions in this subset are fraudulent, the imbalance is evident.

When plotting variable V2 against variable V1, the fraudulent cases, highlighted in red, are distinctly noticeable, indicating a clear imbalance (as seen in Fig. 9.1). For an equal representation of fraudulent and legitimate transactions (50% each), the dataset would require a total of 984 cases, with 492 fraudulent and 492 legitimate transactions. By employing a combination of oversampling (for example, using SMOTE) and undersampling techniques, you can achieve a balanced dataset that is optimal for training machine learning models.

This plot of V2 against V1 shows fraudulent transactions highlighted in a darker shade of red and legitimate transactions highlighted in blue. This visualization should give you an idea of how these two classes are distributed with respect to these two variables, and it clearly illustrates the imbalance between fraudulent and legitimate transactions. While techniques like random oversampling can be instrumental in addressing class imbalances, it's paramount to evaluate their efficacy judiciously. Factors like potential information loss, overfitting, and the nature of the dataset itself play pivotal roles. Advanced methods like the synthetic minority over-sampling technique (SMOTE) and adaptive synthetic sampling (ADASYN) can create synthetic examples to further balance the dataset.

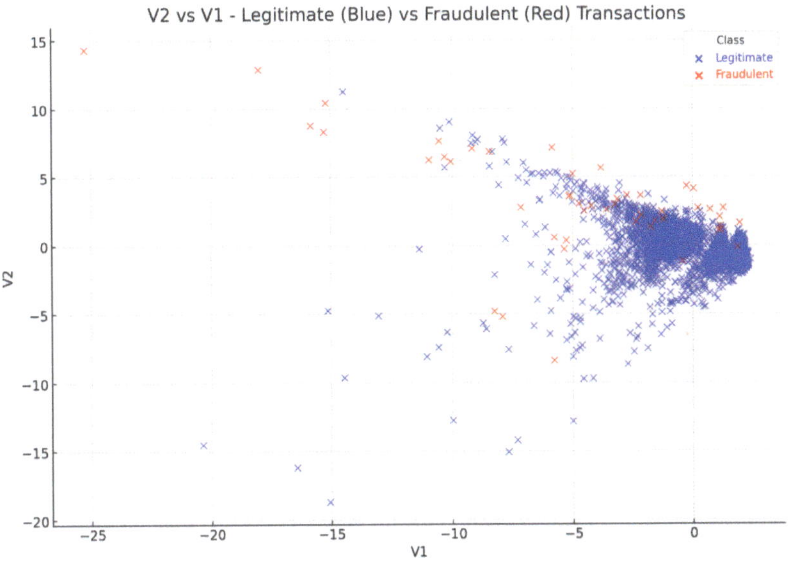

Fig. 9.1 Visualizing the imbalance and the oversampling effect

TIP
In fraud detection, where the stakes are high, and the margin for error is slim, ensuring a balanced dataset and an unbiased model is not just beneficial—it's imperative.

Oversampling in Python

In Python, the imbalanced-learn library offers specialized resampling algorithms for handling imbalanced datasets. Compatible with scikit-learn, it allows for streamlined integration of these techniques. The library includes methods like oversampling, mainly using the SMOTE algorithm, to boost the representation of the minority class. This strategy aids in improving model precision by creating a balanced training data distribution.

Figure 9.2 presents two distinct plots for visualizing 2-dimensional data. The first plot, titled "Original Dataset," displays the initial data points. The second plot, named "Resampled Dataset with Overlapping

Points in Red," illustrates two sets of data: the original dataset is indicated by red points, and the resampled dataset is represented by blue points. This layout helps in clearly distinguishing between the original and the resampled datasets. Overlapping data points, resulting from the oversampling process, appear darker where the red and blue points coincide. After resampling, both class 0 (non-fraud) and class 1 (fraud) have an equal number of instances, showcasing the effect of the oversampling technique.

TIP
You can modify the loss function to penalize the misclassification of the minority class more than the majority class. This is a form of cost-sensitive learning where the costs of different types of errors are not considered equal.

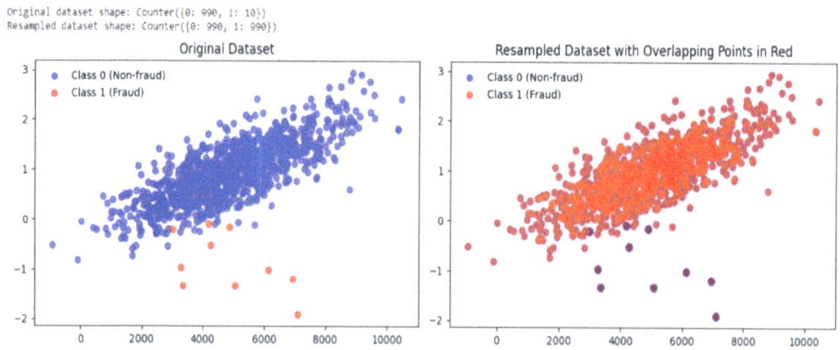

Fig. 9.2 Visualizing the oversampling effect: Two X-Y charts compare datasets. The left chart, titled "Original Dataset," shows blue dots for Class 0 (Non-fraud) and red dots for Class 1 (Fraud), with a sparse distribution of red dots. The right chart, titled "Resampled Dataset with Overlapping Points in Red," displays a more balanced distribution of blue and red dots, indicating resampling. Legends identify the classes. Text above the charts notes the original dataset shape as 990 non-fraud and 10 fraud, and the resampled dataset shape as 990 non-fraud and 990 fraud

Synthetic Minority Over-Sampling Technique (SMOTE)

SMOTE, introduced by Chawla et al. in 2002, is a machine learning technique designed to handle imbalanced datasets. In such datasets, the number of observations in one class, such as fraudulent transactions, is significantly fewer than in the other class, like normal transactions. SMOTE addresses the limitations of random oversampling, which can lead to overfitting by merely replicating minority class instances.

SMOTE creates synthetic samples that are similar to, but not identical to, the minority class instances. The algorithm selects a minority class instance and then finds its k-nearest neighbors in the feature space. SMOTE then creates new instances by interpolating between the *selected instance and its neighbors.*

The *sampling ratio*, a user-defined parameter that specifies the quantity of generated synthetic samples, controls the level of interpolation. To illustrate, suppose you set the sampling ratio at 50% with a synthetic minority oversampling technique (SMOTE). This process will generate synthetic samples until the minority class has half the instances as the majority class.

Consider a dataset comprising 1000 phone calls. Of these, 950 are regular calls, while the remaining 50 are spam calls. This dataset's imbalance is evident, with a mere 5% of calls being spam. This disparity is vividly illustrated in Fig. 9.3, where you plot call duration against the number of calls. Here, spam calls are distinctly marked in red.

To address class imbalances, the synthetic minority over-sampling technique (SMOTE) is a valuable tool. The steps for applying SMOTE are as follows:

1. *Initial selection*: Start by identifying the minority class, in this case, fraudulent calls. From this class, randomly select an observation. For illustration, let's choose a fraudulent call made by "Tom." Then, determine the number of nearest neighbors (K) for the SMOTE algorithm. Here, K is set to 5, as shown in Fig. 9.4.

2. *Determine nearest neighbors:* Using the Euclidean distance metric, identify the k-nearest neighbors for the chosen observation. For

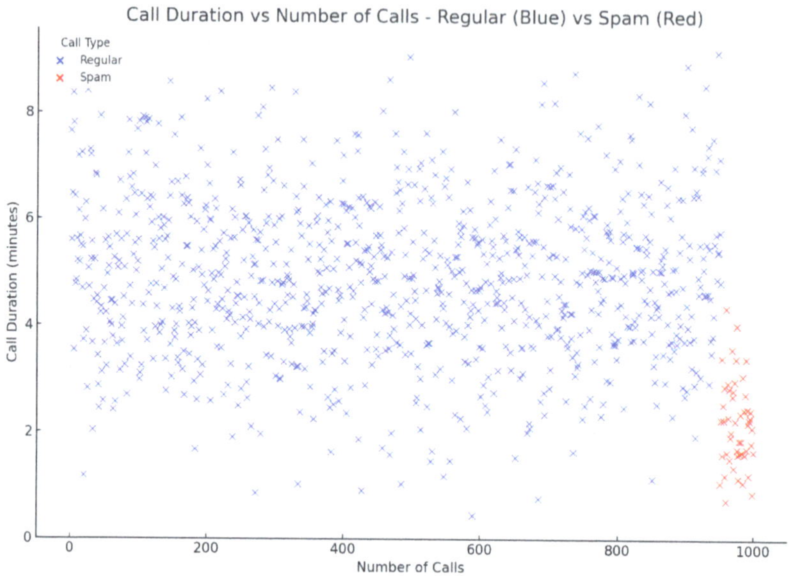

Fig. 9.3 Visualization of the imbalanced dataset: Figure showing a simulated dataset of 1000 phone calls, including 950 regular calls and 50 spam calls. The x-axis represents the number of calls from 0 to 999, and the y-axis shows call duration in minutes. Regular calls are plotted as green "X" marks, while spam calls appear as red circles. The plot highlights the significant imbalance between the two classes, emphasizing the challenge in training models without resampling techniques like SMOTE

"Tom," this means finding the K closest neighbors who also made fraudulent calls, as shown in Fig. 9.5.

3. *Random neighbor selection:* From the nearest neighbors, randomly select one. For this example, we'll choose "John" from Tom's neighbors, as depicted in Fig. 9.6.

   3.a Synthetic sample generation: Create a synthetic instance by taking the difference between the features of the selected observation and its neighbor, multiplying this difference by a random number between 0 and 1, and adding the result to the original

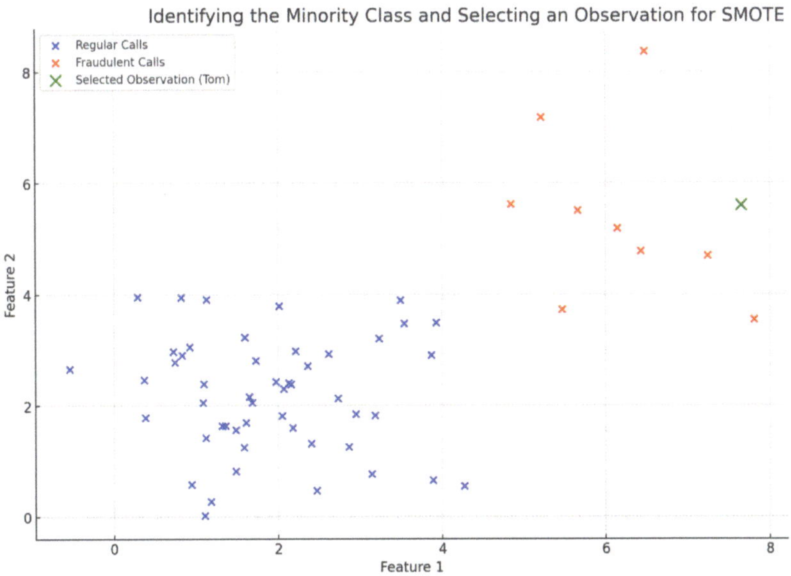

Fig. 9.4 Identifying the minority class and selecting an observation for SMOTE: Plot illustrating the first step in applying SMOTE by identifying the minority class and selecting an observation to oversample. Regular calls are shown as blue points, while fraudulent calls appear as red points grouped toward the upper right corner. Among the fraudulent calls, one observation representing "Tom" is highlighted with a large green "X," signaling it has been chosen for synthetic data generation. This visual sets the stage for the next steps in SMOTE, where Tom's call and its nearest neighbors will be used to create new examples to balance the dataset

observation's features. For instance, to generate a synthetic fraudulent call, you might use a random number (such as 0.7) and multiply it by the difference in features (like call duration) between Tom and John. Adding this to Tom's features yields the synthetic instance, as illustrated in Fig. 9.7.

4. *Dataset augmentation:* Repeat this process for multiple minority class observations to create synthetic samples. Adding these to the

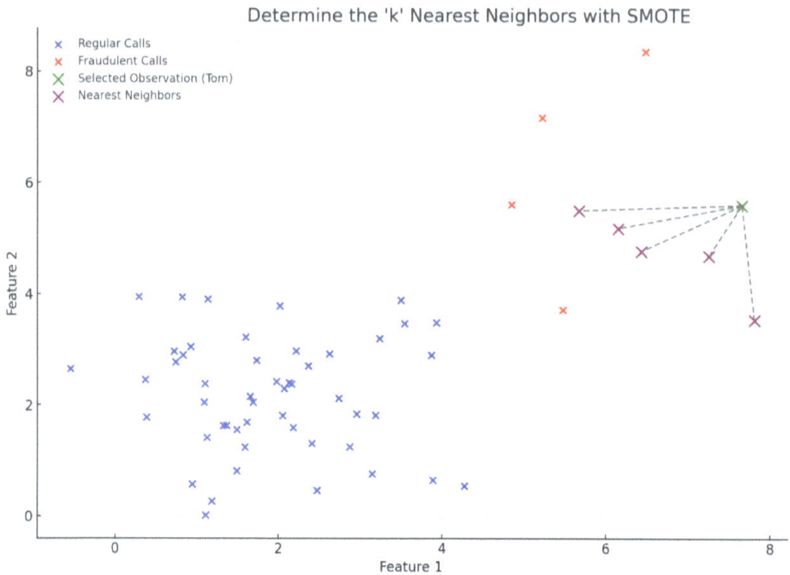

Fig. 9.5 Determine the "k" nearest neighbors with SMOTE: Plot showing the identification of the k-nearest neighbors for SMOTE. Regular calls are displayed as blue points and fraudulent calls as red points, similar to the earlier figure. The nearest neighbors of the selected fraudulent call (Tom) are highlighted in purple, and dashed gray lines connect each neighbor to Tom. This visualization captures the process of selecting the closest fraudulent observations based on Euclidean distance

original dataset ensures a balanced representation of both classes. In our example, using SMOTE with k = 5 produces five synthetic samples for each genuine fraudulent call. Starting from 50 original fraudulent calls, this generates 250 synthetic instances, bringing the total number of fraudulent calls to 300. The resulting oversampled dataset contains 1,250 calls in total—950 regular and 300 fraudulent—meaning fraudulent calls now represent 24% of the dataset, up from the original 5%. This improved representation can enhance classifier performance in detecting fraudulent calls, as visualized in Fig. 9.8.

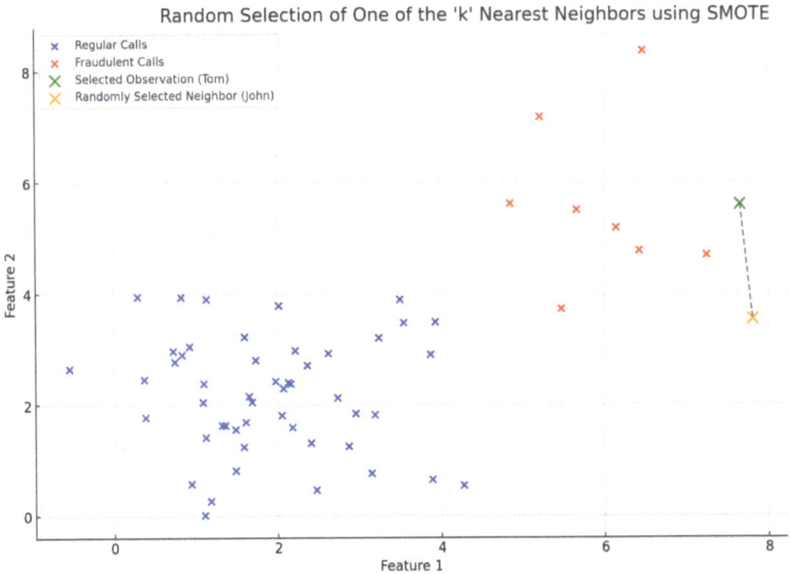

Fig. 9.6 Random selection of one of the "k" nearest neighbors using SMOTE: Plot illustrating the random selection of one neighbor from the k-nearest neighbors identified in the previous step. The selected observation, Tom, remains highlighted in green, while the randomly chosen neighbor, John, is marked in orange. A dashed gray line connects Tom and John, indicating the two points that will be used to create a synthetic sample through interpolation

In the realm of insurance, consider a dataset of claims where fraudulent activities are significantly underrepresented. To illustrate the SMOTE process in this context, let's focus on two insurance claims, one made by Alicia and the other by Hakeem. Alicia's claim details an amount of \$3000 and a frequency of 0.85, indicating the frequency of her claims, while Hakeem's claim includes an amount of \$2880 and a frequency of 0.95.

To create a new synthetic fraudulent claim using SMOTE, we begin by selecting a random number between 0 and 1; for this example, let's use 0.7. This number will be instrumental in interpolating between Alicia and Hakeem's claim data for each attribute:

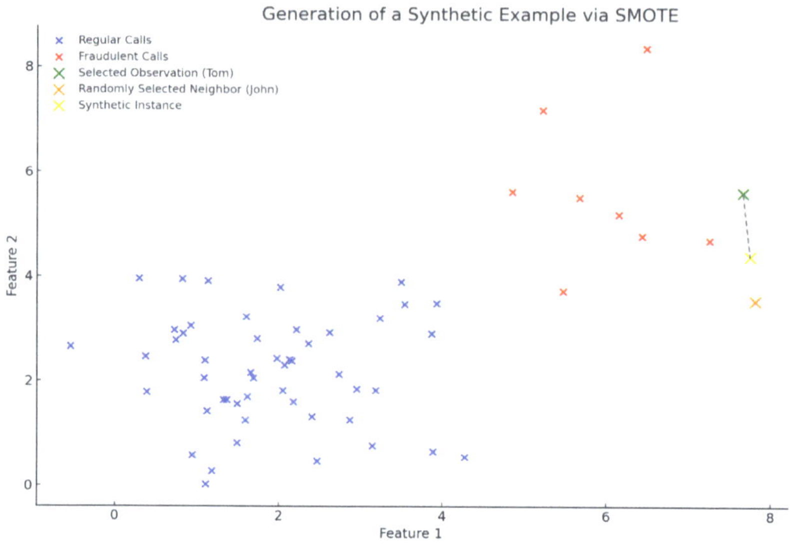

Fig. 9.7 *Generation of a synthetic example* via *SMOTE:* Plot showing the generation of a synthetic sample using SMOTE. The regular calls in blue, original fraudulent calls in red, selected observation (Tom) in green, and selected neighbor (John) in orange are displayed. A new synthetic point appears in yellow between Tom and John, created by interpolating their feature values based on a random factor. This synthetic instance represents a new artificial fraudulent call used to balance the dataset

For the amount, the synthetic sample is calculated as Alicia's amount plus 0.7 times the difference between Hakeem's and Alicia's amounts. The formula is $3000 + 0.7 * ($2880 - $3000), resulting in a synthetic claim amount of $2,916.

For the frequency, the synthetic sample is derived by taking Alicia's frequency plus 0.7 times the difference between Hakeem's and Alicia's frequencies. Applying this, we get 0.85 + 0.7 * (0.95–0.85), resulting in a frequency of 0.92.

Thus, the synthetic insurance claim generated using SMOTE will have an amount of $2916 and a frequency of 0.92. This example underscores SMOTE's utility in balancing class distribution within datasets, especially in scenarios where fraudulent claims are significantly underrepresented. By generating synthetic samples based on the characteristics of existing

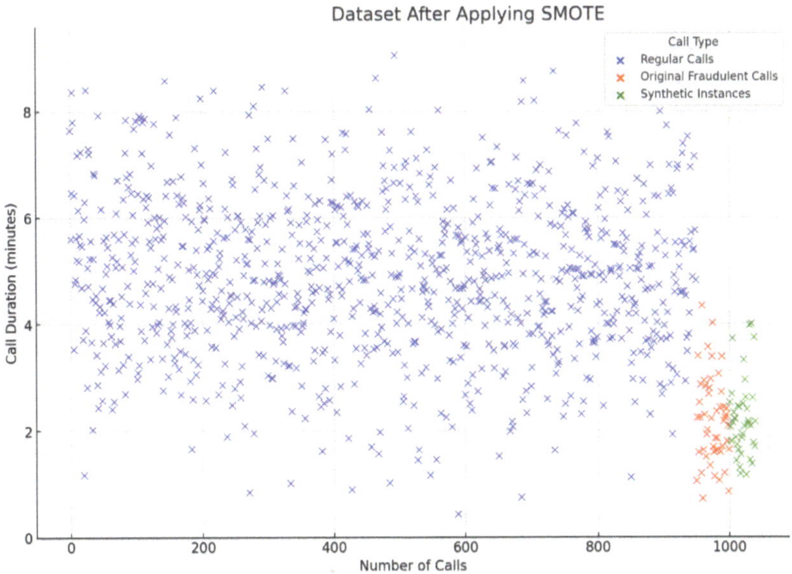

Fig. 9.8 *Visualization of the dataset post-SMOTE application*: Visualization of the dataset after applying SMOTE to create a more balanced class distribution. Regular calls are displayed in blue, original fraudulent calls are shown in red, and newly created synthetic samples are represented in green. The x-axis shows the number of calls, and the y-axis represents the call duration in minutes. This figure demonstrates how the addition of synthetic instances addresses the class imbalance, helping to improve the training of machine learning models
Applying SMOTE: A Mathematical Example in Insurance Fraud Detection

minority class instances like Alicia's and Hakeem's claims, SMOTE contributes to creating a more balanced dataset. This enhanced dataset can then be used to train machine learning models more effectively, improving their accuracy in detecting fraudulent insurance claims.

TIP
For the synthetic insurance claim:
The amount is calculated as $3,000 + 0.7 * ($2,880 - $3,000) = $2,916.
The frequency is calculated as 0.85 + 0.7 * (0.95 - 0.85) = 0.92.
These values represent a synthetic claim that has been interpolated between Alicia's and Hakeem's claims, demonstrating how SMOTE can be used to generate new instances in datasets with class imbalances.

SMOTE offers several advantages over traditional data augmentation techniques. First, it mitigates the risk of overfitting by generating synthetic instances that are variations of real instances, ensuring they aren't mere duplicates. Secondly, it can cause a substantial number of synthetic instances, aiding in achieving a balanced dataset. Finally, its implementation is straightforward across various machine learning platforms, including Python and R. However, SMOTE has its challenges. It might produce unrealistic samples or fail to capture the true distribution of the minority class. Moreover, its computational demands can be significant, especially for extensive datasets. Thus, when leveraging SMOTE for imbalanced data, especially in fraud analytics, it's imperative to weigh the benefits of data balance against computational efficiency.

To address class imbalances, several SMOTE *variants* have been developed to offer tailored solutions. The *Borderline-SMOTE* variant focuses on oversampling minority instances near the decision boundary, addressing the most challenging cases that are proximal to majority class samples. *ADASYN (adaptive synthetic sampling)*, on the other hand, generates synthetic samples adjacent to minority samples that are misclassified using a K-nearest neighbor classifier, aiding the model in distinguishing between easy and challenging cases. The *Safe-Level SMOTE* uses "safe levels" to selectively sample minority instances. Instances surrounded by a larger safe level are synthesized more, often leading to superior performance compared to traditional SMOTE. The *density-based SMOTE (DBSMOTE)* leverages the concept of density-based clusters, oversampling minority instances within clusters identified by DBSCAN. This results in dense synthetic instances around cluster centroids. *MWMOTE (majority-weighted minority oversampling technique)* identifies challenging minority samples and assigns weights based on their proximity to majority samples. It then employs clustering to produce synthetic samples from these weighted instances.

In fraud analytics, the effectiveness of SMOTE is amplified when synergized with other strategies. The selection of machine learning algorithms, the art of feature engineering, and the choice of evaluation metrics are pivotal. Adjusting parameters, such as the value of k and the volume of synthetic samples, can significantly impact results. Merging SMOTE with other resampling methods or ensemble techniques like RUS boost or SMOTE boost can lead to a more holistic approach. Feature refinement, algorithm exploration, and cross-validation are other avenues to enhance performance. In the context of imbalanced datasets, traditional metrics like accuracy can be misleading. Opting for metrics like precision, recall, or the F1-score provides a more comprehensive view of performance. Adaptive SMOTE versions, such as Borderline-SMOTE or ADASYN, consider the local distribution of data and, in some scenarios, outperform the traditional approach.

Crafting a robust fraud detection model in imbalanced datasets requires continuous learning and adaptation. By integrating SMOTE with these strategies, the unique challenges of each dataset can be effectively addressed.

> TIP
>
> Adjusting the decision threshold after training can help increase the sensitivity of the minority class. Instead of using the default 0.5 cutoff (in a binary classification), you can lower the threshold to classify an instance as the minority class.

Practical Lab: Balancing a Fraud Dataset Using SMOTE and Visualizing Synthetic Fraudulent Samples

Imbalanced datasets present significant challenges in machine learning, notably in fraud detection. SMOTE can mitigate these challenges by generating synthetic samples for the minority class—fraudulent transactions—in order to balance the dataset. Although a detailed lab for this process cannot be included in the book due to space constraints, an online resource is available for you to follow through with the hands-on application of this technique.

The lab's objectives are:

- Load and segregate the dataset into fraudulent and non-fraudulent transactions.
- Choose a fraud case and identify its k-nearest neighbors.
- Interpolate between the chosen fraud case and one of its neighbors to create a synthetic fraud sample.
- Employ SMOTE on the full dataset to achieve class balance.
- Visualize both the original and the resampled dataset, highlighting the synthetic fraud samples.

The lab utilizes a bespoke dataset named SMOTE.csv, featuring two attributes, amount and ratio, and a binary fraud label signifying the transaction's legitimacy.

Lab access: To partake in the lab and access the dataset, please visit the online resource at this https://github.com/Hands-On-Fraud-Analytics/Chapter-09-Handling-Imbalanced-Data-Sets/tree/main

In this lab exercise, you will explore techniques to balance an imbalanced dataset using the synthetic minority over-sampling technique (SMOTE). Here is a step-by-step guide on what you will do in the lab:

Begin by loading the SMOTE.csv dataset. You will select the essential columns for the analysis: amount, ratio, and the target variable fraud. Once selected, categorize the transactions into fraud and non-fraud cases to set the stage for deeper analysis.

Then, choose a random fraud case from your dataset. Let's refer to this case as Alicia for illustration purposes. You will examine Alicia's features and identify her four nearest fraudulent neighbors using the k-nearest neighbors algorithm.

With Alicia and her nearest neighbors identified, select one neighbor to focus on, whom we'll call Hakeem. You will then create a synthetic fraud sample by interpolating between Alicia and Hakeem using the SMOTE algorithm. This involves a calculation that combines their features with a random scalar to produce a new, synthetic data point.

After creating a single synthetic sample, you will apply SMOTE to the entire dataset. This process will generate additional synthetic fraud cases, thereby balancing the class distribution between fraud and non-fraud cases. A balanced dataset is crucial for effectively training and evaluating machine learning models for fraud detection.

Construct two plots for visualization. The first plot will include the original dataset with Alicia, Hakeem, and the synthetic fraud case you created. The second plot will show the dataset after applying SMOTE, demonstrating the newly achieved balance.

Examine the plots to evaluate the effectiveness of the nearest neighbors algorithm in generating plausible synthetic cases. Confirm that the synthetic cases produced by SMOTE integrate well with the actual fraud cases, indicating the method's suitability for creating training data for fraud detection models.

Proceed with the lab, carrying out each of these steps. Once you've completed the exercise, return to this discussion to reflect on what you've done and to understand how SMOTE improves the machine learning model's ability to detect fraud by creating a balanced dataset.

In examining the dataset, a significant class imbalance between non-fraud and fraud cases is evident (refer to Fig. 9.9). This disparity poses challenges in developing a reliable model for accurately identifying fraudulent transactions. Figure 9.9 highlights the sparsity of fraud cases (represented by red points) compared to non-fraud cases.

The synthetic fraud case, denoted by a blue "X" and created using SMOTE, appears to be well-integrated within the cluster of actual fraud cases in Fig. 9.9, indicating SMOTE's effectiveness. Alicia and Hakeem are marked by purple and green "X"s, respectively, and their close positioning within the fraud cluster signifies the nearest neighbor algorithm's efficiency.

After applying SMOTE, the resampled dataset (Fig. 9.10) presents a more balanced distribution between fraud and non-fraud cases. The "Resampled Dataset" plot demonstrates an increase in red points, showing a distribution that more closely mirrors that of non-fraud cases. This balanced dataset is a more robust foundation for training and evaluating machine learning models tailored for fraud detection.

Given these observations, it is advisable to use SMOTE to balance the dataset before training machine learning models for fraud detection. Experimenting with various SMOTE parameters, such as the number of nearest neighbors, could further optimize the synthetic data generation process. It might also be beneficial to incorporate additional features or engage in feature engineering to enhance model efficacy. Lastly, evaluating a range of machine learning models on this balanced dataset will help identify the most suitable model for fraud prediction.

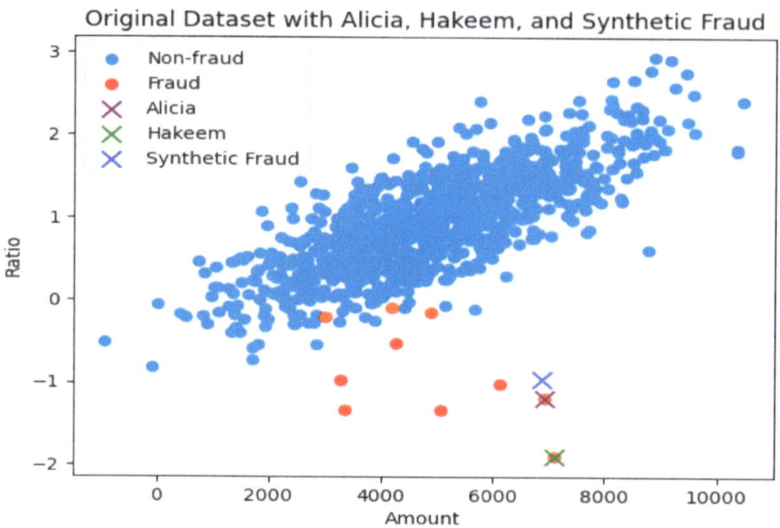

Fig. 9.9 Visualization of the Original Dataset Including Alicia, Hakeem, and a Synthetic Fraudulent Claim: This figure presents the original dataset featuring two genuine fraudulent insurance claims submitted by Alicia and Hakeem, alongside a newly created synthetic fraudulent claim generated through the SMOTE process. Alicia's and Hakeem's claims are plotted as original data points, while the synthetic claim, produced by interpolating between their attributes, is distinguished separately. The visualization demonstrates how SMOTE introduces synthetic examples without modifying the integrity of the original dataset

WARNING

When using SMOTE, ensure the following:

- *Handle missing values:* Before applying SMOTE, ensure that all missing values in your dataset have been appropriately addressed. Missing values can impact the quality of the synthetic samples generated.
- *Ensure the class is categorical:* SMOTE is designed specifically for classification problems, not regression. The target variable should be categorical, meaning it should have discrete values, such as 0 and 1 for binary classification.
- *Beware of data distribution:* SMOTE creates synthetic samples based on the existing data. Ensure that the original data distribution is representative of the true distribution to avoid introducing noise or bias.

Let's recap a bit.

Which resampling method should you use?

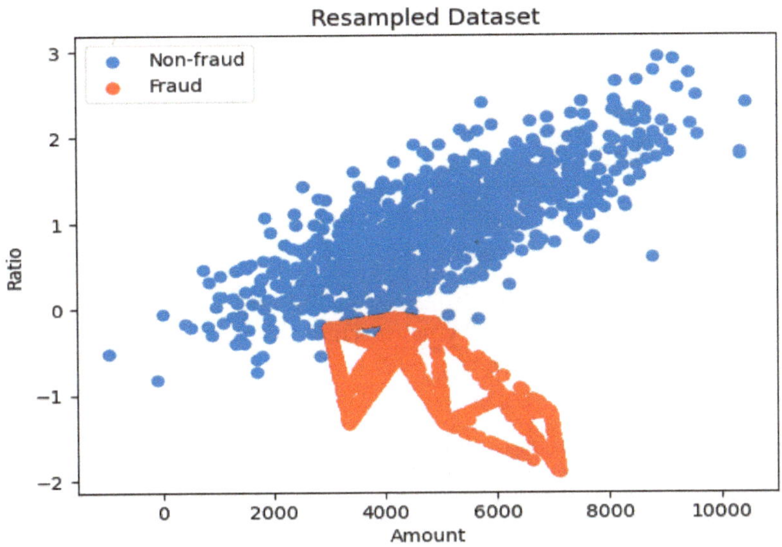

Fig. 9.10 Visualization of the Resampled Dataset Following SMOTE Application This figure illustrates the dataset after broader application of SMOTE to balance the distribution of fraudulent and legitimate claims. The dataset now includes an expanded number of synthetic fraudulent instances, complementing the original observations. The resulting resampled dataset achieves improved class balance, providing a more reliable foundation for training machine learning models in fraud detection

- The best method depends on the specific situation.
- Under-sampling may be computationally easier for large datasets with many fraud cases, but discarding data is generally not desirable.
- SMOTE is a more sophisticated oversampling method since it does not duplicate data, but it works well only if fraud cases are quite similar. If fraud cases are spread out and not very distinct, using SMOTE may introduce noise in the data.

When should you use resampling methods?

- Always resample only the training set, not the test set.

- The goal is to better train the model by providing balanced data, not to predict synthetic samples.
- To use resampling methods properly:

  1. Split the data into training and testing sets.
  2. Resample the training set only.
  3. Fit the model to the resampled training data.
  4. Evaluate the model on the original (non-resampled) test data to obtain performance metrics.

Following these guidelines can effectively address class imbalances and improve the performance of your machine learning models for fraud detection tasks.

> TIP
>
> In cases of extreme class imbalance, it might be more effective to approach the problem as one of anomaly detection rather than as a traditional classification problem. Chapters 13 and 14 provide in-depth explorations of this approach, where you will dive into the nuances of anomaly detection and its application in fraud analytics.

Different Approaches for Dealing with an Imbalanced Dataset

As discussed earlier in this chapter, imbalanced datasets present a unique challenge in the field of data analytics, particularly in applications where the outcome of interest is infrequent, such as in cases of fraud detection. A range of methodologies have been discussed to tackle this imbalance, ensuring that the predictive models maintain sensitivity to the less prevalent yet significant minority class.

This section introduces additional strategies, including class weight balancing, and provides insights into their practical application and efficacy in the context of fraud detection.

Leveraging Class Weight Balancing in Fraud Detection

Class weight balancing is an important technique when dealing with imbalanced datasets, such as fraud detection. In fraud detection, legitimate transactions (the majority class) typically outnumber fraudulent transactions (the minority class) by a large margin. This imbalance can lead to models that are biased toward predicting the majority class, resulting in poor performance in identifying fraudulent transactions.

Class weight balancing involves adjusting the weights of the classes in the cost function that the model optimizes. By assigning higher weights to the minority class (fraudulent transactions), misclassifying a fraudulent transaction incurs a higher penalty during training, forcing the model to pay more attention to the minority class.

Class weight balancing offers a strategic approach to handling imbalanced datasets in fraud detection. By adjusting the weights of classes during model training, it seeks to improve the model's sensitivity toward the minority class:

- It helps the model to focus more on the minority class (fraudulent transactions) without the need for oversampling or under-sampling.
- It's computationally efficient as it doesn't require the creation of synthetic samples or removal of existing samples.

Despite its advantages, class weight balancing also presents certain challenges that need consideration. The method may sometimes require fine-tuning and might not be compatible with all algorithms:

- The choice of class weights might require tuning to find the optimal balance.
- Some algorithms might not provide options for class weight adjustments.

The following code sets up a RandomForestClassifier with class weights adjusted to be balanced, which can help when dealing with imbalanced datasets.

```
from sklearn.ensemble import RandomForestClassifier

# Instantiate the classifier with balanced class weights
clf = RandomForestClassifier(n_estimators=100, class_weight='balanced')

# Train the classifier
clf.fit(X_train, y_train)
```

Comparative Analysis: SMOTE vs. Class Weight Balancing

The comparison between SMOTE and class weight balancing can be elucidated along several dimensions. In terms of *data alteration*, SMOTE addresses class imbalance by generating synthetic samples for the minority class, augmenting the original dataset. In contrast, class weight balancing modifies the cost function during model training to emphasize the minority class without altering the dataset itself.

When considering *computational complexity*, SMOTE can be more demanding as it creates new synthetic instances, leading to an increase in the size of the training set and potentially longer training times. On the other hand, class weight balancing is usually more computationally efficient as it doesn't increase the dataset size and simply adjusts the learning process to be more sensitive to the minority class.

Regarding flexibility, SMOTE is versatile and can be applied to any dataset before training, regardless of the algorithm used. In contrast, class weight balancing might be limited to certain algorithms that allow for the adjustment of class weights.

In *practice*, the choice between SMOTE and class weight balancing depends on various factors, such as dataset characteristics, the problem domain, and available computational resources. It can be beneficial to experiment with both methods, evaluating the model's performance to determine which approach is more suitable for a specific task.

Both methods have found successful applications in various fields, such as fraud detection, where addressing class imbalance is crucial for model performance. In *real-world scenarios*, while both SMOTE and class weight balancing offer unique advantages, it's essential to consider the context and requirements of the task to make an informed decision on the most appropriate method to use.

SIDEBAR

Optimizing Gradient Boosting Algorithms for Handling Imbalanced Datasets

XGBoost and LightGBM are advanced implementations of gradient boosting algorithms that have built-in features to handle imbalanced datasets, but they do not handle imbalanced datasets by default. You need to configure them properly to tackle the imbalance issue. Here's how they can be adjusted:

XGBoost has a parameter called `scale_pos_weight`, which helps balance the positive and negative weights. It's used to scale the gradient for the positive class (minority class) and is typically set to the inverse of the class ratio. For example, if you have a dataset with 20 times more negative classes than positive classes, you would set `scale_pos_weight` to 20.

Additionally, XGBoost allows for custom objective functions where you can implement your own logic to handle imbalances, such as creating a cost-sensitive objective function.

LightGBM also provides a similar parameter called `is_unbalance` or `scale_pos_weight` to deal with imbalanced data.

When `is_unbalance` is set to true, LightGBM will automatically adjust weights inversely proportional to class frequencies in the input data, which is a quick way to manage imbalance.

The `scale_pos_weight` can be used to set the weight for the positive class manually.

Both XGBoost and LightGBM also support weighted datasets directly, where you can assign a higher weight to the minority class instances in your training set.

Additional strategies for XGBoost and LightGBM:

- *Custom loss functions:* Both frameworks allow you to define custom loss functions more sensitive to the minority class.
- *Early stopping*: Use early stopping to prevent the model from overfitting to the majority class.
- *Hyperparameter tuning:* Optimize hyperparameters that control the model complexity, such as `max_depth`, `min_child_weight`, and gamma in XGBoost or `min_data_in_leaf` and `min_sum_hessian_in_leaf` in LightGBM.
- *Ensemble methods*: Combining models using different resampling techniques can sometimes yield better results.

While XGBoost and LightGBM have parameters to help with imbalanced datasets, it's important to note that simply setting these parameters is not always sufficient. You should still consider employing additional techniques like resampling or using appropriate evaluation metrics to ensure that your model is handling the imbalance effectively. It's also crucial to validate the model's performance with cross-validation and on a separate test set to ensure it generalizes well to unseen data.

Adjusting Posterior Probability Estimates

In machine learning classification, models often rely on posterior probability estimations. These models gauge class posterior probabilities and then select the class with the highest probability for the final prediction. However, these estimates might not always be accurate or beneficial for predictions, especially in datasets with imbalanced class distributions. In such cases, the model might exhibit a bias toward the majority class, leading to skewed posterior probability estimates. To counteract this, adjusting the posterior probabilities becomes essential, aiming to align the estimates more with the actual class distribution or to enhance the model's sensitivity to the minority class.

Several techniques can be employed to adjust these probabilities:

- *Threshold moving*: Typically, in binary classification, a threshold of 0.5 is set. If the estimated posterior probability for the positive class surpasses this threshold, the instance is classified as positive. However, by adjusting this threshold, say to 0.3, the classifier becomes more attuned to the minority class. While this can increase sensitivity, it might also elevate the false-positive rate.
- *Resampling techniques*: Oversampling and under-sampling adjust the class distribution in the training data, indirectly influencing the posterior probability estimates. Oversampling replicates minority class instances, whereas under-sampling reduces majority class instances, aiming to diminish the model's majority class bias.
- *Cost-sensitive learning*: Here, different misclassification costs are assigned to classes. The model is then optimized to minimize the overall misclassification cost, making it more receptive to classes with higher misclassification costs.
- *Calibration methods*: Platt scaling and isotonic regression recalibrate the posterior probabilities. They fit either a sigmoid function or a non-decreasing function to the estimated probabilities, refining them to mirror true probabilities more closely.

Incorporating techniques like SMOTE for oversampling can alter class priors, potentially leading to biased classifier outcomes. As highlighted by Saerens et al. (2002), adjusting the probability estimates can address this. When class priors change, it aids machine learning algorithms in differentiating between classes, such as fraudsters and non-fraudsters. While these adjustments might skew class posteriors, it's less of an issue if the primary goal is to rank observations based on their risk. However, for well-calibrated fraud probabilities, posterior probabilities need recalibration. A straightforward method employs the formula:

$$p'(x) = pt(x) \times p(Ci)/pt(Ci)$$

Here, $p'(x)$ denotes the adjusted posterior probability for observation x belonging to class Ci.

This formula rectifies the biased predictions resulting from resampling techniques or methods like SMOTE and ROSE. It bolsters classification performance in datasets that demand well-calibrated fraud probability.

Although adjusting posterior probabilities can be beneficial, it's not universally applicable. The necessity and impact depend on the dataset, the model, and the problem at hand. Furthermore, using a separate validation dataset to validate any adjustments is paramount to avoiding overfitting.

> WARNING
>
> When employing sampling techniques such as SMOTE, under-sampling, or oversampling for class imbalance correction, ensure that these methods are applied only to the training portion of your dataset, not the testing part. Such techniques are crucial for balancing class distribution in the training data, thereby enhancing the model's learning from underrepresented classes. However, modifying the test set with these sampling methods can lead to a misrepresentation of real-world data distribution and, consequently, to misleading evaluation results. The test set should remain as a true representation of real-world data for an accurate assessment of the model's performance.

Summary

This chapter looked closely at the challenges posed by imbalanced data sets and the methodologies employed to handle them. These data sets, where one class significantly outnumbers the other, are common in areas such as fraud detection and rare disease diagnosis. Such imbalances can lead to biased machine learning models that give priority to the majority class and disregard the minority class.

Various techniques to address data imbalances were discussed. These included resampling methods, cost-sensitive learning, ensemble methods, transfer learning, and hybrid methods. Each approach has its benefits and limitations, along with appropriate use cases.

Practical examples and case studies reinforced the theoretical concepts, demonstrating how these techniques can be effectively used to manage imbalanced datasets. Now, a comprehensive understanding of imbalanced datasets, their impact on machine learning models, and a set of techniques to handle these challenges should be at your disposal.

The foundation laid in Chapter 9 paves the way to applying these concepts in Chapter 10. This upcoming chapter provides practical examples of data preparation, including projects that employ machine learning techniques in real scenarios.

The first lab project in Chapter 10 revolves around analyzing human resources data, performing data wrangling, and exploratory data analysis (EDA) using Pandas.

The final lab project offers an in-depth credit card transaction dataset analysis. This project applies machine learning techniques to detect fraudulent transactions, a significant concern in today's digital world.

In Chapter 10, datasets will be imported, EDA performed, class imbalances addressed, data prepared for machine learning, and model performance evaluated. By the end of this chapter, a holistic understanding of the practical aspects of data preparation and analysis should be attained.

CHAPTER 10

Data Preparation for Fraud Analytics: Lab Projects

Building upon the theoretical knowledge acquired so far, this chapter brings the opportunity to dive into hands-on applications and practical examples in data preparation. The chapter introduces two distinct projects, each focusing on a different aspect of data analysis.

You will begin with a project centered on analyzing human resources data. Utilizing the IBM HR analytics employee attrition and performance dataset, this project provides a platform to exercise data wrangling skills and perform a comprehensive exploratory data analysis (EDA) using Pandas, a powerful open-source data analysis tool in Python. The goal is to delve deep into various factors influencing employee behavior and performance, extracting actionable insights and understanding employee dynamics.

As a significant undertaking of this chapter, the final capstone project shifts attention to the crucial issue of credit card fraud detection. This task involves an in-depth analysis of a credit card transaction dataset, applying machine learning techniques to identify fraudulent transactions among a sea of legitimate ones. The analysis dives into the intricacies of the dataset, addressing class imbalances, preparing the data for machine learning, and evaluating the performance of trained models.

Both projects encourage active engagement with datasets, guiding you through importing and understanding the data, performing EDA, addressing class imbalances, preparing the data for machine learning, and

A. Al Aqqad, *Fraud Analytics in Action*
https://doi.org/10.1007/978-3-032-16023-2_10

finally, evaluating the performance of trained models. By the end of the chapter, a more profound, practical understanding of data preparation and analysis in real-world scenarios should be achieved, transitioning learned concepts from abstract ideas into tangible skills.

Lab Project: In-Depth Analysis of Human Resources Data

The business landscape today is increasingly driven by data, with employee attrition and performance metrics standing out as key areas of focus. This project offers a deep dive into the IBM HR Analytics dataset to unearth patterns that influence employee turnover and productivity. By leveraging Python's Pandas library, you are tasked with conducting a detailed analysis to extract meaningful insights from complex employee data.

Approaching the HR Dataset

In this lab, you will engage with the HR dataset, delving into the myriad facets of employee relationships and performance indicators. You will cleanse and curate the data, ensuring its integrity, and transform it into a form that is primed for detailed analysis. Your mission includes the following tasks:

- Conducting statistical analysis on HR data to surface insightful trends.
- Handling missing data to preserve the dataset's completeness.
- Implementing one-hot encoding for categorical data to facilitate modeling.
- Scaling numerical data through normalization and standardization.
- Utilizing advanced Pandas operations and filters to refine the dataset.
- Computing correlation matrices and constructing heatmaps to visualize the interconnections within the data.

Lab access: I invite you to embark on this analytical journey and explore the intricacies of human resources data. To start your exploration, click here for lab access, and go ahead and complete the lab.

Post-Lab Insights

Upon concluding the lab, you have traversed the complexities of the IBM HR analytics dataset, starting with the importation of data, moving through the meticulous examination of its structure, and addressing missing values by imputation to avoid the loss of valuable information.

Your journey continued with the transformation of categorical data through one-hot encoding and the careful scaling of numerical data to ensure comparability across all metrics.

With custom functions and targeted Pandas operations, you refined the dataset, and through the computation of correlation matrices followed by heatmap visualizations, you illuminated the intricate relationships among various factors.

As a result of this project, you have gained a nuanced understanding of employee dynamics and the factors that drive attrition and performance. You have seen first-hand how data visualization can paint a vivid picture of the interplay between different elements, guiding you to informed conclusions about workforce management.

The skills you have honed in transforming HR data into actionable insights are not just an academic exercise but a potent tool in the corporate world, enhancing your ability to make data-driven decisions.

Lab Project: Credit Card Transaction Analysis

In this culminating project, you will dive into a dataset encompassing 5,050 credit card transactions, differentiating between legitimate and fraudulent activities. With 50 fraudulent and 5,000 legitimate cases, each transaction is detailed by 30 features (V1–V28, Amount, and Class), where V1–V28 are anonymized predictors, Amount reflects the transaction's value, and Class indicates a transaction's legitimacy. Your mission is to employ machine learning to detect fraud, sharpening your analytical prowess on this critical task in financial security.

Approaching Credit Card Fraud Detection

In this detailed investigation, you are tasked with extracting clarity from the complex dataset, shedding light on the subtleties of fraudulent behavior. To achieve this, you will:

1. *Dataset exploration:* Initiate your analysis by loading the dataset and conducting exploratory data analysis to understand its structure and distribution.
2. *Class imbalance assessment:* Gauge the extent of imbalance between fraudulent and non-fraudulent transactions to inform subsequent data processing strategies.
3. *Data preprocessing:* Engage in normalization and oversampling to counteract class imbalance and refine your dataset for predictive modeling.
4. *Predictive modeling:* Divide the dataset, train a classifier, like a Random Forest, and validate its performance using precision, recall, and AUC-ROC metrics.
5. *Model optimization:* Test various algorithms to enhance your model, seeking out the most effective method for identifying fraudulent transactions.

Data source: Kaggle's Credit Card Fraud Detection dataset is your playground for this exercise.

Lab access: Click here to embark on your capstone project.

Post-Lab Insights

After deep dives into the credit card transaction dataset and applying machine learning finesse, you made significant strides in distinguishing fraud. The RandomForestClassifier emerged as a robust tool, boasting precision in identifying both fraudulent and non-fraudulent transactions. However, its recall for fraudulent transactions fell short, missing some fraudulent activities. The logistic regression model, while perfect in recall, was prone to false positives, highlighting the delicate balance between sensitivity and specificity in fraud detection.

To further refine your fraud detection toolkit, consider the following enhancements:

- Address the class imbalance more effectively to give the models a fair representation of both classes.
- Explore a broader spectrum of machine learning algorithms, perhaps venturing into deep learning territories.

- Integrate cost-sensitive learning to prioritize the cost of misclassification, especially for fraudulent transactions.
- Augment the dataset with new features that may offer additional insights into transaction authenticity.
- Regularly update and retrain the models to adapt to new fraudulent tactics.
- Engage domain experts in iterative feedback loops to align model predictions with real-world complexities.
- Experiment with unsupervised and semi-supervised learning models to detect anomalies in transaction patterns.

Implementing these strategies can sharpen your detection capabilities, making your system an unwavering sentinel against credit card fraud.

Summary

This chapter enabled you to explore data preparation with practical example lab projects based on human resources analysis and credit card transaction analysis. The chapter explored the IBM HR analytics dataset using data wrangling and EDA with Pandas. Then it shifted to a capstone project on credit card fraud detection using machine learning techniques. The chapter concluded by discussing improvements and recommendations for fraud detection processes.

The chapters in the next three parts of the book explore data-driven techniques for fraud detection, covering unsupervised learning, supervised learning approaches, and social network analysis. You will learn how machine learning models can outperform traditional rule-based systems in detecting fraud. By the end of Part 5, you will have gained insights into crafting a comprehensive fraud detection system using these approaches.

PART III

Unsupervised Learning for Fraud Detection

One of the most persistent challenges in fraud analytics is the absence of labelled data. In many real-world settings, organisations cannot reliably distinguish past fraudulent transactions from legitimate ones—whether because fraud went undetected, records were incomplete, or schemes were too new to have generated confirmed cases. Supervised models, which depend on labelled examples to learn from, cannot operate effectively under these conditions. Unsupervised learning can. By identifying structure, patterns, and deviations within data without requiring predefined labels, unsupervised techniques offer a powerful entry point for fraud detection—and a critical complement to the supervised approaches introduced in Part IV. Their particular strength lies in uncovering anomalies and hidden groupings that deviate from normal behaviour, making them especially valuable for detecting emerging or previously unseen fraud patterns. Part III covers this approach across two focused chapters. Chapter 11 introduces the core techniques of unsupervised learning—including anomaly detection, principal component analysis (PCA), and the foundational concepts that distinguish this family of methods from supervised and rule-based approaches—examining how each can be applied to surface suspicious behaviour in fraud datasets. Chapter 12 narrows the focus to clustering, exploring how algorithms such as K-means group transactions and entities by similarity, enabling analysts to identify irregular segments that warrant further investigation. Together, these chapters equip you with the tools to find fraud signals even when no one has told the model what fraud looks like.

CHAPTER 11

Unsupervised Learning Techniques

This chapter introduces unsupervised learning, a crucial tool for fraud detection in contexts where labeled data is not readily available. The chapter presents a detailed exploration of diverse unsupervised learning techniques and their applications. Anomaly detection, for example, is used to spot irregular patterns in financial transactions that stand out from usual activity, potentially signaling fraud. Dimension reduction techniques are highlighted for their ability to distill complex data into simpler forms, uncovering covert patterns indicative of fraudulent schemes in voluminous datasets. Market basket analysis is discussed for its utility in identifying unusual item combinations in transactions that could hint at fraud, while clustering is shown to be effective in grouping similar transactions to unearth suspicious activities.

Real-world examples bring these concepts to life. Credit card companies utilize anomaly detection to monitor for purchases that diverge significantly from a customer's typical spending habits, potentially pointing to card theft or unauthorized transactions. Banks may employ dimension reduction to navigate through vast numbers of transactions in search of atypical patterns that suggest intricate fraud. E-commerce platforms leverage market basket analysis to detect improbable purchase patterns that may indicate compromised accounts. Insurance companies use clustering to categorize claims, aiding in the detection of patterns that could suggest fraudulent claims.

A. Al Aqqad, *Fraud Analytics in Action*
https://doi.org/10.1007/978-3-032-16023-2_11

The chapter continues with an overview of anomaly detection techniques like the Isolation Forest or one-class SVMs, which are critical for isolating irregular transactions. It delves into *association rule mining*, illustrating how algorithms such as Apriori or Eclat can uncover concealed fraudulent patterns within transaction data. Clustering algorithms like K-means and DBSCAN are discussed for their role in grouping transactions and aiding in fraud detection. The discussion extends to the application of Benford's Law in identifying financial fraud by recognizing unnatural data distributions.

By the end of this chapter, you should possess a deep understanding of these unsupervised learning methods. More importantly, you should appreciate the practicality of these methods in the real world, where they are applied to detect and mitigate fraud across different sectors. The chapter emphasizes the value of these techniques in enhancing the capabilities of organizations to safeguard against fraudulent activities, underscoring the adaptability and potency of unsupervised learning in the ongoing battle against fraud.

Fraud Detection Without Labels: Unsupervised Learning Approaches

Unsupervised learning operates without explicit supervision and is a pivotal category of machine learning (ML) techniques. It is especially useful in scenarios like fraud detection. USL allows models to autonomously uncover hidden patterns, relationships, and structures within datasets that lack predetermined labels. This attribute is particularly beneficial in detecting fraudulent activities, as it enables the revelation of such activities without prior knowledge of their characteristics.

In the realm of machine learning, the terms X and y usually denote the features and labels of a dataset, with X representing the *input* data used to train models in supervised learning and y symbolizing the output data that the model is tasked with predicting. In fraud detection, X might encompass features such as transaction amounts, the number of transactions, and transaction times. However, unlike supervised learning, where y would indicate whether each transaction is fraudulent, unsupervised learning lacks this component. The absence of y in unsupervised learning signifies that the data is unlabeled, and the goal shifts to inferring the natural structure present within the data points.

When it comes to fraud detection, unsupervised learning begins with a selection of features that describe the transactions. These features form the X dataset, which does not include labels to indicate fraudulent transactions. From here, algorithms strive to learn the data structure without labels, which may involve identifying clusters of similar transactions, detecting anomalies, or reducing the dimensionality of the data. Fraudulent transactions, being relatively rare, may manifest as anomalies. Algorithms like K-Means clustering, DBSCAN, or isolation forest are employed to detect such outliers on the premise that fraudulent transactions will exhibit different characteristics compared to legitimate ones.

The challenge of detecting fraud using unsupervised learning stems from the absence of reliable labels to validate the model's results, making it a complex process that often exceeds the complexity of supervised learning. Despite this, such an approach is valuable in numerous fraud detection cases where labeled data is not available. The anomalies identified by the algorithms need to be investigated by domain experts to determine their legitimacy, underscoring the importance of human expertise in interpreting results and verifying potential fraud. The next section discusses some of the most prevalent unsupervised learning techniques.

WARNING

The main difference between supervised and unsupervised learning lies in the type of data they deal with. Supervised learning works with *labeled* data, enabling tasks such as classification and regression, while unsupervised learning deals with *unlabeled* data, with clustering being a prime example of its methods. While supervised learning offers a variety of models and evaluation techniques to ensure accuracy, unsupervised learning provides a less predictable environment as the machine determines outcomes autonomously, making it more challenging but equally fascinating.

Anomaly Detection Techniques

Anomaly detection finds unique patterns that defy expectations and can be beneficial for fraud detection, system health monitoring, and defect detection. For instance, in credit card fraud detection, unusual activities, such as a card being used in a different location than usual or a sudden surge in high-value transactions, may be flagged as suspicious. Similarly, in insurance, a policyholder who suddenly files multiple high-value claims after years of no claims might raise suspicions. In e-commerce, accounts making bulk purchases of high-end electronics or rapid purchases of gift cards may be deemed unusual.

In the context of banking and account takeovers, multiple login attempts during unusual hours or rapid changes to account credentials can be indicative of suspicious activity. Mobile and online payment systems may flag accounts that typically make small retail payments but suddenly engage in large transfers to unfamiliar accounts. Tax return fraud may be suspected in cases of sudden changes in reported income or large deductions that do not align with an individual's previous returns.

Telecom fraud may involve phone numbers that suddenly show a spike in international calls, especially to high-risk countries, or a sudden increase in data or SMS consumption. Supply chain and invoice fraud detection may involve flagging businesses that place large orders for unrelated products or new supplier invoices with round-number quantities or unusual order patterns.

In all these cases, anomaly detection is a tool to preemptively identify potentially fraudulent activities by recognizing patterns that significantly deviate from established behaviors.

Unsupervised Anomaly Detection Techniques

Unsupervised anomaly detection techniques focus on identifying unusual patterns that do not conform to expected behavior. Such methods are invaluable for tasks like fraud detection, system health monitoring, and fault detection. Among the techniques and algorithms employed for anomaly detection are several noteworthy approaches:

- *Statistical methods* serve as foundational techniques that assess the statistical properties of datasets. General approaches consider any data point significantly deviating from the mean or median as a potential anomaly, with methods such as the Z-score or the interquartile range (IQR) being common.
- *Univariate anomaly detection using robust statistics* deals with detecting anomalies in a single variable or feature, where patterns within one attribute are considered independently of others. Techniques might involve using measures like the median *or* IQR, which are less susceptible to extreme values. For instance, anomalies in credit card spending might be detected by only considering the spending amount while ignoring factors like location or type of purchase.

- *Multivariate anomaly detection using robust statistics*, in contrast, considers multiple attributes simultaneously. Anomalies in this context might appear normal when variables are considered individually but can be detected when multiple variables are considered together. Techniques such as the minimum covariance determinant (MCD) method provide robust estimators of multivariate location and scatter. For example, monitoring transactions by looking at both the amount spent and the location of the purchase can help identify anomalies that wouldn't be apparent when considering these variables separately.
- *Isolation Forest* is an algorithm that isolates anomalies instead of profiling normal data points, operating on the principle that anomalies are data points that are few and different and thus easier to "isolate" than normal points. *One-class support vector machine (SVM)*, usually used for classification tasks, can be employed in a one-class mode to find the best boundary that separates data points in a high-dimensional space. *The local outlier factor (LOF)* calculates the local density deviation of a data point with respect to its neighbors, considering both the density of a point and its neighbors to classify it as an inlier or outlier.

Methods like Isolation Forest or one-class SVMs excel at identifying data points that significantly deviate from the norm. Such anomalies could suggest fraudulent activities distinct from typical transactions or behaviors. By flagging these unusual data points, analysts can investigate further to ascertain if they indicate fraud.

Example: Isolation Forest for Credit Card Fraud Detection

A bank aims to enhance its fraud detection system by examining transaction data to pinpoint potential credit card fraud. The bank intends to utilize unsupervised machine learning techniques to spot anomalous transactions, which may indicate fraudulent activities.

The primary objective is to apply the Isolation Forest algorithm to the credit card transaction data to flag potentially fraudulent transactions for further investigation.

The bank provides a dataset containing credit card transaction information. The dataset includes the following columns (see Table 11.1):

- Transaction ID
- Transaction Time
- Transaction Amount
- Location
- Merchant Details

A small sample of the dataset is shown in Table 11.1.

The isolation forest algorithm operates under the premise that anomalies are data points that are uncommon and distinctly different from normal transactions. By leveraging this perspective, the algorithm can identify unusual patterns that could be symptomatic of fraudulent activities.

Upon implementing the Isolation Forest algorithm, the transactions are assigned an anomaly score. Transactions that procure high anomaly scores are flagged as potential frauds. For instance, the algorithm could flag the transactions in Table 11.2.

In this situation, transaction 3 has obtained a high anomaly score, suggesting a significant deviation from the norm. This transaction could indicate fraudulent behavior, such as an unauthorized purchase, warranting further investigation by the bank.

By employing the Isolation Forest algorithm on credit card transaction data, the bank can flag potential fraudulent transactions for additional examination. This approach can considerably fortify the bank's fraud

Table 11.1 Dataset: Isolation Forest for credit card fraud detection

Transaction ID	*Transaction time*	*Transaction amount*	*Location*	*Merchant details*
1	2023 March 15 09:15:32	150	New York	Electronics store
2	2023 March 15 11:45:18	75	New York	Supermarket
3	2023 March 15 14:33:07	2000	Los Angeles	Luxury boutique
4	2023 March 15 16:21:50	20	New York	Coffee shop
5	2023 March 15 19:10:15	80	New York	Restaurant

Table 11.2 Example of a high-risk transaction identified by the isolation forest algorithm

Transaction ID	*Transaction time*	*Transaction amount*	*Location*	*Merchant details*	*Anomaly score*
3	2023 March 15 14:33:07	2000.00	Los Angeles	Luxury boutique	0.85

This table illustrates a transaction flagged by the Isolation Forest algorithm as potentially fraudulent. The anomaly score of 0.85 indicates a strong deviation from typical transaction behavior, suggesting that this purchase—recorded in Los Angeles at a luxury boutique—may represent an unauthorized or suspicious activity requiring further investigation

detection system, enabling it to identify and address fraudulent activities more promptly.

Dimensionality Reduction Techniques

After we find something odd in the data, the next question is why. Fraud data can have hundreds of details—numbers, times, locations, customer traits. Looking at all of them at once is like trying to read a whole library in one sitting. So, we shrink the story. That's what dimensionality reduction does—it keeps the important chapters and removes the clutter.

Think of it as turning noise into a picture. Instead of hundreds of messy columns, we create just a few powerful views that show how transactions relate to each other. Tools like PCA, t-SNE, or autoencoders do the heavy lifting—they compress the data so patterns start to appear.

Why It Matters in Fraud Detection

In most fraud datasets, not every feature carries value. Some add noise, some overlap, and some simply distract. Dimensionality reduction acts as a spotlight—focusing the model on what truly matters. It improves accuracy, speeds up training, and reduces overfitting by removing redundant variables.

Even better, it helps us see what we couldn't before by shrinking a big, messy dataset into two or three simple views, so hidden groups and lonely points pop out—and those lonely points are often real warnings. Because this process also cuts noise, the model can focus on the real signals, which means cleaner data, faster training, and better results.

Techniques in Action

- *Principal Component Analysis (PCA) highlights features with the most variance—the key ingredients that explain most behavior. In fraud detection, these components often reveal hidden correlations or subtle shifts that signal manipulation.*
- *Autoencoders serve a dual role. They learn compact internal representations of data and, through reconstruction error, can flag anomalies that don't fit the learned pattern.*
- *t-SNE excels at visualization by preserving local relationships, allowing analysts to spot natural groupings or outliers in two-dimensional plots.*
- *Linear Discriminant Analysis (LDA), although technically supervised, is useful when partial labels exist, as it maximizes separability between genuine and fraudulent cases.*
- *Feature Agglomeration groups similar attributes, adapting models to evolving fraud tactics by merging features that behave alike.*

Practical Example

Imagine a bank analyzing thousands of loan applications. By applying **LDA**, the bank can highlight the most discriminative features—say, income-to-loan ratio or application timing—creating a clearer boundary between legitimate and suspicious applications. The result: faster screening, fewer false positives, and more confident decision-making.

Challenges to Watch

Simplifying data has trade-offs. Methods like PCA can make things harder to explain, because the new "axes" don't always have clear meanings. And if we shrink too much, we might throw away real fraud signals. That's why standardizing the data, testing settings carefully, and checking results with domain experts are essential before trusting the output.

The Bigger Picture

When we combine a few dimensionality reduction tools, the view gets sharper. Noise turns into a clear picture, slow work turns into quick insight, and confusion turns into discovery. This helps fraud teams spot new, evolving schemes early—before they spread.

Market Basket Analysis

Market Basket Analysis (MBA) started in retail, where it's used to see what products customers often buy together. But its power goes far beyond shopping carts—the same logic can uncover hidden relationships in transactions that may point to fraudulent behavior. At its core, MBA relies on association rule learning, a method that finds "if → then" patterns in big datasets. Algorithms such as Apriori and FP-Growth scan thousands of records to spot strong connections between variables.

In retail, this produced the famous "diapers → beer" rule: shoppers buying diapers were often found purchasing beer as well. When applied to fraud detection, the story changes but the logic stays the same. The rules might reveal that high-value transactions combined with express shipping or new accounts linked to multiple refunds occur together more often than chance would allow. Those links become red flags that invite deeper review.

In this way, MBA turns from a retail marketing tool into an early warning system for suspicious activity. It helps analysts see combinations of behavior that would look harmless on their own but become meaningful when viewed together.

Example: Apriori Algorithm for Market Basket Analysis in a Grocery Store

Consider a bank that wants to analyze its transaction data to identify potentially fraudulent activities. The objective is to apply the Apriori algorithm to the bank's transaction dataset to uncover relationships and patterns indicative of fraud.

The bank's transaction dataset (see Table 11.3) contains attributes such as transaction ID, items purchased, transaction amount, and so on. By applying the Apriori algorithm with a suitable minimum support

Table 11.3 Identifying fraudulent patterns using the Apriori algorithm in bank transactions

Transaction ID	*Account age (days)*	*Transaction amount (USD)*	*Transaction type*
1	10	5000	Online purchase
2	365	100	In-store purchase
3	7	4500	Online purchase
4	1000	150	In-store purchase
5	15	4800	Online purchase

threshold and confidence threshold, the bank can identify frequent item sets and generate association rules that might point to fraud.

For instance, the algorithm might uncover the rule that a sudden surge in transaction amounts is strongly associated with newly opened accounts, which could be a red flag for fraud.

Association rules such as *account age → high transaction amounts* with high confidence could indicate potentially fraudulent behavior. The bank can use this information to flag such transactions for further investigation, thereby preventing potential fraud.

In this manner, techniques like MBA, traditionally used in retail, can be effectively repurposed for fraud detection, offering organizations a means to safeguard against fraudulent activities while ensuring legitimate transactions proceed unhindered.

When applying data mining techniques like the Apriori algorithm in fraud detection, understanding the concept of frequent itemsets is crucial. A *frequent itemset* is a combination of items (in this context, attributes of transactions) that occur together frequently in a dataset. For instance, by using the Apriori algorithm, let's say a bank identifies certain frequent itemsets with a minimum support threshold of 0.4 (40%). This means these combinations of items appear in at least 40% of all transactions analyzed. An example of such an item could be {Online Purchase, High Transaction Amount}, which has been found to occur together in 60% of the transactions.

The algorithm then progresses to generate association rules from these frequent itemsets. These rules are formed with a confidence level above a minimum threshold, say 0.6 (60%). For example, one such rule could be New Account → High Transaction Amount, with a confidence level of 0.75 (75%). This rule implies that there is a 75% chance that transactions involving high amounts are linked with newly opened accounts, considering an account age of less than 30 days as new. Such a pattern is significant in fraud detection, as it could indicate a potential red flag. Newly opened accounts engaging in high-value transactions might be suggestive of malicious intent.

Equipped with this information, the bank can take proactive steps to mitigate fraud risks. For instance, it could implement additional verification measures for transactions that fit this pattern. This approach helps in curbing fraudulent activities while ensuring that legitimate transactions proceed smoothly and efficiently. By analyzing frequent itemsets and the resulting association rules, banks and other financial institutions can enhance their fraud detection capabilities, making their systems more secure and reliable.

Example: Eclat Algorithm for Identifying Fraud Patterns in an Online Store

Lately, an online store has seen more chargebacks. The business management fears some customers are using stolen credit cards or exploiting return policy loopholes. They want to study transaction data for fraud patterns.

The objective is to apply the Eclat algorithm to the store's transaction dataset to uncover relationships and patterns between items purchased and high chargeback rates, which might suggest a specific type of fraud.

The online store has a transaction dataset (see Table 11.4) containing the following attributes:

- Transaction ID
- Items Purchased
- Chargeback (Yes/No)

Sample Data

By applying the Eclat algorithm, let's say the store identifies the following frequent itemsets with a minimum support threshold of 0.4 (40%):

Table 11.4 Dataset: Eclat algorithm for identifying fraud patterns in an online store

Transaction ID	*Items purchased*	*Chargeback*
1	Laptop, mouse, keyboard	No
2	Smartphone, charger, earphones	Yes
3	Laptop, printer, ink	No
4	Smartphone, screen protector	Yes
5	Laptop, mouse, headphones	No

1. {Smartphone, Charger, Earphones, Chargeback: Yes} with a support of 0.4 (40%)
2. {Smartphone, Screen Protector, Chargeback: Yes} with a support of 0.4 (40%)

The algorithm then identifies association rules indicating high chargeback rates:

1. {Smartphone, Charger, Earphones} → {Chargeback: Yes} with a support of 0.4 (40%)
2. {Smartphone, Screen Protector} → {Chargeback: Yes} with a support of 0.4 (40%)

In this example, the rules suggest that transactions involving smartphones and their accessories (chargers, screen protectors, and earphones) are more likely to result in chargebacks. This could indicate potential fraudulent behavior, such as using stolen credit cards or exploiting return policy loopholes.

The online store can use this information to implement additional security measures for smartphone transactions and related accessories. For instance, they could introduce additional verification steps or closely monitor such transactions for signs of suspicious activity. By doing so, the store can mitigate fraud risk and ensure a seamless experience for genuine customers.

Density Estimation

Density estimation is an approach focused on exploring data to discern its underlying structure. It is a foundational step in many machine learning tasks, helping to determine data distribution. In fraud detection, density estimation can be used in various ways. For instance, financial institutions might analyze the distribution of transaction amounts to identify unusually large or small transactions that could indicate fraud. Online platforms may study the distribution of user login times, where an unusual density of logins during off-peak hours might signal bot activity or unauthorized access. Insurance companies can use density estimation to understand the distribution of claim amounts or the frequency of claims by a single entity, with outliers potentially indicating fraudulent claims. Similarly, a high density of credit applications from a single source in a short time might be considered suspicious by financial institutions. E-commerce platforms might analyze the distribution of purchase frequencies from a single account, where a sudden spike could indicate an account takeover or fraudulent activities.

Several techniques are used for density estimation:

- A *histogram* is useful for getting a quick overview of data distribution, such as by visualizing transaction amounts to highlight unusual transactions.
- *Kernel density estimation (KDE)* can smooth out transaction data to identify unusual peaks or troughs indicating fraud.
- *Parametric estimation* is applied when certain transaction behaviors are known to follow a specific distribution, helping to fit the data and identify anomalies.
- The *Gaussian mixture model (GMM)* is useful when fraudulent and legitimate transactions might follow different distributions, helping segregate these distributions.
- *Neural network-based density estimation*, such as variational autoencoders (VAEs), can be used to understand complex transaction patterns and identify potential fraud.

Clustering

Clustering is an indispensable technique in the data analysis arsenal, leveraging the power of similarity to segment and group data points. This method finds its application across various domains, from refining customer profiles in the banking sector to categorizing diverse music libraries. Its utility spans structure discovery, effective data summarization, and the crucial task of anomaly detection. The most prevalent clustering algorithms include K-Means, hierarchical clustering, and DBSCAN, each with its unique approach to grouping data.

Within the sphere of fraud detection, clustering emerges as a key strategy for sifting through data to isolate patterns that may signify fraudulent behavior. For example, in a cluster of bank transactions—those that feature anomalous characteristics such as abnormally high values, repeated occurrences from a single source, or timings that deviate from the norm—could point to fraudulent activities. These insights form a core part of Chapter 12 "Clustering for Fraud Detection", which discusses the specifics of utilizing clustering for detecting fraud.

The following sections illustrate the practical application of clustering in various fraud detection contexts.

Credit Card Fraud Detection with K-Means Clustering

A bank might deploy K-means clustering to categorize credit card transactions by attributes such as transaction amount, time, and merchant category. Post-clustering, a distinct group of high-value transactions might emerge, clustered due to their occurrence at atypical hours and association with high-risk merchants like online gambling sites. This could raise red flags, prompting further scrutiny of these transactions to confirm or dispel suspicions of credit card fraud.

Insurance Claims Fraud Detection with DBSCAN

An insurance company might use DBSCAN to analyze clusters in auto insurance claims, considering factors such as claim amount, frequency of claims, and nature of the reported damage. A dense cluster of claims with suspiciously high amounts for minor damages or claims filed in quick succession might be identified. Such a pattern could suggest a scheme of inflated or repetitive false claims, signaling the need for a deeper dive into these particular cases.

Social Network Fraud Detection with Hierarchical Clustering

A social media platform could employ hierarchical clustering to examine user accounts based on metrics like friend counts, posting behavior, and follower ratios. The algorithm might reveal a cluster of accounts with an excessively high follower count, sparse content sharing, and an abnormal follower-to-following ratio. These characteristics could indicate the presence of a network of fake or bot-driven accounts, leading to interventions such as account suspension to preserve the authenticity of interactions on the platform.

By actively engaging in pattern recognition through these algorithms, organizations are empowered to discern hidden relationships and behaviors, enabling fraud analysts to preemptively address potential issues and mitigate risks. Real-world examples and case studies further illustrate its practical application in fraud detection.

> TIP
>
> The effectiveness of clustering in fraud detection is evaluated using precision, recall, and silhouette scores. It faces challenges like handling high-dimensional data and complex cluster interpretation. Clustering is often integrated with other techniques like classification and anomaly detection to improve accuracy, especially in real-time fraud detection, which demands quick and dynamic data handling.

Generative Models

Generative models are a sophisticated branch of machine learning that specializes in creating new data samples resembling original datasets. Their capacity to generate realistic data has been famously showcased in *generative adversarial networks* (GANs), which have become a mainstay in tasks like image generation and beyond.

In the fraud detection domain, these generative models address challenges like the scarcity of fraudulent data needed for training. They generate synthetic fraudulent transactions that blend with actual data to train detection algorithms, enhancing the model's anomaly detection capabilities. This method is crucial for maintaining the model's accuracy, ensuring it remains adept at identifying irregularities that could indicate fraud.

Moreover, generative models play a pivotal role in feature learning, where they identify and recreate important data characteristics. This is particularly valuable in fraud detection algorithms, where distinguishing features are crucial for identifying suspicious activities. For example, a credit card company might employ variational autoencoders (VAEs) to discern a baseline of normal transaction patterns. Transactions that deviate from this baseline with a high reconstruction error signal potential fraud, prompting further investigation.

These models are not just limited to data generation and feature learning; they are also instrumental in simulating transactions to forecast and understand emerging fraudulent patterns. This proactive approach is exemplified by financial institutions using generative models to anticipate and adapt to the continuously evolving tactics of fraudsters.

Several techniques fall under generative models:

- GANs are popular for generating synthetic data and can be trained to create synthetic fraudulent transactions to augment datasets. For illustration, a bank uses GANs to generate synthetic financial transactions that mimic fraudulent activities. The synthetic data is then mixed with real data to train a fraud detection model, improving its performance in identifying fraud patterns in imbalanced datasets.
- VAEs can be used for feature learning and dimensionality reduction in fraud detection tasks and can also generate new samples to analyze for potential fraud patterns. For example, a credit card company uses VAEs to learn a compressed representation of normal transactions. When a new transaction is processed, it is encoded and decoded by the VAE. If the reconstruction error is high, the transaction is flagged as an anomaly, possibly indicating fraud.
- *Restricted Boltzmann machines* (RBMs) can be used for feature learning and generating new data samples and are useful in understanding complex transaction patterns. An insurance company uses RBMs to learn important features from a claims dataset. The learned features, which include patterns of claim amounts, frequencies, and types, are then used to train a classifier to identify potentially fraudulent claims.
- *Bayesian networks* are probabilistic graphical models that generate data based on the learned joint probability distribution, aiding in

understanding and predicting fraudulent behaviors. An e-commerce platform uses Bayesian networks to model the probabilistic relationships between various transaction features, such as user behavior, transaction amount, and item category. By observing the joint probabilities, the model can predict the likelihood of fraudulent transactions.

- *Mixture models* can generate data based on multiple underlying distributions, which is useful when fraudulent and legitimate transactions follow different distributions. A financial institution uses a mixture of models to understand the distribution of transactions. The model identifies that legitimate and fraudulent transactions follow different distributions. By identifying which distribution a new transaction is likely to come from, the institution can flag potential frauds for further investigation.

Integrating various generative models allows organizations across different sectors to significantly enhance their fraud detection systems, making them more adept at identifying and preventing fraudulent activities. This holistic approach to fraud detection, powered by the generative capabilities of these models, stands as a testament to the innovative applications of machine learning in safeguarding financial and data integrity.

If you use generative models to identify unusual patterns by generating what normal transactions should look like and then flagging deviations from this norm, you are using them in an *unsupervised* manner.

If you have labeled data for both fraudulent and non-fraudulent transactions and you train a generative model to generate new examples of each class, you are incorporating elements of *supervised* learning.

Generative models are particularly useful in situations where you might not have a lot of labeled data (common in fraud detection), allowing them to utilize the principles of unsupervised learning to augment datasets or identify patterns indicative of fraud.

WARNING

While unsupervised learning algorithms are powerful tools for detecting fraud, they are not infallible. The insights and contextual knowledge that domain experts provide are indispensable for interpreting the outputs of unsupervised learning and for ensuring that the actions taken based on these outputs are accurate, relevant, and compliant with regulatory standards.

First-Digit Phenomenon: Harnessing Benford's Law to Spot Financial Fraud

The *first-digit law*, also known as *Benford's Law*, is a statistical phenomenon that defines the distribution of leading digits in many naturally occurring datasets. It asserts that the leading digit d (d 1,...,9) appears with a probability $P(d) = \log10(1 + 1/d)$ in a dataset. This means that smaller digits, such as 1, 2, and 3, are more likely to appear as the initial digit of a number, whereas larger digits, such as 8 and 9, are less likely to appear.

The distribution of the initial digits in many real-world datasets, such as financial transactions, market prices, or population statistics, closely follows Benford's Law. This observation can be used to detect fraud by examining the distribution of leading digits in a dataset for probable anomalies or fraudulent activity.

When individuals manipulate data, such as in cases of financial fraud, they often fail to consider the natural distribution of digits, which results in a deviation from the expected distribution according to Benford's Law. By comparing the actual distribution of the leading digits in a dataset to the expected distribution given by Benford's Law, it is possible to identify potential anomalies that may indicate fraudulent activities.

For instance, auditors and investigators can apply Benford's Law to analyze financial data, such as company revenues, expenses, or tax declarations. If the distribution of the first digits significantly deviates from the expected distribution, it may suggest that the data has been manipulated or tampered with, prompting further investigation.

Benford's Law identifies statistical abnormalities that may serve as warning indicators—it does not, by itself, confirm fraud. It is often used as a preliminary analysis tool to drive future investigations, but it should be combined with other analytical methods for more extensive fraud identification.

Example: Detecting Financial Fraud Using Benford's Law: A Comparative Analysis of Leading Digit Distribution

Auditors examine a company's financial statements for fraud. The corporation may have falsified financial records to evade taxes.

The objective is to examine the distribution of the leading digits in the company's financial records to identify any significant deviations from

Table 11.5 Detecting financial fraud using Benford's law dataset

Transaction ID	*Transaction amount*
1	12,500
2	7430
3	1850
4	2275
5	9180
...	...

the expected distribution according to Benford's Law, which may indicate manipulation or fraud.

The dataset (see Table 11.5) consists of 1000 recorded transaction amounts from the company's financial records over the past year. The leading digits of these transaction amounts are extracted for analysis.

Sample Data Snapshot

For every transaction amount, the first number you see is the "leading digit." For example, (see Table 11.6) in the amount $12,500, the leading digit is 1. In $7430, the leading digit is 7. This step is about extracting the first number from each transaction amount.

When you do the analysis, first the observed frequency distribution of the leading digits is calculated: After extracting the leading digits from all transactions, you need to count how many times each digit (from 1 to 9) appears as the leading digit (see Table 11.7). This count gives you the "observed" frequency for each digit. It's like taking a survey and noting down how many times people chose a particular option.

Table 11.6 Leading digits extraction

Transaction ID	*Leading digit*
1	1
2	7
3	1
4	2
5	9
...	...

Table 11.7 Observed frequency distribution

Leading digit	*Observed frequency*
1	345
2	210
3	160
4	95
5	85
6	50
7	30
8	15
9	10

Next, the expected frequency distribution according to Benford's Law is calculated (see Table 11.8) Benford's Law predicts how often each digit (from 1 to 9) should appear as the leading digit in many real-world datasets. It provides a set of percentages for each digit. For instance, it predicts that the digit 1 will appear as the leading digit about 30.1% of the time. By applying these percentages to our dataset, we can calculate the "expected" frequency for each digit. It's like having an answer key or a benchmark to compare against.

The auditor detects large variations in some leading digits, particularly digits 6 through 9, when comparing the observed and expected frequency distributions. This shows possible financial record falsification and calls for an additional inquiry.

In the context of the example:

- The "*observed*" frequencies are the actual counts of leading digits from the company's financial records.
- The "*expected*" frequencies are what Benford's Law predicts those counts should be if there was no tampering or fraud.

If there's a significant difference between the observed and expected frequencies, it might indicate that the financial records were manipulated. However, it's just an indicator, not a definitive proof.

Table 11.8 Expected frequency distribution (Benford's Law)

Leading digit	*Expected frequency*	*Probabilities predicted by Benford's Law (%)*	*Expected frequency*
1	Expected frequency of 1	1000 × 30.1	301
2	Expected frequency of 2	1000 × 17.6	176
3	Expected frequency of 3	1000 × 12.5	125
4	Expected frequency of 4	1000 × 9.7	97
5	Expected frequency of 5	1000 × 7.9	79
6	Expected frequency of 6	1000 × 6.7	67
7	Expected frequency of 7	1000 × 5.8	58
8	Expected frequency of 8	1000 × 5.1	51
9	Expected frequency of 9	1000 × 4.6	46

TIP

The expected frequency for each leading digit, as per Benford's Law, is determined by considering the total number of observations and the likelihood of a particular digit appearing as the leading digit. Benford's Law anticipates that in a dataset, the leading digits 1 to 9 will manifest with the following approximate frequencies: 1 occurs 30.1% of the time, 2 occurs 17.6% of the time, 3 occurs 12.5% of the time, 4 occurs 9.7% of the time, 5 occurs 7.9% of the time, 6 occurs 6.7% of the time, 7 occurs 5.8% of the time, 8 occurs 5.1% of the time, and 9 occurs 4.6% of the time.

Benford's Law posits that in many naturally occurring datasets, the leading digit d (where $\in\{1,\ldots,9\}d\in\{1,\ldots,9\}$) appears with a probability $P(d)$ determined by the formula:

$$P(d) = log_{10}(d+1) - log_{10}(d) = log_{10}(1+\frac{1}{d})$$

These probabilities indicate that the leading digit is more likely to be 1 than any other digit and is least likely to be 9. It's crucial to recognize that these percentages are not arbitrary but stem from the logarithmic distribution proposed by Benford's Law.

However, it is also essential to acknowledge that not every dataset will comply with Benford's Law. The law typically applies to naturally occurring datasets, such as financial data, population numbers, stock prices, and others that span several orders of magnitude.

> WARNING
>
> It is vital to remember that a divergence from Benford's Law does not show fraud on its own. This conclusion should serve as a starting point for the auditor to perform a more in-depth investigation, combining different analytical approaches and obtaining further evidence to validate or reject the allegation of fraud.

Example: Detecting Anomalies in Financial Transactions Using Benford's Law in Python

A financial company wants to detect anomalies in their transaction data that may indicate potential fraud. They have a dataset containing multiple features related to financial transactions.

The objective is to apply Benford's Law to the transaction dataset to identify whether there are any significant deviations in the distribution of leading digits, which could indicate possible anomalies or fraudulent activities.

The original dataset is a subset of the "Credit card fraud detection" dataset from Kaggle. It contains multiple columns (V1, V2, …, V28) representing anonymized features for each transaction. You can access the resampled dataset for this example using this link.

1. Import the dataset and inspect its structure. Import the necessary libraries and read the dataset (assuming you have downloaded it to your local directory and named it *creditcard.csv*)

```
import pandas as pd
import numpy as np
import matplotlib.pyplot as plt
import seaborn as sns

# Read the dataset
data = pd.read_csv('creditcard.csv')
print(data.head())
```

2. Create a new column `Amount_sum` to store the sum of the anonymized features (V1, V2, ..., V28) for each row:

```
data['Amount_sum'] = data.loc[:, 'V1':'V28'].sum(axis=1)
print(data.head())
```

3. Define the `leading_digit` function to extract the leading digit from a number. This function is essential for applying Benford's Law:

```
def leading_digit(x):
    x = abs(x)  # Take the absolute value to handle negative numbers
    while x >= 10 or x < 1:  # Adjust the condition to handle decimals
        if x < 1:
            x *= 10
        else:
            x //= 10
    return int(x)
```

4. Recompute the `leading_digit` column. Apply the `leading_digit` function to the `Amount_sum` column and store the result in a new column:

```
# Recompute the Leading_Digit column
data['Leading_Digit'] = data['Amount_sum'].apply(leading_digit)
```

5. Recompute the `actual_distribution`. Calculate the distribution of leading digits in the dataset:

```
# Recompute the actual_distribution
actual_distribution =
data['Leading_Digit'].value_counts(normalize=True).sort_index()
```

6. Ensure that the `actual_distribution` has all digits from 1 to 9. This is important because if any digit is missing from the actual distribution, it will cause issues when plotting or comparing with Benford's distribution:

```
# Ensure all digits from 1 to 9 are present
if len(actual_distribution) != 9:
    missing_digits = set(range(1, 10)) - set(actual_distribution.index)
    for digit in missing_digits:
        actual_distribution.loc[digit] = 0
    actual_distribution = actual_distribution.sort_index()
# Expected distribution according to Benford's Law
benford_distribution = [np.log10(1 + 1/digit) for digit in range(1, 10)]
benford_series = pd.Series(benford_distribution, index=range(1, 10))
```

7. Visualize the distributions. Plot the actual distribution of leading digits alongside the expected distribution according to Benford's Law (see Fig. 11.1):

```
# Visualizing the distributions
plt.figure(figsize=(10, 6))
plt.bar(range(1, 10), actual_distribution, label='Actual Distribution',
alpha=0.7)
plt.plot(range(1, 10), benford_series, color='red', marker='o',
linestyle='-', label="Benford's Law")
plt.xlabel('Leading Digit')
plt.ylabel('Probability')
plt.title("Actual vs. Benford's Distribution of Leading Digits")
plt.legend()
plt.show()
```

8. Analyze deviations. Compute the deviations between the actual distribution and Benford's Law and calculate the Z-scores for these deviations:

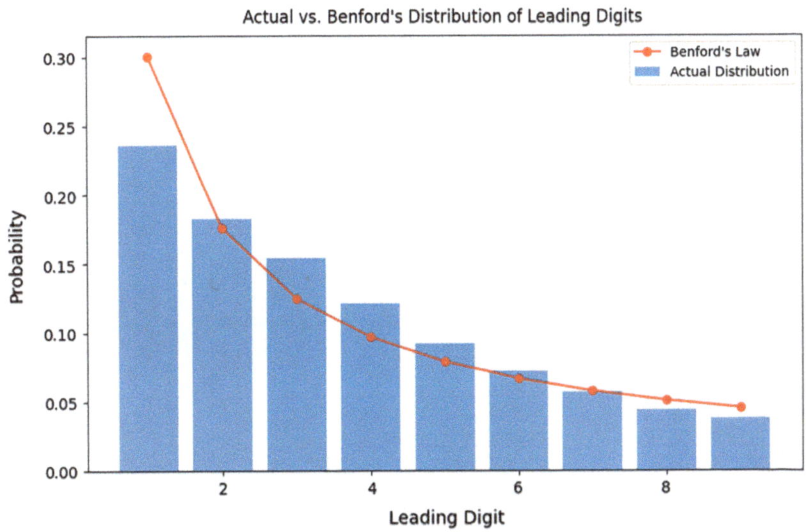

Fig. 11.1 Actual vs. Benford's distribution of leading digits: This figure presents a visual comparison between the actual distribution of leading digits in a dataset and the theoretical distribution predicted by Benford's Law. The x-axis displays the leading digits from 1 to 9, while the y-axis represents their corresponding probability. The blue bars illustrate the observed frequencies of each leading digit in the actual dataset, while the red line with markers overlays the expected probabilities according to Benford's Law. The highest probability is concentrated at the digit "1," and the probability decreases steadily toward "9," following a logarithmic pattern. This chart is useful for identifying anomalies or irregularities in numerical datasets, commonly applied in forensic accounting, audit investigations, and fraud detection to assess data authenticity

```
# Step 8 - Analyze deviations and Z-scores
deviations = np.abs(np.array(actual_distribution) -
                    np.array(benford_series))
n = len(data)
z_scores = (np.array(actual_distribution) - np.array(benford_series)) / \
           np.sqrt(np.array(benford_series) *
                   (1 - np.array(benford_series)) / n)

# Create results DataFrame
results = pd.DataFrame({
    'First_1_Dig': range(1, 10),
    'Expected': benford_series,
    'Found': actual_distribution,
    'Deviation': deviations,
    'Z_score': z_scores
})

# Figure 2: Comparison of Expected vs Found distribution
fig, ax = plt.subplots(figsize=(10, 6))
bar_width = 0.35
r1 = np.arange(len(benford_series))
r2 = [x + bar_width for x in r1]

plt.bar(r1, benford_series, width=bar_width, color='blue',
        edgecolor='grey', label="Expected (Benford's Law)")
plt.bar(r2, actual_distribution, width=bar_width, color='orange',
        edgecolor='grey', label='Found (Actual Distribution)')

plt.title('Comparison of Expected vs. Found Distribution of Leading
Digits',
          fontweight='bold')
plt.xlabel('Leading Digit', fontweight='bold')
plt.ylabel('Frequency', fontweight='bold')
plt.xticks([r + bar_width/2 for r in range(len(benford_series))],
           ['1', '2', '3', '4', '5', '6', '7', '8', '9'])
plt.legend()
plt.show()

# Display results
print(results)
```

In total, this code performs an analysis based on Benford's Law to check the distribution of leading digits in the `Amount_sum` column of the dataset. The actual distribution is compared with the expected distribution according to Benford's Law, and deviations are quantified using Z-scores. The results are visualized using a bar plot and presented in a dataframe.

The last piece of code in step 8 creates a side-by-side bar chart that compares two distributions: the actual observed distribution of leading digits in a dataset and the expected distribution according to Benford's Law (see Fig. 11.2).

Observations on the analysis of the data using Benford's Law reveal several insights. The analysis focused on the `Amount_sum` column, derived by summing the values across the feature columns V1–V28 for each record. Benford's Law anticipates the distribution of the first digits in naturally occurring datasets, suggesting that the digit 1 should appear as the leading digit approximately 30.1% of the time, while 9 should appear about 4.6% of the time. However, the data shows deviations from this expected distribution. Digit 4 appears as the leading digit more frequently than expected, with a Z-score of 0.148, representing the most pronounced overrepresentation. Digits 2, 3, and 5 also appear slightly more often than expected, with Z-scores of 0.017, 0.031, and 0.048 respectively, though these deviations are minor. In contrast, digit 6 exhibits the largest overall deviation, with a Z-score of −0.355, indicating it appears significantly less frequently than Benford's Law predicts. Digits 7, 8, and 9 are also underrepresented, with Z-scores of −0.187, −0.043, and −0.039 respectively. Digit 1, while the most common leading digit in both distributions, carries a Z-score of −0.153, suggesting slight under-representation relative to the Benford benchmark. The most analytically significant signals are the strong underrepresentation of digit 6 and the overrepresentation of digit 4, both of which warrant closer examination.

Based on these observations, several recommendations can be made. It would be beneficial to examine the records with deviations from Benford's Law, especially those starting with the digits 4 and 6, as these deviations could indicate anomalies or inconsistencies in the dataset. A root cause analysis should be conducted to understand the reasons behind these deviations, which could stem from the inherent nature of the dataset, data entry errors, or potentially fraudulent activities. Additionally, data preparation efforts should be enhanced, including improved data preprocessing and feature engineering, to ensure the data is highly quality and suitable for further analysis or modeling. Since Benford's Law might not be universally applicable, other statistical methods or machine learning algorithms should also be considered for detecting anomalies. Finally, if

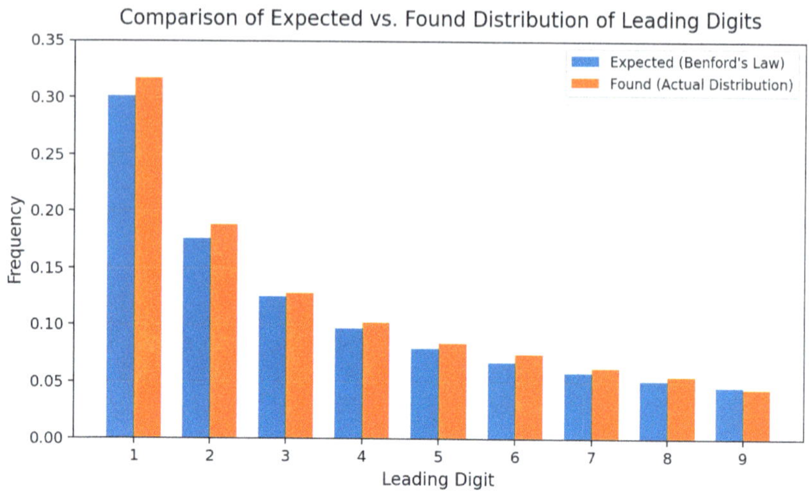

First_Dig	Expected	Found	Z_score
1	0.301030	0.316600	-0.153016
2	0.176091	0.187921	0.016585
3	0.124939	0.127681	0.031058
4	0.096910	0.101880	0.148347
5	0.079181	0.083684	0.048130
6	0.066947	0.074256	-0.354599
7	0.057992	0.061840	-0.187129
8	0.051153	0.054780	-0.042956
9	0.045757	0.043880	-0.038922

Fig. 11.2 Benford's Law Analysis for Leading Digit Distributions: Comparison of expected vs. found distribution of leading digits: This figure compares the expected distribution of leading digits according to Benford's Law (blue bars) against the actual distribution found in the dataset (orange bars). Benford's Law predicts a logarithmic distribution where lower digits, especially 1, appear more frequently as leading digits. Deviations from this expected pattern—particularly for digits 1 and 3—may indicate anomalies or potential data manipulation. The table below the chart details the expected vs. actual frequency, along with Z-scores for each digit. Significant Z-score deviations suggest areas where the observed digit distribution may warrant further forensic investigation, making this analysis a valuable tool in fraud detection and audit analytics

fraudulent activities are suspected, collaboration with domain experts is advised to validate the findings and devise effective countermeasures.

Understanding the Limitations of Benford's Law in Data Analysis

SIDEBAR

Benford's Law is indeed an interesting phenomenon used in various fields, including fraud detection, but it's important to note that it isn't universally applicable. Its applicability largely depends on the nature of the data being analyzed. Here are some scenarios where Benford's law might not be applicable or as effective:

1. *Uniformly distributed data*: Benford's Law is most effective for datasets where the numbers are naturally distributed across orders of magnitude. If the data is uniformly distributed or constrained within a small range, Benford's law may not hold. For instance, data like phone numbers or social security numbers, which are arbitrarily assigned, wouldn't follow Benford's Law.
2. *Human-generated data*: Numbers that are influenced by human thought or decision-making processes, such as set prices or psychological pricing in retail (like $9.99), may not conform to Benford's Law.
3. *Small datasets:* Benford's Law is more accurate for larger datasets. In smaller datasets, the distribution of the first digits may not align well with the logarithmic distribution predicted by Benford's Law.
4. *Data with Inherent biases*: Datasets that have built-in minimums or maximums, or where the numbers are not naturally occurring (like interest rates or inventory levels that are often rounded to specific numbers), may not follow the distribution pattern outlined in Benfords Law.

When deviations from Benford's Law are observed, especially for digits 3, 4, and 5, it's crucial to conduct a thorough investigation. These deviations could indicate anomalies, but they might also be due to the inherent characteristics of the data, entry errors, or fraudulent activities. Therefore, a root cause analysis is essential to determine the reasons behind these discrepancies.

Further, it's advisable to supplement Benford's Law analysis with other statistical methods or machine learning algorithms for a more comprehensive approach to anomaly detection. Data preparation efforts, including preprocessing and feature engineering, should be prioritized to enhance data quality.

If fraud is suspected, collaboration with domain experts becomes crucial. They can help validate the findings and develop appropriate strategies to address any fraudulent activities detected through the analysis. This multifaceted approach, combining Benford's Law with other techniques and expert insights, is key to effective fraud detection and data integrity assurance.

Summary

In this chapter, you explored the landscape of unsupervised learning techniques often used in fraud detection when labeled data is limited. We examined clustering, anomaly detection, association rule mining, and dimensionality reduction, highlighting how these methods uncover hidden patterns and irregular behaviors.

You learned how clustering algorithms such as K-Means and DBSCAN group similar transactions to expose suspicious deviations, while anomaly detection techniques like Isolation Forest and One-Class SVM pinpoint outliers that may represent fraudulent activity.

You also discovered how association rule mining tools such as Apriori and Eclat reveal covert relationships within data, and how Benford's Law can detect accounting irregularities by identifying unnatural digit distributions. Together, these techniques provide a solid foundation for detecting anomalies and behavioral shifts in complex datasets—an essential capability for uncovering hidden fraud patterns.

As you move into Chapter 12—Clustering for Fraud Detection, you'll take a deeper dive into one of these unsupervised methods. This next chapter focuses on how clustering algorithms group data points, define normal behavior, and spotlight the outliers that may signal fraudulent activity.

Through theory, visualization, and hands-on Python examples, you'll learn to translate clustering results into practical fraud detection insights that can be applied to real-world financial and transactional data.

CHAPTER 12

Clustering for Fraud Detection

Imagine an analyst at a mid-sized bank reviewing yesterday's transactions. Among 50,000 records, only a handful are flagged by the existing rules engine—but the analyst knows from experience that several others feel wrong. They don't match the typical pattern. They aren't labeled as fraud, but they aren't behaving like normal transactions either. How can these subtle anomalies be surfaced systematically, without waiting for the eventual chargeback or customer complaint that confirms the fraud? This is the problem that clustering is uniquely suited to solve. Clustering is a branch of unsupervised machine learning that groups similar data points together based on their inherent characteristics—no labels required. By learning what "normal" customer behavior looks like, clustering algorithms allow us to spot the transactions that don't fit the mold. These outliers may be perfectly innocent. They may also be the first sign of a fraud scheme that hasn't yet been categorized. In this chapter, you will work through the complete clustering workflow for fraud detection. You'll start by defining normal behavior through customer segmentation and exploratory data analysis, then meet the K-means algorithm—the workhorse of unsupervised fraud analytics. You'll learn how to choose the right number of clusters using the elbow method, how to flag suspicious points based on their distance from cluster centroids, and—critically—how to evaluate whether your model is actually catching fraud or just chasing noise. Finally, you'll see how DBSCAN, a density-based alternative to K-means,

A. Al Aqqad, *Fraud Analytics in Action*
https://doi.org/10.1007/978-3-032-16023-2_12

can detect fraud in datasets where the shape and number of clusters aren't known in advance. By the end of the chapter, you'll have applied both methods to a real banking dataset and developed the judgment to decide which tool fits which problem.

Defining Normal Behavior

To effectively recognize unexpected behavior in data, a detailed understanding and analysis are paramount. This process begins with a comprehensive exploratory data analysis (EDA), encompassing distribution plots, outlier detection, and correlation studies. Engaging with fraud analysts can be instrumental in evaluating typical data values and pinpointing characteristics indicative of fraudulent behavior.

A key aspect to consider is the homogeneity of your data. It's essential to determine whether different customer types exhibit distinct behavior patterns. What constitutes normal activity for one group may not apply to another. For example, older demographics may naturally have higher health insurance claims than younger individuals. Similarly, the spending habits of a millionaire are likely to differ from a student's. Recognizing these nuances is crucial. If your data reveals such disparities, identifying homogeneous subgroups becomes vital for accurately detecting anomalies within each segment.

Customer Segmentation: Tailoring Detection to Normal Behavior Within Segments

In the realm of customer segmentation, consistency in data types is crucial. Whether dealing with individuals, groups, companies, or governmental entities, it's important to ensure that the data points within each segment are comparable. Analyze varying factors such as spending patterns, age, geographic location, or transaction frequency to understand each segment better.

Geolocation, for instance, plays a critical role in fraud detection scenarios like credit card fraud or e-commerce activities. An effective strategy is to compare the IP address location with the shipping destination of the products. Significant discrepancies in these locations might signal unusual activity, although there can be legitimate exceptions.

When creating models for each segment to detect suspicious behavior, a challenge arises in integrating the insights from multiple models. Developing an effective method to consolidate these diverse findings into a single, coherent outcome is crucial for a comprehensive fraud detection strategy.

Remember, the goal is to tailor the detection mechanism to the unique behavioral patterns of each segment, ensuring that the nuances of each group are accurately captured and analyzed. This bespoke approach significantly enhances the ability to detect and prevent fraud effectively.

Practice Opportunity 1: Customer Segmentation

In these exercises, you will explore a dataset of bank payment transactions that categorize financial transactions by type and amount, along with client characteristics such as age group and gender. Your primary goal is to use unsupervised learning techniques to identify potentially fraudulent transactions.

The dataset includes crucial data like age group and gender, but it lacks extensive client information, particularly regarding wealth levels. Some transactions are labeled as fraud, which will be instrumental in validating the results of your analysis.

Your first step will be to understand the dataset's nature and characteristics, focusing particularly on analyzing age data to uncover behavioral differences across age groups. This understanding is key to distinguishing normal transactions from abnormal ones, which may indicate fraud.

You will also assess whether the data needs to be segmented into distinct groups based on client characteristics or if the dataset exhibits enough homogeneity to be analyzed as a whole. This initial exploration sets the stage for a more in-depth analysis and the application of unsupervised learning techniques to detect and understand fraudulent activities in the dataset.

Instructions:

1. Import the Pandas library and use it to read the dataset from a CSV file.
2. Store the resulting dataframe in `banksim_df`.
3. Obtain a statistical overview of the dataset to familiarize yourself with its characteristics.

4. Group the data by the "category" column and calculate the mean for each group. This will give insights into the average behavior per category.
5. Group the dataset by the "age" column and calculate the mean for each age group to understand average behaviors.
6. Use `value_counts()` on the "age" column to assess the age distribution within the dataset.

Lab access: Embark on an analytical expedition with the *banksim_df* dataset to unravel customer behaviors and detect potential fraud through unsupervised learning techniques. Begin by dissecting the dataset's characteristics, particularly age data and transaction categories, to identify behavioral patterns. Assess the need for data segmentation based on client attributes and prepare the groundwork for advanced fraud detection analysis. Click here for lab access to start your journey into customer segmentation and fraud analysis.

Discussion question: Based on your analysis, does it make sense to segment the data into different age groups before running a fraud detection algorithm?

Possible answers:

- *No:* The larger age groups exhibit relatively similar behaviors in terms of average spending and fraud occurrence.
- *Yes:* The age group "0" shows distinct behavior, warranting separate analysis.

Answer explanation: The correct answer is no. The analysis indicates that the behaviors, including average spending and fraud rates, are fairly consistent across different age groups. Although age group "0" appears distinct, it represents only a small portion of the dataset (40 cases), which is insufficient to justify a separate model. Therefore, treating the data as homogenous is more practical for model development and evaluation.

Practice Opportunity 2: Examining Statistics to Identify Normal Behavior

In the previous exercises, you discovered that fraud is more common in specific transaction categories, but there wasn't a clear way to segment the data, such as by age groups. Now, let's explore the average amounts spent on normal transactions compared to fraudulent transactions. This will help you understand how fraudulent transactions structurally differ from normal transactions (see Fig. 12.1).

Instructions:

1. Make two new dataframes: one for fraud observations and one for non-fraud observations. To create the additional dataframes, `use the.loc function` to locate the data in the `df` dataframe and set criteria "where fraud is 1" and "where fraud is 0."
2. Plot the amount column of the newly produced dataframes using histogram plot functions and label the plots `fraud` and non-fraud.

Lab access: Deepen your analysis of the *banksim_df* dataset by comparing transaction behaviors for fraudulent and non-fraudulent activities. This exercise involves creating separate datasets for fraud and non-fraud transactions to explore structural differences in spending patterns. Engage in visual analysis using histogram plots to discern between fraud and

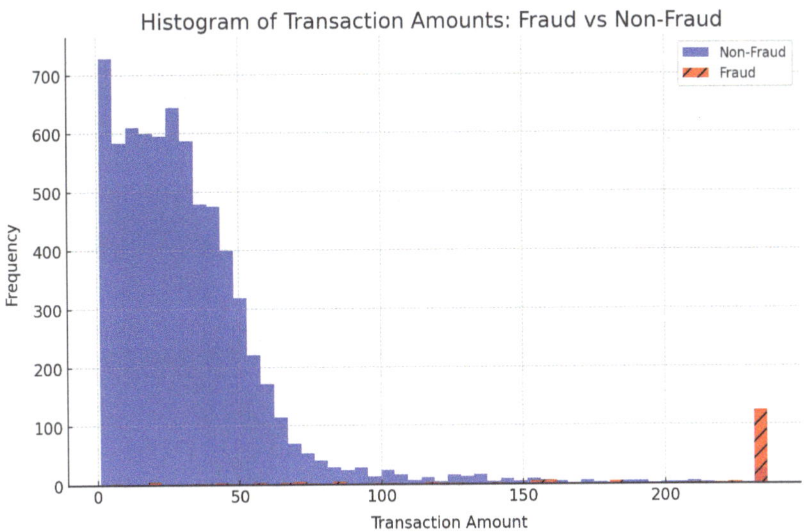

Fig. 12.1 Histogram of transaction amounts in the banksim_df dataset

non-fraud transactions. Click here for lab access to enhance your understanding of transactional anomalies and typical behaviors.

This histogram provides a comparative visualization of transaction amounts categorized by fraud status within the banksim_df dataset. Non-fraudulent transactions are shown in solid blue, while fraudulent transactions are overlaid using a red color (with diagonal hatching where visible) for clear differentiation. The x-axis represents transaction amounts, and the y-axis indicates transaction frequency. Transparency (alpha) is applied to allow overlapping areas to remain visible. The plot reveals that while non-fraudulent transactions are heavily concentrated at lower amounts, fraudulent transactions—although fewer in number—are skewed toward larger transaction values. This observed pattern offers critical insights for developing fraud detection strategies, especially when distinguishing between normal and suspicious transaction behaviors in unlabeled datasets. The histogram uses distinct markers or patterns to differentiate between these two categories:

1. *Transactions labeled as fraud:* These are represented by a specific pattern of diagonal lines), clearly distinguishing them from non-fraud transactions.
2. *Transactions labeled as non-fraud*: These are represented by a no pattern, making it easy to visually separate them from fraudulent transactions.

The histogram uses transparency, or alpha, to enhance visualization, particularly in areas where the categories overlap. This allows for a clearer view of how fraud and non-fraud transactions are distributed across different transaction amounts.

The x-axis of the histogram details the range of transaction amounts, and the y-axis shows the frequency of transactions within each amount range. This visualization reveals distinct patterns in transaction amounts between fraudulent and non-fraudulent activities, providing valuable insights into the behavioral patterns associated with fraud.

While the number of fraud observations in Fig. 15.1 is comparatively smaller and less visually prominent, it is noticeable that fraudulent transactions tend to have larger amounts than standard non-fraudulent transactions. This characteristic is crucial for analyzing and understanding fraud trends and will aid in distinguishing between normal and abnormal transactions in later analyses, even when explicit fraud labels are not available.

Clustering for Fraud Detection

Clustering algorithms play a crucial role in identifying suspicious patterns and anomalies in data, particularly in the context of fraud detection. By segmenting data into distinct groups based on similarities, clustering helps unveil unusual patterns that could indicate fraudulent activities. This section delves into how clustering techniques can be leveraged to detect and analyze fraudulent transactions within large datasets. You will explore various clustering methods, their applications in fraud detection, and the process of identifying and interpreting the results these methods yield.

Identifying Patterns in Data

Clustering uses features to group similar data points in unsupervised machine learning. For fraud detection, it helps uncover anomalous trends or behaviors in customer, account, and transaction data.

Data patterns are the clustering models' main purpose. In particular, clustering models divide data into clusters of points that are related yet distinct. For fraud detection, we can use this method to find data that is comparable to cluster data and data that is difficult to assign to any cluster. Unusual or questionable data might be detected. In practice, this can help discover data clusters that may indicate fraud (see Fig. 12.2).

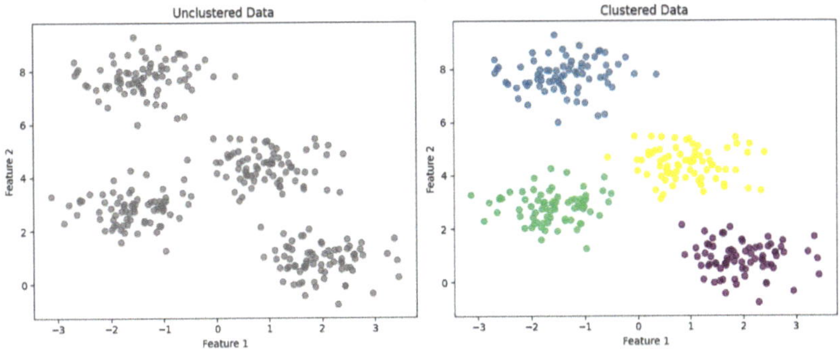

Fig. 12.2 Unclustered vs Clustered data representation for fraud detection

Figure 12.2 consists of two plots that illustrate the impact of clustering on data analysis for fraud detection:

1. *Left plot—unclustered data:* This plot visualizes the dataset before any clustering algorithm is applied. The data points are marked with a uniform pattern or shading (such as dots), without any differentiation. In this state, the data appears random with no evident patterns or groupings.
2. *Right plot—clustered data*: After the application of K-means clustering, the same data points are organized into distinct clusters. These clusters are represented by colors (such as blue, teal, yellow, and purple) to differentiate them from one another. This organization of data into clusters makes underlying patterns and relationships more apparent. The plot highlights areas of dense grouping (potential clusters) and points that stand apart from these groups (potential outliers or anomalies), which could be indicative of fraudulent activities.

The contrast between the two plots in Fig. 12.2 demonstrates the power of clustering in data analysis. It shows how a seemingly random and unstructured collection of data points can be transformed into well-defined groups through clustering techniques. This ability to identify clusters and outliers is critical in fraud detection, especially in large datasets where such patterns are not immediately visible.

Types of Clustering Techniques

Understanding different clustering techniques is essential for effectively analyzing and interpreting complex data sets. This section discusses hierarchical clustering, a method that organizes data into a tree-like structure, revealing natural groupings and relationships within the data. We will explore the agglomerative and divisive approaches to hierarchical clustering, their specific uses, and how they can be employed to uncover patterns indicative of fraud. Additionally, we'll touch upon other clustering methods like K-means and self-organizing maps (SOMs), examining their unique applications and benefits in various data analysis scenarios.

Hierarchical Clustering

This method is a versatile tool in data analysis, organizing data into a hierarchical tree structure known as a *dendrogram*. It's ideal for gaining insights into the data structure and discovering closely connected data points. Hierarchical clustering can be approached in two main ways:

- *Agglomerative (bottom-up) approach:* This method treats each data point as an individual cluster and merges them progressively based on their similarity. Preferred for its computational efficiency, it is particularly useful for handling large datasets. The dendrogram, which is a visual output of this method, serves as an insightful tool for understanding the clustering process and helps determine the optimal number of clusters.
- *Divisive (top-down) approach:* In this approach, the analysis starts with a single cluster encompassing all data points, which is then iteratively divided into smaller clusters. While it is computationally more demanding, it offers a thorough analysis of data structures and is effective for detailed explorations. Figure 12.3 compares the two approaches.

This figure compares two major hierarchical clustering approaches used in data analysis and fraud detection. The left panel illustrates the agglomerative (bottom–up) clustering process through a dendrogram, where each data point initially forms its own cluster and merges iteratively based on

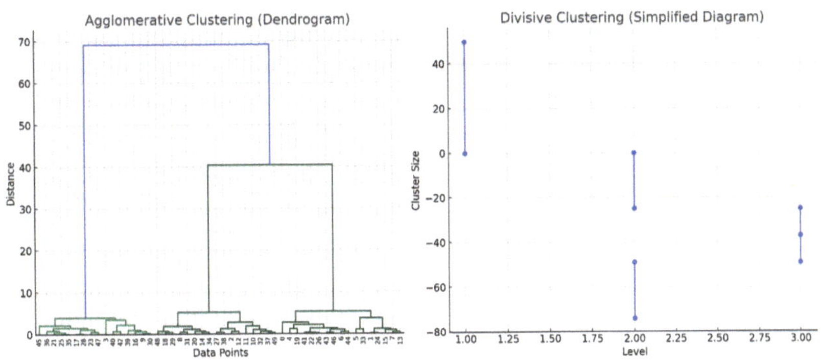

Fig. 12.3 Hierarchical Clustering Representations for Data Analysis

similarity. The vertical axis measures the distance or dissimilarity at which clusters are merged. The right panel presents a simplified divisive (top–down) clustering diagram, starting with all data points grouped in a single cluster and progressively splitting into smaller clusters across hierarchical levels. Dots represent clusters at each stage, while vertical lines indicate the division process. Both methods provide valuable structural insights, helping analysts identify natural groupings, anomalies, and patterns critical to fraud detection and other complex data investigations.

Dendrograms and Scree Plots

In data analysis, dendrograms, and scree plots are vital tools used with hierarchical clustering. By contrast, ***non-hierarchical*** or ***partitional*** clustering methods like K-means and self-organizing maps (SOMs) offer alternative approaches for data segmentation.

Dendrograms play a crucial role in hierarchical clustering by graphically representing clusters' formation and similarity levels. They are instrumental in visually inspecting the data and determining the appropriate number of clusters. However, interpreting a dendrogram can be subjective, as it depends on the specific context and objectives of the data analysis.

Complementing dendrograms with scree plots is another graphical tool used in hierarchical clustering. *Scree plots* depict the variance each hierarchy level explains relative to the number of clusters. The "elbow" in a scree plot is particularly significant as it indicates the optimal number of clusters—the point where adding more clusters does not significantly improve the variance explanation.

Shifting to non-hierarchical clustering methods, these approaches lack a hierarchical structure and instead focus on partitioning the data into distinct clusters. Among these methods, K-means clustering is widely recognized for its effectiveness, especially with large datasets. It segments the data into a predefined number of clusters, starting with the random selection of centroids. Data points are assigned to the nearest centroid, and centroids are recalculated iteratively until the clustering process stabilizes. However, the effectiveness of K-means clustering can be influenced by the initial selection of centroids and the distance measure used.

Self-organizing maps (SOMs) offer a unique perspective within non-hierarchical clustering. As a type of neural network trained using unsupervised learning, SOMs are adept at simplifying and visualizing high-dimensional data. They are particularly valuable for providing an understandable low-dimensional representation of complex datasets, aiding in the visualization and understanding of intricate data structures.

Each of these clustering methods, whether hierarchical or non-hierarchical, has its specific applications and considerations. The choice between them hinges on the requirements of the data analysis project, such as dataset size, complexity, and the desired depth of exploration. Combining these methods provides a comprehensive toolkit for data analysts, enabling them to uncover meaningful patterns and insights from their datasets.

Understanding the Theory and Intuition Behind K-means

K-means is an unsupervised learning algorithm renowned for its efficiency in clustering data. Unlike supervised learning, it doesn't require pre-labeled data, making it versatile for a range of applications where data categorization is essential but explicit labels are not available. The core objective of K-means is to group data points based on their inherent similarities, with the aim of minimizing variance within each cluster. This is achieved by calculating the Euclidean distance between data points; the closer the points, the more likely they are to belong to the same cluster.

K-means Algorithm Steps

Figure 12.4 provides a step-by-step graphical representation of the K-means clustering algorithm:

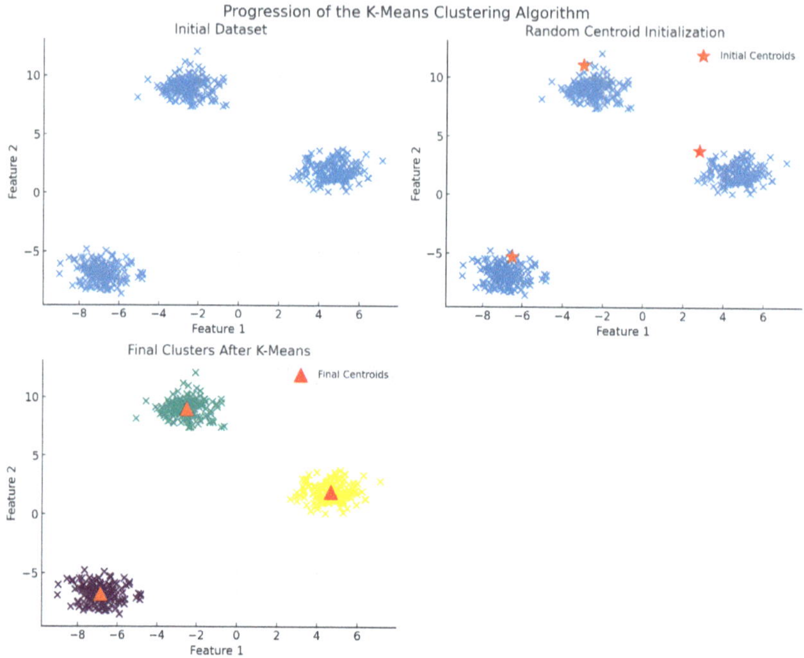

Fig. 12.4 K-Means Clustering Algorithm Process. This figure illustrates the sequential stages of the K-means clustering algorithm. The top-left panel shows the initial dataset distribution without clustering. The top-right panel displays the initial random selection of K centroids, marked by red stars, prior to any cluster assignment. The bottom panel visualizes the outcome after applying K-means clustering: data points are assigned to the nearest centroids, forming distinct color-coded clusters, with centroids repositioned at the mean of their respective clusters. Through iterative reassignments and centroid recalculations, the algorithm converges to stable clusters. This visual walkthrough highlights the sensitivity of K-means to centroid initialization and the importance of selecting an appropriate number of clusters (K) for meaningful results. Adapted from https://www.geeksforgeeks.org/machine-learning/k-means-clustering-introduction/

1. *Initial selection of centroids*: The figure starts by showing the initial random selection of K centroids. These centroids are marked with distinct symbols or patterns (such as stars, triangles) to differentiate them from the data points.
2. *Assignment of data points to nearest centroids:* The next stage illustrates how each data point in the dataset is assigned to the nearest centroid. Lines or arrows might be used to connect data points to their closest centroids, indicating the formation of initial clusters.
3. *Recalculation of centroids:* The figure then demonstrates the recalculated positions of the centroids after the initial assignment. This can be shown by moving the centroid symbols (stars, squares, triangles) to new positions that represent the mean of all points in their respective clusters.
4. *Reassignment of data points:* The diagram may display the re-examination and possible reassignment of data points to the clusters with the closest recalculated centroids. This can be represented by adjusting the lines or arrows to connect data points to their new centroids.
5. *Iteration and convergence:* The final part of the figure shows the iterative process of recalculating centroids and reassigning data points. This is represented by a series of iterations where centroids shift positions until they stabilize, indicating the formation of stable clusters.

WARNING

Key points to remember:

- The initial selection of centroids can significantly affect the final clusters. Therefore, K-means is often run multiple times with different initial centroids to ensure a good result.
- Choosing the right value for K is critical. If K is too small or too large, it may not capture the natural clusters in the data effectively.
- K-means assumes that clusters are spherical and of similar size. This might not always be the case with real-world data, affecting the algorithm's performance.
- K-means is a straightforward yet powerful algorithm for clustering data points into groups based on their similarities. It is widely used across various fields for its efficiency and ease of understanding.

How to Select the Optimal Number of Clusters (K) Using the Elbow Method

The elbow method is a widely recognized approach to determining the optimal number of clusters (K) for K-means clustering. This method is particularly useful because it provides a visual way to assess the trade-off between the number of clusters and the within-cluster variance (often measured as the *within-cluster sum of squares*, or WCSS). The goal is to find a balance where increasing the number of clusters does not yield a significant reduction in within-cluster variance.

To effectively utilize the elbow method, the following steps are typically followed:

1. *Calculate WCSS for different K values:* Start by calculating the WCSS for a range of K values. WCSS is the total sum of squared distances between each data point and the centroid of its cluster. Initially, when the number of clusters is small, WCSS tends to be high because the centroids are relatively far from many of the data points.
2. *Decrease in WCSS with increasing K:* As you increase the number of clusters, each centroid becomes closer to the data points in its cluster, leading to a decrease in WCSS. This trend continues as K increases, but the rate of decrease in WCSS diminishes.
3. *Plot WCSS against K:* Create a plot with the number of clusters on the x-axis and the corresponding WCSS on the y-axis. This plot

will typically show a steep decline in WCSS as the number of clusters increases from a small number, followed by a point where the decline becomes more gradual.

4. *Identify the elbow point:* The optimal value of K is found at the "elbow" of the plot. This is the point where the rate of decrease in WCSS shifts from being rapid to more gradual. Beyond the elbow point, adding more clusters does not provide a significant reduction in WCSS, indicating that the additional clusters are not capturing substantial new information.
5. *Choose the optimal K:* Once the elbow point is identified, select the number of clusters that correspond to this point as the optimal K for the K-means clustering algorithm. This ensures a balanced approach where the model is neither overfitting by having too many clusters nor underfitting by having too few.

> TIP
>
> It's important to note that the elbow method is somewhat subjective, as the "elbow" point may not always be sharply defined, and different analysts might interpret the plot slightly differently. Additionally, the method assumes that a lower WCSS is always better, which might not hold true in all contexts. Despite these limitations, the elbow method remains a practical and commonly used technique to guide the selection of K in K-means clustering, helping to ensure that the model is appropriately fitted to the data.

K-means Clustering in Python

To utilize K-means clustering effectively in Python, it's crucial to start by importing the necessary tools from scikit-learn, which include the K-means model and a suitable scaling technique. Remember, before applying K-means clustering or any distance-based technique, scaling your data is essential. Without scaling, features with higher scales can disproportionately influence the algorithm's outcome, leading to skewed results. To ensure that all features contribute equally, you must scale them to a similar range.

The process begins with two critical steps:

1. Convert your dataframe `df` into a NumPy array. This conversion involves extracting the values from `df` and making sure they are all of the float type.

2. Apply `MinMaxScaler` to the data. `MinMaxScaler` adjusts the feature values to a common scale, typically between 0 and 1, ensuring that no single feature dominates due to its scale.

Here's how you can execute these steps in Python

```
import numpy as np
import pandas as pd
from sklearn.preprocessing import MinMaxScaler
from sklearn.cluster import KMeans

# Load your DataFrame (assuming it's already loaded in df)
# df = pd.read_csv('path_to_your_data.csv')

# Convert the DataFrame to a NumPy array and ensure all data is float
X = np.array(df).astype(float)

# Scaling the data using MinMaxScaler
scaler = MinMaxScaler()
X_scaled = scaler.fit_transform(X)

# Define the K-means model with six clusters
kmeans = KMeans(n_clusters=6, random_state=42)

# Fit the model to the scaled data
kmeans.fit(X_scaled)

# You can now use the fitted model to make predictions or analyze the
clusters
```

WARNING

Remember to replace `'path_to_your_data.csv'` with the actual path to your data file, and `df` with the name of your `dataframe` variable.

For the effective application of K-means clustering, it is crucial that the data is entirely numerical. In cases where your dataset includes categorical features, these must be converted into numerical values before proceeding with K-means. This conversion can be accomplished using techniques like one-hot encoding or label encoding, as detailed in Chapter 9. The choice between these encoding techniques hinges on the nature of the categorical data—whether it is ordinal or nominal. One-hot encoding is ideal for nominal categories without an intrinsic order, while label encoding is suitable for ordinal categories with a defined sequence.

Determining the Right Number of Clusters

A drawback of K-means clustering is that you need to assign the number of clusters beforehand. There are multiple ways to determine the right number of clusters, such as the silhouette method or the elbow curve. Let's quickly review the elbow curve. The objective of K-means is to minimize the sum of all distances between data samples and their associated cluster centroids. The score is the negative of that minimization, so you want the score to be close to zero. By running a K-means model on clusters ranging from 1 to 10 and saving the scores for each model under `score`, you can obtain the elbow curve. Then simply plot the scores against the number of clusters. The resulting plot is shown in Fig. 15.5 in chapter "Lab: Classification Techniques for Fraud Detection":

> **NOTE**
>
> The silhouette method is a technique used to determine the optimal number of clusters in algorithms like K-means. It measures how similar each data point in a cluster is to points in its own cluster versus points in other clusters. This is quantified by the silhouette score, which ranges from -1 to +1. A high score indicates that data points are well-clustered, a score near 0 suggests overlapping clusters and a negative score implies incorrect clustering. The optimal number of clusters is often considered to be the one that maximizes the average silhouette score across all data points. This method provides insight into the separation distance between the resulting clusters, aiding in the validation of the clustering model.

```
import matplotlib.pyplot as plt
from sklearn.cluster import KMeans
from sklearn.preprocessing import MinMaxScaler
import numpy as np

# Assuming 'X_scaled' is your scaled data from the previous step
# If not, first scale your data:
# scaler = MinMaxScaler()
# X_scaled = scaler.fit_transform(X)

# Calculating sum of squared distances for different values of k
sum_of_squared_distances = []
K = range(1,11)
for k in K:
    km = KMeans(n_clusters=k, random_state=42)
    km = km.fit(X_scaled)
    sum_of_squared_distances.append(km.inertia_)

# Plotting the elbow curve
plt.plot(K, sum_of_squared_distances, 'bx-')
plt.xlabel('k')
plt.ylabel('Sum of Squared Distances')
plt.title('Elbow Method For Optimal k')
plt.show()
```

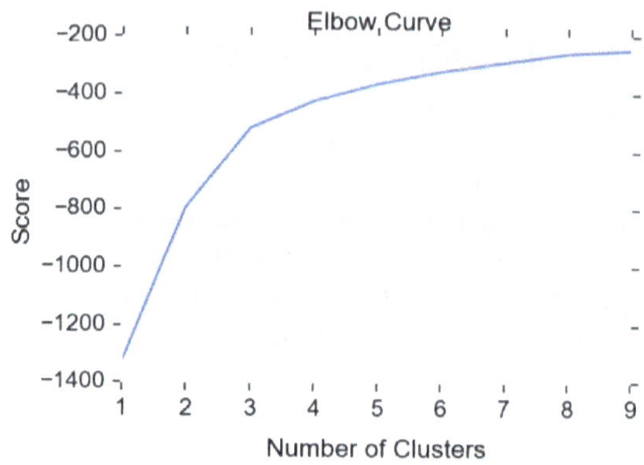

Fig. 12.5 Determining the Optimal Number of Clusters Using the Elbow Method

This figure illustrates the elbow method used to determine the ideal number of clusters in K-means clustering. The x-axis represents the number of clusters (k), while the y-axis shows the sum of squared distances (inertia) between data points and their assigned centroids. As the number of clusters increases, the sum of squared distances decreases. A noticeable bend or "elbow" is observed at **k = 3**, indicating that three clusters could provide a suitable balance between model complexity and performance. Although the elbow is not sharply pronounced, it suggests that adding more clusters beyond k = 3 yields diminishing improvements. This technique helps guide the selection of an appropriate number of clusters to avoid overfitting or underfitting in clustering applications (Fig 12.5).

Practice Opportunity 3: Clustering Method to Deducting Fraud

In the complex and ever-evolving field of fraud detection, clustering methods have emerged as powerful tools for identifying fraudulent activities. Clustering, a type of unsupervised machine learning, groups similar data points together based on certain characteristics, making it particularly useful in detecting anomalies such as fraud. In this practice opportunity, you will explore the application of K-means clustering, a popular clustering method, to a dataset for fraud detection. Your focus will be on preparing the data, implementing the clustering algorithm, and optimizing the number of clusters to efficiently detect potential fraud cases.

Task 1: Scaling the Data

Scaling your data is essential for machine learning algorithms that use distance-based metrics, as features of different magnitudes can significantly impact the results. Since K-means clustering relies on Euclidean distance to determine the separation between cluster centroids, scaling your data is a crucial preliminary step before implementing the algorithm. In this exercise, we'll focus on this important step.

You will be working with the dataframe (df) from the last exercise, which has already undergone some basic data preparation to make it suitable for use with sklearn's machine learning tools. The labels for potential fraud cases are stored separately in the `labels` variable, which you will use later for validation purposes. Additionally, NumPy has been imported as `np`.

Instructions:

1. Import the `MinMaxScaler` from `sklearn.preprocessing`.
2. Convert your dataframe (`df`) into a Numpy array X. This can be done by extracting the values from `df` and ensuring they are all of type float.
3. Instantiate the `MinMaxScaler` and apply it to X to obtain the scaled values in `X_scaled`. This process will normalize all your features to a scale of 0 to 1.

Lab access for task 1: Begin your exploration into fraud detection by scaling your data, a crucial step for distance-based machine learning algorithms like K-means. Work with the pre-prepared `banksim_df` dataframe and get hands-on experience with data normalization. Click here for lab access and start transforming your data for optimal algorithm performance.

Task 2: K-means Clustering

K-means clustering is a widely used technique, especially effective for fraud detection due to its simplicity and efficiency. However, transaction data in fraud detection cases is often voluminous, making standard K-means clustering computationally intensive. To address this, we will use the MiniBatch K-means variant in this exercise, which is more suitable for large datasets.

You will continue working with the scaled data (`X_scaled`) from the previous exercise. Let's explore how MiniBatch K-means can be applied in this context.

Instructions:

1. Import `MiniBatchKMeans` from `sklearn.cluster`.
2. Initialize the MiniBatch K-means model, specifying 8 clusters. Set a random state for reproducibility, if desired.
3. Fit the model to the scaled data, X_scaled.

Lab access for task 2: Continue your journey in fraud detection with the application of MiniBatch K-means clustering to the scaled data. This task focuses on implementing an efficient clustering method suitable for large datasets. Click here for lab access to fit the model and explore its clustering capabilities in a high-volume data context.

NOTE
You have now fitted your MiniBatch K-means model to the data.

Task 3: Elbow Method

In the previous task, we arbitrarily chose 8 clusters for the MiniBatch K-means model without determining the optimal number of clusters. For an effective initial fraud detection strategy, it's crucial to find the right number of clusters, particularly if you plan to identify outliers within these clusters for fraud prediction. The elbow method is a technique that helps in determining the most appropriate number of clusters. You will apply this method to identify the optimal cluster count.

`MiniBatchKMeans` is already imported from `sklearn.cluster`, and you have the scaled data `X_scaled` available for this task.

Instructions:

1. Define a range for the number of clusters to try, varying from 1 to 5.
2. Use a list comprehension to create and store a MiniBatch K-means model for each cluster count within the defined range.
3. Fit each MiniBatch K-means model to the scaled data X_scaled and compute their scores.

4. Plot the number of clusters against their respective scores. This visual representation will help you observe the "elbow" point, indicating the optimal number of clusters.

Lab access for task 3: Advance your understanding by determining the optimal number of clusters for fraud detection using the elbow method. This task involves experimenting with different cluster counts and observing their impact on the model's performance. Click here for lab access and take a deep dive into refining your clustering strategy.

As you can see in Fig. 12.6 the optimal number of clusters should probably be around 3 clusters, as that is where the elbow is in the curve. You'll use this in the next exercise as our baseline model and see how well it does at detecting fraud.

Assigning Fraud vs. Non-Fraud

In this section, we explore the transition from clustering data to its application in fraud detection. The focus is on how to leverage clustered data, particularly using algorithms like K-means, to pinpoint potential fraudulent activities.

Visualizing Clustered Data and Identifying Outliers (Figs. 12.7, 12.8, 12.9 and 12.10).

Flagging Fraud Based on Distance to Centroid

In Python, follow the next code block to flag potential fraud based on the distance to the centroid. Start with your trained clustering model (e.g., K-means) and use the `predict` function to assign each data point to a cluster. Save the results and the cluster centers. Then, calculate the distance of each data point to its cluster centroid using NumPy's linear algebra package's `norm` function. Finally, use percentiles of distances to determine outliers. For example, flag data points beyond the 93rd percentile with a one. These are the final fraud predictions:

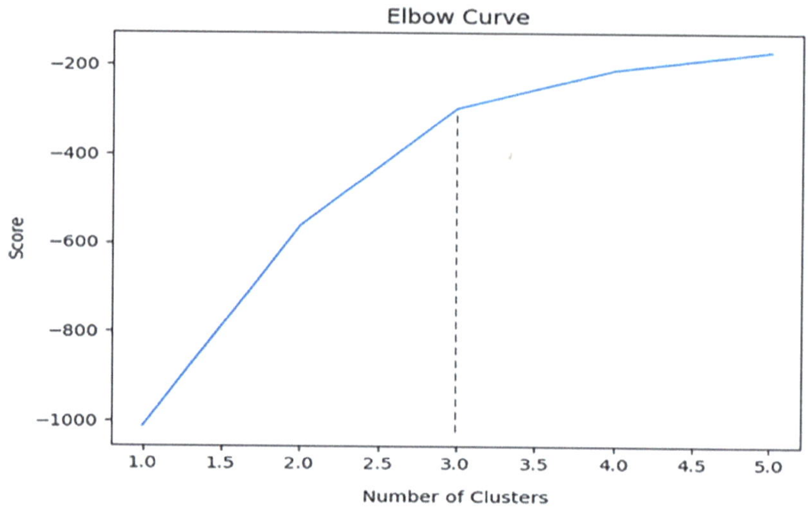

Fig. 12.6 Elbow Curve Indicating Optimal Cluster Selection for MiniBatch K-Means: This figure visualizes the elbow method applied to determine the optimal number of clusters for MiniBatch K-Means clustering in fraud detection. The x-axis represents the number of clusters, while the y-axis shows the corresponding model score (sum of squared distances). A noticeable "elbow" appears around k = 3, where the rate of improvement slows significantly. A dashed vertical line is plotted at k = 3 to highlight this inflection point, suggesting that three clusters likely provide a balance between underfitting and overfitting. Identifying this elbow point is essential for constructing an effective fraud detection model by selecting an appropriate number of clusters based on data structure

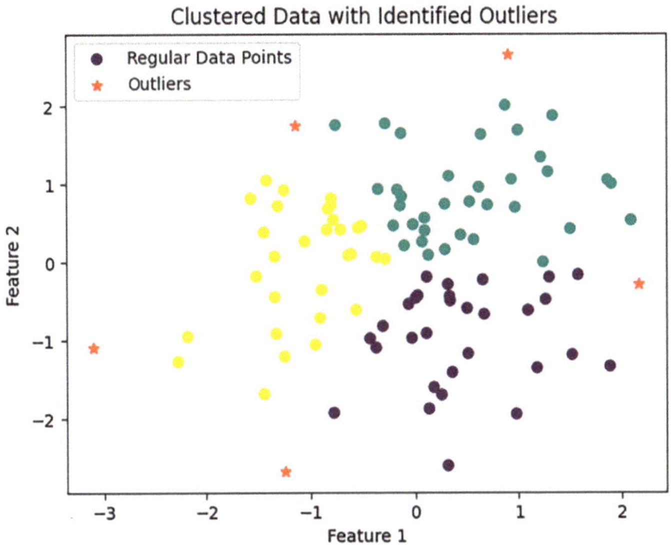

Fig. 12.7 Clustered Data with Identified Outliers: This figure visualizes data that has been clustered using a technique such as K-means clustering. Regular data points are grouped into distinct clusters, each represented with a different color. Outliers—data points that significantly deviate from the main cluster structures—are marked separately using red star symbols. These outliers may signal potential fraudulent activities or unusual behavior patterns. The x-axis and y-axis correspond to two features used in the clustering process. This visualization supports fraud detection efforts by isolating anomalies that warrant further investigation, illustrating how clustering can be effectively used to segment normal behavior from suspicious activities

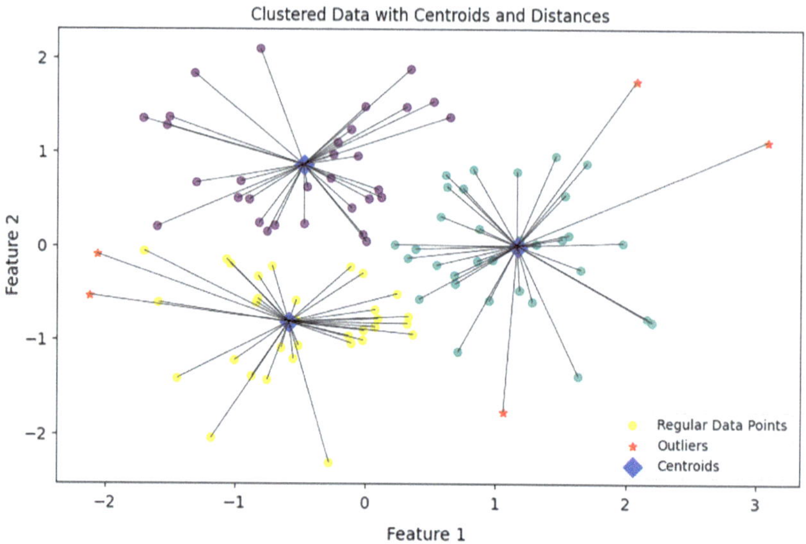

Fig. 12.8 Clustered Data with Centroids and Distance Calculations: This figure visualizes clustered data with an emphasis on cluster centroids and the distances between individual points and their respective centroids. Regular data points are grouped into distinct clusters, while outliers are marked with red stars. Cluster centroids are represented by blue diamond symbols, indicating the mean position of each group. Black lines connect each regular data point to its assigned centroid, representing the calculated distance used to assess the deviation of each point from its cluster's center. Larger deviations may indicate potential anomalies. This distance-based analysis is a crucial step for detecting outliers and understanding cluster compactness, supporting enhanced fraud detection and anomaly identification efforts

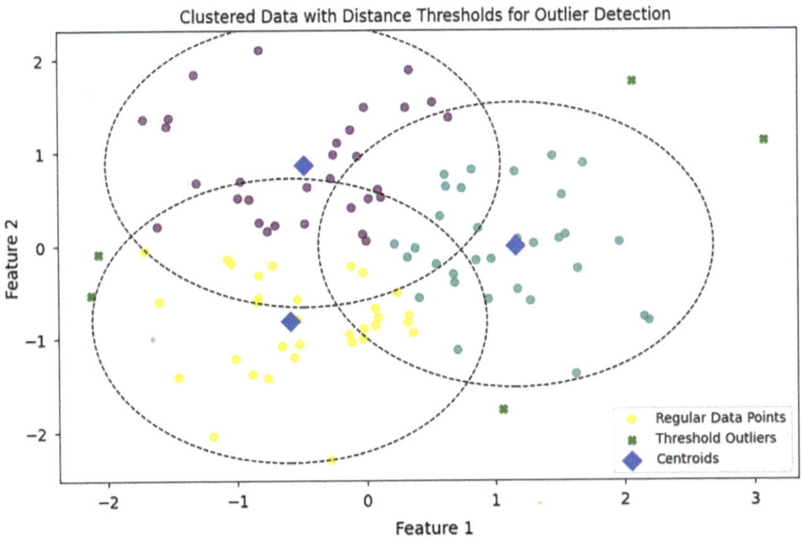

Fig. 12.9 *Clustered Data with Distance Thresholds for Outlier Identification:* This figure demonstrates the application of distance thresholds to detect outliers within clustered data. Regular data points are displayed within distinct clusters, and cluster centroids are represented by blue diamond markers. Dashed black ellipses depict the distance thresholds around each cluster centroid. Data points falling outside these threshold boundaries are flagged as outliers, highlighted with green cross markers. This method enhances fraud detection and anomaly analysis by systematically identifying data points that exhibit significant deviations from expected cluster behavior based on their distance from the centroid

Fig. 12.10 Clustered Data Highlighting Flagged Outliers and Cluster Boundaries. This figure visualizes the final stage of the clustering-based fraud detection process. Data points are grouped into clusters, with centroids marked as blue diamonds and dashed ellipses outlining the approximate cluster boundaries. Red highlighted markers identify the most distant outliers relative to their assigned cluster centroids—these flagged points represent atypical behavior that warrants further investigation. While these outliers are not confirmed fraud cases, they serve as critical starting points for deeper review. This visualization emphasizes the systematic transition from clustering to targeted anomaly detection, reinforcing the role of contextual analysis in refining fraud detection efforts

```
import numpy as np
from sklearn.cluster import KMeans
from sklearn.preprocessing import StandardScaler

# Assuming you have your data in a DataFrame 'df'
# Replace 'features' with the actual names or indices of your features
X = df[['feature1', 'feature2', 'feature3']].values

# Scale the features
scaler = StandardScaler()
X_scaled = scaler.fit_transform(X)

# Train a K-means clustering model
kmeans = KMeans(n_clusters=3, random_state=42)  # Adjust n_clusters as
needed
kmeans.fit(X_scaled)

# Assign each data point to a cluster
cluster_labels = kmeans.predict(X_scaled)

# Get cluster centroids
cluster_centers = kmeans.cluster_centers_

# Calculate the distance of each data point to its cluster centroid
distances = np.linalg.norm(X_scaled - cluster_centers[cluster_labels],
axis=1)

# Determine the threshold for flagging outliers (e.g., beyond the 93rd
percentile)
threshold = np.percentile(distances, 93)

# Flag data points as potential fraud (1) if they are beyond the threshold
fraud_predictions = np.where(distances > threshold, 1, 0)

# Optional: Add predictions to your DataFrame
df['fraud_prediction'] = fraud_predictions

# Now 'df' contains a new column 'fraud_prediction' with 1 for suspected
fraud and 0 otherwise
```

Validating the Model Results

If you don't have original fraud labels, validating results can be challenging since standard performance metrics are unavailable. To verify your results, collaborate with a fraud expert to review the predictions, and investigate further. Understand why cases are outliers; are they genuinely fraudulent or just rare instances of legitimate data? To reduce the number of non-fraudulent outliers being flagged, consider engineering features differently or removing legitimate outliers from the training data after analyst review. If you have historical fraud cases, test your model on that data to see if it can predict them accurately. In the practice opportunity, you will use original fraud labels to evaluate model performance but remember that this is typically not feasible. See Chapter 15 ('Fraud Detection Excellence—A Deep Exploration of Model Metrics, Optimization, and Governance') for more information on model performance concepts.

Practice Opportunity 4: Detecting Outliers

In the next exercises, you will use the K-means algorithm to detect fraud and validate the results by comparing the predictions to the saved labels. The method commonly used to identify fraudulent transactions involves marking the observations that are farthest from the cluster centroid as suspicious. This exercise will show you how to do it and identify the threshold that will be used to confirm the results in future exercises. You can access the scaled observations X_scaled as well as the labels kept in the variable y.

Instructions

1. Split the scaled data and labels y into a training and testing set.
2. Create a MiniBatch K-means model with three clusters and fit it to the training data.
3. Obtain the cluster predictions from the test data and determine the cluster centroids.
4. Set the threshold for identifying fraud as 95% of the distance distribution and above.

Lab access for practice opportunity 4: Explore fraud detection using K-means clustering in the banksim_df dataset. Your challenge involves splitting the data, creating a MiniBatch K-means model, and setting a threshold to identify outliers as potential fraud. Dive in and apply your clustering skills to uncover unusual transactions. Click here for lab access.

Post-Lab Insights

In the practice opportunity 4 lab, you explored the application of the K-means clustering algorithm to detect potential fraudulent transactions in the `banksim_df` dataset. The dataset contained key features such as age, gender, category, and amount, along with the label "fraud."

Key findings:

- The method of marking observations farthest from the cluster centroid as suspicious proved effective in flagging potentially fraudulent transactions.
- By setting a specific threshold, the model could identify the most extreme outliers, which were the most likely to be fraudulent.

The K-means algorithm, with its ability to detect anomalies in transaction data, demonstrated a systematic approach to fraud detection. Identifying transactions that deviated significantly from established patterns it provided a valuable tool for flagging potential fraud. This method's efficacy lies in its simplicity and its focus on transactions that are markedly different from the majority, thereby pinpointing possible areas of concern in financial datasets like `banksim_df`.

Practice Opportunity 5: Checking Model Results

Let's evaluate the model's performance. In the previous exercise, you flagged all observations as fraud if they were in the top 5% by distance from the cluster centroid, meaning these are the extreme outliers of the three clusters. You already have the scaled data and labels separated into training and test sets for this experiment, so y_test is available. The prior exercise's forecasts, `fraud_prediction`, are also available. Let's compute some performance measures to see how well the model did.

Instructions:

1. Compute the area under the ROC curve using the test labels and predicted labels.
2. Calculate the confusion matrix using the test labels and predicted labels, and then visualize the results.

Lab access for practice opportunity 5: Advance your analysis in `banksim_df` by evaluating the performance of your fraud detection model. Focus on computing the ROC curve and visualizing a confusion matrix to assess the precision of your outlier detection. Enhance your skills in model evaluation and validation. Click here for lab access.

Post-Lab Insights

The K-means model employed for fraud detection in the dataset exhibits certain performance metrics, as detailed in the following analysis. For a comprehensive understanding of these concepts, see Chapter 15 ('Fraud Detection Excellence—A Deep Exploration of Model Metrics, Optimization, and Governance')

- *ROC Score:* 0.711
- *Precision:* 0.22
- *Recall:* 0.46
- *F1-score:* 0.30

According to the classification report, the K-means model achieves an overall accuracy of approximately 94.81% for the entire dataset. But note the disparity in precision and F1-score when it comes to detecting fraud (class 1), which are comparatively lower. This discrepancy highlights the model's tendency to correctly identify the majority of non-fraudulent transactions while struggling to accurately pinpoint fraudulent transactions without a significant number of false positives.

The confusion matrix reveals the following insights (see Fig. 12.11):

- The model correctly identified 2024 non-fraud cases as true negatives and 24 fraud cases as true positives.
- However, there were 84 instances where non-fraud transactions were incorrectly flagged as fraud (false positives), and 28 fraud transactions were missed, being classified as non-fraud (false negatives).

These results suggest that while the model can identify a reasonable portion of fraudulent transactions (recall = 0.46), it also misclassifies a significant number of non-fraudulent transactions as fraudulent (yielding low precision = 0.22). This aspect is crucial in contexts like fraud detection, where both false positives and false negatives carry significant implications.

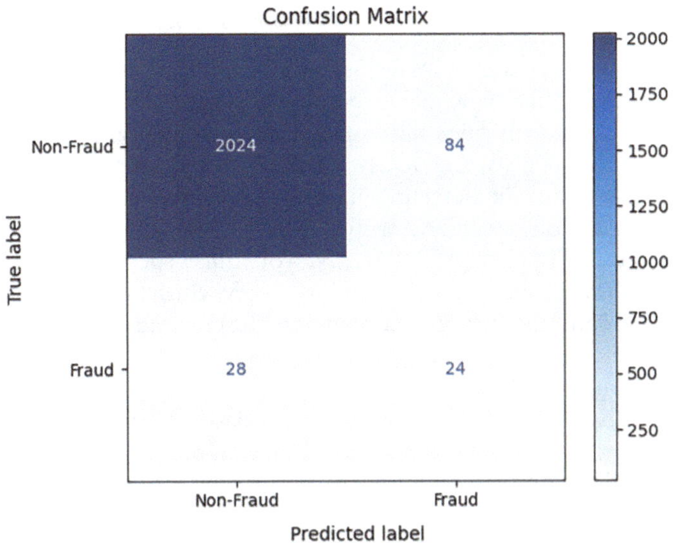

Fig. 12.11 Confusion Matrix for K-Means Model Fraud Detection Performance. This figure presents the confusion matrix evaluating the performance of the K-means-based fraud detection model. True negatives (2024) represent non-fraudulent transactions correctly identified, while true positives (24) represent correctly detected fraudulent transactions. False positives (84) correspond to legitimate transactions incorrectly flagged as fraud, and false negatives (28) are fraudulent transactions missed by the model. The matrix highlights the model's strength in identifying non-fraudulent cases, but also shows a moderate number of misclassifications, emphasizing the balance between recall and precision—a critical consideration in fraud detection contexts where both types of errors carry significant operational and financial consequences

Other Clustering Fraud Detection Methods

Aside from K-means clustering, a variety of clustering methods can be used to detect fraud. Each clustering approach has advantages and disadvantages, and the choice is determined by the nature of the data and the specific situation at hand.

Alternative Clustering Methods

DBSCAN (density-based spatial clustering of applications with noise) is an appealing alternative to K-means because it does not require a specified number of clusters. It finds high-density core samples and expands clusters from them. This works nicely on data with similar density clusters. DBSCAN is useful for detecting fraud in very small clusters. It outperforms K-means on irregularly shaped data but is computationally more demanding. To implement DBSCAN, you must specify the maximum allowable distance between data points inside clusters (epsilon) as well as the minimum number of data points in clusters (`min_samples`).

Implementing DBSCAN

The following Python code demonstrates a basic DBSCAN implementation. It standardizes a small sample dataset, applies the algorithm with defined epsilon and min_samples parameters, and visualizes the resulting clusters along with any noise points identified as outliers.

```
import numpy as np
from sklearn.cluster import DBSCAN
from sklearn.preprocessing import StandardScaler
import matplotlib.pyplot as plt

# Sample data - replace this with your dataset
X = np.array([[1, 2], [2, 2], [2, 3],
              [8, 7], [8, 8], [25, 80]])

# Standardizing the data is often good practice for clustering algorithms
X = StandardScaler().fit_transform(X)

# Defining the DBSCAN parameters
epsilon = 0.5  # maximum distance for two points to be considered in the
same neighborhood
min_samples = 2  # minimum number of points required to form a cluster

# Creating the DBSCAN model
dbscan = DBSCAN(eps=epsilon, min_samples=min_samples)

# Fitting the model
dbscan.fit(X)

# Extracting labels
labels = dbscan.labels_

# Plotting the results
plt.scatter(X[:, 0], X[:, 1], c=labels, cmap='viridis')
plt.xlabel('Feature 1')
plt.ylabel('Feature 2')
plt.title('DBSCAN Clustering')
plt.show()
```

Checking the size of the clusters

After fitting the DBSCAN model, it is useful to inspect the size of each resulting cluster, including the count of noise points (labeled as -1). The following code uses NumPy's unique function to count and print the number of points assigned to each cluster.

```
# Counting the number of points in each cluster
unique_labels, counts = np.unique(labels, return_counts=True)

# Printing cluster sizes
for label, count in zip(unique_labels, counts):
    if label == -1:
        print(f"Noise points: {count} points")
    else:
        print(f"Cluster {label}: {count} points")
```

Practice Opportunity 6: Detecting Outliers Using DBSCAN

You can adapt the existing process to use DBSCAN (Density-Based Spatial Clustering of Applications with Noise) instead of K-means. DBSCAN is a density-based clustering algorithm that doesn't require specifying the number of clusters beforehand, and it can identify outliers as points in low-density regions.

Instructions:

1. Create and fit a DBSCAN model to the training data.
2. Identify core samples and noise points (outliers) in the test data.
3. Since DBSCAN doesn't use centroids like K-means, you'll identify the outliers directly based on the DBSCAN labels.
4. Compute the area under the ROC curve using the test labels and predicted labels.
5. Calculate the confusion matrix using the test labels and predicted labels, and then visualize the results.

Lab access for practice opportunity 6: Dive into the`banksim_df` dataset to identify potential fraud using DBSCAN, a robust unsupervised learning technique. Your challenge is to analyze transaction data, validate results with fraud labels, and visualize findings through ROC curves and confusion matrices. Click here to start exploring and applying your skills to uncovering hidden patterns of financial fraud.

Post-Lab Insights

The DBSCAN algorithm, applied to the `banksim_df` dataset for detecting outliers, offers a unique approach compared to traditional methods like K-means. Unlike K-means, DBSCAN does not require a predetermined number of clusters and works effectively by identifying outliers as points in low-density areas.

Key findings and metrics: (see Fig. 12.12):

- The DBSCAN model was able to detect all fraudulent transactions (true positives) without missing any (zero false negatives), achieving a recall score of 1.0.

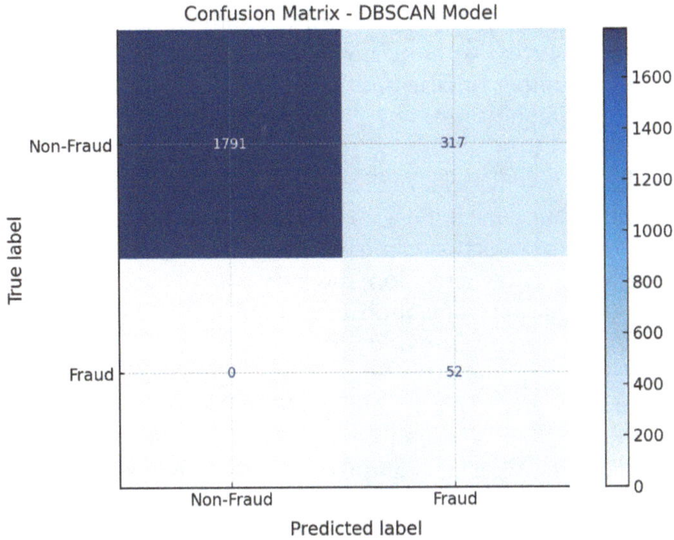

Fig. 12.12 Confusion Matrix for DBSCAN Model Performance. This figure presents the confusion matrix for the DBSCAN-based fraud detection model. The model correctly identified all fraudulent transactions (52 true positives) without any false negatives, achieving a recall score of 1.0. However, 317 legitimate transactions were incorrectly flagged as fraudulent (false positives), resulting in a precision of approximately 0.14. The overall accuracy was about 85.32%, and the F1-score, balancing precision and recall, was approximately 0.25. The confusion matrix visually highlights the model's sensitivity to detecting fraud but also underscores the high rate of false positives, an important consideration when balancing fraud detection effectiveness against operational impact in real-world applications

- However, the precision was low, at approximately 0.14, indicating that a significant number of non-fraudulent transactions were incorrectly flagged as fraudulent. This resulted in 317 false positives out of 2160 total test transactions.
- The F1-score, balancing precision and recall, was approximately 0.25, reflecting the trade-off between these two metrics.
- The overall accuracy of the DBSCAN model on the dataset was about 85.32%.

As indicated, the model has successfully identified all fraudulent transactions (true positives) without any false negatives, but at the cost of a relatively high number of false positives.

Here are the implications:

- The DBSCAN model's high recall implies it is highly sensitive to detecting fraud, making it a valuable tool for scenarios where missing a fraudulent transaction can have severe consequences.
- However, the low precision suggests a high rate of false alarms, which could lead to operational inefficiencies and potential customer dissatisfaction in a real-world setting.
- The results highlight the importance of considering the balance between sensitivity (recall) and specificity (precision) in fraud detection systems. The choice of model and parameters should align with the specific requirements and tolerance for false positives in a given application.

The DBSCAN model's ability to identify all fraudulent transactions is commendable, but its high false positive rate necessitates careful consideration of its application in practice. Its effectiveness in outlier detection, particularly in scenarios where missing a fraudulent transaction is not an option, is noteworthy, but it should be complemented with additional measures or models to reduce false positives.

You can plot (see Fig. 12.13) the ROC curves for both the K-means and DBSCAN models to visually compare their performance. For comprehensive coverage of these concepts, see Chapter 16 "Knowledge Assessment Lab".

The plot illustrates the receiver operating characteristic (ROC) curves for both the K-means and DBSCAN models. To differentiate between the two models:

1. K-means model: The ROC curve for the K-means model is depicted as the blue line above the dashed diagonal line. This curve has an area under the curve (AUC) of 0.71, as previously calculated.
2. DBSCAN model: The ROC curve for the DBSCAN model is shown as the uppermost line, above the K-means curve. This model's ROC curve has a higher AUC of 0.925.

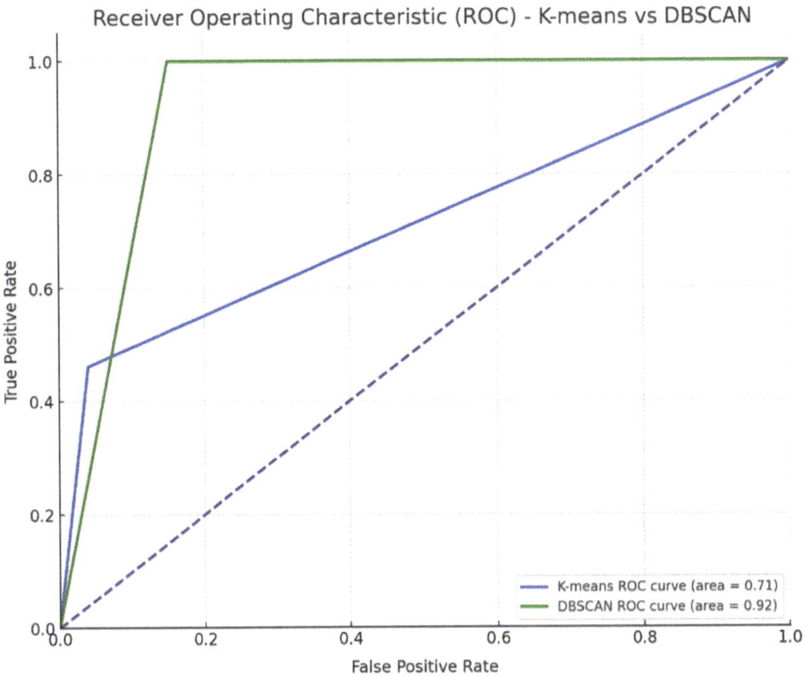

Fig. 12.13 ROC Curves for K-Means and DBSCAN Models in Fraud Detection

This visualization enables comparing the two models' ability to distinguish between fraudulent and non-fraudulent transactions. The AUC measures a model's predictive accuracy, with a higher value indicating better performance. In this scenario, the DBSCAN model demonstrates a higher AUC, suggesting it more effectively identifies fraud.

Flagging Fraud Using Smallest Clusters

Instead of identifying fraud based on cluster outliers, you can use the smallest clusters as an indication of fraud. This approach works when fraudulent behavior shares common features and forms small clusters in the data. Visualizing data using techniques like PCA (covered later in this chapter) can help reveal such clusters.

Challenges in Real-World Data

Detecting fraud in real-world data may be more difficult than in well-separated clusters. Multiple small to medium-sized clusters may be closely connected to larger ones, making it difficult to determine which clusters represent fraudulent behavior.

Performance metrics: Metrics such as the average silhouette score can be used to evaluate the performance of the clustering model, like DBSCAN. To calculate the size of each cluster, you can use functions like NumPy's `bincount`, which counts the occurrences of each value in an array. You can then sort by size and decide how many of the smaller clusters to flag as fraud.

> TIP
>
> Clustering approaches can detect fraud based on the situation and data. DBSCAN is a popular alternative to K-means for irregular data and unknown clusters. Detecting fraud by identifying the smallest clusters can also work. Real-world data may require more research and a mix of ways to solve this problem.

Self-organizing maps (SOMs) are neural networks that visualize and cluster high-dimensional data on a low-dimensional neural grid. SOMs have input, competitive, and output layers. In the competitive layer, neurons compete to be the best matching unit (BMU) for each input vector. A low-dimensional grid of output layer neurons represents clusters. SOMs employ a similarity measure to compare input vectors to neuron weight vectors and alter BMU and neighbor weights using a learning method. SOMs can display clusters and handle high-dimensional data, but they are computationally expensive and need numerous parameters.

> TIP
>
> Non-hierarchical clustering methods can be useful for identifying clusters in large datasets without building a hierarchy of clusters. K-means clustering is a popular and efficient method that requires the number of clusters to be specified beforehand, while SOMs provide a visual representation of the clusters and can handle high-dimensional data. The choice of non-hierarchical clustering method depends on the specific problem domain and the characteristics of the data.

Reducing the Dimensionality of the Data with PCA

Reducing the dimensionality of data is a crucial step in many machine learning applications, and principal component analysis (PCA) is a widely used unsupervised approach for this purpose. PCA is particularly effective in transforming high-dimensional data into a lower-dimensional representation while retaining essential information. Here are the key aspects of PCA:

- *Independence from labeled data:* PCA does not require labeled data for its training or analysis process. This makes it a versatile tool for exploratory data analysis and preprocessing, applicable even when the dataset does not have defined target variables.
- *Dimensionality reduction*: The primary function of PCA is to reduce the dimensionality of data. It achieves this by projecting the original high-dimensional data onto a new, lower-dimensional subspace. The goal is to retain as much variance or information as possible from the original dataset.
- *Component discovery*: PCA identifies principal components, which are linear combinations of the original input features. These components capture different aspects or variations in the data.
- *Orthogonality of components*: An essential characteristic of PCA is that these components are orthogonal and uncorrelated. This orthogonality ensures that each component captures unique variance in the data, thereby reducing feature redundancy.
- *Variance and dimensionality reduction*: PCA selects the principal components that account for the most variance in the data. By focusing on these components, PCA effectively reduces the dimensions of the data. This is particularly beneficial for visualization purposes, enhancing computing efficiency, and improving the performance of certain machine learning algorithms that struggle with high-dimensional data.

TIP

Although PCA is primarily a technique for dimensionality reduction rather than clustering, its ability to simplify data without losing critical information makes it an invaluable tool when combined with clustering algorithms. When used in conjunction with hierarchical or non-hierarchical clustering methods, PCA can facilitate the discovery of more distinct cluster structures. It helps mitigate the challenges posed by the curse of dimensionality, which can significantly hamper the performance of clustering algorithms in high-dimensional spaces. By simplifying the data structure, PCA can lead to more efficient and effective clustering outcomes.

Understanding Autoencoders

Autoencoders are a unique and powerful type of unsupervised machine learning algorithm that employ artificial neural networks to learn representations or encodings of data. Central to their architecture are two interconnected networks: an encoder and a decoder.

- *Encoder network:* The encoder's role is to compress or reduce the dimensionality of the input data. It accomplishes this by transforming the input into a compressed representation, often referred to as the code layer or bottleneck. This compressed form represents a distilled essence of the input data.
- *Decoder network*: The decoder network takes over from the point of compression. Its job is to reconstruct the original input data from this compressed code layer. The process involves upsampling the compressed data back to the original input space. Since the original input data is also used as the target for output, this self-referential nature classifies autoencoders as an unsupervised learning technique.
- *Utility of autoencoders:* Autoencoders are incredibly versatile and find applications in dimensionality reduction, feature extraction, and representation learning. They are particularly effective when the input data exhibits a high degree of correlation. However, their performance can degrade when dealing with independent input data, as they thrive on identifying and leveraging patterns and relationships in the data.
- *Mathematical mechanics*: The functioning of both the encoder and decoder networks involves a series of mathematical operations. These include multiplying the input data by weights, adding a bias, and applying an activation function. A noteworthy aspect is the concept

of tied weights, where the weights of the encoder and decoder are mirrored or matched.

- *Discovery of hidden patterns*: One of the most compelling aspects of autoencoders is their ability to uncover hidden patterns, structures, or relationships within the input data without explicit supervision. This makes them particularly useful in scenarios where the underlying structure of the data is complex and not immediately apparent.

TIP

Autoencoders, through their dual network structure of encoding and decoding, offer a sophisticated approach to understanding and representing complex data. Their ability to distill and reconstruct data gives them a unique place in the machine learning landscape, especially for tasks involving data compression, reconstruction, and unsupervised pattern discovery.

Summary

This chapter explored the use of clustering in fraud detection, focusing on the K-means algorithm and its role in grouping data to identify outliers that could indicate fraud. It introduced DBSCAN, an alternative clustering method, and emphasized the careful analysis of outliers, as they are not inherently indicative of fraud. The chapter combined theoretical insights with practical Python examples, aiming to equip you with skills for applying clustering in real-world scenarios.

In Chapter 13, the focus shifts to applying your knowledge to real-world situations. The chapter presents scenarios where a bank seeks to gain a deeper understanding of its customers' spending habits and credit card usage patterns. This insight is crucial for the bank to develop targeted marketing strategies. The chapter promises to offer hands-on experiences demonstrating how data analysis can directly impact and enhance customer relationship management and marketing efficacy in the banking sector.

PART IV

Supervised Learning for Fraud Detection

Where unsupervised learning finds patterns without guidance, supervised learning learns from experience. By training on historical data in which fraud cases have already been identified and labelled, supervised models develop the ability to recognise the signatures of fraudulent behaviour and apply that recognition to new, unseen transactions. This makes supervised learning the most widely deployed family of techniques in operational fraud detection—and the one that delivers the most directly actionable predictions. Part IV covers the full arc of supervised learning for fraud across four chapters. Chapter 13 introduces regression as a fraud detection tool, examining how regression models quantify risk, how XGBoost extends classical regression through ensemble learning, and how these techniques adapt across different fraud contexts. Chapter 14 broadens the toolkit to classification, working through the core algorithms used in practice—logistic regression, support vector machines, decision trees, random forests, K-nearest neighbours, naïve Bayes, gradient boosting, and artificial neural networks—alongside the essential mechanics of model preparation, data splitting, and training. Chapter 15 moves from building models to evaluating and governing them, covering classification metrics, ROC curves, hyperparameter optimisation, bias-variance trade-offs, overfitting, model deployment, governance frameworks, and automated machine learning through AutoGluon. Chapter 16 consolidates everything through a capstone knowledge assessment lab, applying advanced machine learning to a real insurance fraud detection scenario using AutoGluon—bridging theory and production-ready practice. Together, these chapters transform supervised learning from a concept into a deployable fraud detection capability.

CHAPTER 13

Regression in Fraud Detection

In this chapter you embark on an in-depth exploration of supervised learning and its critical role in fraud detection. Supervised learning, a cornerstone of predictive analytics, involves training models on labeled datasets to predict outcomes accurately. This chapter delves into the regression and classification aspects of supervised learning, illuminating their applications in the nuanced field of fraud detection.

This chapter takes you through various facets of supervised learning, starting with the fundamental principles of regression and classification. You will explore the nature of the target variable in these contexts, understand how continuous variables are used in regression for nuanced risk assessments, and how categorical variables in classification help identify fraudulent vs. non-fraudulent activities.

A significant portion of this chapter addresses the inherent challenges in fraud detection, from the ambiguity and noise in the data to the complexities of defining the target variable. You'll learn about the intricate processes of feature engineering and selection and their vital role in enhancing model performance and interpretability.

You will also confront the practical challenges of applying these models, such as managing data imbalances and ensuring the ethical use of algorithms. The chapter emphasizes the importance of robust techniques to

A. Al Aqqad, *Fraud Analytics in Action*
https://doi.org/10.1007/978-3-032-16023-2_13

navigate through the uncertainties characteristic of fraud detection, highlighting the need for models that are not just precise but also adaptable and resilient.

A key highlight of this chapter is the focus on XGBoost (extreme gradient boosting), an advanced ensemble learning technique. We delve into the mechanics of XGBoost, its strengths in handling complex datasets, and its adaptability to both regression and classification tasks. You will gain insights into how XGBoost, with its ensemble approach, excels in fraud detection, offering a potent combination of efficiency, accuracy, and flexibility.

The chapter culminates with a practical example: employing XGBoost in predictive analysis for university admissions. This section will solidify your understanding of the algorithm and regression techniques and showcase their real-world application in predictive modeling.

By the end of this chapter, you'll have a comprehensive understanding of supervised learning, its challenges, and its profound impact on fraud detection. Armed with this knowledge, you'll be well-equipped to apply these concepts and techniques in various professional contexts, setting a strong foundation for advanced exploration in subsequent chapters.

Supervised Learning

What Is Supervised Learning?

Supervised learning, which uses a labeled data, is an important component of predictive analytics and plays an important role in fraud detection. This method involves training a machine learning model on a labeled dataset with known values for the target variable (fraud or non-fraud). The model can learn to predict outcomes based on novel, unexpected data by mapping input features to the target variable. There are two types of predictive analytics based on the measurement level of the target: *regression and classification.*

Nature of the target variable: The nature of the target variable in supervised learning can be either continuous (regression) or categorical (classification). In fraud detection:

- *Regression:* The target variable in regression is continuous and fluctuates within a set interval. This interval can be limited (between

0 and 1) or infinite (between 0 and infinity). An example of fraud detection is predicting the amount of fraud.

- *Classification:* Classification in supervised learning uses a categorical target variable with
  - o *Binary classification*: featuring two categories (e.g., fraud vs. no fraud) and
  - o *Multiclass classification*: involving more than two (e.g., severe fraud, medium fraud, no fraud). For instance, in insurance fraud detection, a classification model estimates the probability of fraud, while a regression model forecasts potential loss given fraud. These calculations together estimate expected fraud loss.

However, supervised learning in fraud detection is not without challenges. Accurately labeling fraudulent activities can be difficult due to their complex and deceptive nature. Additionally, the risk of mislabeling and noisy data can complicate the model's training process.

The Imperative for Robust Techniques

Given the complexities in fraud detection, employing robust supervised learning techniques is crucial. Key strategies include:

- *Feature Engineering and Selection:* This foundational step, detailed in Chapter 7, (Feature Engineering) involves creating and choosing the most relevant features to improve model performance and reduce the risk of overfitting.
- *Choosing the Right Methodology:* A range of algorithms, from linear regression to neural networks, can be employed, each with its strengths. Ensemble methods like XGBoost and LightGBM are particularly effective.
- *Performance Evaluation:* Rigorously evaluating model performance using metrics like precision, recall, and the F1 score is essential, as detailed in Chapter 15 (Fraud Detection Excellence—A Deep Exploration of Model Metrics, Optimization, and Governance) Balancing sensitivity (identifying true fraud cases) with specificity (not mislabeling non-fraudulent cases) is crucial.

TIP

Supervised learning is pivotal for fraud detection in predictive analytics, as it helps organizations identify potentially fraudulent activities based on historical data. Yet, its success hinges on the model's ability to manage uncertainties and the quality of the features used in the modeling process.

Defining the Target Variable in Fraud Detection

In predictive analytics for fraud detection, the precision in defining the target variable is crucial. The target variable represents the likelihood of fraudulent activity and is central to guiding the predictive model. However, accurately defining this variable can be complex, considering various factors such as direct and indirect costs, reputational damage, and the time value of money.

Types of Target Variables:

- Binary variable (fraud vs. non-fraud): This categorical distinction labels transactions as fraudulent or non-fraudulent. For example, transactions with unusual patterns might be flagged as Fraud, while those aligned with typical customer behavior could be labeled non-fraud.
- Continuous variable (probability score): Some models use a continuous probability score, ranging from 0 (low likelihood of fraud) to 1 (high likelihood). This approach is valuable for nuanced assessments, allowing for varying levels of scrutiny and detailed risk analysis.

Importance of Continuous Scores: Unlike binary classifications, continuous probability scores offer a more detailed perspective of transactional risk. This granularity enables more informed decision-making, tailoring responses to the specific risk level of each transaction. These scores can be especially beneficial for identifying subtle fraud indicators in financial transaction data, aiding in proactive fraud detection strategies.

By adopting a binary or continuous target variable, models in fraud detection can be customized to meet specific operational requirements. This customization is pivotal in balancing the need for accurate fraud detection against the risk of false positives, ensuring that the models are effective and efficient.

> TIP
>
> Ultimately, the choice between binary and continuous target variables in fraud detection depends on the specific system requirements and objectives. Both methods provide valuable insights but cater to different operational and analytical needs. The subsequent sections of this book will delve into various techniques and their applications in fraud detection, considering these complexities.

Direct and Indirect Expenses in Defining the Target Variable for Fraud Detection

In predictive analytics for fraud detection, accurately defining the target variable is a nuanced process complicated by factors such as direct and indirect expenses, reputational damage, and the time value of money. These elements introduce layers of complexity, especially in labeling transactions accurately.

Direct expenses are the immediate, quantifiable costs resulting from fraudulent activities, like monetary loss from unauthorized transactions. While these costs are typically straightforward to quantify, the challenge lies in transactions where direct costs are not immediately evident, demanding a deeper analysis to determine their fraudulent nature.

Indirect expenses, on the other hand, are more elusive and challenging to quantify. They encompass long-term consequences such as increased security measures, legal fees, investigative costs, and the need for additional resources to prevent future fraud. The subtlety and the delayed manifestation of these costs make accurately labeling transactions complex. The full extent of indirect costs often becomes clear only after comprehensive analysis, impacting the ability to identify and categorize fraudulent transactions swiftly and accurately.

Reputational damage also plays a significant role in complicating the labeling process. The long-term impact of a fraud incident on an organization's reputation can lead to a loss of customer trust, reduced business, and a decline in market value. This damage is not directly measurable in the short term, posing challenges in labeling transactions based on potential long-term effects.

Furthermore, the *time value of money* adds another layer of complexity. It involves considering the future financial impact of fraud, which affects an organization's long-term financial planning and stability. Incorporating this aspect into the labeling process requires predictive analysis and adds to the complexity of accurately identifying and categorizing fraud.

Collectively, these factors underscore the challenges in defining the target variable in fraud detection. They highlight the need for sophisticated models capable of immediate fraud evidence and long-term implications. This necessitates advanced data analysis techniques, machine learning models adept at handling ambiguity, and a comprehensive fraud detection approach considering immediate and future impacts.

Understanding the Challenges in Supervised Learning

In fraud detection, a major challenge is the imbalanced nature of datasets, where fraudulent transactions are much fewer than legitimate ones. Addressing this requires techniques like oversampling or using the Synthetic Minority Over-sampling Technique (SMOTE), as explored in Chapter 9 (Handling Imbalanced Data Sets) Furthermore, the evolving nature of fraud tactics necessitates continuous model updating and refinement.

TIP

Defining the target variable in supervised fraud detection models is intricate and multifaceted. It demands careful consideration of the nature of fraud and a meticulous approach to data handling, model training, and evaluation. This complexity underscores the need for comprehensive strategies that address noise, uncertainty, data imbalance, and ethical considerations to create effective and reliable fraud detection systems.

SIDEBAR

Practical Considerations in Implementing Fraud Detection Models

Implementing fraud detection models in real-world scenarios involves several practical considerations:

- Real-time Detection: Models must be capable of analyzing transactions instantaneously for real-time fraud detection.
- Integration with Existing Systems: Models should seamlessly integrate with existing transaction processing systems, considering data compatibility, scalability, and latency.
- Evolving Fraud Tactics: Continuous model training and adaptation are necessary to keep up with sophisticated fraudulent strategies.
- Collaboration with Domain Experts: Combining technical expertise with domain knowledge ensures models are both accurate and relevant to real-world fraud patterns.

Regression Analysis in Fraud Detection

Regression analysis, a cornerstone of predictive analytics, is crucial in fraud detection. This statistical method estimates a continuous dependent variable based on various independent variables. It's especially effective in discerning relationships between multiple factors and the probability of fraudulent activities.

Regression models can predict the risk associated with financial transactions in fraud detection. For instance, variables like transaction amount, time since the last transaction, geographical location, and frequency of transactions can be analyzed to estimate a continuous probability of fraud. This nuanced approach provides more detailed risk assessments than binary classifications, enhancing informed decision-making.

Applications and Adaptability of Regression Models

Regression analysis is not confined to fraud detection alone; its versatility extends to sectors like banking, economics, healthcare, and weather forecasting. The adaptability of regression models to specific patterns in financial transaction data is key to their effectiveness. They can be trained to identify subtle fraud indicators, thereby enhancing predictive accuracy and aiding in developing proactive anti-fraud strategies.

Challenges and Solutions in Regression Analysis

Despite its strengths, regression in fraud detection faces challenges like data imbalance, evolving fraud patterns, and the need for model interpretability. Techniques like weighted regression address data imbalance, common in fraud detection scenarios where legitimate ones often outnumber fraudulent transactions.

Model interpretability, particularly in linear regression, provides transparency in decision-making, which is essential for trust and regulatory compliance. The application of regression models also demands integration into existing transaction processing systems, necessitating considerations for real-time data processing and low latency.

Ethical Considerations

Ethical and privacy considerations are paramount in regression analysis. Models must be developed with an awareness of potential biases and a commitment to fair treatment. Ensuring privacy compliance and regular audits are crucial for maintaining transparency and fairness.

Regression analysis in fraud detection is a multifaceted approach beyond predictive modeling. It involves addressing complex challenges and integrating ethical practices, forming a comprehensive strategy for effective fraud detection.

> TIP
>
> The subsequent sections of this book will explore various regression techniques and their applications in designing effective fraud detection models, addressing the challenges and nuances detailed above.

XGBoost in Fraud Detection

"If I have seen further, it is by standing on the shoulders of giants," Isaac Newton

XGBoost, or extreme gradient boosting, is a highly favored algorithm among data scientists for its adaptability to regression and classification problems. Renowned for its effectiveness, XGBoost has claimed victories in several Kaggle competitions and stands out for its practical utility in fraud detection scenarios.

As a supervised learning algorithm, XGBoost necessitates labeled data for training. It employs the gradient-boosted trees algorithm, a concept we will delve into more comprehensively. The essence of XGBoost lies in its ability to enhance predictions by combining outputs from a series of weak models in an ensemble approach. This incremental learning from previous weaker models underpins the strength of XGBoost.

A key aspect of XGBoost is its robustness to various data distributions and relationships. It offers an extensive array of hyperparameters that, while allowing for tailored model customization, also present challenges in tuning for optimal performance. An entire section of our discussions will explore hyperparameter optimization strategies for XGBoost, emphasizing its flexibility and adaptability in fraud detection tasks.

XGBoost's capabilities extend to efficient memory usage and accelerated processing speeds. It's built on the principle of iteratively improving accuracy by learning from past mistakes, reflecting Isaac Newton's idea of building upon the knowledge of predecessors (See Fig. 13.1).

Advantages of XGBoost in Fraud Analytics

- No need for feature scaling.
- Effective with datasets containing missing values.
- Resilience to outliers.
- Applicable for both regression and classification tasks.
- High computational efficiency and fast predictions.
- Facilitates distributed training across multiple machines.

Challenges and Limitations

- XGBoost sometimes struggles with extrapolation, particularly for data points outside the range of the training set.
- Extensive tuning requirements, which can be time-consuming.
- Slower training speeds, although distributed training options, can mitigate this.

For instance, as illustrated in (see Fig. 13.2), while linear regression and artificial neural networks can perform reasonable extrapolation outside their training range, XGBoost and algorithms like Random Forest may not. This limitation becomes evident when the model is tested on data points beyond its trained range, resulting in subpar performance or unreasonable predictions. This characteristic is crucial when employing XGBoost in fraud detection, especially when dealing with data that may extend beyond familiar ranges.

Here's the visualization illustrating how different models perform when extrapolating beyond their training range:

- The gray dots represent the training data confined to a specific range (up to the black dashed line).

Fig. 13.1 Medieval Illustration of the Philosophy of Knowledge Transmission: This illuminated manuscript page visually represents the allegory of intellectual inheritance, echoing the principle behind XGBoost's iterative learning approach. Derived from Greek mythology, it depicts a crowned figure symbolizing "Philosophia" (Philosophy), embodying divine wisdom and scholarly tradition. A smaller scholar stands atop Philosophy's shoulders, illustrating the concept of building upon the knowledge of predecessors — an idea famously captured by Isaac Newton's quote, "If I have seen further, it is by standing on the shoulders of giants." The detailed Gothic script, rendered in red and black ink, conveys theological and philosophical teachings about the divine origin of wisdom. The refined parchment background enhances the clarity and historic authenticity of the illustration, making it an apt metaphor for XGBoost's strength: progressively learning from prior models to achieve superior outcomes. Adapted from: Wikimedia Commons, Library of Congress, Rosenwald 4, Bl. 5r. Available at: https://commons.wikimedia.org/wiki/File:Library_of_Congress,_Rosenwald_4,_Bl._5r.jpg

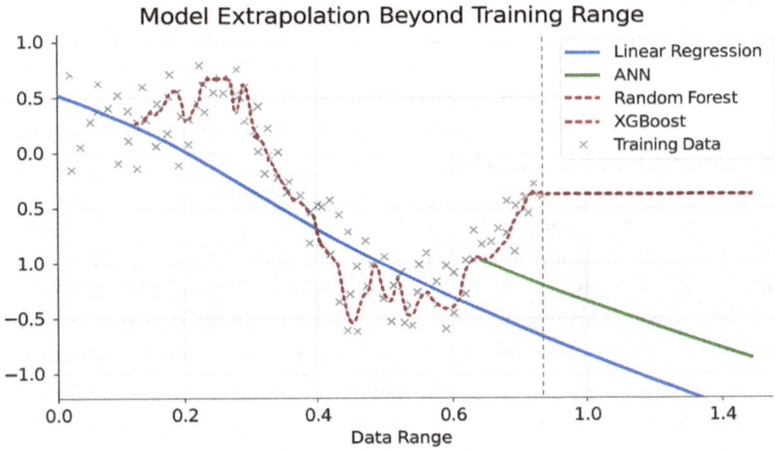

Fig. 13.2 Model Extrapolation Beyond Training Range. Comparison of how Linear Regression, ANN, Random Forest, and XGBoost behave when predicting beyond their training range (marked by the vertical dashed line). The figure highlights the importance of understanding model limitations when extrapolating beyond observed data

- The *linear regression* (blue line) and *artificial neural network (ANN)* (green line) models show a reasonable level of extrapolation beyond the training range.
- Conversely, the *random forest* (red dashed line) and *XGBoost* (purple dashed line) models demonstrate limitations in extrapolation. Their predictions become less reliable as the data extends beyond the range they were trained on.

TIP

"When in doubt, just use XGBoost!" Owen Zhang, 1st place Kaggle Winner

XGBoost is a powerful tool in the arsenal of fraud detection techniques. Its advantages in handling complex datasets efficiently are counterbalanced by the need for careful tuning and awareness of its extrapolation limits. With this understanding, XGBoost can be leveraged effectively to uncover and predict fraudulent activities in financial transactions.

XGBoost: What Is Boosting?

Boosting is an ensemble machine learning technique that significantly enhances the accuracy of predictions in fraud detection by systematically learning from past mistakes. It operates by sequentially training weaker models, each honing in on the errors of its predecessors, to collectively improve the predictive capability.

Consider a typical scenario in fraud detection involving a binary classification problem. The initial model attempts to separate the classes with a basic linear boundary. Due to its inherent simplicity, this model assigns equal weight to all data points, leading to some misclassifications. Subsequent models then focus on these inaccuracies, adjusting their parameters specifically to correct these errors. This iterative refinement process continues, with each new model aiming to reduce the errors of the ones before it.

The culmination of the boosting process is a final model that encapsulates the learning from all previous models. This model is more than just a sum of its parts; it's an ensemble that leverages the collective insights gained throughout the process, resulting in a robust and precise tool for detecting fraud.

This method is exemplified in algorithms like XGBoost (eXtreme gradient boosting), a staple in fraud analytics due to its versatility in handling diverse data types and scenarios. XGBoost thrives in classification and regression problems, making it a preferred choice for tackling complex patterns in fraud detection. Its success is evident in numerous real-world applications and competitions, highlighting its effectiveness in predictive modeling in fraud detection and analytics.

In essence, boosting represents a strategic fusion of multiple models, each contributing to a more refined and accurate prediction. Its ability to iteratively improve and adapt makes it an invaluable approach in the nuanced and challenging field of fraud detection.

XGBoost: What Is Ensemble Learning?

Ensemble learning, a foundational concept for understanding XGBoost, is crucial in advanced fraud detection systems. XGBoost, standing for eXtreme gradient boosting, embodies ensemble learning techniques, particularly boosting. This approach harnesses the collective intelligence of multiple models, enhancing predictive accuracy and robustness.

Ensemble learning, comprising methods like bagging and boosting, integrates multiple models to improve decision-making capabilities. The process involves synthesizing input from various sources rather than relying on a single predictive model. This collective approach is akin to the parable of the blind men and the elephant, where each individual, touching a different part of the elephant, contributes to a more accurate understanding of the whole (See Fig. 13.3).

XGBoost, an exemplar of ensemble learning techniques, stands out in fraud detection for its methodical integration of insights from multiple models, particularly those that are individually weak or average. This integration is key to its success, as it harnesses the collective strength of these models, leading to significantly enhanced predictive accuracy and robustness. Central to XGBoost's methodology is the principle of boosting, a specialized form of ensemble learning that systematically addresses and corrects the errors of preceding models through sequential training.

This approach markedly reduces variance and the risk of overfitting and ensures that the model's capacity to generalize is continuously improved. Such a dynamic and adaptive process is crucial in fraud detection, where the ability to learn from past mistakes and adapt to evolving fraudulent patterns is essential for effective and reliable predictions. This makes XGBoost a powerful tool for detecting complex fraudulent activities, surpassing the capabilities of traditional single-model approaches with its ability to refine accuracy and adapt over time.

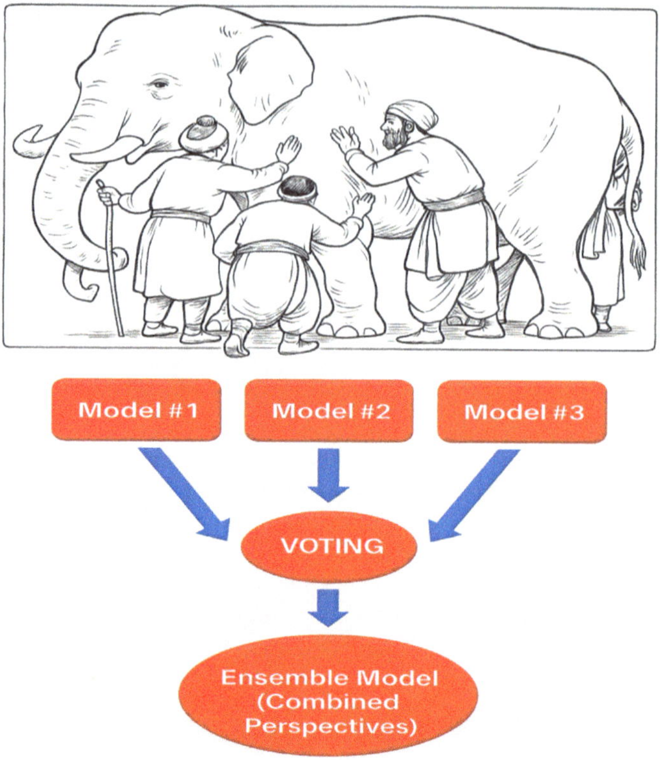

Fig. 13.3 Ensemble learning illustrated through the parable of the blind men and the elephant. This figure uses the classic parable of the blind men and the elephant to illustrate the concept of ensemble learning, a foundational principle underlying XGBoost. Each individual interacts with a different part of the elephant, symbolizing how separate models (Model #1, Model #2, and Model #3) each capture only a partial perspective of the underlying reality. Through a structured aggregation or voting process, these individual perspectives are combined into a single ensemble model with improved accuracy and robustness. This mirrors XGBoost's approach in fraud detection, where multiple weak learners are sequentially integrated to produce a highly accurate and adaptive predictive system. The visual reinforces the idea that combining diverse viewpoints leads to a more complete and reliable understanding, which is essential when addressing complex and evolving fraud patterns. Adapted from: Wikimedia Commons, 'Blind men and elephant.' Available at: https://commons.wikimedia.org/wiki/File:Blind_men_and_elephant.png

Decision Trees and Their Ensemble in Fraud Detection
Multiple decision trees (classification and regression trees, or CART) are combined in an ensemble model. Each tree makes its prediction based on different conditions, and these individual predictions are aggregated to form a more accurate final prediction. This ensemble approach amplifies the strength of each tree, compensating for any individual weaknesses, and culminates in a robust model capable of handling the complexities of fraud detection.

In practical terms, consider the application of decision tree ensembles in XGBoost for fraud detection. These trees, part of supervised learning models, analyze transaction data based on specific conditions or parameters. For example, a decision tree might categorize transactions based on transaction amount, frequency, and location deviations. Each tree in the ensemble focuses on different aspects, contributing insights to the overall analysis.

One tree might evaluate transactions based on the amount, looking for unusually large transactions that deviate from a customer's typical spending pattern. Another tree might focus on the geographical location of transactions, identifying those that occur far from the customer's usual area of activity. A third tree could analyze the frequency and timing of transactions, flagging those that occur suspiciously close together or at unusual times.

By aggregating the predictions from all these trees, XGBoost forms a comprehensive decision-making tool for fraud detection. The final prediction score, a cumulative result of assessments from each tree, represents the likelihood of a transaction being fraudulent. This score might consider various risk factors, such as abnormal transaction sizes, atypical locations, or unusual timings.

The strength of XGBoost in fraud detection primarily lies in its comprehensive approach. This method integrates multiple models, enabling a nuanced understanding of potential fraud risks. By learning from the errors of previous models, XGBoost continuously adapts to new patterns and complexities in fraudulent activities, enhancing its detection capabilities. Its ability to combine insights from various models and learn from past mistakes positions it as an effective tool for identifying complex fraudulent patterns in financial transactions, offering a significant advantage over traditional single-model approaches.

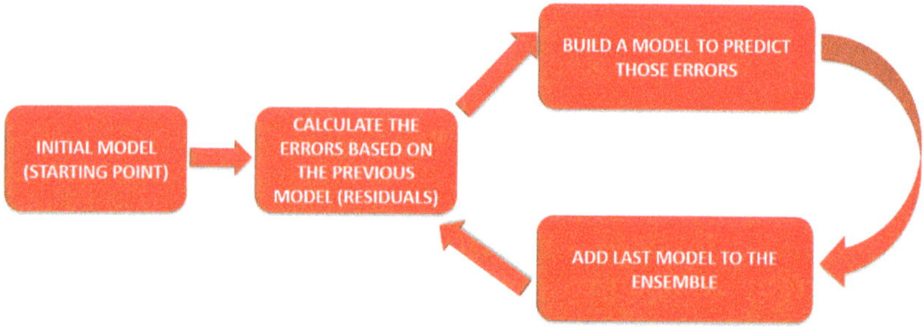

Fig. 13.4 The Iterative Boosting Process in XGBoost: This figure visually illustrates the core iterative process of XGBoost's boosting methodology. It starts with an initial model (the starting point) that generates baseline predictions. The residual errors—the differences between the model's predictions and the actual outcomes—are then calculated. In response, a new model is built specifically to predict these residual errors. This model is subsequently added to the ensemble. The process repeats cyclically, with each new model progressively correcting the mistakes of the previous ones. This continuous learning from prior errors significantly enhances the model's overall predictive power and robustness, making XGBoost particularly effective in complex tasks like fraud detection

SIDEBAR

XGBoost in Fraud Detection: A Deep Dive

XGBoost (eXtreme gradient boosting) is a cornerstone in modern fraud detection, offering a nuanced approach to predictive modeling. Its methodology revolves around ensemble learning, where multiple weak models combine to form a robust predictive system. This section delves into the intricate workings of XGBoost and its application in fraud detection.

Building models sequentially: XGBoost starts with a basic model, making initial predictions based on the available data. The model's performance is assessed by comparing these predictions against the ground truth from labeled data, identifying errors or residuals (See Figure 13-4).

Learning from errors: XGBoost's distinctive feature is its ability to learn from past mistakes. Each subsequent model it builds focuses on correcting the residuals from the previous one. This process of iterative improvement is key to XGBoost's efficiency.

Regularization and learning rate: XGBoost incorporates a learning rate, acting as a regularization term to prevent overfitting. This learning rate, a critical parameter, scales the contribution of each new model, ensuring that the ensemble gradually improves without fitting too closely to the training data.

Consider a fraud detection scenario where XGBoost is employed to analyze transaction data. The initial model might use simple averages or basic classifications. Subsequent models then focus on refining predictions where the first model faltered, like identifying unusual transaction patterns or locations.

Ensemble of Decision Trees: The ensemble comprises multiple decision trees, each evaluating different aspects of the data. For instance, one tree might assess transaction amounts while another focuses on the frequency of transactions. The final output is an aggregated score that reflects the collective assessment of all trees.

Optimizing predictions: XGBoost continuously optimizes its predictions, balancing the need for accuracy with the risk of overfitting. This is achieved through its learning rate and the ensemble approach, where each model adds incremental improvements.

XGBoost's Strengths:

- *Scalability:* It can handle large datasets efficiently.
- *Speed:* XGBoost is faster than many traditional models, making it suitable for real-time fraud detection.
- *Accuracy:* By focusing on errors and iteratively improving, XGBoost achieves high predictive accuracy.

Application in fraud detection: XGBoost's ability to handle complex and nuanced patterns makes it particularly effective in fraud detection. It can adapt to evolving fraud strategies and offers detailed insights into each transaction, significantly enhancing fraud detection capabilities.

XGBoost stands out for its accuracy, efficiency, and adaptability, making it a powerful tool against financial fraud. The upcoming sections will further explore its practical applications and demonstrate its effectiveness in real-world fraud detection scenarios.

Lab Project: Predictive Analysis in University Admissions

In the ever-evolving landscape of education, the prediction of university admissions plays a pivotal role in shaping the future of students and educational institutions. This project offers an insightful exploration into using the XGBoost algorithm for predicting university admission chances based on a diverse range of student profiles. By harnessing the power of Python and libraries such as XGBoost, Seaborn, and Matplotlib, you will delve into the world of regression analysis to forecast admission probabilities.

Engaging with the admissions dataset: Your journey in this lab involves engaging with a dataset that captures various aspects of a student's profile, including academic scores, university ratings, and other relevant attributes. You will undertake the following key tasks:

1. *Understanding regression analysis:* grasping the fundamentals of regression in data science and its relevance in predictive modeling
2. *Implementing the XGBoost algorithm*: exploring and applying the XGBoost algorithm, a powerful tool known for its efficiency in handling regression tasks.
3. *Data visualization and preprocessing:* leveraging Seaborn and Matplotlib for data visualization and preparing the dataset for modeling
4. *Model training and evaluation*: building and training an XGBoost model to predict admission chances and evaluate its performance rigorously.

Lab Access Dive into the intriguing world of predictive analysis in university admissions. Click here for lab access to begin your exploration and complete the lab.

Post-Lab Insights: Upon completion of this lab, you will have journeyed through the critical stages of predictive modeling in the context of university admissions. Starting with an understanding of regression analysis, you moved on to the practical application of the XGBoost algorithm, a cornerstone in modern data science for regression problems.

Your path led you through effective data visualization techniques essential for understanding the underlying patterns and relationships. The hands-on experience in training the XGBoost model and evaluating its predictive prowess highlighted the nuances of machine learning in practical scenarios.

As a result, you've gained a robust understanding of the XGBoost algorithm and regression analysis and the broader implications of predictive modeling in the educational sector. This project enhances your analytical skills and equips you with knowledge directly applicable to real-world situations, like aiding university admission offices in streamlining their admission processes.

The skills and insights garnered from this project transcend academic learning, offering you a valuable toolkit for data-driven decision-making in various professional contexts (Fig. 13.5).

> TIP
>
> XGBoost (Extreme Gradient Boosting) does not require feature scaling. Tree-based XGBoost is indifferent to the magnitude of input characteristics. Tree-based models are split by feature value rather than feature distance.

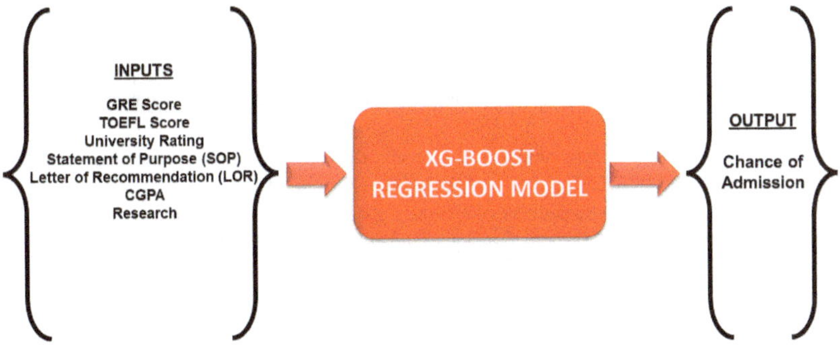

Fig. 13.5 XGBoost model input and output

CAUTION

When retraining the XGBoost model with a lower max_depth, be aware of the potential impact on performance.

After retraining with a max_depth of 2, a decline in the R2 score may be observed, indicating a decrease in the model's performance, this decline occurs because lowering the max_depth reduces the complexity of the model, thereby limiting its ability to capture complex relationships in the data.

However, it is crucial to balance model complexity and performance. An overly complex model may overfit the training data, leading to poor generalization on new, unseen data. This is where the art of hyperparameter tuning becomes essential. It involves finding the optimal combination of hyperparameters that yields the best performance while minimizing the risk of overfitting. In future projects, consider employing more systematic approaches such as grid or random search for a more comprehensive optimization of your model's hyperparameters.

Summary

Chapter 13 goes into supervised learning, with a focus on fraud detection. It discusses challenges such as defining the target variable, given the inherent complexities and noise in fraudulent activities. To counter these, robust learning algorithms, data cleaning, outlier detection, and ensemble learning methods are suggested.

The chapter also highlighted the issue of imbalanced datasets, common in fraud detection. It also emphasizes the importance of model evaluation using metrics like precision, recall, F1 score, and AUC-ROC.

The chapter introduces various regression algorithms, including linear regression as a valuable tool but also acknowledges its limitations, suggesting the need for other models and techniques.

Finally, the chapter explores XGBoost, detailing its advantages, limitations, and practical implementation. It provides an illustrative example of how XGBoost uses boosting to make improved predictions.

Chapter 13 serves as a comprehensive guide to fraud detection using supervised learning, setting the stage for further exploration of classification techniques in Chapter 14.

In conclusion, Chapter 13 explored the complexities of fraud detection, starting from defining the target variable to employing regression models for the same. You learned about the benefits and drawbacks of the XGBoost algorithm, visualizing data, and the practical implementation of XGBoost for university admission prediction. As you move on to Chapter 14, you will continue to build on this knowledge, focusing on different classification techniques within supervised learning for more efficient fraud detection.

CHAPTER 14

Classification Techniques in Supervised Learning

Welcome to this chapter, a deep dive into the diverse landscape of classification techniques in supervised learning, with a spotlight on their crucial role in fraud data analytics (FDA). This chapter is designed to guide you through the various classification methods, shedding light on their specific applications and effectiveness in the context of fraud detection.

Classification tasks, as a fundamental aspect of supervised machine learning, are focused on predicting categorical target variables. Within this realm, we explore both binary and multiclass classification, each presenting unique challenges and applications. The selection of an appropriate classification algorithm, whether logistic regression, decision trees, random forests, support vector machines (SVM), or neural networks, depends on various factors. These include the nature of the fraud detection task, dataset characteristics, and the required balance between model accuracy and interpretability.

Logistic regression, for instance, is a staple in binary classification problems such as fraud detection, offering simplicity and efficiency. SVMs, with their exceptional ability to distinguish between classes, are particularly valuable in fraud detection tasks. However, their complexity often categorizes them as black-box models, posing challenges in interpretability.

We also delve into the random forest classifiers, known for their ensemble approach. By creating multiple decision trees during training

A. Al Aqqad, *Fraud Analytics in Action*
https://doi.org/10.1007/978-3-032-16023-2_14

and aggregating their predictions, they enhance accuracy and mitigate the risk of overfitting, a common challenge in handling extensive fraud data analytics.

The chapter also introduces other techniques like k-nearest neighbors (KNN) and Naïve Bayes. KNN, though straightforward, effectively manages both binary and multiclass classification problems and is widely used in various fraud detection scenarios. Naïve Bayes, despite its simplicity, often excels in practice, particularly in text classification tasks relevant to fraud data analytics. Gradient boosting methods, including XGBoost, LightGBM, and CatBoost, round out the toolkit, offering powerful performance on complex, high-dimensional fraud datasets.

As you journey through this chapter, you will gain insights into the intricacies of each classification method and its strategic importance in the ever-evolving field of fraud detection. This exploration is not just about understanding different algorithms but also about learning how to apply them effectively in real-world scenarios to detect and prevent fraudulent activities.

Classification

Classification, a fundamental supervised machine learning task, revolves around predicting categorical target variables. It operates on the principle of using labeled training data to discern patterns that can be applied to predict class labels from new, unseen data.

In binary classification, the model navigates a scenario where the target variable manifests in one of two possible outcomes. The essence of binary classification lies in its ability to differentiate between these two classes based on various input features. Typical applications include fraud detection, where transactions are classified as either fraudulent or non-fraudulent; spam detection, distinguishing between spam and non-spam emails; and medical diagnosis, identifying the presence or absence of a specific disease.

Multiclass classification extends this concept to scenarios where the target variable can fall into more than two categories. Here, the model is trained to recognize and predict among multiple classes for new data points. This type of classification finds utility in diverse fields such as risk assessment, categorizing risk levels as high, medium, or low; handwritten digit recognition, classifying digits from 0 to 9; and news categorization, assigning articles to various categories like politics, sports, or technology.

There is a plethora of algorithms suitable for tackling classification tasks. Logistic regression is particularly favored for binary classification problems due to its efficiency and simplicity. Support vector machines (SVM) shine in high-dimensional spaces and are excellent when the classes are distinctly separable. For scenarios requiring interpretable models and handling of both numerical and categorical data, decision trees and random forests are go-to options. Neural networks, especially those leveraging deep learning, are potent for complex classification tasks involving large datasets.

The selection of an appropriate algorithm hinges on several factors, including the specific nature of the problem, the dataset's size and characteristics, computational constraints, and the desired balance between model accuracy and interpretability. This decision-making process is crucial to ensure that the chosen model aligns well with the problem's requirements and the available data, thereby maximizing the effectiveness and efficiency of the classification task.

Logistic Regression

Logistic regression is a binary classification model primarily used to estimate the probability of an instance belonging to a specific class, such as determining whether a transaction is fraudulent or non-fraudulent. It utilizes the logistic function, also known as the sigmoid function, to output probabilities that lie between 0 and 1, making it well-suited for binary outcomes. logistic regression can also be adapted for multiclass classification problems through techniques like one-vs-rest (OvR) or multinomial logistic regression. In the OvR approach, separate binary classifiers are trained for each class, while multinomial logistic regression extends the logistic regression model to handle multiple classes directly.

> TIP
>
> Logistic regression is a powerful tool for classifying transactions in the realm of financial fraud detection. It operates by estimating the probability of a transaction being fraudulent or legitimate, using a logistic function to output probabilities between 0 and 1.

Context and Application

As a data scientist at a leading financial institution in Chicago, you are tasked with utilizing logistic regression to identify fraudulent transactions. This scenario involves examining diverse transaction data, where your objective is to accurately distinguish between fraudulent (class 1) and legitimate (class 0) transactions, focusing on key indicators like transaction amounts, frequency, and customer behavioral patterns.

Understanding Logistic Regression

Logistic regression transforms the linear regression equation, $\Upsilon = B_0 + B_1X$, through the sigmoid function: $P(X) = \frac{1}{1+e^{-(B_0+B_1X)}}$. (See Fig. 14.1). This adaptation converts the linear output into a probability score between 0 and 1, ideal for binary classification (Fig. 14.2).

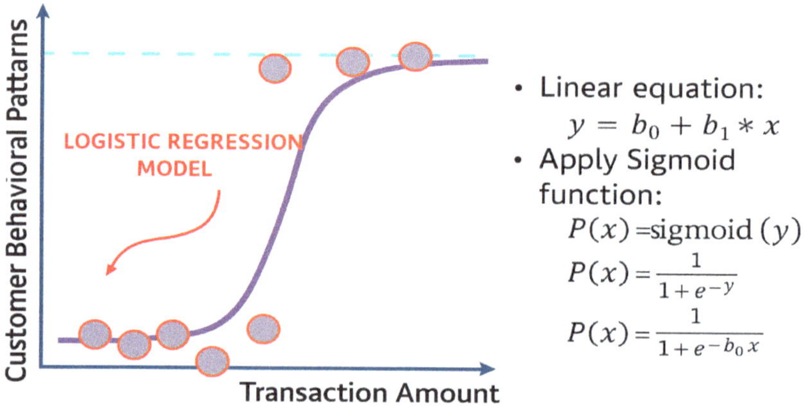

Fig. 14.1 Logistic regression: This figure illustrates the behavior of a logistic regression model when analyzing customer behavioral patterns in relation to transaction amounts. On the left side, the S-shaped (sigmoid) curve shows how the probability of a customer behavior shifts with increasing transaction values. Individual data points are highlighted to represent observed customer behaviors. The logistic regression model fits these points, transitioning smoothly between binary outcomes (e.g., fraudulent vs. legitimate transactions). On the right, the corresponding mathematical formulation is presented: a basic linear equation is first computed, followed by the application of the sigmoid function to transform predictions into probabilities between 0 and 1. This visualization emphasizes the process of converting linear relationships into probability-based classifications, which is foundational in many fraud detection models

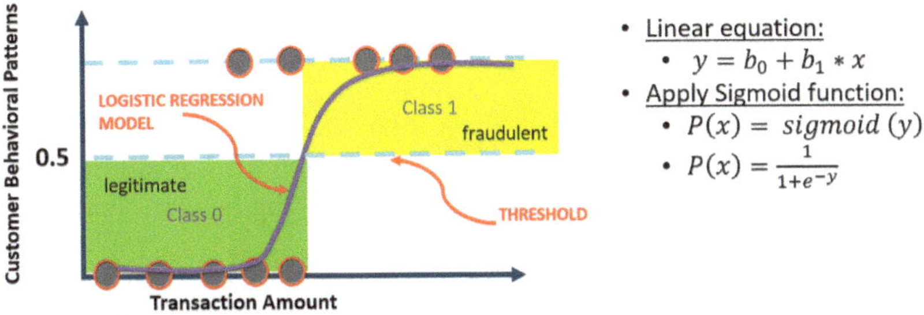

Fig. 14.2 Logistic regression classification for fraud detection. This figure illustrates the logistic regression process for classifying transaction amounts based on customer behavioral patterns. The x-axis represents the transaction amount, while the y-axis captures customer behavior. A purple S-shaped sigmoid curve separates two distinct zones: "Class 0—legitimate" (green area) and "Class 1—fraudulent" (yellow area). The decision boundary, or threshold, is set at 0.5 on the y-axis, indicating the probability cutoff used to distinguish between classes. Data points are mapped and classified according to their predicted probabilities. On the right, the figure presents the mathematical foundation of logistic regression, showing the linear equation and the application of the sigmoid function to convert outputs into probabilities between 0 and 1. This visual emphasizes how logistic regression models are used to distinguish legitimate from fraudulent transactions based on behavioral patterns and probability scoring

TIP

- Logistic regression algorithm works by implementing a linear equation first with independent predictors to predict a value.
- We then need to convert this value into a probability that could range from 0 to 1. (See Figure 14.2)

Training and Testing the Model

The process begins with data collection and preprocessing, where you gather historical transaction data, address any missing values, scale the features, and categorize transactions as either fraudulent or legitimate. Once the data is prepared, it is divided into two sets: a training set to develop the logistic regression model and a testing set to evaluate its performance.

The next step is model development, where the logistic regression model is trained on the training set. The performance of the model is then evaluated using various metrics such as accuracy, precision, recall, and the F1 score. This evaluation helps in understanding how well the model can generalize its predictions to new data.

After developing the model, it's crucial to interpret the probability scores it generates. A typical threshold is set at 0.5 to classify transactions based on their probability scores, distinguishing between fraudulent and legitimate transactions.

The final step involves continuous improvement of the model. Regular updates with new data are essential to keep the model effective against evolving fraud patterns.

> TIP
>
> Logistic regression offers a balance between interpretability and accuracy, crucial for adapting to new fraud trends in fraud detection.

Distinguishing Logistic and Linear Regression

- *Logistic regression*: Suitable for binary classification tasks. It outputs probability scores constrained between 0 and 1, ideal for distinguishing between two categories like fraudulent and non-fraudulent transactions.
- *Linear regression*: Used for predicting continuous outcomes and is inappropriate for binary classification tasks like fraud detection. It predicts a continuous dependent variable based on independent variables and is not limited to a range between 0 and 1.

> TIP
>
> Choose logistic regression for binary classification (e.g., fraud detection), and linear regression for predicting continuous outcomes (e.g., forecasting sales).

Support Vector Machines (SVM)

Support vector machines (SVM) stand as an exceptional classification tool, particularly effective in distinguishing between fraudulent and non-fraudulent cases in various domains, including financial fraud detection. At their core, SVMs aim to find the optimal decision boundary, or hyperplane, that maximizes the margin between different classes. They are versatile enough to handle both binary and multiclass classification challenges and can effectively manage non-linearly separable data using kernel functions such as linear, polynomial, and radial basis function (RBF). For more information about SVM, please visit this site https://www.statlearning.com/.

Originally developed for classification tasks, SVMs are also adaptable for regression problems. Their ability to handle both linearly and non-linearly separable cases, as well as transforming non-linear scenarios into a higher-dimensional feature space for linear separation, makes them a robust choice for a wide array of applications.

In the context of fraud analytics, SVMs offer several advantages. They are capable of managing non-linear instances and benefit from convex optimization properties, making them a strong candidate for such applications. To address this, techniques such as variable selection, rule extraction approaches, and two-stage models can be employed to enhance the interpretability of SVM models.

For instance, imagine you're a data scientist at a major bank in New York City. Your primary responsibility involves analyzing customer transactions to identify potentially fraudulent activities. The task at hand is to classify transactions as either fraudulent or legitimate, utilizing customer transaction data. Two main features could be considered: *feature 1*, representing the transaction amount, and *feature 2*, the frequency of transactions. The goal is to categorize transactions into two groups: legitimate transactions (gray class) and fraudulent transactions (red class). See Fig. 14.3.

The challenge is effectively distinguishing between legitimate and fraudulent transactions. Support vector machines (SVM) excel in this context. SVMs aim to find the optimal separating line, known as the *maximum margin hyperplane*, to distinctly separate the two classes (See Fig. 14.3).

In fraud detection, support vectors are critical transactions that lie on the boundary between legitimate and fraudulent activities, and they are often the most challenging to classify. SVM focuses on these borderline cases to establish the maximum margin hyperplane—a line that maximizes the distance between the nearest points (support vectors) of each class, ensuring a clear and distinct separation.

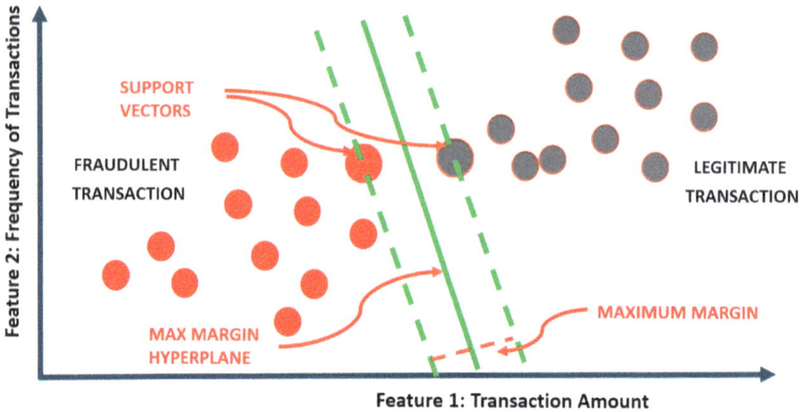

Fig. 14.3 Maximum margin hyperplane: This figure demonstrates how a Support Vector Machine (SVM) model separates fraudulent transactions from legitimate transactions using two features: transaction amount (Feature 1) and frequency of transactions (Feature 2). Fraudulent transactions are plotted on the left side, while legitimate transactions appear on the right. The SVM identifies support vectors—the critical data points closest to the decision boundary—and constructs a maximum margin hyperplane (solid green line) that optimally separates the two classes. Two parallel dashed green lines represent the boundaries of the margin. The space between them is the maximum margin, which the SVM seeks to maximize to improve classification robustness. This visualization highlights how SVMs are used to distinguish between transaction types by maximizing the separation between classes based on transaction characteristics

Training and Testing the SVM Model

Start with collecting and preprocessing the data. This involves gathering historical transaction data, which includes transaction amounts, patterns, and labels indicating whether they were fraudulent. Preprocessing steps include handling missing values, scaling the features, and encoding the target variable for fraudulent and non-fraudulent transactions.

Next, divide this preprocessed data into training and test sets. The training set is where the SVM model learns from the data, while the test set is reserved for evaluating the model's performance (Fig. 14.4).

TIP

In practice, data is divided into training and testing sets. The SVM algorithm is trained with the training set, which includes examples of both legitimate and fraudulent transactions. After training, the model is evaluated with a separate set of transactions that were not part of the training phase (See Figure 14.4) green color dataset. This strategy assesses the model's ability to generalize and accurately classify new, unseen transaction data.

Selecting the right kernel function is crucial. You can choose from linear, polynomial, or radial basis function (RBF) kernels. The decision depends on the nature of your data, and it's typically best to experiment to see which kernel works best for your specific case.

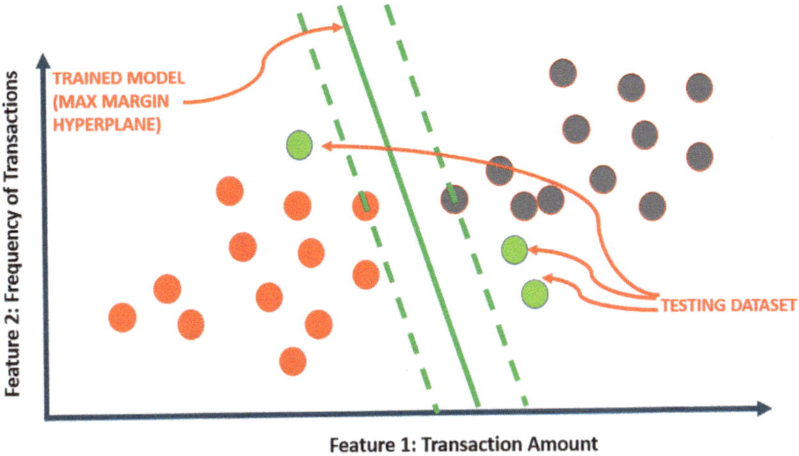

Fig. 14.4 SVM model evaluation using unseen transaction data: Unseen new transaction data (the green dataset). This figure illustrates the practical application of Support Vector Machine (SVM) classification by dividing data into training and testing datasets. The training dataset consists of labeled transactions (fraudulent and legitimate), used to train the model and define the maximum margin hyperplane (solid green line). The green-colored points represent the unseen testing dataset—transactions that were not part of the training phase—introduced to evaluate the model's performance. The model aims to classify these new transactions based on their position relative to the hyperplane and margins. This visual highlights the importance of using separate training and testing sets to assess a model's generalization ability and classification accuracy on unseen data, a critical step in real-world fraud detection systems

Hyperparameter tuning is an essential step in this process. Utilize cross-validation techniques to determine the optimal regularization parameter (C) and any kernel-specific parameters. This fine-tuning is key to achieving the right balance between the model's complexity and its ability to generalize well (Figs. 14.5 and 14.6).

> TIP
>
> *C parameter:* Controls trade-off between classifying training points correctly and having a smooth decision boundary (See Figure 14.5).
>
> - *Small C (loose)* makes cost (penalty) of misclassification low (soft margin)
> - *Large C (strict)* makes cost of misclassification high (hard margin), forcing the model to explain input data stricter and potentially overfit.

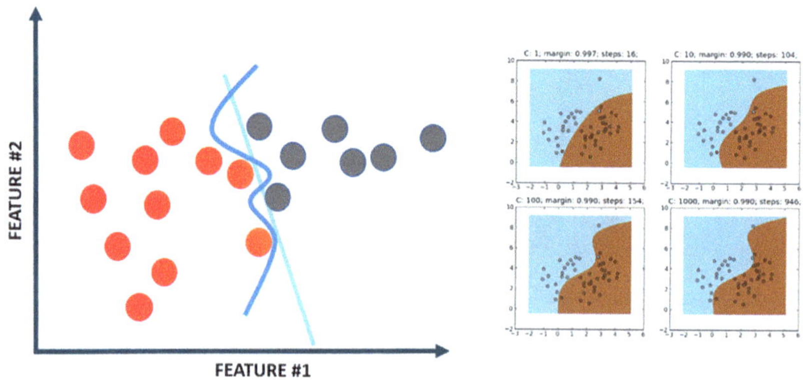

Fig. 14.5 Support Vector Machines (SVM): effect of the C parameter on decision boundaries. This figure illustrates how varying the regularization parameter C influences the shape and flexibility of the SVM decision boundary. Lower values of C prioritize a wider margin, allowing more classification errors but improving generalization. Higher values of C reduce tolerance for misclassification, resulting in tighter margins and more complex decision boundaries that closely fit the training data. In fraud detection, careful tuning of C is critical to balancing underfitting and overfitting, particularly when dealing with noisy or highly imbalanced datasets. Adapted from: mlpy documentation, Support Vector Machines. https://mlpy.sourceforge.net/docs/3.4/svm.html

TIP

The gamma parameter: controls how far the influence of a single training set reaches (See Figure 14.6).

- Large gamma: close reach (closer data points have high weight)
- Small gamma: far reach (more generalized solution)

Once the kernel and hyperparameters are set, you move to training the SVM model on the training data. After training, the model's performance needs to be evaluated on the test set. Key performance metrics such as accuracy, precision, recall, and F1-score help in understanding how well the model generalizes to unseen data.

WARNING

Choosing the right kernel: The selection of the kernel function is critical and should be based on the specific nature of the data. Different kernels can lead to significantly different results, and inappropriate kernel selection can lead to overfitting or underfitting.

After training and evaluation, the SVM model is ready to make predictions. Use it to classify new transactions based on their amount and pattern, identifying potentially fraudulent activities.

However, because fraud patterns can change over time, it's essential to continuously monitor the model's performance. Regularly updating

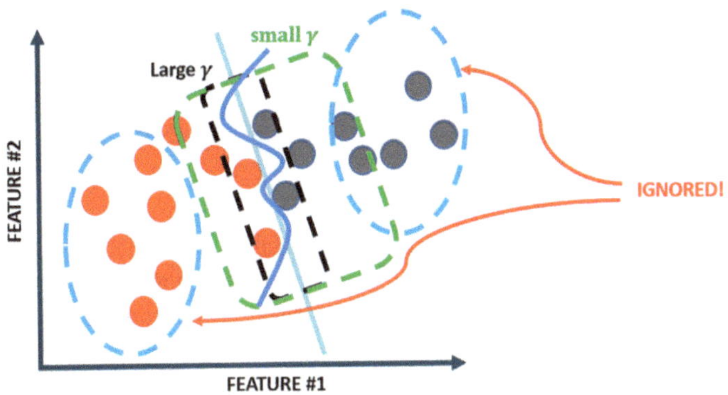

Fig. 14.6 Support vector machines: parameters optimization—gamma parameter

the model with new data ensures that it stays effective and relevant in detecting the latest trends in fraudulent transactions.

Given that SVMs are often considered black-box models, their interpretability can be limited. To enhance the model's transparency, particularly for stakeholders, you might need to employ techniques like rule extraction or local interpretable model-agnostic explanations (LIME). See Chapters 5 and 15 for more information.

WARNING

Model complexity and interpretability: SVMs, particularly with non-linear kernels, can be complex and are often seen as black-box models. This complexity can pose challenges in interpretability, which is a crucial aspect in fraud detection where understanding the rationale behind decisions is often as important as the decisions themselves.

SVMs serve as a robust and versatile tool for fraud detection. They are particularly effective in scenarios where transaction data shows clear patterns distinguishing between legitimate and fraudulent activities. However, their success in a real-world setting like a major bank in NYC relies heavily on continuous monitoring and adaptability to evolving fraud patterns.

Decision Trees

A decision tree is a flowchart-like structure in which each internal node represents a feature (or attribute), each branch represents a decision rule, and each leaf node represents an outcome. The topmost node in a decision tree is known as the root node. It learns to partition based on the attribute value. It partitions the tree recursively in a top-down, recursive, divide-and-conquer manner.

Advantages in Fraud Detection

- *Interpretability:* Decision trees are easy to understand and interpret. They provide a clear visualization of the features that are most important for classification, which is crucial for understanding the reasons behind a fraud detection decision.
- *Handling different data types:* They can handle both numerical and categorical data, making them versatile for various fraud detection scenarios.
- *Non-linearity:* Decision trees can capture non-linear relationships in the data, which might be prevalent in complex fraud patterns.

Imagine you're a data scientist working for a large bank, tasked with developing a model to detect potentially fraudulent activities among customer transactions. Decision trees are a supervised machine learning technique that splits data according to certain conditions or parameters, which can be extremely useful in this context.

Practical Application: Fraudulent Transaction Classification
Suppose you need to classify transactions based on their likelihood of being fraudulent. Each transaction comes with various features, such as transaction amount, customer account history, transaction frequency, and geographical location.

Let's visualize this with a decision tree: (See Fig. 14.7)

1. *Initial decision node (question):* The first question might be whether the transaction amount exceeds a certain threshold, say $10,000. This threshold is determined based on historical data indicating that high-value transactions have a higher likelihood of being fraudulent.
2. *Subsequent nodes:* If the transaction is above this amount, the next question might involve the frequency of transactions. For instance, is this large transaction a one-off event or part of a regular pattern? Irregularly large transactions might be flagged for further review.
3. *Leaf nodes (outcomes):* If a transaction meets certain criteria (e.g., high value and irregular occurrence), it might be classified as potentially fraudulent (Class 1). Conversely, transactions that don't meet these criteria would be considered legitimate (Class 0).
4. *Further analysis:* For transactions flagged as potentially fraudulent, additional details might be scrutinized, such as the geographical location. If the transaction occurs in a location known for high fraud rates, this could further validate the initial classification.

As you can see from the figure, the X-axis has the transaction amount, while the Y-axis represents the frequency of transactions for each customer.

The collected data points from all the bank's customers are plotted, revealing patterns of normal and suspicious activities.

Through a series of questions (decision nodes), transactions are classified into either potentially fraudulent or legitimate. These nodes are

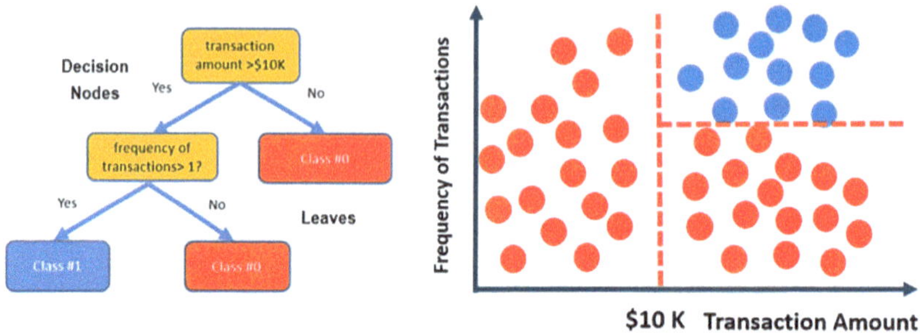

Fig. 14.7 Decision tree: classification of transaction

based on historical data patterns and expert knowledge in banking fraud detection.

In practical, this is represented as shown below.

The visualization provided (Fig. 14.8) illustrates a decision tree's approach to classifying transactions as either normal or fraudulent based on two features: transaction amount and frequency. Below is a detailed description of the various components of this visualization:

Scatter plot clusters:

- Green dots: These represent normal transactions. The position of each dot is determined by the transaction's amount (along the x-axis) and frequency (along the y-axis).
- Red crosses: These symbolize fraudulent transactions, plotted similarly to the normal transactions but typically showing different patterns in terms of amount and frequency.

Blue vertical dashed line (decision boundary for transaction amount):

- This line is set at a transaction amount of $10,000.
- It serves as a critical decision boundary in the decision tree algorithm. Transactions with amounts greater than this value may be scrutinized more closely for potential fraud.

Orange horizontal dashed line (frequency threshold):

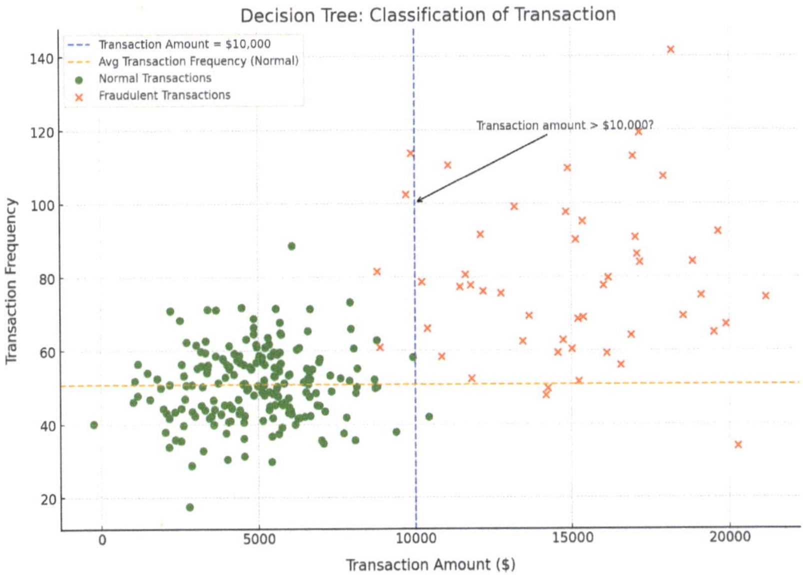

Fig. 14.8 The decision tree for fraudulent transaction classification

- This line represents the average transaction frequency of normal transactions.
- It is used to compare individual transactions against a benchmark frequency. Transactions with a much higher frequency than this average might be flagged for further investigation.

Annotation (decision node query):

- The annotation poses a question that forms part of the decision-making process in the tree: "Is the transaction amount greater than $10,000?"
- This question helps in segregating transactions into different branches of the decision tree based on their amount.

This visualization effectively demonstrates how a decision tree algorithm could use transaction amount and frequency to categorize transactions. The decision boundary and frequency threshold are key in dividing the data, allowing the algorithm to identify patterns that might suggest fraudulent activity. This visual representation aligns closely with the theoretical steps of decision tree analysis, offering a clear and intuitive understanding of the process.

Advanced Application: Customer Segmentation for Marketing Campaigns

In a different scenario, such as launching a marketing campaign, decision trees can also help segment customers based on their income and credit score. For example, (See Fig. 14.9) customers with high incomes and excellent credit scores might be targeted for premium banking services, while those with lower scores might be offered different products.

> TIP
>
> The decision tree method provides a straightforward yet powerful way to categorize transactions, making it a valuable tool in fraud detection. It helps to break down complex decision-making processes into simpler, more manageable steps, leading to more effective and accurate fraud detection strategies.

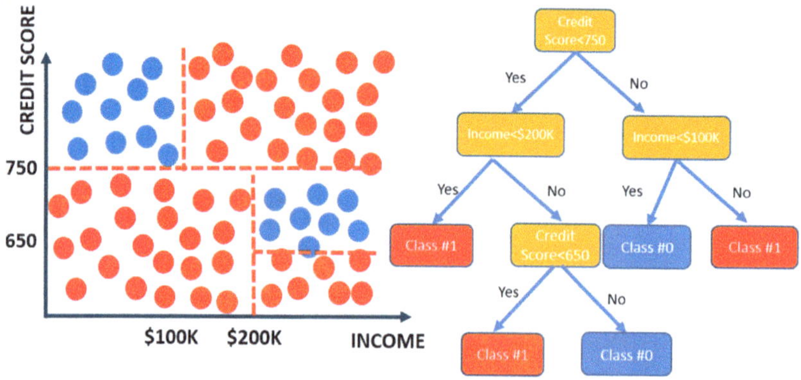

Fig. 14.9 Decision tree: customer segmentation

Random Forest

Random forest is an ensemble machine learning method that creates a "forest" of multiple decision trees during the training phase and merges their predictions for more accurate and robust classification. This technique is effective for both binary and multiclass classification problems and is particularly adept at addressing the issue of overfitting, common with single decision trees.

The method involves several key processes. *Bootstrap aggregating*, or *bagging*, where each decision tree is trained on a distinct subset of the data, drawn with replacement, is fundamental to random forest. This diversity in training data for each tree ensures a robust model. Additionally, when making splits in these trees, random forest only considers a random subset of features. This *feature of randomness* helps in de-correlating individual trees, reducing overfitting.

For classification tasks, random forest employs a voting system where each tree casts a vote for a class label, and the class with the majority of votes becomes the model's prediction. In regression tasks, the predictions of all trees are averaged to determine the output.

In practice, suppose you have a dataset of 100 data points. The random forest algorithm would select a random subset of these points, say 20, and train a decision tree on them. This process is repeated multiple times, each time selecting a different subset of data points and training a new tree. The final decision is made based on the majority vote from all these individual trees.

This collective wisdom approach allows random forest to provide more reliable and robust predictions compared to a single decision tree. By diversifying the training data for each tree, the algorithm effectively reduces the risk of overfitting, which is a common problem in machine learning models where the algorithm becomes too tailored to the training data and fails to generalize to new data.

For example, in fraud detection, a random forest classifier can be trained on a dataset of credit card transactions. Each decision tree in the forest would make a prediction based on its subset of data, and the final classification of a transaction as fraudulent or legitimate would be determined by the majority vote across all trees. This process significantly enhances the model's ability to accurately detect fraud, considering the diverse patterns and anomalies present in such datasets (See Fig. 14.10).

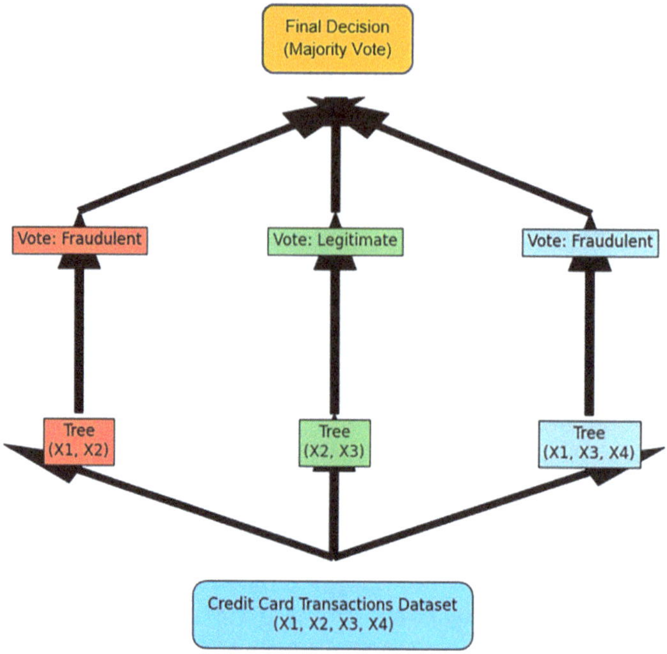

Fig. 14.10 Random forest classifier aggregation for fraud detection

To elaborate further, imagine training three distinct decision trees using three different subsets of a dataset containing features X1, X2, X3, and X4, labeled L1, L2, L3, and L4. Each tree is trained with a unique combination of these features, resulting in different perspectives on the data. The final decision is made by aggregating the votes from these trees, ensuring a well-rounded analysis.

This diagram represents how the random forest classifier combines the outcomes of individual trees to make a well-rounded final decision, enhancing the ability to accurately detect fraud in the dataset.

Random forest's is more resilient to *noise* in data compared to individual trees. Since it averages the predictions from multiple trees, it can filter out the noise, making it particularly useful in fraud detection, where subtle fraudulent activities can be obscured by noisy data.

Random forest also offers interpretability by ranking features based on their importance in prediction, highlighting critical features like transaction amount, location, or time of day. The method can handle large, high-dimensional datasets efficiently and is scalable as it can train trees in parallel. Known for producing highly accurate classifiers, Random Forest is a valuable tool in fraud detection, where misclassification can have significant consequences.

Its versatility also allows it to be used not only for classification (identifying fraudulent transactions) but also for regression tasks (such as predicting the amount of a fraudulent transaction).

Application in Fraud Detection

Consider a scenario where a dataset of credit card transactions, each with features like transaction amount, location, time of day, and merchant category, exists. Some transactions are labeled as fraudulent based on past investigations. A random forest classifier trained on this dataset learns from patterns of past fraudulent activities. For every new transaction, the classifier predicts its probability of being fraudulent. By aggregating predictions from multiple decision trees, the Random Forest model achieves higher accuracy, minimizing false positives and negatives (See Fig. 14.11).

Random forest classifiers are a potent tool in the arsenal of fraud detection. By leveraging the collective strength of multiple decision trees and sidestepping challenges like overfitting, they offer a dependable and scalable solution for pinpointing potentially fraudulent activities in extensive datasets. More details can be found at https://www.statlearning.com/.

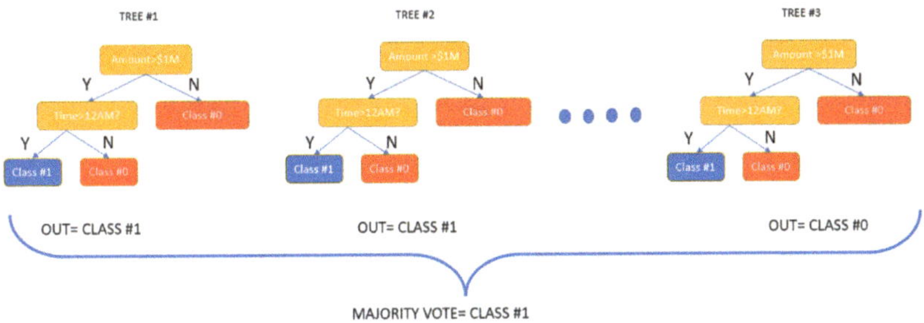

Fig. 14.11 Majority vote—credit card transaction

K-Nearest Neighbors (KNN)

KNN is a straightforward, non-parametric classification technique that predicts a given transaction's legitimacy based on the majority vote of its k-nearest neighbors in the feature space. In the context of fraud detection, KNN can be used to classify transactions as fraudulent or legitimate by comparing them to historical transaction data. The algorithm is applicable to binary classification problems, such as fraud detection, where transactions are classified as either fraudulent (1) or legitimate (0). The choice of k (number of neighbors) and the distance metric, such as Euclidean, Manhattan, or Minkowski distance, can significantly impact the KNN classifier's performance in detecting fraud (See Fig. 14.12).

Key Points

- K-nearest neighbors (KNN) algorithm is primarily a classification algorithm.
- In fraud detection, KNN works by finding the most similar historical transaction data points to a new transaction and making an educated guess based on their classifications.

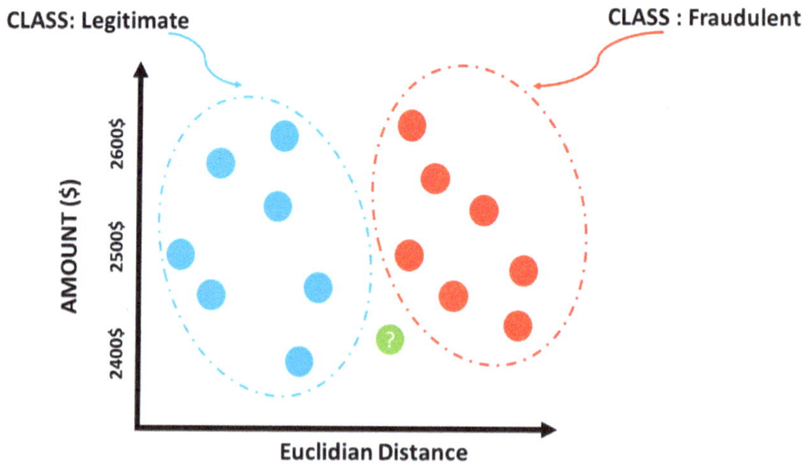

Fig. 14.12 K-Nearest neighbors (KNN) classifier

- The effectiveness of KNN in fraud detection depends on the choice of k and the distance metric used.

KNN Algorithm Step for Fraud Detection

1. *Choose a value for k*: Select an appropriate number for k, the number of nearest neighbors to consider. Common choices for k include small integers, such as 1, 3, 5, etc. The choice of k can significantly impact the algorithm's performance, with smaller values making the model more sensitive to noise and larger values potentially smoothing out the classification too much.
2. *Calculate Euclidean distances*: For the transaction you wish to classify, calculate the Euclidean distance to each point in the training dataset. The Euclidean distance is a measure of the straight-line distance between two points in Euclidean space.
3. *Identify k-nearest points:* From the calculated distances, identify the k closest points. These are the points in the training dataset with the smallest Euclidean distances to the transaction you are classifying.
4. *Majority voting for classification:* Perform a majority vote among the k selected points. The classification (fraudulent or legitimate) most common among these points is assigned to the transaction being classified. This step assumes a binary classification where each transaction is categorized as either fraudulent or legitimate.
5. *Repeat for each point:* Repeat the above steps for each new transaction point that needs to be classified. This ensures that every transaction is evaluated based on its nearest neighbors in the training dataset (See Fig. 14.3) for visual representation.

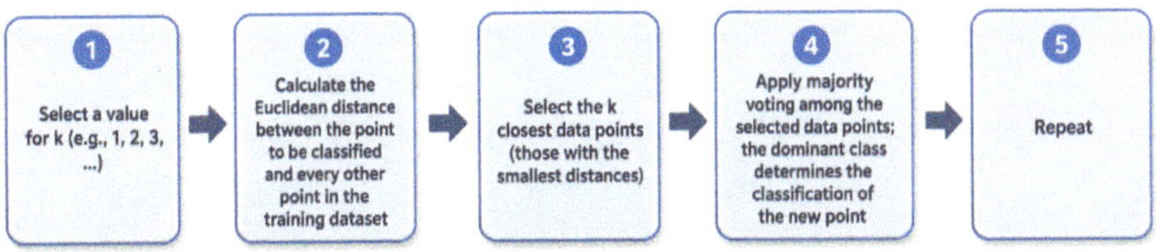

Fig. 14.13 KNN algorithm step for fraud detection

TIP

The efficiency and accuracy of KNN in fraud detection depends on the choice of k and the characteristics of the dataset. In fraud detection, where the data might be highly imbalanced (with fraudulent transactions being much rarer than legitimate ones), careful consideration must be given to how k is chosen and how the voting mechanism is implemented to avoid bias toward the majority class.

The *Euclidean* distance formula (See Fig. 14.14) is a commonly used metric in mathematics and data science, particularly in machine learning algorithms like K-Nearest Neighbors (KNN). It calculates the straight-line distance between two points in Euclidean space. This metric is often used to determine how similar or dissimilar two entities (like data points) are based on their features.

$$d = \sqrt{(x_2 - x_1)^2 + (y_2 - y_1)^2}$$

where:

- $(x1, y1)$ and $(x2, y2)$ are the coordinates of the two points between which the distance is being measured.
- The differences between the x-coordinates and y-coordinates are squared and summed, and then the square root of the sum is taken to find the distance.

This distance measure is fundamental in various applications, from calculating distances on maps to clustering and classification in machine learning.

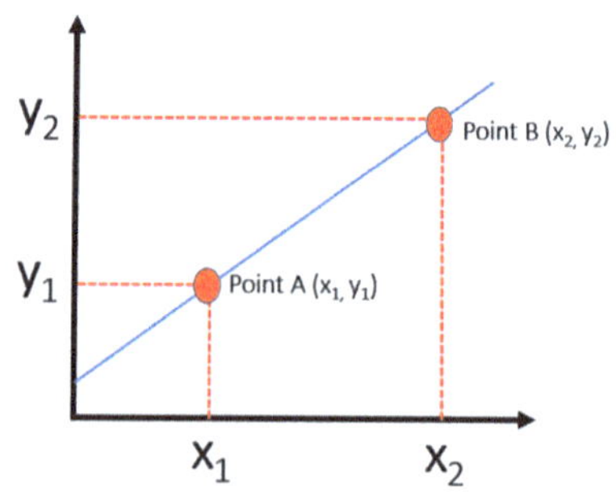

Fig. 14.14 Euclidean distance metric

A Contextual Scenario for KNN in Fraud Detection

You are a data scientist working at CyberSafe Bank, a financial institution renowned for its robust online banking services. The bank has recently experienced a surge in online transaction activity, raising concerns about potential fraud. Your task is to enhance the bank's fraud detection system using machine learning techniques, with the KNN algorithm being a key component of your strategy.

Your objective is to develop a system that can quickly and accurately classify new online transactions as either fraudulent or legitimate, based on historical transaction data. This classification is crucial to prevent fraudulent activities and to ensure customer trust in the bank's online services.

Implementation:

1. *Data collection*: You have access to a comprehensive dataset of past online transactions, which includes details such as transaction amounts, locations (indicating whether a transaction was made online or at a physical location), and the times of transactions. Each transaction in this dataset is labeled as either "legitimate" or "fraudulent," based on thorough investigations conducted by the bank's security team.
2. *KNN algorithm setup:* To implement the KNN algorithm, you decide to use the transaction amount, location, and time as key features to compare transactions. The 'k' value is set to 5, meaning the algorithm will consider the 5 nearest transactions in the feature space to classify a new transaction.

Practical Example:

- A new online transaction occurs at 2:00 a.m. with an amount of $2500. This transaction needs to be classified as either fraudulent or legitimate.
- Using the KNN algorithm, you calculate the Euclidean distance between this new transaction and all previous transactions in the dataset. (The KNN algorithm calculates the Euclidean distance between this new transaction and each transaction in the historical dataset.)

- The 5 nearest transactions with the smallest Euclidean distances (based on amount, location, and time) are identified. Let's say four of these are labeled as "legitimate" and one as "fraudulent."
- A majority vote among these 5 transactions suggests that the new transaction is likely to be legitimate. The KNN algorithm here employs majority voting among the nearest neighbors to classify the new transaction. In this case, since four out of the five closest transactions are classified as "legitimate," the new transaction is also likely to be legitimate.
- The bank's fraud detection system, therefore, classifies this new transaction at 2:00 a.m. for $2500 as "legitimate." However, it remains under surveillance for any subsequent unusual activities, ensuring continuous monitoring.

In this scenario, the KNN algorithm serves as an effective tool for classifying transactions in real-time, aiding CyberSafe Bank in maintaining the security of its online banking services. This method allows for dynamic and adaptable fraud detection, which is crucial in the ever-evolving domain of online financial transactions (Table 14.1).

Naïve Bayes

Naïve Bayes is a classification technique grounded in Bayes' theorem, a key concept in probability theory. It's termed "naïve" due to its assumption of conditional independence between features within a class. Essentially, it considers each feature's contribution to the probability of a class (like fraudulent or legitimate transactions) as independent of other features.

Despite its simplicity, Naïve Bayes often performs effectively, especially when its assumption of conditional independence is approximately true. This makes it suitable for binary and multiclass classification problems. Its common applications include text classification tasks such as spam detection and sentiment analysis. However, in contexts like fraud detection, where features may have interdependencies, its assumption might be a limitation.

In fraud detection, Naïve Bayes treats features such as transaction amount, location, and time independently, even though they may be interrelated in reality. For instance, frequent large purchases of luxury

Table 14.1 KNN classification example for fraud detection: nearest neighbors voting

Amount	Location	Time	Classification	Euclidean Dist.	Rank
$2,400	Online	1:50 AM	Legitimate	3.16227766	
$2,450	Online	1:55 AM	Legitimate	2.236067977	
$2,550	Online	2:05 AM	Legitimate	2.236067977	
$2,490	Online	2:01 AM	Legitimate	1.414213562	2
$2,510	Online	2:03 AM	Legitimate	1	1
$2,520	Online	2:04 AM	Legitimate	1.414213562	2
$2,530	Online	2:06 AM	Legitimate	2	4
$2,600	Online	2:10 AM	Fraudulent	3.16227766	5
$2,580	Online	2:08 AM	Fraudulent	4	
$2,570	Online	2:07 AM	Fraudulent	4.123105626	
$2,560	Online	2:09 AM	Fraudulent	5.656858249	

New transaction information: Amount: $2500, Location: Online, Time: 2:00 am; assume k= 5

items might be more indicative of fraud than the algorithm assumes if it treats purchase frequency and item type as independent.

Using Naïve Bayes in fraud detection typically involves:

- *Prior probability:* assessing the initial likelihood of transactions being fraudulent based on historical data.
- *Likelihood assessment*: Comparing new transactions with historical fraudulent patterns.
- *Posterior probability calculation*: integrating prior probability and likelihood to make a final prediction.

In the context of fraud detection, the Naïve Bayes formula calculates the probability of a transaction being fraudulent (posterior probability) given its attributes (features). The formula is:

$$P(\text{Fraud} \mid \text{Features}) = \frac{P(\text{Features} \mid \text{Fraud})\, P(\text{Fraud})}{P(\text{Features})}$$

While Naïve Bayes is efficient and straightforward, it's crucial to be aware of its "naïve" assumption, especially when dealing with interdependent features in fraud detection. Effective use in this field might require careful feature engineering and ongoing model evaluation to counteract potential oversimplifications.

TIP
While Naïve Bayes is efficient and straightforward, it's crucial to be aware of its "naïve" assumption, especially when dealing with interdependent features in fraud detection. Effective use in this field might require careful feature engineering and ongoing model evaluation to counteract potential oversimplifications.

In the Naïve Bayes context, the formula would look like this: (See Fig. 14.15).

Here's a breakdown of each component:

- (Fraud| Features): This is the posterior probability, the probability of a transaction being fraudulent given its features (like transaction amount, location, time, etc.).
- (Features| Fraud): This is the likelihood, the probability of observing these specific features in transactions that are fraudulent.
- *P* (Fraud): This is the prior probability, the general likelihood of transactions being fraudulent, independent of the current transaction's features.

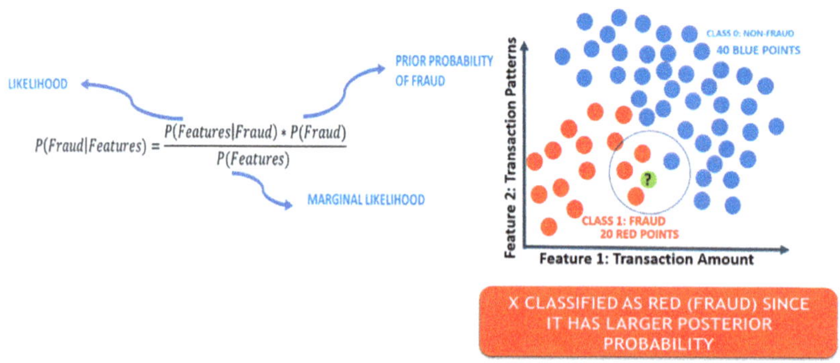

Fig. 14.15 Naïve Bayes formula

- *P* (Features): This is the marginal likelihood or evidence, the probability of observing these features in any transaction, fraudulent or not.

This formula represents how Naïve Bayes combines prior knowledge (the general likelihood of fraud) with specific evidence (the features of a particular transaction) to assess the probability of fraud.

Gradient Boosting

Gradient boosting is a key tool in a data scientist's arsenal, particularly effective with nonlinear, high-dimensional data. Its strength lies in handling missing data more gracefully than linear regression and similar algorithms. This method is versatile, adept at both classification and regression tasks, and has proven to be highly effective in areas like fraud detection. By efficiently identifying complex patterns and anomalies, gradient boosting algorithms can play a crucial role in detecting fraudulent activities in financial transactions or insurance claims.

Among gradient boosting algorithms, *XGBoost* is known for its efficiency and ease of tuning, making it a popular choice for large datasets. (See Chapter 13 for more details on XGBoost.) It primarily uses tree-based models, which are beneficial in detecting intricate patterns indicative of fraud. *LightGBM* offers greater efficiency, using gradient-based one-side sampling for faster training and reduced memory usage. It combines tree-based models with this unique sampling approach, enhancing its capability to handle large-scale fraud detection problems where speed and memory efficiency are crucial.

Other notable algorithms include *CatBoost*, designed specifically for categorical data and excelling with sparse categorical datasets often encountered in fraud detection scenarios. CatBoost and LightGBM can be used together in stacked or ensembled pipelines to combine CatBoost's native handling of categorical features with LightGBM's training-time efficiency—a useful pattern for fraud detection tasks involving a mix of categorical and numerical data. *H2O AutoML* extends beyond just gradient boosting, integrating various algorithms like random forests and neural networks. This comprehensive approach can be particularly beneficial in fraud detection, where a combination of different machine learning techniques might be necessary to capture the complexity of fraudulent behaviors.

The choice between these algorithms often depends on the specific nature of the data and the problem at hand, such as the subtleties involved in fraud detection. In the dynamic field of machine learning, understanding the nuances of these tools allows practitioners to select the most appropriate algorithm for their projects, including the challenging and critical task of detecting fraudulent activities.

Artificial Neural Networks (ANNs)

In the realm of fraud detection, artificial neural networks (ANNs) offer a powerful tool for analyzing complex data patterns and making predictive decisions. Let's delve into how ANNs, inspired by the human brain, can be adapted for fraud detection tasks.

The concept of ANNs is rooted in emulating the function of neurons in the human brain. Just as neurons process and transmit signals, ANNs use artificial neurons to process data and make predictions or decisions. In fraud detection, these artificial neurons can be trained to recognize patterns indicative of fraudulent activities (Fig. 14.16).

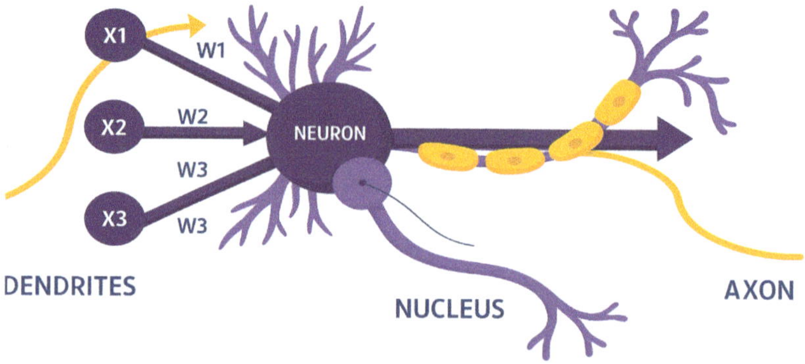

Fig. 14.16 Artificial neural networks: Emulating brain function for predictive analysis

Understanding the Structure of an ANN

A typical ANN is structured with layers of interconnected artificial neurons, or nodes. Neurons within one layer are connected to multiple neurons in the subsequent layer, forming a network. Each connection is assigned a weight that quantifies the influence of one neuron's signal on another. These weights are the adjustable parameters of the network and are fine-tuned during the training process to optimize the ANN's performance for specific tasks, such as fraud detection.

The diagram (See Fig. 14.17) and accompanying description below show the basic operation of an artificial neuron used in neural networks, which are a cornerstone of many machine learning tasks, including fraud detection.

In the context of fraud detection, an ANN might be configured to process various transaction attributes, which serve as inputs to the neurons in the initial layer (denoted as X1, X2, X3). These could include transaction amounts, the ages of customer accounts, and transaction frequencies. The associated weights (W1, W2, W3) determine the impact of each input on the neuron's output, effectively shaping the decision-making process of the network. Additionally, a bias term (b) is introduced to shift the activation function, allowing the network to better model the data and handle cases that are not linearly separable. In a network with multiple hidden neurons, this notation expands so that each weight carries two subscripts — one indexing the input and one indexing the destination neuron (See Fig. 14.18).

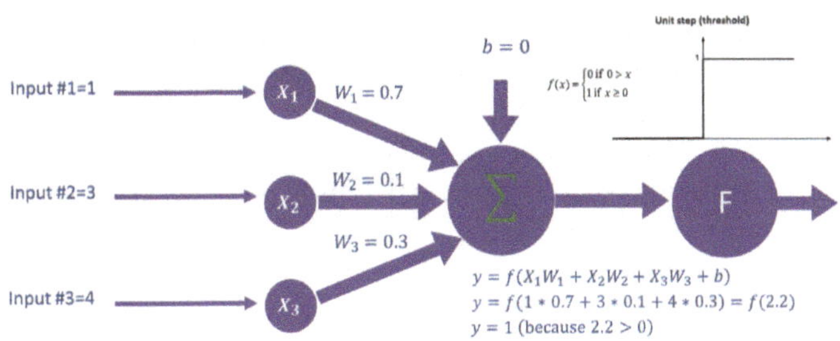

Fig. 14.17 The basic operation of ANN

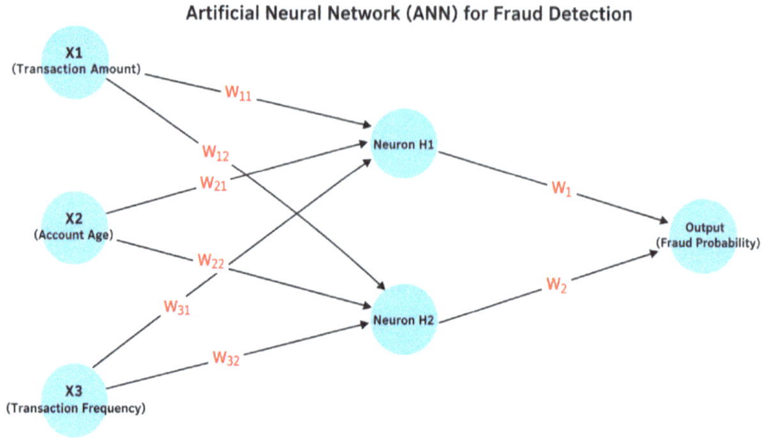

Fig. 14.18 Artificial neural networks for fraud detection

Training ANNs for Fraud Detection

The process of training an artificial neural network (ANN) for fraud detection involves inputting a myriad of data points, such as detailed transaction records, into the network. This data is then used by the ANN to fine-tune the weights of its connections through an iterative process known as backpropagation. As the ANN is exposed to a diverse set of labeled data—identifying which transactions are fraudulent and which are not—it incrementally improves its capacity to recognize fraud, thus enhancing its predictive accuracy over successive training cycles.

Take, for instance, an ANN that has been fed historical data on credit card transactions. Through training, the network becomes adept at identifying subtle and overt patterns that are indicative of fraudulent behavior. This enables the network to spot potential fraud in future transactions based on its learned experiences.

Expanding this application, let's consider an ANN being trained on a comprehensive dataset of banking transactions. This dataset encompasses key transaction attributes such as the amounts, the times they were conducted, the locations involved, and the historical data of the accounts. Through the training process, the ANN learns to discern what characterizes a normal transaction versus one that might be suspicious. It's this ability to differentiate and learn from the data that makes ANNs invaluable tools in the fight against fraud in the financial sector.

The Role of Neurons and Activation Functions in Fraud Detection

Within an ANN, the neuron's role is pivotal—it integrates multiple inputs, each weighted according to its relevance, and then applies an activation function (F). This function serves as a mathematical "gate," deciding whether the neuron's output signals the presence of a characteristic pattern. The non-linear nature of the activation function allows the neuron to make complex decisions beyond simple linear thresholds, which is particularly useful in fraud detection where subtleties and patterns in data need to be discerned accurately.

For example, in fraud analytics, the activation function evaluates the weighted sum of transaction attributes—like amount, frequency, and customer history. If the output exceeds a certain threshold, which is determined during the training phase, the neuron activates to flag the transaction as potentially fraudulent. This mechanism enables the ANN to effectively isolate and identify transactions that deviate from established patterns of normal activity, signaling possible fraud.

Practical Application

When new transaction data is fed into the trained neural network, each neuron processes the inputs through its weights and bias, then applies the activation function. The output layer compiles these signals to make a final decision about the transaction's legitimacy. The neural network's ability to consider complex, non-linear interactions between features makes it a powerful tool for detecting fraud.

In a practical scenario, suppose you have an ANN trained to detect credit card fraud. When a new transaction comes in, the ANN processes it through its layers of neurons, each assessing different aspects of the transaction. The final output layer would give a prediction—if the transaction is likely to be fraudulent or not.

The ANN's ability to learn from past data and adapt to new patterns makes it an invaluable asset in fraud detection. It can continuously evolve its understanding of what constitutes fraud, becoming more adept at identifying even the most subtle signs of fraudulent activity over time.

> TIP
>
> ANNs offer a sophisticated and dynamic approach to fraud detection. By simulating the nuanced decision-making processes of the human brain, they serve as essential tools in the ongoing battle against fraudulent activities, capable of adapting to new patterns and strategies employed by fraudsters.

Shuffling in Machine Learning Model Preparation for Fraud Detection

The following two sections address data preparation steps that apply across all the classification algorithms discussed above. The primary goal of shuffling is to eliminate any potential biases or patterns associated with the sequence in which data is presented. This step is essential to ensure that the model's learning process is not influenced by the order of the data.

In fraud analytics, datasets are typically divided into training, testing, and validation subsets. Shuffling the data before this division helps in distributing patterns and anomalies more evenly across these subsets. This balanced distribution is crucial for the model to learn effectively and generalize well to new, unseen data.

Benefits for Machine Learning Models

- Enhanced model quality and performance: By randomizing the order of data points, shuffling helps in creating a more robust model. This process aids the model in capturing a wide range of patterns and behaviors indicative of both legitimate and fraudulent transactions, which might otherwise be overlooked if the data were ordered in a specific way.
- Reduction in overfitting: Overfitting occurs when a model learns the specific details and noise in the training data to the extent that it

negatively impacts the model's performance on new data. Shuffling mitigates this risk by preventing the model from learning patterns that are a result of the sequential order of data rather than inherent characteristics of the data itself.

> TIP
>
> *Shuffling* is a key preprocessing step in the development of machine learning models for fraud detection. It ensures that the models are trained on data that is representative of the real-world scenarios they will encounter, thereby enhancing their accuracy and reliability in identifying fraudulent activities.

Dividing Data Into Training, Testing, and Validation Sets for Fraud Detection

Preparing a dataset for fraud detection model training involves a critical step: dividing the data into training, testing, and sometimes validation sets. This segmentation is crucial for the learning process and for evaluating the model's performance.

Strategies for Data Division

1. *Training and testing split:* A prevalent strategy is to allocate a substantial portion of the dataset, typically 70–80%, for training purposes. The remaining 20–30% is designated for testing. It's imperative that the testing data remain entirely unseen by the model during its training phase. This delineation is vital to accurately gauge the model's capacity to generalize and effectively detect fraudulent activities beyond the confines of the training data.
2. *Including a validation set:* An alternative strategy includes a three-way data division, integrating a validation or cross-validation dataset. For instance, the dataset can be segmented into 60% for training, with the remaining 40% equally split between validation and testing. The precise percentages may be adjusted based on the dataset's characteristics and the specific requirements of the fraud detection task.

Understanding the Role of Each Data Set

- *Training data:* This is the primary phase where models are trained, utilizing data to calculate gradients and update weights. During training, models are exposed to various fraud and legitimate transaction scenarios, which allows them to learn and identify distinguishing patterns.
- *Validation data*: Utilized in tandem with the training process, the validation dataset aids in assessing the quality of the training and ensures that models do not succumb to overfitting. Overfitting is a phenomenon where models excessively learn the specifics of the training data, including its noise and anomalies, thereby losing their ability to generalize. The validation set helps monitor the model's performance on unseen data. A model's decreasing error on the training set, coupled with increasing error on the validation set, signals overfitting. In such cases, strategies like early stopping are implemented to cease further training.
- *Testing data:* This dataset is critical for evaluating the trained model's proficiency in fraud detection. Testing data, never utilized during the training phase, offers an unbiased assessment of the model's ability to generalize. This set confirms the model's efficacy in identifying fraudulent transactions that it hasn't previously encountered.

TIP

Segmenting data into training, validation, and testing sets is a fundamental process in preparing models for fraud detection. This division ensures that models not only assimilate historical data but also develop the ability to generalize and accurately identify emerging patterns of fraud. Correct understanding and implementation of these data divisions are key to developing effective and reliable fraud detection systems.

Summary

Chapter 14 in the series on fraud data analytics (FDA) stands as an in-depth exploration of classification techniques within supervised learning, focusing on their crucial role in detecting fraudulent transactions. The chapter delves into a range of algorithms, each dissected for its unique strengths and limitations, as well as specific scenarios where they are most effective in fraud detection.

The discussion begins by laying the groundwork for understanding binary and multiclass classification. It explains how these methods categorize transactions into fraudulent or legitimate classes and extends to other applications like risk assessment and customer behavior prediction.

In terms of algorithms, logistic regression is emphasized for its effectiveness in binary classifications, such as distinguishing between fraudulent and non-fraudulent transactions. The chapter lauds its balance between interpretability and predictive accuracy. Support vector machines (SVM) are explored for their ability to handle high-dimensional spaces and effectiveness in distinct class separations, especially in identifying fraudulent transactions based on transaction amounts and patterns.

Further, decision trees and random forests are highlighted for their interpretability and capability to handle both numerical and categorical data. They are adept at capturing non-linear relationships, making them suitable for complex fraud patterns. The K-Nearest Neighbors (KNN) methodology is reviewed for its straightforward approach to classifying transactions based on the majority vote of nearest neighbors in the feature space, with practical examples demonstrating its application in real-world fraud detection scenarios.

Naïve Bayes is discussed for its probabilistic approach and simplicity, especially where conditional independence is a reasonable assumption. The chapter also coversgradient boosting methods, including an introduction to XGBoost, LightGBM, and CatBoost. These are recognized for their efficiency in identifying complex patterns indicative of fraud.

Chapter 14 of the series on fraud data analytics (FDA) introduces artificial neural networks (ANNs) as a sophisticated tool for fraud detection. This section of the chapter elaborates on how ANNs, inspired by the functionality of the human brain, can be adapted to analyze complex data patterns and make predictive decisions in the context of fraud.

Looking ahead, Chapter 15 goes into advanced topics in fraud detection, extending beyond the basics of machine learning models to cover model optimization, hyperparameter tuning, and the crucial role of model governance in deployment. This upcoming chapter is designed to equip readers with the skills to navigate the complexities of model development, optimization, and governance in the dynamic and critical field of fraud detection. Chapter 15 promises to provide deeper insights and more sophisticated techniques, preparing readers for the nuanced and evolving challenges in fraud detection analytics.

CHAPTER 15

Fraud Detection Excellence—A Deep Exploration of Model Metrics, Optimization, and Governance

This chapter explores the complexities of fraud detection, focusing on transforming theoretical models into effective tools for identifying and preventing fraud. This chapter emphasizes advanced metrics, optimization techniques, and the crucial role of governance, guiding readers through the nuanced process of model tuning and deployment. It highlights the importance of understanding classification model metrics, balancing model explainability with accuracy, and mastering optimization strategies, including the pivotal role of learning rate and challenges in non-convex objective functions.

Key aspects such as adaptive learning rates, early stopping, advanced tuning methods like grid search and Bayesian optimization, and deployment challenges are thoroughly explored. Emphasizing model governance, the chapter ensures models remain transparent, compliant, and performant. The introduction of AutoGluon, a tool for automated machine learning, marks a significant advancement, particularly for managing large, imbalanced datasets common in fraud detection.

In essence, this chapter serves as a comprehensive guide through the advanced stages of model development, deployment, and governance in fraud detection, equipping readers with the knowledge to effectively navigate and leverage opportunities in this evolving field.

A. Al Aqqad, *Fraud Analytics in Action*
https://doi.org/10.1007/978-3-032-16023-2_15

Understanding Classification Metrics for Fraud Detection

Before diving deep into the performance metrics, it's crucial to grasp basic terminologies related to classification:

- *True positives (TP):* Correctly predicted fraud cases.
- *False positives (FP):* Non-fraud cases incorrectly flagged as fraud (Type I error).
- *False negatives (FN):* Fraud cases that went unnoticed by the model (Type II error).
- *True negatives (TN):* Correctly predicted non-fraud cases.

TIP

Understanding these terms is foundational, as they're referenced in various classification metrics.

Classification Model KPIs

In fraud detection, understanding the confusion matrix (see Fig. 15.1) is crucial. This matrix is a tabular representation that contrasts the predicted classes with the actual ones, providing a clear picture of a model's performance. Key metrics derived from the *confusion matrix* include *classification accuracy, misclassification rate, precision, and recall.*

- *Classification accuracy* is a measure of the overall correctness of the model, calculated by the formula $(TP + TN)/(TP + TN + FP + FN)$. It tells us the proportion of true results (both true positives and true negatives) among the total number of cases examined.
- The *misclassification rate*, often referred to as the error rate, is the opposite of accuracy. It indicates the proportion of incorrect predictions and is computed as $(FP + FN)/(TP + TN + FP + FN)$. This metric is crucial for understanding the instances where the model has erred in prediction.
- *Precision* in the context of fraud detection denotes how many of the cases predicted as fraud were actually fraudulent. It is calculated

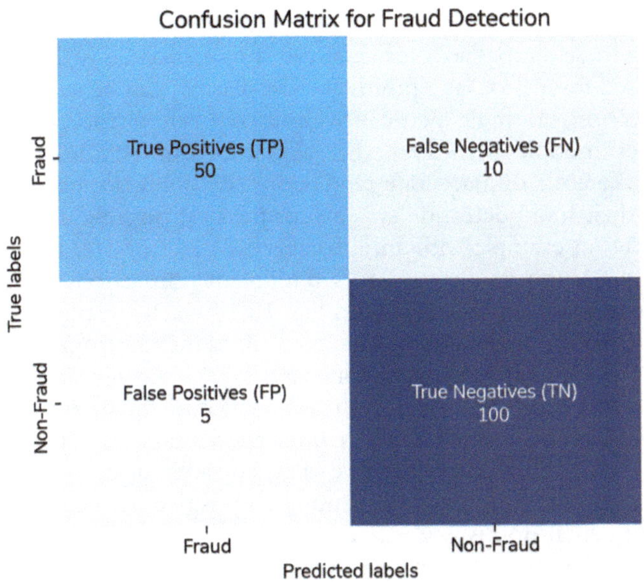

Fig. 15.1 Confusion matrix for fraud detection

by $TP/(TP + FP)$ and provides insight into the model's ability to minimize false positives. (When model predicted fraud class, how often was it right?)

- *Recall*, also known as sensitivity, is about capturing the proportion of actual fraud cases that the model successfully detected. The formula $TP/(TP + FN)$ is used to calculate recall. It's a critical measure, especially in scenarios where missing out on actual fraud cases can have significant implications. (When the class was actually fraud, how often did the classifier get it right?)

Together, these metrics, derived from the confusion matrix, offer a comprehensive view of a model's performance, guiding the fine-tuning process for optimal fraud detection.

In fraud detection, the importance of *precision* versus *recall* can vary based on the specific business needs. For example, a credit card company might prioritize high recall to catch most frauds, accepting lower precision as a trade-off. In contrast, an insurance firm might focus on high precision to minimize resource-intensive false alarms. Understanding and leveraging these metrics are crucial, as the costs associated with false negatives (missed frauds) or false positives (false alarms) can be substantial. In fraud detection, no single metric provides a complete picture; it's essential to consider multiple metrics together, aligning them with business objectives and the costs of inaccurate predictions. By doing so, businesses can optimize their fraud detection systems for the best possible performance.

Consider an example with an imbalanced dataset of 100 transactions, comprising 91 non-fraudulent and 9 fraudulent transactions. (Note: this example uses different numbers from Fig. 15.1, which illustrates a distinct dataset of 165 transactions.). The confusion matrix from a machine learning classifier might show certain metrics like classification accuracy, precision, and recall. While a high accuracy rate might initially seem impressive, it can be misleading in imbalanced datasets. Precision and recall provide a more comprehensive view, considering both the proportion of actual positive predictions among all positive predictions and the fraction of actual positives identified correctly. Tools like the precision-recall curve, F-score, ROC curve, and detailed classification reports are vital for a nuanced understanding and improvement of a model's performance, especially in imbalanced datasets like those common in fraud detection.

> TIP
>
> *Accuracy limitations:* It's important to note that accuracy alone can be misleading, especially in unbalanced datasets where one class significantly outnumbers the other. This is common in fraud detection, where legitimate transactions vastly outnumber fraudulent ones.
>
> *Importance of recall:* Recall becomes a crucial metric in scenarios where the cost of missing true positive cases (such as actual fraud) is high. In unbalanced datasets, such as a small number of fraud cases compared to non-fraudulent ones, recall helps to measure how effectively the model detects the minority class.

ROC (Receiver Operating Characteristic Curve)

ROC is a statistical tool used in the field of decision-making and, more broadly, in machine learning for evaluating binary classification models. Let's break down the concept:

The ROC curve is a graphical representation (see Fig. 2) that shows the performance of a *fraud detection system* as its discrimination threshold varies. It plots the *fraud detection rate (FDR)* against the *false alarm rate (FAR)* at different threshold settings. FDR, also known as *sensitivity* or *recall*, is the proportion of actual frauds correctly identified by the system. FAR, on the other hand, is the proportion of legitimate non-fraud transactions that the system incorrectly flags as fraudulent.

ROC curves are particularly useful for *comparative analysis* as they allow for the simultaneous evaluation of multiple classifiers on the same graph. The effectiveness of a classifier is generally indicated by how close its ROC curve is to the top-left corner of the plot. An important aspect of the ROC curve is its use in *threshold selection* for fraud detection systems. By analyzing the curve, one can choose a threshold that offers the best balance between detecting genuine fraud (FDR) and avoiding false alarms (FAR) (Fig. 15.2).

The ROC curve not only serves as a tool to visually assess the performance of a fraud detection system across all possible thresholds but also illustrates how a system that performs no better than random would have an ROC curve resembling a 45-degree diagonal line. In contrast, an ideal system that perfectly detects fraud will have an ROC curve that passes through the top-left corner of the chart.

AUC (Area Under Curve)

The area under the curve (AUC), as illustrated in Fig. 15.3, summarizes the overall ability of the system to differentiate between fraudulent and non-fraudulent transactions. A system with an AUC of 0.5 performs no better than random guessing, whereas an AUC of 1.0 indicates perfect differentiation between fraud and non-fraud. The figure highlights various aspects of the ROC curve, including the light blue area representing the AUROC, the diagonal dashed red line depicting a model with random outcomes, and the position of different predictors indicating their comparative effectiveness.

Here's the visualization of the area under curve (AUC) for fraud detection:

- The blue line represents the ROC curve, plotting the fraud detection rate (FDR) against the false alarm rate (FAR).
- The light blue shaded area under the ROC curve symbolizes the AUC. This area quantifies the overall ability of the system to differentiate between fraudulent and non-fraudulent transactions.
- The AUC value is indicated in the legend. An AUC of 0.5, depicted by the diagonal dashed red line, corresponds to a model performing

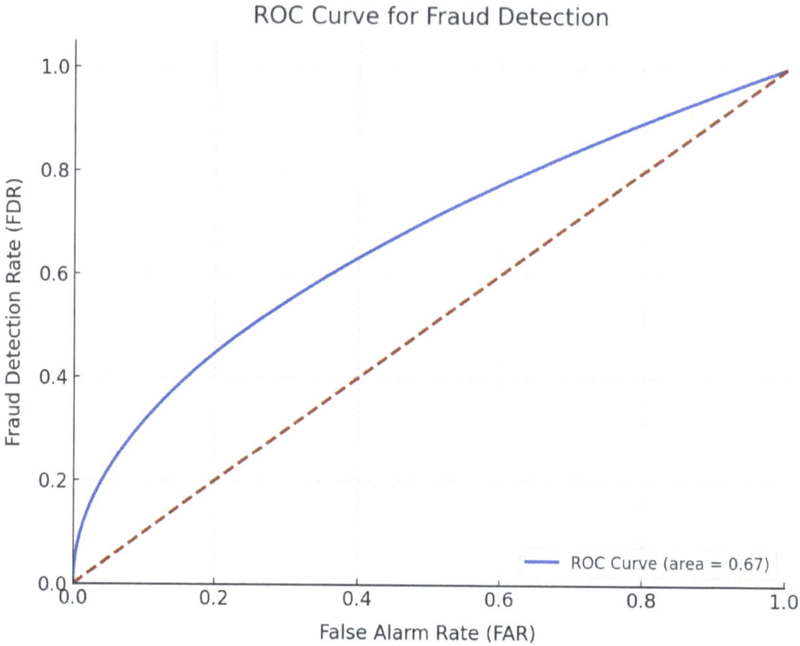

Fig. 15.2 Receiver Operating Characteristic (ROC) Curve for Fraud Detection. This figure illustrates the Receiver Operating Characteristic (ROC) curve, which evaluates the performance of a binary classification model by plotting the Fraud Detection Rate (True Positive Rate) against the False Alarm Rate (False Positive Rate) across different decision thresholds. The dashed diagonal line represents the performance of a random classifier, while the solid curve demonstrates the model's discriminatory power. The Area Under the Curve (AUC) provides a single summary metric of overall model effectiveness, with higher values indicating stronger classification performance. Adapted from: Wikimedia Commons, "ROC Curves," available at: https://commons.wikimedia.org/wiki/File:Roccurves.png

no better than random guessing. On the other hand, an AUC of 1.0 would indicate perfect differentiation.

- The position and shape of the ROC curve relative to the dashed line demonstrate the comparative effectiveness of the system in distinguishing between fraud and non-fraud cases.

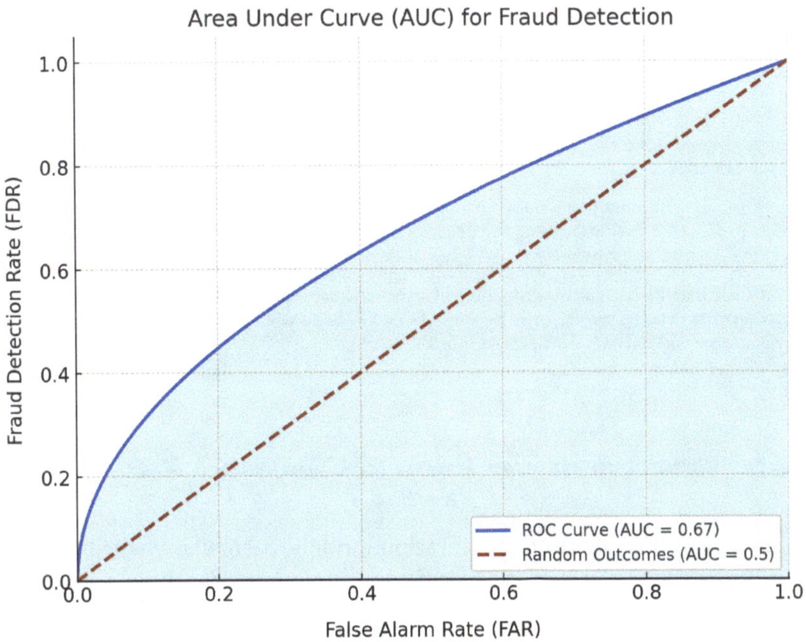

Fig. 15.3 AUC (area under curve) for fraud detection. This figure visualizes the area under the ROC curve for a fraud detection model. The solid blue line plots the Fraud Detection Rate (FDR) against the False Alarm Rate (FAR), with the light blue shaded region beneath representing the AUC—a single metric quantifying the model's overall ability to distinguish fraudulent from legitimate transactions. The dashed red diagonal line represents a random classifier (AUC = 0.5). The model shown achieves an AUC of 0.67, indicating moderate discriminatory power above chance. An AUC of 1.0 would indicate perfect classification.

The AUC is a crucial metric in evaluating the performance of classification models, especially in complex scenarios like fraud detection where the cost of misclassification can be significant.

TIP

While ROC curves are invaluable for evaluating the performance of fraud detection systems, it's important to interpret them judiciously. The ROC curve and the area under the curve (AUC) provide insights into the trade-offs between the fraud detection rate (FDR) and the false alarm rate (FAR). However, the optimal balance between these rates can vary depending on the specific context and requirements of the fraud detection system.

For instance, in scenarios where the cost of missing a fraudulent transaction is very high, a higher FDR might be preferable, even at the expense of a higher FAR. Conversely, in situations where false alarms can lead to significant disruption or costs, minimizing the FAR might be more critical.

Therefore, while the ROC curve is a powerful tool for assessing and comparing the effectiveness of different fraud detection models, the choice of the threshold for fraud detection should be made considering the unique operational and business requirements of the system.

Comprehensive Evaluation Metrics for Classification Models: Beyond the Basics

In the realm of evaluating classification models, particularly when dealing with imbalanced datasets or specific application needs, there are several metrics beyond the commonly discussed KPIs that can significantly aid in performance evaluation.

Specificity, for instance, is a crucial metric calculated as TN/(TN + FP). It indicates the fraction of true negatives among all actual negatives, focusing on the model's ability to correctly identify the negative class in binary classification.

Another important metric is the *F1 Score*, which represents the harmonic mean of precision and recall. It provides a balanced measure between these two metrics, ranging from 0 to 1, where 1 signifies perfect precision and recall, and 0 indicates the absence of either. The F1 Score is particularly useful as it's formulated by (2 x precision x recall)/(precision + recall).

Balanced accuracy also plays a significant role, especially in the context of imbalanced datasets. It averages sensitivity (recall) and specificity, offering a holistic view of the classifier's effectiveness across classes. Calculated as (sensitivity + specificity)/2, it ensures that both classes are equally represented in the performance assessment.

The *Matthews correlation coefficient* (MCC) is another metric that considers all elements of the confusion matrix (TP, TN, FP, and FN). It provides a balanced view of classifier performance and is particularly valuable in scenarios involving imbalanced datasets. MCC values range from −1 to 1, where 1 indicates perfect prediction, 0 represents random prediction, and −1 indicates inverse prediction.

Cohen's kappa extends the understanding of model performance by measuring the agreement between model predictions and actual labels, adjusting for random chance. Its scores range from −1 to 1, with 1 implying perfect concordance, 0 indicating chance agreement, and negative values suggesting worse-than-chance agreement.

Utilizing these metrics allows for a comprehensive assessment of a classification model's capabilities, addressing the specific nuances of the dataset or application requirements. Such insights are invaluable for understanding a model's strengths and limitations, facilitating informed decisions in model selection or tuning.

TIP

In assessing classification models, it's crucial to have a keen understanding of various KPIs, including accuracy, precision, recall, specificity, the F1 Score, balanced accuracy, the Matthews Correlation Coefficient, and Cohen's Kappa. Understanding the significance of each metric and how it relates to the dataset or application at hand is pivotal in choosing, fine-tuning, and contrasting different classification models, ensuring a well-rounded approach to model evaluation.

Navigating the Trade-Off Between Explainability and Accuracy in Fraud Detection

In fraud detection, practitioners are often tasked with navigating the delicate balance between explainability (Black Box and Glass Box issues) and accuracy, a theme that's also extensively explored in chapter 5 "Techniques and Approaches in Fraud Analytics".

Explainability in models is vital for several reasons. First and foremost, it addresses the need for accountability. When transactions are flagged as potentially fraudulent, both the affected customers and merchants naturally seek explanations. A model that offers clear insights into its decision-making not only builds trust but also ensures clarity in communication. Moreover, financial institutions are often under regulatory scrutiny that requires them to clearly explain their decision-making processes, particularly in instances where transactions are flagged. This need is underscored by regulations like the U.S. Fair Credit Reporting Act (FCRA), which mandates businesses to justify adverse actions stemming from a consumer's credit report. Operationally, when a model flags transactions, these are typically reviewed by human analysts. An interpretable model can greatly assist these analysts by providing valuable insights, thereby enabling quicker and more accurate reviews.

On the flip side, the importance of accuracy in fraud detection is paramount. The financial risks associated with false negatives, where fraudulent transactions slip through the net, are significant. Equally, false positives—legitimate transactions wrongly identified as fraudulent—can lead to lost sales and customer dissatisfaction, not to mention damage to a company's reputation. Frequent errors in identifying fraud or mistakenly blocking genuine transactions can severely impact a company's public image and trustworthiness.

This tug-of-war between explainability and accuracy is evident in the selection of models for fraud detection. Logistic regression models, for example, offer a degree of transparency by assigning weights to various features, making their decisions easier to interpret. However, they may not always capture the more complex patterns hidden within the data. In contrast, deep learning models, like neural networks, excel at identifying complicated patterns and relationships, potentially offering greater accuracy. But their decision-making process is often less transparent, making it hard to articulate the reasoning behind flagged transactions.

To effectively balance these two critical aspects, several strategies are adopted in practice. Hybrid models are one approach where a complex model first detects potential fraud, and a simpler model subsequently provides the rationale behind these decisions. Interpretation tools such as SHAP (SHapley additive explanations) and LIME (local interpretable model-agnostic explanations) also play a significant role. These tools help demystify the decisions of complex models, offering insights into the reasoning behind specific outcomes. Both SHAP and LIME are applied practically in the classification lab at the end of this chapter. Additionally, incorporating feedback mechanisms, where insights from human evaluators are used to continually refine the model, proves to be invaluable. If analysts consistently question or challenge the model's decisions on certain types of transactions, this feedback can be utilized to further train and enhance the model.

In essence, the journey of balancing explainability and accuracy in fraud detection is a continuous and evolving process, demanding a blend of sophisticated modeling, regulatory compliance, and practical operational considerations.

> TIP
>
> In the world of fraud detection, both explainability and accuracy are of paramount importance. It's not merely about identifying as many suspicious transactions as possible but also understanding the reasoning behind each flag. Achieving this balance requires a combination of the right models, interpretative tools, and feedback mechanisms.

Model Optimization in Fraud Detection

In the domain of fraud detection, the stakes are incredibly high. It's not just about identifying unauthorized transactions; it's about safeguarding trust, ensuring financial security, and maintaining the integrity of financial systems. The financial sector and businesses are constantly under threat of fraudulent activities. Given these high stakes, the models employed for fraud detection must be both accurate and timely. They need to recognize patterns in vast amounts of transactional data, discerning legitimate transactions from fraudulent ones. However, when a machine learning model is initially trained for this purpose, it might not always yield the desired results. This could be due to various factors, such as imbalanced datasets, noise in the data, or the ever-evolving nature of fraudulent tactics. An under-optimized model can lead to:

- *False negatives:* This means the model misses out on detecting actual fraudulent transactions, leading to potential financial losses.
- *False positives:* legitimate transactions are incorrectly flagged as fraudulent, causing inconvenience to customers and potentially leading to a loss of trust or business.

Given these challenges, post-training model optimization becomes not just beneficial but essential. It ensures that the model is fine-tuned to detect fraudulent activities with higher precision and recall.

Hyperparameter Optimization in Machine Learning for Fraud Detection

Hyperparameters and Parameters

- *Hyperparameters:* These are settings configured before training begins, like the learning rate, which dictates the model's learning aggressiveness. High learning rates mean larger, quicker steps but risk overshooting the optimal solution, while low rates offer more precision at the cost of speed.
- *Parameters:* Values derived during training, such as weights in neural networks or slope and intercept in linear regression. Unlike hyperparameters, these are not preset but learned from data.

Applying Optimization in Fraud Detection

In fraud detection, the primary goal is to minimize error and enhance the accuracy of models, necessitating meticulous hyperparameter tuning. These models typically start with initial parameter values and undergo iterative adjustments to find the global minimum (see Fig. 15.4), the point of least error. Central to this process is the learning rate, a critical hyperparameter that requires careful balancing to achieve optimal model performance.

When applying hyperparameter optimization in fraud detection, particularly with regard to the learning rate, striking a delicate balance is essential. A *high learning rate* can speed up the exploration of the parameter space and potentially accelerate convergence to the optimal solution. However, this approach carries the risk of rapid movements that might overshoot the ideal solution.

In contrast, a *low learning rate* helps in avoiding such overshooting by allowing the model to make smaller, more precise steps. This approach, while reducing the chance of skipping the best solution, can significantly slow down the process, which may not be ideal in time-sensitive scenarios typical of fraud detection.

To address this balancing act, *adaptive learning rate* strategies are often employed. These strategies involve starting with larger steps to quickly cover ground in the parameter space and then gradually reducing the step size as the model approaches the optimal solution. This method enables the model to efficiently bypass less promising areas while making

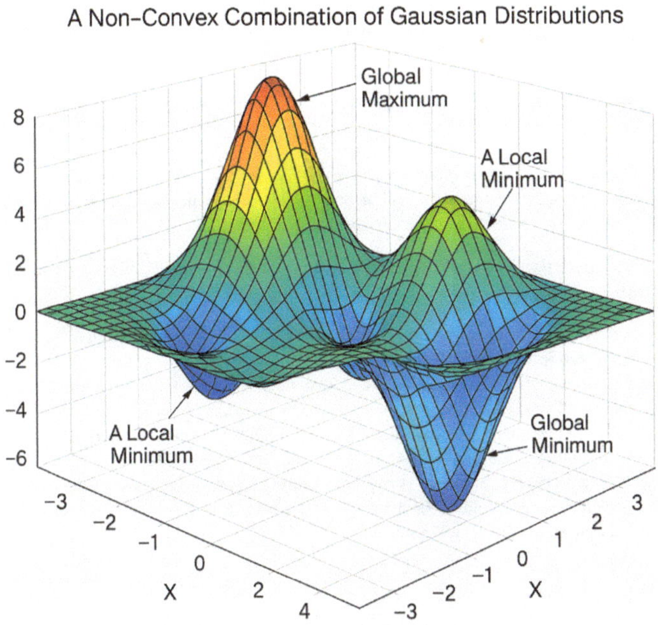

Fig. 15.4 Non-Convex Objective Functions. This figure illustrates a non-convex objective surface formed by the combination of multiple Gaussian distributions. The surface contains several local minima and maxima alongside a global optimum, highlighting the challenges faced by optimization algorithms when navigating complex loss landscapes. Such non-convexity is common in machine learning models, particularly in deep learning and ensemble methods, where gradient-based optimization techniques may converge to suboptimal local solutions rather than the global optimum. Adapted from: Wikimedia Commons, Non-Convex Objective Function https://commons.wikimedia.org/wiki/File:Non-Convex_Objective_Function.gif

careful and precise adjustments as it nears the point of least error, ensuring accuracy without compromising speed.

Addressing Non-convex Objective Functions in Fraud Detection

WARNING

Addressing non-convex objective functions in fraud detection

When navigating the complex landscape of fraud detection models, it's crucial to be aware of the following challenges:

- *Local minima and saddle points:* Using conservative learning rates can lead to models becoming trapped in suboptimal solutions or saddle points. This is particularly pertinent in deep learning, where the function space is high-dimensional and complex.
- *Overshooting risks:* Conversely, aggressive learning rates carry the risk of overshooting. This can cause the model to bypass the optimal solutions, leading to less effective fraud detection.
- *Balancing strategies:* To manage these risks effectively, consider using adaptive algorithms like Adam and RMSprop, which are optimization algorithms used in deep learning model training. Adam combines the benefits of AdaGrad and RMSprop, adapting learning rates based on a moving average of gradients, while RMSprop adjusts rates by maintaining a moving average of the square of gradients. These algorithms are essential for adjusting the learning rate during training, aiding in quicker and more efficient convergence. Additionally, strategies like learning rate annealing, scheduled adjustments, and early stopping are crucial. These methods enable the model to adaptively traverse the complex parameter space, striking a balance between swift convergence and precise localization of the global minimum.

TIP

In fraud detection, the choice of hyperparameters, particularly the learning rate, plays a pivotal role. Models need to be agile yet accurate, capable of adapting to evolving fraud patterns while minimizing errors. This discussion underscores the importance of strategic learning rate management and generalization strategies to develop efficient and reliable fraud detection systems.

Understanding Batch Size in Machine Learning for Fraud Detection

Batch size is a crucial hyperparameter in the training of machine learning models, particularly in the domain of fraud detection and analytics. It determines the number of samples processed before the model's internal parameters are updated.

Definition and Role: The batch size specifies how many data points (such as transaction records or customer profiles) are fed into the algorithm during one iteration of training. For instance, if you're training a model with 1000 data points and set a batch size of 50, the model initially processes the first 50 data points. Subsequently, the next sets of 50 data points are processed in sequence until the entire dataset is covered.

Impact on Training Dynamics:

- Small Batch Size: Using a smaller batch size, like the aforementioned batch of 50, can increase the model's ability to escape from local minima during training. This is because smaller batches provide more frequent updates to the model's parameters, introducing a degree of randomness that helps in exploring the parameter space more effectively. In fraud detection, this could mean better identification of subtle or rare fraud patterns that might be missed with larger batches.
- Large Batch Size: Conversely, larger batch sizes can lead to faster computational times as more data is processed in each iteration. However, there's a risk of the model converging to local minima, potentially missing nuanced patterns in the data. This might result in the model not identifying certain types of fraudulent activities as effectively.

Experimentation with Batch Sizes: In practice, especially in fraud analytics, finding the optimal batch size often involves experimentation. You can start with a certain batch size and adjust it based on the model's performance and the computational resources available. The goal is to strike a balance between efficient learning, model accuracy, and computational feasibility.

In summary, selecting the right batch size is a vital aspect of model training in fraud detection. It influences how the model learns from the data and can significantly impact its ability to detect fraudulent activities accurately. The choice of batch size should be informed by both the nature of the data and the specific requirements of the fraud detection task at hand.

Model Optimization Strategies in Fraud Detection

When it comes to *hyperparameter tuning*, three common strategies are grid search, *randomized search, and Bayesian optimization*. Let's briefly explore each.

Grid Search

Given the high stakes in fraud detection, an exhaustive search like a grid search can be beneficial to ensure no stone is left unturned.

What Is a Grid Search?
Grid search is a method for hyperparameter tuning that systematically builds and evaluates a model for each combination of algorithm parameters specified in a grid. This approach can be thought of as an "exhaustive search" because it leaves no stone unturned in exploring parameter space.

How Does Grid Search Work in Fraud Detection?
Suppose you're using an XGBoost model for detecting fraudulent activities. Key hyperparameters might include `max_depth` (depth of the tree), `learning_rate`, `n_estimators` (number of trees), and subsample (fraction of samples to be used for fitting individual trees).

You define a grid of potential values for these parameters. For example: models like XGBoost are used in applications such as credit card fraud detection.

- `max_depth`: [3, 6, 10]

  Description: This parameter determines the maximum depth of each tree in the model. A deeper tree can model more complex relationships by creating more decision nodes.

  Impact on fraud detection: In credit card fraud detection, a deeper tree (higher `max_depth`) might capture more complex patterns of fraudulent transactions, but there's also a risk of overfitting (modeling the noise in the training data).

  Example: A `max_depth` of 3 might be too shallow to capture complex fraud patterns, while 10 might be more effective but could overfit if not carefully validated.
- `learning_rate`: [0.01, 0.05, 0.1]

  Description: Also known as the shrinkage or step size, this parameter scales the contribution of each tree. A smaller learning rate requires more trees but can lead to a more robust model.

  Impact on fraud detection: A lower learning rate might require more iterations but can incrementally improve the model's ability to detect fraud.

  Example: A learning rate of 0.01 implies a very gradual improvement per tree, potentially leading to a more nuanced model, while 0.1 would result in faster but potentially less refined learning.
- `n_estimators`: [100, 500, 1000]

Description: This represents the number of trees built before stopping. More trees can lead to a more accurate model, but they increase computational complexity.

Impact on Fraud Detection: More trees might improve the model's ability to detect fraud by considering more scenarios, but too many can lead to overfitting.

Example: 100 trees might be insufficient for complex fraud detection patterns, whereas 1000 trees might capture more subtle patterns, but at the cost of longer training time and the risk of overfitting.

- `subsample`: [0.3, 0.7]

  Description: This parameter defines the fraction of samples to be used for fitting each individual tree. It's a form of stochastic boosting that helps reduce overfitting.

  Impact on fraud detection: Subsampling can prevent overfitting by ensuring that individual trees are trained on different subsets of data, potentially capturing diverse patterns of fraudulent behavior.

  Example: A subsample value of 0.3 means only 30% of the data is used to train each tree. This introduces randomness but can help in generalizing the model better.

Grid search will then create and evaluate models for every possible combination of these parameters. With the values given above, this results in 3 x 3 x 3 x 2 = 54 different combinations.

Performing cross-validation: To robustly assess the performance of each model, grid search often incorporates cross-validation. For instance, specifying fivefold cross-validation means each model will be trained and evaluated 5 times on different subsets of the data.

Thus, the total number of model training and evaluation runs would be 54 combinations x 5 folds = 270 runs.

Application in fraud detection: In fraud detection, where the cost of misclassification can be high, optimizing the hyperparameters to get the best possible model is crucial.

Grid search allows for a thorough exploration of the hyperparameter space, increasing the likelihood of finding the most effective model for identifying fraudulent activities.

TIP

- *Exhaustive nature:* Grid search can be computationally expensive, especially with large datasets or complex models like XGBoost. The number of combinations increases exponentially with the addition of more parameters and their values.
- *Balance between precision and recall:* In fraud detection, it's often important to find a balance between precision (the proportion of true positive identifications) and recall (the proportion of actual positives correctly identified). Grid search can help in fine-tuning the model to achieve this balance.

Model optimization using grid search

```
#Step 1:Import Necessary Libraries

from sklearn.model_selection import GridSearchCV
import xgboost as xgb
from sklearn.metrics import r2_score, mean_squared_error, mean_absolute_error
from math import sqrt
import numpy as np

#Step 2:Define the Parameters Grid
parameters_grid = { 'max_depth': [3, 6, 10],
             'learning_rate': [0.01, 0.05, 0.1],
             'n_estimators': [100, 500, 1000],
             'subsample_bytree': [0.3, 0.7]}

#Step 3:Initialize the XGBRegressor Model
model = xgb.XGBRegressor(objective ='reg:squarederror')

# Note that we used the "neg_mean_squared_error" since GridSearchCV() ranks all the algorithms (estimators)
# and specifies which one is the best. We are trying to minimize the error.

#Step 4:Configure GridSearchCV
xgb_gridsearch = GridSearchCV(estimator = model,
                    param_grid = parameters_grid,
                    scoring = 'neg_mean_squared_error',
                    cv = 5,
                    verbose = 5)

#Step 5:Fit GridSearchCV to the Training Data
```

Randomized Search
After exploring grid search, let's turn our attention to randomized search, the second strategy in hyperparameter tuning. While grid search offers a comprehensive approach by evaluating every possible combination of specified hyperparameters, it can become impractical in scenarios with a large number of hyperparameters or extensive ranges of values. For instance, a model with 30 hyperparameters, each with about 50 possible values, would result in an overwhelming number of combinations to test.

Efficiency of Randomized Search in Extensive Hyperparameter Spaces
Randomized search effectively addresses the limitations of grid search, especially when dealing with vast hyperparameter spaces. It operates by randomly sampling a subset of the parameter space, significantly reducing the number of combinations evaluated. This method is particularly useful in scenarios with expansive search spaces, as it strikes a balance between thoroughness and computational feasibility.

How Does a Randomized Search Function? In randomized search, instead of evaluating every possible combination of hyperparameters, a predetermined number of random combinations are selected and tested.

For example, in a model with hyperparameters like `n_estimators`, `max_depth`, `learning_rate`, and `min_child_weight`, randomized search might evaluate 50 random combinations from a range of specified values.

Advantages of Randomized Search:

- *Efficiency:* It's more efficient than grid search in large parameter spaces, as it avoids evaluating every single combination.
- *Speed:* Often, it can find a sufficiently effective solution faster than grid search.
- *Focus:* The process involves a more focused approach compared to the exhaustive nature of grid search.

Applying Randomized Search in Fraud Detection Context:

Consider developing a machine learning model for detecting fraudulent credit card transactions using an algorithm like XGBoost.

You define ranges for hyperparameters such as `n_estimators`, `max_depth`, `learning_rate`, and booster.

Rather than trying all combinations, you use a randomized search to randomly sample and assess, for example, 50 different configurations.

The objective is to fine-tune the model to accurately identify fraudulent activities, balancing the need for precision and recall.

Benefits in Fraud Detection:

- *Rapid model development:* Randomized search's speed is crucial in fraud detection, where models may need to adapt quickly to evolving fraud patterns.
- *Resource optimization*: It is more resource-efficient, an important consideration given the computational demands of fraud detection models.
- *Exploration of possibilities*: The method allows for the exploration of a broad range of hyperparameter settings, accommodating the complex and often non-linear patterns characteristic of fraudulent activities.

> TIP
>
> In fraud detection, where timely and accurate identification of fraudulent transactions is critical, randomized search stands out as a practical and efficient tool for model tuning. It enables the rapid deployment of robust models that effectively balance the detection of fraud with the avoidance of false positives.

Model Optimization Using Random Search

```
#Step 1:Import Necessary Libraries

from sklearn.model_selection import RandomizedSearchCV
import xgboost as xgb
from sklearn.metrics import r2_score, mean_squared_error, mean_absolute_error
from math import sqrt

#Step 2:Define the grid of hyperparameters to search
# you can choose which booster you'd like to choose:
# Two options are available: gbtree, gblinear
# gbtree uses tree based models while gblinear uses linear functions

grid = {
  'n_estimators': [100, 500, 700],
  'max_depth': [2, 3, 5],
  'learning_rate': [0.1, 0.5, 1],
  'min_child_weight': [1, 2, 3]
      }

# grid = {
#   'n_estimators': [100, 500, 700],
#    'max_depth': [2, 3, 5],
#    'learning_rate': [0.1, 0.5, 1],
#     'min_child_weight': [1, 2, 3],
#    'booster': ['gbtree','gblinear']}


#Step 3:Initialize the XGBRegressor Model
model = xgb.XGBRegressor(objective ='reg:squarederror')

#Step 4: Set up the random search
random_cv = RandomizedSearchCV(estimator = model,
                  param_distributions = grid,
                  cv = 5,
                  n_iter = 50,
                  scoring = 'neg_mean_absolute_error',
                  verbose = 5,
                  return_train_score = True)

#Step 5:Fit Random Search to the Training Data
# Replace X_train and y_train with your actual training data
random_cv.fit(X_train, y_train)

#Step6: Retrieve the Best Estimator
random_cv.best_estimator_

#Step 7: Predict and Evaluate the Model

# Replace X_test and y_test with your actual test data
y_predict = random_cv.predict(X_test)

# Calculate various performance metrics
k = X_test.shape[1]
n = len(X_test)
RMSE = float(format(np.sqrt(mean_squared_error(y_test, y_predict)),'.3f'))
MSE = mean_squared_error(y_test, y_predict)
MAE = mean_absolute_error(y_test, y_predict)
r2 = r2_score(y_test, y_predict)
adj_r2 = 1-(1-r2)*(n-1)/(n-k-1)

# Print performance metrics
print('RMSE =',RMSE, '\nMSE =',MSE, '\nMAE =',MAE, '\nR2 =', r2, '\nAdjusted R2 =', adj_r2)
```

Bayesian Optimization
Bayesian optimization marks a significant shift from the somewhat blind trial-and-error approach of grid and randomized searches. It introduces a more intelligent way of navigating hyperparameter space, learning from past results to make better-informed decisions about where to search next.

How Bayesian Optimization Works

- *Intelligent search*: Instead of randomly or exhaustively exploring the hyperparameter space, Bayesian optimization focuses on areas that show promise. It uses a probabilistic model to predict which hyperparameter combinations are most likely to yield the best performance.
- *Example*: Consider hyperparameters like learning rate and subsample in an XGBoost model for fraud detection. Bayesian optimization starts by sampling a few points in the parameter space and evaluating their performance. If it finds a particular range of learning rate leading to lower errors, it will focus more on that range in subsequent iterations, refining the search based on previous outcomes.

Application in Fraud Detection:

In fraud detection, where the patterns can be highly intricate and the cost of misclassification is significant, Bayesian optimization can be especially advantageous.

When the model identifies promising hyperparameter values that lead to accurate identification of fraudulent transactions, Bayesian optimization will concentrate its efforts in similar ranges, thereby improving efficiency.

You can define the search space with specific ranges or distributions for each hyperparameter. For instance, you might specify that the `learning_rate` follows a log-uniform distribution, allowing the search to cover a wide range of values efficiently.

Advantages of Bayesian Optimization in Fraud Detection:

- *Learning from past evaluations*: Unlike grid or randomized Search, Bayesian optimization actively learns which areas of the parameter space are worth exploring further.
- *Efficiency:* This method can often find optimal or near-optimal hyperparameter settings faster than other search strategies, especially in complex models.
- *Balanced search:* It strikes a balance between exploring new areas and exploiting known promising regions, which is crucial in fraud detection where model performance has significant implications.

> TIP
>
> Bayesian optimization offers a smart and efficient approach to hyperparameter tuning in fraud detection models. By focusing on promising areas of the hyperparameter space and learning from each evaluation, it can significantly reduce the time and computational resources required to find the optimal model configuration. This efficiency is vital in fraud detection, where adapting quickly to evolving patterns is crucial for maintaining high detection accuracy. In our upcoming session, we will delve into how to set up and run Bayesian optimization, exploring different ways to define the search space and the practical aspects of implementing this technique in real-world scenarios.

Model optimization using Bayesian optimization.

```
# Let's install a library called Scikit-Optimize (Skopt) which is used to perform bayesian optimization
# BayesSearchCV class is used in a similar fashion to GridSearchCV
# You secify the search space as a distribution instead of discrete values

#Step 1:Install Scikit-Optimize

! pip install scikit-optimize

#Step 2:Import Necessary Libraries
from skopt import BayesSearchCV
import xgboost as xgb

#Step 3:Initialize the XGBRegressor Model
model = xgb.XGBRegressor(objective ='reg:squarederror')

#Step 4: Define the Search Space for Bayesian Optimization

search_space = {
    "learning_rate": (0.01, 1.0, "log-uniform"),
    "max_depth": (1, 50),
    "n_estimators": (5, 500),
}


#Step 5: Configure BayesSearchCV
xgb_bayes_search = BayesSearchCV(model,
                    search_space,
                    n_iter = 50,
                    scoring = 'neg_mean_absolute_error',
                    cv = 5)


#Step 6: Fit BayesSearchCV to the Training Data

result = xgb_bayes_search.fit(X_train, y_train)

#Step 7: Predict and Evaluate the Model
# Replace X_test and y_test with your actual test data
y_predict = xgb_bayes_search.predict(X_test)

# Calculate various performance metrics
k = X_test.shape[1]
n = len(X_test)
RMSE = float(format(np.sqrt(mean_squared_error(y_test, y_predict)),'.3f'))
MSE = mean_squared_error(y_test, y_predict)
MAE = mean_absolute_error(y_test, y_predict)
r2 = r2_score(y_test, y_predict)
adj_r2 = 1-(1-r2)*(n-1)/(n-k-1)

# Print performance metrics
print('RMSE =',RMSE, '\nMSE =',MSE, '\nMAE =',MAE, '\nR2 =', r2, '\nAdjusted R2 =', adj_r2)
```

When it comes to fraud detection, the optimization of machine learning models is paramount. Given the dynamic nature of fraudulent techniques, models need to be not only accurate but also adaptable. The right combination of hyperparameters can make the difference between catching a fraudulent transaction and letting it slip through the cracks.

The Concept of Bias and Variance

Bias: Refers to the error due to overly simplistic assumptions in the learning algorithm. A high-bias model might oversimplify, failing to capture key patterns in the data. For example, a linear regression model might not flexibly fit complex fraud detection data, leading to high bias.

Variance: Refers to the error due to too much complexity in the learning algorithm. High-variance models overfit the training data, performing well on this data but poorly on unseen data. For instance, a high-order polynomial model might fit the training data perfectly but fail to generalize well, leading to high variance.

Practical example: Let's consider two models: a simple linear regression (high bias) and a complex high-order polynomial (high variance).

- The linear model, due to its simplicity, might not fit the fraud detection data perfectly, resulting in significant residuals and hence, high bias.
- The complex model, while fitting the training data perfectly (low bias), performs poorly on unseen test data, indicating high variance.

The Trade-Off

The key is to find a balance between bias and variance. The ideal model for fraud detection should neither oversimplify the data (high bias) nor overfit to the training data (high variance). This balance ensures the model performs consistently well on both training and unseen data, providing reliable fraud detection.

TIP

- A model with high bias oversimplifies, unable to capture complex fraud patterns.
- A model with high variance overfits, failing to generalize to new data.
- The optimal model in fraud detection strikes a balance, providing consistent and reliable performance.

This bias-variance tradeoff is critical in machine learning for fraud detection, guiding data scientists to build models that are not just accurate on training data but also effective in predicting and identifying real-world fraudulent activities.

The Perils of Overfitting in Fraud Detection Model Optimization

Models that perform well on training data but poorly on unseen data can be misleading, creating a false sense of security in fraud detection.

In fraud detection, missing actual fraud (false negatives) can have significant financial and trust implications. Fraud patterns are dynamic, requiring models to be adaptable to new and emerging patterns.

Underfitting model: Imagine a scenario where we have a set of data points, and our objective is to discern a relationship between two features. An underfitting model, characterized by its simplicity, might take a straightforward approach, like fitting these points with a straight line. However, this simplicity often fails to capture the complexity inherent in the data, resulting in a model that doesn't accurately represent the problem at hand. To remedy underfitting, we can increase the model's complexity, perhaps moving from a linear to a higher-order polynomial model, or extend the training time to enhance its learning capacity.

Overfitting: Conversely, overfitting represents the other extreme. An overfitting model, while appearing perfect at a high level, essentially memorizes the training data, adapting its parameters to fit each data point precisely. This approach, although it might seem ideal initially, lacks the ability to generalize. When new, unseen data is introduced (for example, in a testing set), the model's performance often deteriorates significantly. This is because it has tailored itself too closely to the specific details of the training data, at the expense of its ability to adapt to new information.

The goal in machine learning, especially in the context of fraud detection, is to strike a balance between these two extremes. We seek a model that is complex enough to learn from the training data accurately but also possesses the flexibility to adapt and perform well on new, unseen data. This balance is akin to a student who not only learns from provided examples but can also apply this knowledge to different, unseen problems.

The ideal model is one (see Figs. 15.5 and 15.6) that generalizes well, performing effectively on both the training and testing datasets, thereby ensuring reliability and robustness in real-world fraud detection scenarios.

These visualizations (Fig. 15.5) illustrate the *trade-offs* between bias and variance in model training and testing. An underfitting model oversimplifies the problem (high bias), while an overfitting model is overly complex and sensitive to the specifics of the training data (high variance). The goal in machine learning is to find a balance between these two extremes to achieve good generalization on unseen data.

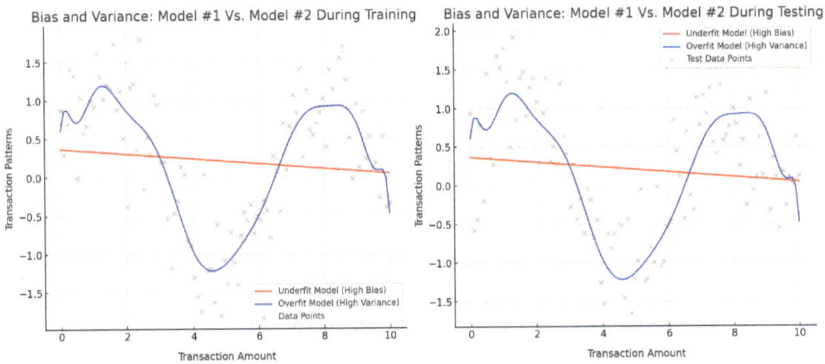

Fig. 15.5 Bias and variance: Model performance during training and testing

Fig. 15.6 Ideal model performance: Balancing bias and variance for effective generalization

These plots (Fig. 15.6) demonstrate the ideal scenario in model training and testing—a model that performs well on both training and unseen data. This balance minimizes both bias (not being too simple) and variance (not being too complex), leading to a model that generalizes well to new data, which is the ultimate goal in machine learning and predictive modeling.

Effective Strategies for Preventing Overfitting in Fraud Detection Machine Learning Models

1. *Early stopping:* is a technique used to prevent overfitting during model training. It is applied when the accuracy on the training dataset continues to increase, but the accuracy on the validation dataset begins to decrease. Early stopping ensures that the network can generalize well, meaning it will perform effectively not just on the training dataset but also on unseen testing data.
2. *Regularization:* Techniques like L1 and L2 regularization are methods used to prevent overfitting in machine learning models by penalizing large coefficients. L1 regularization, also known as lasso regularization, adds the absolute value of coefficients as a penalty to the loss function, encouraging sparsity in the model. L2 regularization, known as ridge regularization, adds the square of the coefficients as a penalty, promoting smaller, more distributed coefficient values. Both methods help in creating simpler models that generalize better to new data.
3. *Cross-validation:* Using methods like k-fold cross-validation, which involves dividing the dataset into "k" number of subsets and then iteratively using each subset as a test set while the remaining subsets serve as the training set, ensures diverse evaluation and reduces the likelihood of overfitting. This technique provides a robust way to assess model performance by averaging results over multiple iterations, leading to more reliable and generalizable conclusions.
4. *Utilizing ensemble learning techniques* such as boosting and bagging can significantly enhance model generalization. By aggregating predictions from a variety of models, these methods apply collective decision-making, which often leads to improved accuracy and robustness in predictive performance.
5. *Balancing datasets:* Techniques like SMOTE or ADASYN are crucial for addressing dataset imbalances prevalent in fraud data. (see Chapter 9 for a full discussion).

6. *Feature selection:* Reducing the number of input features can simplify models, making them less prone to overfitting.
7. *Reducing model complexity* is a key strategy in mitigating overfitting. Overfitting occurs when a model is too complex, capturing not just the underlying patterns in the data but also the noise, leading to poor performance on new, unseen data. By simplifying the model, you reduce its tendency to overfit. This can be achieved through various methods such as decreasing the number of layers or neurons in a neural network, reducing the number of features in the dataset, or using simpler models. A less complex model may not capture all the nuances in the training data, but it can generalize better to new data, improving its overall predictive performance.

Each of these methods contributes to creating more robust and effective machine learning models by addressing different aspects of overfitting. This comprehensive approach is particularly effective in fields like fraud detection, where the ability to generalize well to new data is crucial.

Model Deployment in Fraud Detection

Model deployment in fraud detection is a crucial phase where trained and optimized models are implemented in real-world environments to identify and prevent financial fraud actively. This stage is where the model truly begins to add value, applying its learned insights to real transaction data.

The process of model deployment involves several key steps. First is *model serialization*, where the trained model is saved in a format suitable for later use. Formats like PMML (predictive model markup language), ONNX (open neural network exchange), and platform-specific ones like TensorFlow's *SavedModel* or *PyTorch's TorchScript* are commonly used.

Integration with existing *production systems* is the next step. Here, the serialized model is incorporated into the business's transaction processing systems. This often involves creating APIs (application programming interfaces) that allow transaction data to be fed into the model for prediction.

Real-time monitoring is critical in fraud detection. The deployed model must process transactions instantly, identifying and flagging suspicious activities as they occur. An essential aspect of this phase is the feedback loop. As the model operates in the real world, it's vital to have a system where human experts can review and provide input on its predictions. This feedback helps in continuously refining the model.

Fraudulent tactics are ever evolving; thus, *continuous deployment and updating* of the model are necessary. Automated pipelines for periodically retraining the model with new data and deploying the updated version are crucial for maintaining its effectiveness.

However, several *challenges* accompany model deployment. Latency is a significant concern; predictions must be made quickly to prevent fraud without delaying legitimate transactions. Scalability is also vital, as the system must handle large volumes of transactions. Additionally, model drift, where the transaction data's distribution changes over time, may affect the model's performance. Regular monitoring and updates are necessary to address this.

To mitigate these challenges, certain best practices are recommended. A/B testing allows for comparing the performance of the new model against the existing one in a live environment. Rollback mechanisms are crucial for reverting to a previous model version in case of issues with the new deployment. Lastly, thorough logging and monitoring of all predictions, especially false positives and negatives, are essential for ongoing troubleshooting, performance assessment, and model improvement.

TIP

Model deployment in fraud detection is the final, critical step in the machine learning pipeline. It involves not just the technical implementation of the model but also its continuous evaluation and enhancement to ensure that it remains effective against the dynamic landscape of financial fraud.

Model Governance in Fraud Detection

Model governance in fraud detection encapsulates the comprehensive approach to overseeing, tracking, and maintaining machine learning models post-deployment. It focuses on ensuring these models remain effective, transparent, trustworthy, and compliant with both organizational and legal standards.

In the realm of finance and similar industries, the accuracy and reliability of predictive models are paramount due to stringent regulatory requirements. Effective model governance plays a critical role in adhering to these regulations, thereby maintaining legal compliance and building trust. It involves explaining model decisions clearly, which is crucial in gaining stakeholders' trust, especially when errors could lead to significant consequences.

Key aspects of model governance include rigorous pre-deployment testing, such as out-of-sample evaluations and cross-validation, to ensure model robustness. It also involves constant tracking of model modifications and their impacts, maintaining detailed audit trails for every update or decision made about the model. This practice is essential for transparency and often a legal requirement.

Performance monitoring is another vital component, involving keeping logs of all changes and decisions related to the model. Additionally, comprehensive documentation of the model's functionality, methodologies, and updates is necessary. Open communication channels for feedback from users and stakeholders are crucial for continuous improvement and addressing concerns.

Model governance also demands attention to ethical considerations, ensuring that models do not perpetuate biases and remain fair and just. This aspect is increasingly critical in a world where algorithms can significantly impact individuals and communities.

However, model governance is not without its challenges. The complexity increases with the number of models in use, often requiring a dedicated team and specialized tools. Moreover, the constantly evolving landscape of rules and regulations necessitates frequent updates and adaptations of models to remain compliant.

TIP

Best Practices:

- *Embrace automation:* There are tools out there that can take on tasks like monitoring performance or validating models. Use them.
- *Teamwork makes dreams work:* Data scientists, IT pros, and business folks need to join forces for governance to truly work.
- *Stay updated:* Governance isn't a one-time thing. Policies need regular revisits to keep them current.

When it comes to fraud detection, there's no room for slip-ups. Model governance is the safety net, ensuring that every model is not just efficient but also ethical, transparent, and compliant. It's not just about doing things right but also about doing the right thing.

AutoGluon

AutoGluon, emerging as a potent tool in supervised machine learning, particularly excels in the complex field of fraud detection.

Automated Machine Learning (AutoML) Capabilities

Its automated machine learning (AutoML) capabilities are key to its effectiveness. By streamlining the selection of the best models, fine-tuning hyperparameters, and optimizing feature transformations, AutoGluon addresses the critical challenges in fraud detection, a domain where model performance significantly influences outcomes. This AutoML aspect of AutoGluon is particularly noteworthy, as it simplifies the otherwise complex and time-consuming process of model selection and optimization, making advanced machine learning techniques more accessible and efficient.

Ensemble Learning Techniques

The use of ensemble learning techniques is another standout feature of AutoGluon. It aggregates predictions from multiple models to produce more accurate and robust results. This approach is invaluable in fraud detection scenarios, particularly with imbalanced datasets, a common challenge in this field. AutoGluon's proficiency in managing these imbalances ensures comprehensive learning, including the often-underrepresented fraudulent transactions.

Efficiency and Customization

Efficiency is a cornerstone of AutoGluon's design, allowing it to quickly process large datasets, an essential feature for real-time fraud detection applications. Its automated pipeline, coupled with customization options in data preprocessing, feature engineering, and model selection, allows users to adapt the tool to specific fraud detection needs.

Practical Application and Continuous Adaptation

The structured approach to fraud detection with AutoGluon begins with data preparation, involving transactional data labeled as fraudulent or legitimate, and then involves training various models. The platform's capacity to automatically select and tune models for optimal performance demonstrates its AutoML strength. Furthermore, its ability to identify the most predictive features of fraud enhances strategic approaches to fraud detection.

Once trained, AutoGluon models are deployable for real-time predictions on new transactions, aiding in timely fraud detection. The evolving nature of fraud patterns necessitates continuous model retraining, a process facilitated by AutoGluon to maintain effectiveness over time.

WARNING

- While AutoGluon excels in performance, aspects like data privacy, model interpretability, and integration into existing systems are important.
- Understanding the reasoning behind fraud flags is crucial, necessitating supplementary tools for interpretability.

AutoGluon offers a powerful, efficient, and accessible solution for fraud detection, highlighting the advantages of AutoML in handling large, imbalanced datasets and automating significant portions of the modeling process. Its role in democratizing access to complex machine learning techniques while ensuring adaptability and compliance with essential data privacy and interpretability considerations makes it a valuable asset in the machine learning toolkit.

TIP

- AutoGluon, an open-source library, supports quick prototyping of AI/ML models with minimal coding.
- It works efficiently with diverse data types (text, images, and tabular) and powers AWS SageMaker Autopilot.
- Its modular design allows for tailored installations, with specific sub-modules for different machine learning tasks.
- In fraud detection, the TabularPredictor in AutoGluon.tabular is especially relevant, offering parameters for customization and optimization.

Broader Impact and Industry Relevance

AutoGluon, as part of a larger ecosystem of technological advancements in fraud detection, contributes to the ongoing evolution of the field. Its integration with platforms like AWS SageMaker Autopilot highlights its practicality in real-world applications and underscores its relevance in modern fraud detection strategies. For more detailed information, interested users can explore AutoGluon through its official website here and learn more about its applications from an informative AWS blog article here.

Summary

Chapter 15 goes into the advanced aspects of fraud detection, emphasizing model optimization, the significance of hyperparameters, and the importance of governance in deploying models. It offers an in-depth look at performance metrics, balancing accuracy with model explainability, and advanced model tuning, including learning rate optimization and techniques like grid search and Bayesian optimization.

A key feature of this chapter is the introduction of AutoGluon, showcasing its effectiveness in handling large, imbalanced datasets typical of fraud detection. The chapter also applies practical examples, such as churn prediction in telecoms, to demonstrate the application of various algorithms in predicting customer behavior.

The chapter culminates with labs on predicting the churn rate of customers,
and predicting health insurance costs using AutoGluon, providing a hands-on application of the concepts covered and thereby bridging theoretical knowledge with practical skills in fraud detection.
Chapter 16 builds on these insights, exploring new methodologies and tools in fraud analytics and focusing on the integration of different data types to enhance fraud detection.

Lab: Classification Techniques for Fraud Detection

In this chapter lab, you will go into the practical applications of machine learning, emphasizing advanced tools and techniques in real-world scenarios, with a special focus on AutoGluon in one of the key projects. This chapter presents a series of lab projects demonstrating the application of various machine learning algorithms in different industries, culminating with a project that specifically utilizes AutoGluon's capabilities in predicting health insurance costs.

Lab project: Predicting customer churn in the telecommunications sector: This project involves applying machine learning algorithms such as logistic regression, support vector machines, K-Nearest Neighbors, and random forest classifiers to analyze and predict customer churn rates.

The aim is to understand customer behavior and identify factors contributing to churn using detailed data analysis and strategic model selection.

Final lab project: Predicting health insurance costs with AutoGluon: Here, AutoGluon's automated machine learning features are tested to predict health insurance costs based on individual factors like age, BMI, smoking status, and more.

This project showcases AutoGluon's ability to streamline the model selection and training process, making advanced machine learning techniques more accessible and efficient for practical applications.

Each lab in this chapter provides a hands-on experience in applying machine learning techniques to real-world problems. It's not just an exercise in theory but a journey through applying these technologies in dynamic sectors like telecommunications, finance, and health insurance. You'll learn how tools like AutoGluon can simplify complex processes in model training and optimization, enhancing the efficacy and accessibility of machine learning solutions in tackling practical challenges.

Chapter 15, therefore, is a crucial component in the comprehensive study of machine learning applications, highlighting the fusion of theory and practice in data science. It prepares readers for diverse challenges and opportunities, focusing particularly on fraud detection and predictive modeling in various industry settings.

Lab Project: Predict the Churn Rate of Customers

This project immerses you in studying customer churn within the telecommunications sector, leveraging various classification algorithms, including logistic regression, support vector machine, K-Nearest Neighbors, and random forest classifier. For telecom service providers, understanding and mitigating customer churn is paramount, as maintaining existing customer relationships is often more economical than acquiring new ones. In this project, data science techniques derive valuable insights from diverse customer attributes, such as the types of services subscribed to, customer tenure, demographics, and more. These attributes play a crucial role in addressing the classification challenges presented in customer churn analysis (see Fig. 15.7, for an illustrative representation of the classification problem and its components).

Approach to Predicting Customer Churn

1. *Data preparation and initial analysis:*
    - Import the telecom dataset for exploratory data analysis, understanding its structure and key attributes.
    - Analyze the distribution of factors like tenure rate, service subscriptions, and demographics.
2. *Feature analysis and data visualization:*
    - Determine the significance of different features in predicting customer churn.
    - Utilize data visualization to identify patterns and trends indicative of churn.
3. *Model training and evaluation:*
    - Train multiple classification models and assess their performance using accuracy, precision, recall, and AUC metrics.
4. *Model comparison and selection:*
    - Compare the performance of each model to identify the most effective one, likely based on accuracy and AUC.
5. *Enhancing model performance:*
    - Employ techniques like grid search to optimize the chosen model.
    - Analyze the effects of hyperparameter tuning on model accuracy and churn prediction capability.

Lab Access: I invite you to embark on this analytical journey and explore the intricacies of telecommunication customer data. To start your exploration, click here for lab access, and go ahead and complete the lab (Fig. 15.7).

Post-project Analysis

Upon completing the project, insights reveal the Random Forest Classifier as the standout model, with high accuracy and precision in predicting churn. However, there is potential for enhancing recall for churned

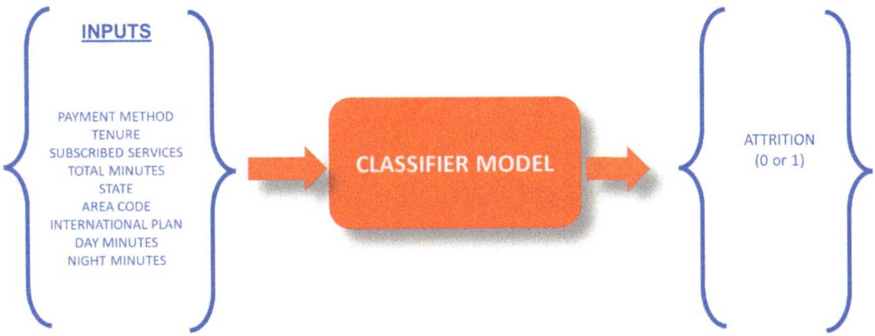

Fig. 15.7 Project input, process, and output

customers, which is achievable through advanced hyperparameter optimization using grid search.

This project comprehensively demonstrates the application of machine learning in analyzing and predicting customer behavior in the telecommunication sector. It emphasizes the importance of detailed data analysis, strategic model selection, and continuous model optimization for improved prediction accuracy and effectiveness.

For more in-depth learning, particularly on grid search and model optimization, refer to machine learning mastery's guide on hyperparameter optimization.

Final Lab Project: Predicting Health Insurance Costs Using AutoGluon

In this project, the goal is to utilize AutoGluon, a powerful tool for automated machine learning, to predict the health insurance costs incurred by individuals. This prediction is based on several factors, including age, gender, BMI, number of children, smoking habits, and geolocation. The practical application of this project lies in its potential use by insurance companies to predict healthcare insurance costs, thereby helping to increase revenues and reduce costs.

Approaching Health Insurance Cost Prediction

You will work with a dataset that includes various inputs such as age, gender, BMI, number of children, smoking habits, and geolocation to predict the output—insurance charges. The dataset contains detailed features like the sex of the insurance contractor, body mass index, number of dependents, smoking status, and the region of residence in the US. The target output to predict is the individual medical costs billed by health insurance.

To effectively carry out the health insurance cost prediction project using AutoGluon, you should follow these essential steps:

1. *Data cleaning and preprocessing:* Start by meticulously cleaning your dataset, removing irrelevant columns, and addressing missing values. This step ensures the integrity of your data, preparing it for effective analysis. Additionally, transform and encode the categorical features to formats that AutoGluon can efficiently process.
2. *Exploratory data analysis (EDA):* Conduct a thorough exploratory analysis to understand the distribution of the features and their relationship with the target variable, "insurance charges." This analysis is crucial for identifying patterns and potential predictors in the dataset.
3. *Model training with AutoGluon:* Split your dataset into training and testing sets, an essential step for model evaluation. Utilize AutoGluon to train models on the training set to predict insurance charges, leveraging its automated machine learning capabilities for efficient data handling and model learning.
4. *Model evaluation:* Evaluate the trained models' performance on the test set. Assess metrics like accuracy, precision, recall, and F1 score to gauge their effectiveness in predicting health insurance costs. Analyze the features that are important to understand which factors most significantly impact insurance charges.

Tools Used

- AutoGluon for automated machine learning.
- Python, along with libraries like Pandas for data manipulation and Matplotlib/Seaborn for visualization.

TIP

Practical Real-World Application: Implementing this model in the insurance sector can significantly optimize the process of predicting healthcare insurance costs. It can lead to more accurate cost predictions, enhanced operational efficiency, and better financial planning for insurance companies.

Input data: The dataset includes age, gender, BMI, number of children, smoking habits, and geolocation.

Output: The outcome is the prediction of insurance charges, represented as a continuous variable.

Model Training and Evaluation

- Utilize AutoGluon's tabular predictor for model training.
- Evaluate the model's performance using a range of metrics to ensure accuracy and reliability.

Lab access: I invite you to embark on this analytical journey and explore the intricacies of health insurance cost data. To start exploring, click here for access and dive into the lab.

Post-project Insights

Upon completing the project, insights into the model's performance and ability to accurately predict health insurance costs will be gathered. This will include understanding the effectiveness of different features in predicting costs, the model's generalization capability to new data, and areas for future improvements to enhance the model's accuracy and reliability. The project aims to refine the prediction model for health insurance costs, maximizing its utility and effectiveness in real-world insurance. It focuses on delivering accurate predictions that aid in better decision-making and financial planning.

Summary: Key Learnings and Insights

Chapter 15's labs have been a deep dive into the practical applications of machine learning across various real-world scenarios, offering learners a rich blend of theoretical knowledge and hands-on experience.

In the Customer Churn Prediction lab focused on the telecommunications sector, participants engaged in understanding the nuances of industry-specific data and challenges. This lab served as a platform to apply diverse classification algorithms, enhancing data preparation, feature analysis, and visualization skills. The experience emphasized the importance of in-depth data exploration before model building and the need to tailor machine-learning approaches to specific industry challenges.

In the Health Insurance Cost Prediction lab, learners were introduced to AutoGluon, experiencing its capabilities in automating the machine learning process. This lab underscored the end-to-end model training process, from data preprocessing to evaluation, highlighting AutoGluon's role in simplifying and streamlining machine learning tasks.

These labs collectively emphasized the versatility and adaptability required in modern data science. They balanced theoretical understanding with practical application, enhancing critical thinking and problem-solving skills. Each lab provided unique insights into industry-specific data challenges, underscoring the importance of contextual understanding in data analysis and model building.

As a whole, Chapter 15's labs equipped learners with both the skills and insights necessary to apply machine learning techniques in complex, real-world scenarios, ensuring a well-rounded understanding that bridges the gap between theory and practical, impactful application.

CHAPTER 16

Knowledge Assessment Lab

This chapter emerges as the culmination of our exploration into fraud detection, where theory and practice converge in a symphony of advanced machine learning techniques. It's a deep dive into the real-world application of sophisticated models and strategies, a masterclass in navigating the nuances of insurance fraud detection. This chapter isn't just about algorithms and data; it's about wielding these tools to sculpt an effective defense against the ever-evolving tactics of fraudsters.

At the heart of this chapter is the challenge of insurance fraud—a complex, multifaceted problem that demands not only technical finesse but also strategic acumen. Here, you embark on an intricate journey through the labyrinth of data, weaving through layers of analysis, prediction, and interpretation. This chapter is a testament to the power of machine learning in transforming raw data into a beacon of insight, casting light on the shadows where fraud lurks.

The journey in Chapter is marked by a series of meticulously crafted stages, each a steppingstone toward mastering fraud detection. It begins with the art of data handling and preprocessing, where the raw, unstructured chaos of data is transformed into a clear, coherent canvas ready for exploration. This sets the stage for the next act—exploratory data analysis (EDA), a crucial process where patterns emerge and the story hidden within the data begins to unfold.

A. Al Aqqad, *Fraud Analytics in Action*
https://doi.org/10.1007/978-3-032-16023-2_16

As the narrative progresses, you delve into the realm of feature engineering and selection, unearthing the most telling indicators of fraudulent activity. This meticulous process is the groundwork for the ensuing chapter of model training and evaluation. Here, sophisticated algorithms like gradient boosting and deep learning are put to the test; their prowess is measured not just in accuracy but in their ability to discern the subtle nuances of fraud.

Interpretability takes center stage as you employ tools like LIME and SHAP. These are not just technical instruments; they are the translators that bridge the gap between complex model outputs and human understanding. They are the key to earning stakeholder trust and turning opaque predictions into transparent insights.

The climax of this chapter is a lab project that encapsulates all these elements—a hands-on application of advanced machine learning to detect fraud in insurance claims. This lab is not merely an exercise; it's a real-world challenge that demands a harmonious blend of skill, knowledge, and creativity. It's where you, the reader, take the helm, applying everything learned to outsmart cunning fraudsters.

Chapter is more than just a knowledge assessment lab of a series; it's a gateway to a new frontier in fraud detection. It equips you with the knowledge, tools, and confidence to tackle fraud head-on, blending the art of data science with the precision of machine learning. This chapter is your map to navigating the complex terrain of fraud detection, where each decision, each analysis, and each prediction is a step toward safeguarding the digital world.

Final Capstone Lab: Advanced Machine Learning in Insurance Fraud Detection

This project focuses on the complex task of detecting insurance fraud using advanced machine learning techniques. The insurance industry faces significant challenges due to fraudulent claims, which not only impact financial stability but also increase premiums for honest policyholders. Employing machine learning in this context offers a sophisticated approach to identifying and preventing fraud effectively.

Objectives:

- To analyze insurance claim data for potential fraud detection using advanced machine learning models.
- To compare the effectiveness of various algorithms like gradient boosting and deep learning in identifying fraudulent activities.
- To explore the balance between model accuracy, interpretability, and operational feasibility in fraud detection.
- To leverage interpretability tools like LIME and SHAP for model transparency and stakeholder trust.

Approach to the Lab

1. *Data handling and preprocessing:* The project begins with comprehensive data preparation, including cleaning, outlier management, and categorical data conversion.
2. *Exploratory data analysis (EDA):* This stage involves visualizing data to uncover trends and relationships between variables.
3. *Feature engineering and selection:* Key features impacting fraud detection will be identified and engineered for model training.
4. *Model training and evaluation*: Employing various models like gradient boosting and deep learning, and evaluating them using metrics such as precision, recall, F1 score, and AUC.
5. *Model Interpretation:* Using LIME and SHAP to interpret model predictions and understand decision-making factors
6. *Prediction:* applying the selected model to new data to predict fraudulent claims.

Lab access: I invite you to embark on this analytical journey and explore the intricacies of insurance claims data. To start your exploration, click here for lab access and dive into the lab.

Post-Lab Insights

- The project demonstrates the efficacy of advanced machine learning models in detecting insurance fraud.
- Interpretability techniques like LIME and SHAP provide essential insights into the models' predictions, enhancing stakeholder trust.

- The findings emphasize the need for balanced model selection, considering factors beyond just predictive performance, such as computational costs and practical deployability.
- Continuous refinement and updating of models are essential in response to evolving fraud tactics.
- Collaborative efforts between data scientists and domain experts are crucial for successful implementation.

Methodology and key findings:

- The lab uses a comprehensive multi-stage methodology, starting from data loading to final predictions.
- Findings suggest significant factors like "Incident Severity," "Insured Hobbies," and "Policy State" play crucial roles in fraud predictions.
- The ROC curve analysis and AUC scores are critical in setting the right threshold for fraud detection.
- Practical implications highlight the importance of model interpretability and balanced model selection in real-world applications.

The project underscores the potential of machine learning to revolutionize fraud detection in the insurance sector, balancing technological advancements with operational and ethical considerations.

Lab Project: Fraud Detection in Insurance Claims Using AutoGluon

This project focuses on using AutoGluon to address the challenging task of detecting fraudulent activities in insurance claims. The complexity of insurance claim data, coupled with the subtleties of fraudulent behavior, makes this a demanding yet crucial endeavor in maintaining financial integrity.

Approaching Insurance Claim Fraud Detection

In this lab, you will engage with a dataset of 1000 insurance claim records, each meticulously detailed by 41 features, including customer demographics, policy details, incident specifics, and claim amounts. Your objective is to harness the power of AutoGluon to accurately identify fraudulent insurance claims, paying special attention to the typical imbalances that characterize fraud detection datasets.

Initial observations have shown that the dataset includes a mix of records labeled as either fraudulent or legitimate. However, it has been noted that there's an extra, irrelevant column, "_c39," filled with nan values. This finding underscores the importance of thorough data cleaning as a preliminary step in your analysis. Your tasks in this lab will not only involve identifying fraudulent activities but also ensuring the dataset's integrity and readiness for a detailed investigation with AutoGluon.

To successfully carry out a fraud detection project using AutoGluon, you should follow these essential steps:

1. *Data cleaning and preprocessing:* Start by thoroughly cleaning your dataset. This includes removing any irrelevant columns that won't contribute to fraud detection and addressing any missing values to ensure data integrity. Make sure to convert date columns into datetime objects, as this will allow you to extract additional useful features such as year, month, and day. This step is crucial in preparing your data for effective analysis. Also, encode categorical features in a format that AutoGluon can process, which will aid in the subsequent modeling phase.
2. *Exploratory data analysis (EDA):* Your next task is to gain a deeper understanding of the dataset. Conduct an exploratory data analysis by examining the distribution of the target variable, "fraud_reported." This will give you a clear picture of the balance between fraudulent and non-fraudulent claims in your dataset. Additionally, analyze the correlations between different features and the target variable. This analysis is key to identifying which features may potentially predict fraudulent behavior.
3. *Model training with AutoGluon:* In this critical phase, split your dataset into training and test sets. This separation is vital for evaluating the performance of your model accurately. With the datasets prepared, employ AutoGluon to train models to predict the "fraud_reported" column. AutoGluon's automated machine learning capabilities will streamline this process, efficiently handling the data and learning from it.

4. *Model evaluation:* The final step in your project is to evaluate the performance of the models you've trained. Assess their performance on the test set to gauge their accuracy and ability to generalize. This evaluation will provide valuable insights into how well your models can identify fraudulent cases. Additionally, perform an analysis of feature importance. This analysis will highlight which aspects of your data are most indicative of fraudulent claims, offering crucial insights into the behavior of your models and guiding you in identifying key areas for future improvements.

Tools Used

- AutoGluon for automated machine learning.
- Python, along with libraries like Pandas for data manipulation and Matplotlib/Seaborn for visualization.

> TIP
>
> *Practical Real-World Application:* Implementing this model can significantly streamline the fraud detection process in insurance companies. It can lead to quicker claim processing, enhanced accuracy in fraud detection, and reduced losses from fraudulent claims.

Input Data: The dataset includes columns such as "months_as_customer," "age," "policy_number," "policy_state," "incident_type," and the target variable "fraud_reported."

Output: The output is a binary classification indicating the presence ('1') or absence ('0') of fraud in a claim.

Model Training and Evaluation

- AutoGluon's TabularPredictor is used for model training, configured to address class imbalance.
- The model's performance is evaluated on the test set using metrics like accuracy, precision, recall, and F1 score.

Lab access: I invite you to embark on this analytical journey and explore the intricacies of insurance claims data. To start your exploration, click here for lab access and dive into the lab.

Post-Project Insights

In the model performance overview of the fraud detection project using AutoGluon, the weighted ensemble model (WEM) emerged as the top performer with the highest validation and test accuracies, 88.12% and 84%, respectively, demonstrating its effectiveness across both fraud and non-fraud cases. Meanwhile, the CatBoost model, while equaling the ensemble model in validation accuracy, fell short in test performance. This highlighted its strength in validation scenarios but also pointed toward a need for better generalization to unseen data.

The key metrics for fraud detection revealed interesting insights. The recall of 75.51% indicated a strong ability of the model to identify fraudulent cases, yet it also suggested the potential to miss some fraud instances. Precision, at 64.91%, showed a reasonable accuracy of the model's fraud predictions but also implied the possibility of false positives—non-fraudulent claims being incorrectly flagged as fraud. The F1 Score, balancing precision and recall, stood at 0.6981, a good score that nevertheless hinted at room for further improvement in the model's reliability.

The project also emphasized the importance of model interpretation and future steps for improvement. Conducting a feature importance analysis was crucial to understanding which factors were most predictive of fraud. Additionally, error analysis, focusing on false positives and negatives, was identified as a key step to understanding where the model fell short and the types of data it struggled with. Model calibration was also noted as a necessary step if the model's probability outputs were to be used in decision-making.

Looking ahead, several enhancement strategies were outlined. *Feature engineering* was marked as a priority to enhance the model's ability to detect fraudulent patterns. *Hyperparameter tuning* was suggested to optimize the model for the specific task of fraud detection. *Cost-sensitive training and* adjusting the model to prioritize the costs associated with misclassification were also recommended. *Exploring advanced sampling techniques* beyond traditional methods like SMOTE (see Chapter 9) was considered important for better handling of the class imbalance. Finally, testing other models, including *deep learning approaches*, was proposed as a means to potentially improve fraud detection capabilities.

Overall, the project aimed at fine-tuning the fraud detection system to maximize its efficiency and reliability in a real-world insurance setting.

The focus was on catching as many fraudulent claims as possible while minimizing false alarms, thus enhancing customer satisfaction and operational efficiency.

WARNING

When you proceed with coding tasks using AutoGluon, the installation of necessary libraries and setting up of the environment will vary depending on where you are working.

1. *In Google colab*: use (!pip) *install autogluon* to install AutoGluon. The exclamation mark (!) is necessary in Colab to execute pip commands for installing Python packages.
2. *In a local Python environment:* if you're working on your local machine, simply use *pip install autogluon* in your command line or terminal. This standard pip command is used for installing Python packages locally.
3. *Other environments:* If you're in a different environment (like a specialized IDE or cloud-based service), you may need to follow specific instructions for that environment. Some environments may have libraries pre-installed, or you may need to use a different method to install AutoGluon.

Once the necessary libraries, including AutoGluon, are installed in your chosen environment, you can then proceed to load your dataset and perform the outlined tasks.

Summary

As you conclude Chapter 16, you reflect on a journey through the advanced and dynamic landscape of fraud detection powered by machine learning. This chapter stood as a testament to the strength of analytical innovation in combating complex frauds—especially within insurance, where deception constantly evolves in the digital era.

You delved deeply into the world of gradient boosting and deep learning, learning to harness their capabilities to detect sophisticated fraud patterns. Through the capstone lab project, you gained practical experience applying these algorithms to real datasets, solidifying your understanding of the complete fraud detection workflow—from preprocessing to prediction.

The chapter also emphasized the importance of model interpretability through tools such as LIME and SHAP, reinforcing that in fraud analytics, transparency is as critical as accuracy. You explored how effective models balance performance, interpretability, and operational feasibility—highlighting that the “best” model is the one that works reliably in real-world conditions, not necessarily the most complex.

Finally, you learned that fraud detection is a continuous journey. As fraudsters evolve, so too must our analytical techniques. Chapter 16 prepared you not only to use today’s tools but also to think critically, adapt, and innovate for tomorrow’s challenges.

With this foundation, you are now ready to move into Part V, where the focus shifts from individual transactions to the broader networks of relationships that underlie fraudulent behavior.

PART V

Fraud Detection in Social Networks

Most fraud analytics focuses on the individual—a single transaction, a single account, a single claim. But fraud is rarely a solitary act. Organised fraud rings, money mule networks, collusive insurance schemes, and coordinated account takeovers all depend on relationships between people, accounts, devices, and institutions. Those relationships leave traces, and Social Network Analysis (SNA) is the discipline designed to find them. By modelling entities and their connections as networks, SNA shifts the analytical lens from individual behaviour to relational structure—revealing coordinated patterns, key influencers, and suspicious clusters that transaction-level analysis would miss entirely. Part V covers this approach across two chapters. Chapter 17 introduces the core principles of social network analysis applied to fraud detection—examining how entities such as customers, accounts, merchants, and devices can be modelled as networks, and how concepts including homophily, dyadicity, heterophilicity, centrality, and graph algorithms expose the structural signatures of organised fraud and identity theft. Chapter 18 translates that theory into practice through Python-based implementations using real-world datasets, building and visualising fraud networks, computing key metrics, and applying subgraph analysis and degree ratios to detect money mule operations and other collusive schemes. Together, these chapters extend your fraud analytics toolkit into the relational dimension where the connections between entities reveal what the data points alone cannot.

CHAPTER 17

Fraud and Social Network Analysis

The rise of digital networks has fundamentally altered societal structure, influencing everything from communication and commerce, to crime. Notably, the phenomenon of fraud has also evolved in this new landscape, necessitating a reevaluation of traditional fraud detection approaches. This chapter delves into the vital intersection of fraud and social network analysis, elucidating how the dynamics of modern networks can be harnessed for more effective fraud detection.

Beginning with a philosophical inquiry into the nature of fraud as a social phenomenon, this exploration critically examines if fraud propagates in a contagious manner across networks and whether fraudsters band together within specific network structures. By unearthing patterns in fraudulent behavior within networks, a foundation for utilizing social network analysis in fraud detection is established.

The analysis presented leads to an intriguing aspect of network theory—Homophily, a pattern observed in networks where nodes with similar properties tend to connect with each other. This pattern is explored in depth within fraud networks, and the discussion demonstrates how a close examination of Homophily can help predict and identify instances of fraud.

Two key measures, dyadicity and heterophilicity, which respectively measure the connectedness among similar and dissimilar nodes, are

A. Al Aqqad, *Fraud Analytics in Action*
https://doi.org/10.1007/978-3-032-16023-2_17

further introduced and applied in a real-world context. This understanding allows for the construction of a theoretical framework, predicting fraudulent behavior based on the network attributes of homophily, dyadicity, and heterophilicity.

The discussion then extends to concrete applications of social network analysis in detecting identity theft and spotting money mules. It elucidates how these instances of fraud manifest within networks and demonstrates how network analysis can effectively identify them.

Finally, the exploration probes into the realm of graph algorithms, essential tools in identifying suspicious patterns and relationships within a network. Using these techniques, the spread of fraudulent activities within a network can be traced, identifying indirect relationships and connections that might otherwise remain hidden. This technique becomes crucial in tracing money flows in complex financial networks, often key in spotting sophisticated fraud and money laundering schemes.

By the end of this chapter, readers will have a comprehensive understanding of the synergistic relationship between fraud detection and social network analysis. It demonstrates how an understanding of network dynamics can augment traditional fraud detection methods and provide invaluable insights into complex fraudulent behavior. Through these insights, a stride can be made toward a more secure and trustworthy digital landscape.

Fraud and Social Network Analysis

Fraud Detection through Social Network Analysis

In this section, we explore how social network analytics can enhance the effectiveness of analytical fraud detection techniques.

Is Fraud a Social Phenomenon?

When analyzing a network for fraud, it is critical to consider whether detection models could benefit from social network analytics. In other words, do interpersonal interactions play a large part in fraud, and does fraud propagate via a network in a contagious manner? Are fraudsters scattered randomly over the network, or can we see patterns that indicate fraud is a social phenomenon?

Looking for Fraud Patterns We look for signs that fraudsters are sharing information on how to commit fraud within a certain social structure. Fraudsters frequently band together because they engage in similar activities, do the same illegal actions, use the same resources, or even take the same identity, like in identity theft instances (Fig. 17.1).

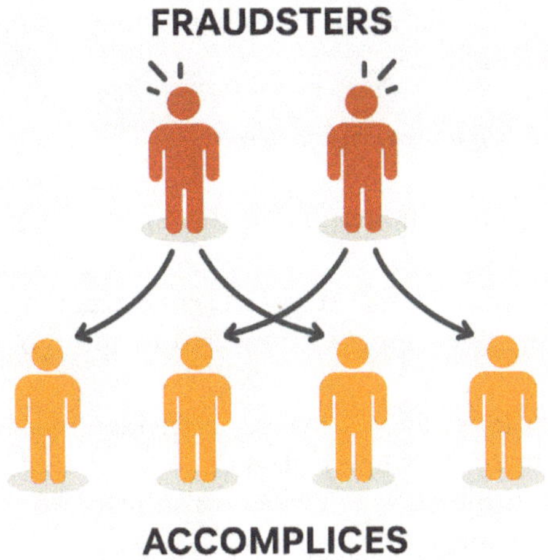

Fig. 17.1 Fraud Network Structure: Fraudsters and Accomplices: This diagram illustrates a simplified fraud network structure, highlighting the relationship between primary fraudsters and their accomplices. At the top, two red figures represent the fraudsters, who act as the central orchestrators of fraudulent activities. Below them, five orange figures denote the accomplices, who assist or enable the fraudulent actions through various roles. Arrows connecting the fraudsters to the accomplices demonstrate the direction of influence or control within the fraud scheme. This visualization helps depict how fraud is often a collaborative effort, with key individuals coordinating with others to execute and conceal their misconduct. The structure is relevant in social network analysis and fraud detection models used to identify organized fraudulent behavior

Homophily in Fraud Networks: Uncovering Hidden Patterns for Predictive Analysis

Homophily—the tendency of individuals to associate with others who are similar to themselves—is a foundational principle in social network theory. In the context of fraud networks, this behavior has significant implications. Fraudsters tend to connect with other fraudsters, while honest individuals often avoid them. This self-organizing tendency can lead to visible partitions in the network, revealing hidden fraud clusters that are ideal targets for investigation.

Ego Networks and Behavioral Signatures

An effective way to study homophily is through ego networks, where:

- Ego is the focal individual (e.g., a user or account),
- Alters are the nodes directly connected to the ego.

In fraud investigations, ego networks help identify clusters of similar behavior. For example, if an ego is flagged as fraudulent, chances are high that several alters in the ego network are also involved in fraud—because of homophilic behavior.

This dramatically reduces investigative complexity, enabling analysts to focus on suspicious pockets within vast datasets instead of scanning the entire network. See Fig .17.2.

Fraud Network Analysis: Using Homophily and Clustering
Let's take a fraud investigation scenario to apply homophily practically. If you, as a fraud investigator, identify a large network of potentially fraudulent individuals, a close look will likely reveal that many of their ego networks are homophilous. This means their friends and associates are likely engaged in similar fraudulent activities.

Such observations provide an excellent starting point for your investigation, where social network analysis (SNA) and machine learning techniques can help analyze the ego networks and uncover fraudulent patterns.

Link Analysis and Identifying Fraud Hubs: One effective technique for analyzing networks is link analysis, which helps identify key individuals (or "hubs") in a network based on their connections. In fraud networks, hubs

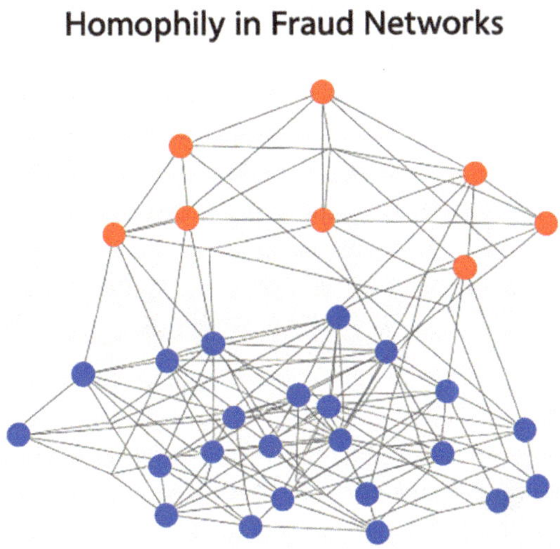

Fig. 17.2 Homophily in Fraud Networks (simulated graph representation): The visualization showcases a simulated network that illustrates the concept of homophily within fraud networks. Red nodes represent individuals involved in fraudulent activities, while blue nodes symbolize honest individuals. Connections between nodes represent observed relationships or interactions

are often central individuals who are connected to many others. Identifying and investigating these hubs can be pivotal in uncovering fraudulent activities.

Fraudsters create links within the network by communicating with others to coordinate their actions. As the network grows, these links typically increase, and homophily ensures that fraudsters are more likely to connect with other fraudsters. By identifying individuals with significant connections, investigators can focus on high-priority suspects.

Homophily vs. Clustering: A Critical Distinction.

Concept	Definition	Example in Fraud
Homophily	Tendency of similar individuals to associate	Fraudsters cluster with other fraudsters
Clustering	Tendency to form tightly knit groups	Fraud rings or syndicates within a larger network

Think of homophily as "birds of a feather flock together," and clustering as the creation of close-knit communities—even among dissimilar types.

Example: Credit Card Fraud Detection
Consider a credit card fraud detection system:

- Homophily would show the tendency of individuals with similar credit scores or behavior to interact with one another.
- Clustering would highlight groups of frequently transacting individuals, revealing potential fraud rings.

To assess whether a network exhibits homophily, we use metrics like **dyadicity** (which measures the connectedness between nodes of the same label) and **heterophilicity** (which evaluates connections between nodes with opposite labels). These metrics provide valuable insights into network topology, which can significantly aid predictive fraud detection.

Once homophily is assessed, analysts can extract node-based attributes for further analysis, such as:

- Node Degree (number of connections),
- Local Clustering Coefficient (ego's local tightness),
- K-core membership (core decomposition), Neighborhood-level features (e.g., local clustering coefficients),
- Global features (e.g., average path length and Centrality Scores).

These features fuel fraud detection models using:

- Unsupervised techniques: clustering, outlier detection,
- Supervised ML algorithms: logistic regression, SVMs, random forests.

A Comparative Analysis of Homophily, Clustering, and Anomaly Detection

This comparative table summarizes the key principles, applications in fraud detection, strengths, and limitations of three major network analysis techniques: *Homophily, Clustering, and Anomaly Detection.*

- *Homophily* is based on the idea that individuals with similar behaviors or characteristics are more likely to be connected. It is effective for uncovering fraud rings by analyzing the relationships among known fraudsters.

- *Clustering* focuses on identifying tightly connected subgroups within a network. These clusters often reveal coordinated groups, potentially indicating organized fraudulent activity.
- *Anomaly Detection* works by identifying individual behaviors that deviate significantly from the norm. This technique is especially useful for spotting isolated fraud cases or novel patterns that do not rely on network connections.

Each approach has unique strengths: Homophily uncovers relational fraud, Clustering simplifies group analysis, and Anomaly Detection isolates irregular patterns. However, they also have limitations such as reliance on behavioral similarity, the need for clear connection patterns, or assumptions about what constitutes "normal" behavior. Used together, these methods provide a robust framework for fraud detection within complex networks (Fig. 17.3).

Example-1: Dyadicity in Social Network Analysis

Let's explore dyadicity—a concept that helps us understand how densely connected nodes with the same label (e.g., color or class) are, relative to a random network.

In this example, we examine two networks, each consisting of 12 nodes:

- 8 blue nodes (e.g., regular accounts)
- 4 green nodes (e.g., suspected or tagged accounts)

The connectance (p), which is the probability that any two nodes are connected, is set to 0.2.

Goal: Measure the dyadicity of green nodes in both networks.

Dyadicity Formula:

$$Dyadicity = \frac{\text{Actual edges between green nodes}}{\text{Expected edges between green nodes in a random graph}}$$

Where:

A Comparative Analysis of Homophily, Clustering, and Anomaly Detection

Homophily	Clustering	Anomaly Detection
The principle that similar individuals (in terms of behavior or characteristics) are more likely to be connected in a network.	The process of grouping closely connected individuals in a network. These clusters represent tightly knit communities within the larger network.	Detects fraud by looking for unusual patterns. If an individual's behavior drastically deviates from what's expected, they might be involved in fraudulent activities.
Use in Fraud Detection Identifies fraudsters through their connections. If one individual is involved in fraud, their connections are likely to be involved as well.	Helps identify groups of fraudsters. If several individuals frequently interact and form a tightly knit group, they could potentially be part of a fraud ring.	Detects fraud by looking for unusual patterns. If an individual's behavior drastically deviates from what's expected, they might be involved in fraudulent activities.
Strengths Effective at uncovering networks of fraudsters through the connections between similar individuals.	Helps investigators focus on groups instead of individuals, making the detection process more manageable.	Requires an understanding of what 'normal' behavior looks like, which can be challenging in complex systems or when dealing with sophisticated fraudsters who are able to mimic normal behavior.
Limitations Not as effective in situations where fraudsters behave differently from each other or if they deliberately hide their connections.	Requires a clear pattern of connections between individuals, which may not always be present or easy to detect.	A way of identifying points in the network that are significantly different from their neighbors (can be used in conjunction with homophily and clustering). The goal is to find anomalies.

Fig. 17.3 A Comparative Analysis of Homophily, Clustering, and Anomaly Detection in Fraud Networks

$$Expectededges = \binom{n}{2} \times p = \frac{n(n-1)}{2} \times p$$

Network 1:

1. Actual green-green edges: 3
2. Expected green-green edges: (4 * 3 / 2) * 0.2 = 1.2
3. Dyadicity: 3 / 1.2 = 2.5 Dyadic (homophilic)

Network 2:

1. Actual green-green edges: 4
2. Expected green-green edges: (4 * 3 / 2) * 0.2 = 1.2 (same calculation)
3. Dyadicity: 4 / 1.2 = 3.33 (More Dyadic)

Interpretation: In both networks, green nodes are **more interconnected** than expected in a random network (Dyadicity > 1), suggesting **homophily**.

Network 2 shows stronger homophily among green nodes.

```
import networkx as nx
import matplotlib.pyplot as plt

def calculate_dyadicity(actual_edges, total_nodes, same_label_nodes,
connectance):
    expected_edges = (same_label_nodes * (same_label_nodes - 1) / 2) *
connectance
    return actual_edges / expected_edges if expected_edges else 0

def draw_network(edges, node_colors, title):
    G = nx.Graph()
    G.add_edges_from(edges)
    pos = nx.spring_layout(G, seed=42)
    nx.draw(G, pos, node_color=node_colors, with_labels=True,
node_size=500)
    plt.title(title)
    plt.axis('off')
    plt.show()

# Parameters
total_nodes = 12
same_label_nodes = 4
connectance = 0.2
node_colors = ['blue'] * 8 + ['green'] * 4

# Network 1
edges_network1 = [(1,2), (1,3), (1,4), (5,6), (5,7), (8,9), (8,10),
(8,11), (8,12), (5,8)]
dyadicity1 = calculate_dyadicity(actual_edges=3, total_nodes=12,
same_label_nodes=4, connectance=0.2)
print(f"Dyadicity for Network 1: {dyadicity1:.2f}")
draw_network(edges_network1, node_colors, "Network 1")

# Network 2
edges_network2 = [(1,2), (1,3), (1,4), (5,6), (5,7), (5,8), (9,10),
(9,11), (9,12), (1,9)]
dyadicity2 = calculate_dyadicity(actual_edges=4, total_nodes=12,
same_label_nodes=4, connectance=0.2)
print(f"Dyadicity for Network 2: {dyadicity2:.2f}")
draw_network(edges_network2, node_colors, "Network 2")
```

Conclusion

- **Dyadicity > 1** = Evidence of **homophily** or clustering within same-labeled nodes.
- Use this metric to identify abnormal social cohesion in fraud detection, insider networks, or clustered criminal behavior.

- Both *Network 1 and Network 2* contain 12 nodes: 8 blue nodes (e.g., regular accounts) and 4 green nodes (e.g., suspected or tagged accounts).
- In *Network 1*, the dyadicity of green nodes is 2.50, calculated as 3 actual green–green connections divided by 1.2 expected connections.
- In *Network 2*, dyadicity rises to 3.33, indicating stronger internal cohesion among the green nodes.

These elevated dyadicity scores (greater than 1) suggest **homophily**—a tendency for similar nodes to form connections, which can be a powerful signal in fraud detection. The figure supports the idea that when suspicious individuals are disproportionately connected to each other, it may point to organized collusion or insider networks (Fig. 17.4).

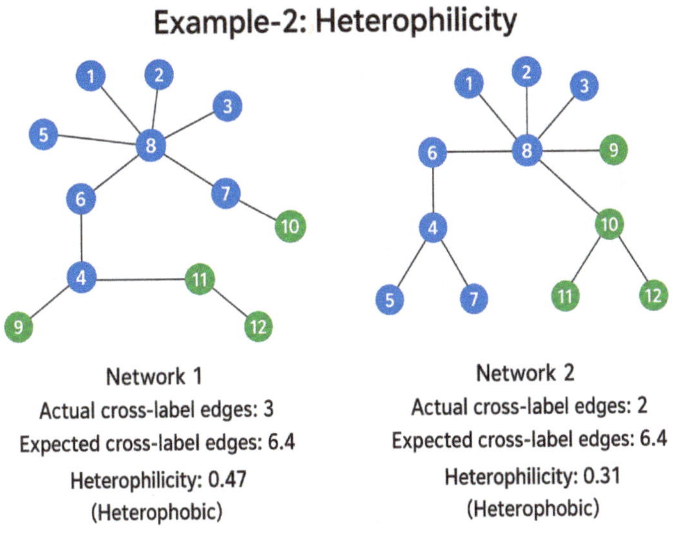

Fig. 17.4 Dyadicity Example in Social Network Analysis: This figure illustrates two example networks to demonstrate the concept of dyadicity, which measures how strongly same-labeled nodes (e.g., fraud suspects) are interconnected compared to what would be expected in a random network

Example-2: Heterophilicity in Social Network Analysis

In this example, we examine two networks composed of 12 nodes each—8 blue (Group A) and 4 green (Group B). These colors represent two different account types or user categories in a fraud detection context. The connectance (p), which represents the probability of connection between any two nodes, is assumed to be 0.2.

Objective: To evaluate whether different types of nodes (e.g., legitimate vs. fraudulent) interact more or less than expected by chance.

In this example, we work with two social networks of 12 nodes:

- 8 blue nodes represent one category (e.g., legitimate users),
- 4 green nodes represent another category (e.g., flagged or fraudulent users),
- Connectance (p) is assumed to be 0.2.

  Heterophilicity is calculated using the formula:

Heterophilicity = Actual cross-type edges / Expected cross-type edges.
Where: Expected = (blue nodes × green nodes) × connectance.

Network 1:

- Blue Nodes: 1–8
- Green Nodes: 9–12
- Cross-label (blue-green) edges: 3
- Expected cross-label edges: (8 × 4) × 0.2 = 6.4
- Heterophilicity = 3 / 6.4 = 0.47 → *Heterophobic*

Network 2:

- Blue Nodes: 1–8
- Green Nodes: 9–12
- Cross-label edges: 2
- Expected cross-label edges: 6.4 (same as above)
- Heterophilicity = 2 / 6.4 = 0.31 → *Strongly Heterophobic*

Interpretation:

- *Values < 1 indicate that nodes tend to connect within their own group, not across types.*
- *Both networks are heterophobic, but Network 2 displays even stronger internal clustering.*

Python Code for Visualization and Calculation

```
import networkx as nx
import matplotlib.pyplot as plt

# Function to calculate heterophilicity
def calculate_heterophilicity(actual_cross_edges, blue_nodes, green_nodes,
connectance):
    expected = blue_nodes * green_nodes * connectance
    return actual_cross_edges / expected

# Draw network utility
def draw_network(edges, node_colors, title):
    G = nx.Graph()
    G.add_edges_from(edges)
    pos = nx.spring_layout(G, seed=42)
    nx.draw(G, pos, with_labels=True, node_color=node_colors,
node_size=500, font_size=10)
    plt.title(title)
    plt.axis('off')
    plt.show()

# Constants
total_nodes = 12
blue_nodes = 8
green_nodes = 4
connectance = 0.2
node_colors = ['blue'] * blue_nodes + ['green'] * green_nodes

# Network 1
edges_network1 = [
    (1, 2), (2, 3), (3, 4), (4, 5),
    (5, 6), (6, 7), (7, 8), (1, 8),
    (9, 10), (10, 11), (11, 12)
]
actual_cross_edges_n1 = 3
h_n1 = calculate_heterophilicity(actual_cross_edges_n1, blue_nodes,
green_nodes, connectance)
print("Heterophilicity for Network 1:", h_n1)
draw_network(edges_network1, node_colors, f"Network 1 - Heterophilicity:
{h_n1:.2f}")

# Network 2
edges_network2 = [
    (1, 2), (2, 3), (3, 4), (4, 5),
    (5, 6), (6, 7), (7, 8), (1, 8),
    (9, 10), (10, 11), (11, 12), (9, 12)
]
actual_cross_edges_n2 = 2
h_n2 = calculate_heterophilicity(actual_cross_edges_n2, blue_nodes,
green_nodes, connectance)
print("Heterophilicity for Network 2:", h_n2)
draw_network(edges_network2, node_colors, f"Network 2 - Heterophilicity:
{h_n2:.2f}")
```

This experiment shows how heterophilicity can reveal inter-group dynamics. In fraud analytics:

- Low heterophilicity may indicate internal fraud rings,
- High heterophilicity might reflect social engineering or coordinated campaigns across user types.

Visualizations + metrics like this are key to early fraud detection in telecom, banking, and social networks (Fig. 17.5).

Each network contains 12 nodes:

- Blue nodes represent one group (e.g., legitimate users),
- Green nodes represent another group (e.g., flagged or fraudulent users),
- The probability of a connection (connectance) is assumed to be 0.2.
- In Network 1, there are 3 actual cross-label (blue–green) connections, compared to 6.4 expected, resulting in a heterophilicity score

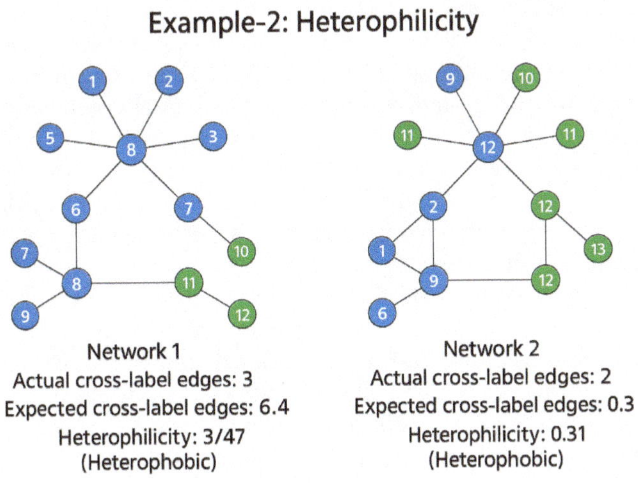

Fig. 17.5 Heterophilicity Example in Social Network Analysis: This figure presents two sample networks used to demonstrate the concept of *heterophilicity*, which measures the degree to which nodes with different labels (e.g., legitimate vs. fraudulent users) are connected, relative to a random network baseline

of 0.47—indicating heterophobic behavior (less cross-type interaction than expected).
- In Network 2, the heterophilicity score drops further to **0.31**, reinforcing stronger separation between groups and more internal clustering within the same group.

Both networks show **heterophobic** tendencies (heterophilicity < 1), suggesting that connections are more likely to form within the same group. This can reveal fraud rings, insular behavior, or low social mixing, which are useful indicators in fraud investigations.

Identity Theft

Social network analysis (SNA) *is a powerful tool for detecting identity theft—an increasingly prevalent fraud scenario in the telecom industry. In such cases, a fraudster gains unauthorized access to a legitimate subscriber's account and uses it to establish fraudulent connections or activate illicit services. Behavioral anomalies and structural shifts in the network can offer early warning signs* (Fig. 17.6).

Figure 17.6 illustrates the evolution of call behavior following identity theft. Initially, the victim account (blue node) interacts with a small, consistent set of trusted contacts (nodes A–D), reflecting normal usage. After compromise, the same account begins calling a completely new set of contacts (nodes E–N), many of which overlap with another individual's network—possibly a known fraudster. This unexpected overlap signals a deviation from typical social behavior and may indicate SIM misuse, shared device usage, or identity takeover. This behavioral shift is a key signal in fraud detection systems.

As fraudulent control of the account escalates, network centrality metrics also change. Figure 17.7 builds on this by analyzing top connected accounts using in-degree and out-degree measures. The victim account now appears among the highest-ranked nodes by in-degree (receiving many contacts), while an associated fraud gateway node (node "1") rises in out-degree, linking the compromised identity to multiple fraudulent SIMs or burner numbers (orange nodes). These structural indicators reveal how a single compromised account can act as an entry point to a larger fraud ecosystem. Edges marked in green represent legitimate historical behavior, while red dashed edges signal suspicious new connections that facilitate fraud propagation (Fig. 17.7).

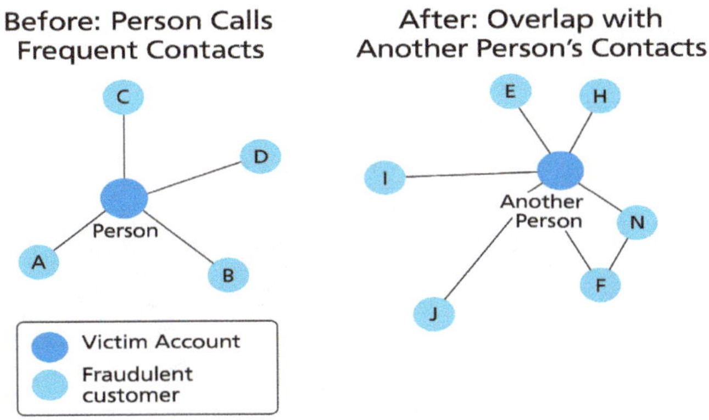

Fig. 17.6 Evolution of call behavior following identity theft: Initially, the victim account (blue node) interacts with a small, consistent set of trusted contacts (nodes A–D), reflecting normal usage. After compromise, the same account begins calling a completely new set of contacts (nodes E–N), many of which overlap with another individual's network—possibly a known fraudster. This unexpected overlap signals a deviation from typical social behavior and may indicate SIM misuse, shared device usage, or identity takeover. This behavioral shift is a key signal in fraud detection systems.

Together, these figures demonstrate how combining behavioral monitoring with degree-based centrality metrics can uncover the early stages of identity theft and expose the networked structure of fraud rings, making intervention more timely and effective.

Graph Algorithms for Fraud Detection

Graph algorithms are essential in identifying suspicious patterns and relationships in a network. For instance, in a financial transaction network, graph algorithms can help identify unusual transaction patterns or groups of interconnected accounts that may suggest fraudulent activities.

Finding Paths

Pathfinding has numerous crucial applications, such as optimization problems that involve finding the shortest path between two nodes for transportation. It also plays a significant role in modeling the spread of

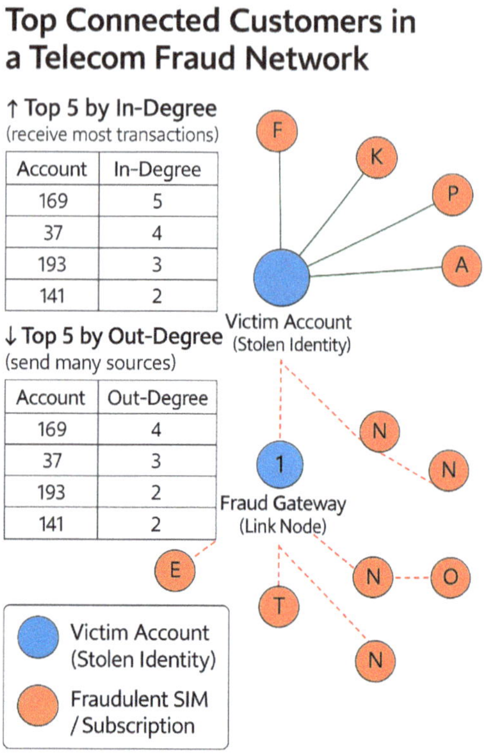

Fig. 17.7 *Top Connected Customers in a Telecom Fraud Network (In-Degree and Out-Degree Analysis)*

various phenomena, like disease outbreaks or information dissemination in a social network. To determine whether a path exists between two nodes and identify the shortest path, we can employ the "breadth-first search algorithm."

In the context of fraud detection, finding paths between nodes can help uncover hidden relationships or indirect connections between entities that might otherwise go unnoticed. Identifying these relationships can help in detecting money laundering schemes, where funds are transferred through multiple accounts to disguise their origins.

Breadth-first search (BFS): The breadth-first search algorithm, developed in the 1950s, initially aimed to identify the shortest path out of a maze.

BFS can be applied in fraud detection to explore the relationships between entities in a network. By analyzing the connections and their distances from a suspected fraudulent account, BFS can help reveal indirect relationships or potential accomplices that might be involved in fraudulent activities. Additionally, BFS can be used to identify accounts or transactions that are close in proximity to known fraudulent activities, which can help prioritize further investigation.

Understanding the shortest path between accounts or transactions can help identify potential fraud rings or money laundering schemes. In these cases, the funds might be transferred through multiple accounts to obscure their source. By using BFS to find the shortest path, investigators can efficiently trace the flow of funds and identify the accounts involved in the fraud (Fig. 17.8).

The BFS algorithm explores the network from the start node, expanding outward through all neighbors and then to their neighbors, iteratively, until it finds the target node. The edges that form the shortest path identified by BFS are highlighted in red, illustrating the sequence of nodes traversed to reach the target node efficiently.

This method is particularly useful in fraud detection to uncover hidden relationships or indirect connections between accounts or entities, helping to reveal complex schemes such as money laundering, where funds might be transferred through a series of intermediaries to obscure their origin. By identifying the shortest path, investigators can trace the flow of illicit funds more directly and potentially uncover the involved parties.

Recall: Neighbors: In the context of fraud detection, identifying the neighbors of a suspicious node can provide insights into potential collaborators or accomplices in fraudulent activities. By examining the neighbors and their connections, investigators can spot unusual patterns or high-risk connections that may warrant further investigation. This can help uncover hidden relationships, identify fraud rings, or trace the flow of funds in money laundering schemes.

In summary, graph algorithms and path-finding techniques, such as BFS, can play a crucial role in fraud detection by helping identify suspicious patterns, uncover hidden relationships, and trace the flow of funds in complex networks.

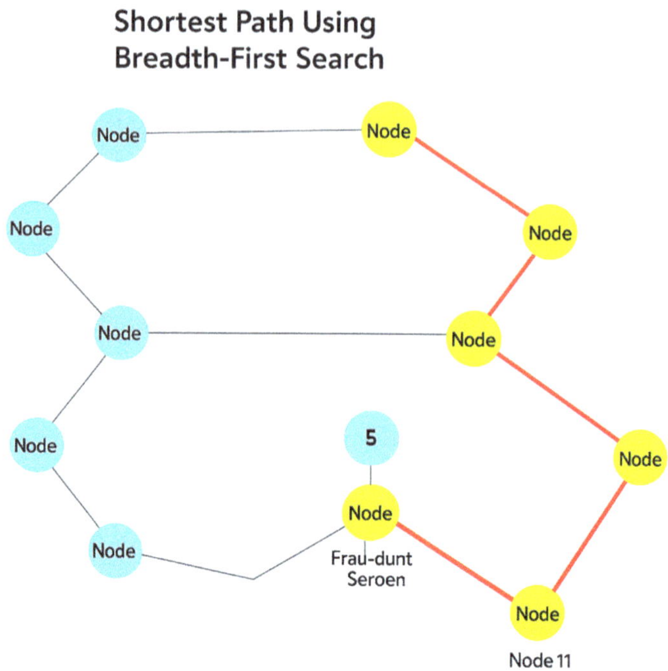

Fig. 17.8 Shortest Path Visualization Using Breadth-First Search (BFS): The visualization demonstrates the process of finding the shortest path between two nodes in a network using the Breadth-First Search (BFS) algorithm. In this example, the network consists of 11 nodes, and we aimed to find the shortest path from ***Node 1*** (the start node, highlighted in yellow) to ***Node 11*** (the target node)

Summary

Chapter 17 explored the intriguing role of Social Network Analysis (SNA) in fraud detection. You explored the critical question of whether fraud is a social phenomenon and whether fraudsters display discernible patterns in their networks. As you learned, interpersonal interactions can be instrumental in fraud propagation, often causing fraud to spread in a contagiously social manner.

You then examined the concept of homophily in fraud networks and its significance in predictive analysis. Homophily—the tendency of individuals to associate with those similar to themselves—can help uncover hidden patterns within fraud networks. You worked through concrete examples measuring dyadicity and heterophilicity, two key metrics that quantify how strongly same-type and cross-type nodes connect relative to a random network. You also explored how identity theft manifests in telecom networks through behavioral shifts in call patterns and degree-centrality analysis.

Finally, you applied graph algorithms—particularly breadth-first search—to trace hidden relationships and money flows within complex financial networks, reinforcing how SNA complements traditional machine learning in fraud detection.

CHAPTER 18

Social Network Analysis Practical Examples

Building directly on the principles introduced in this chapter 17, this chapter moves from concept to practice. You'll now create transaction-based network graphs, compute assortativity and degree ratios, and visualize how suspicious accounts cluster together. Through Python coding examples and real datasets, you'll see how Social Network Analysis can turn theoretical insight into actionable fraud detection.

In this chapter, you will be introduced to the application of *Social Network Analysis* for fraud detection in financial transactions. This critical technique has gained prominence in the current digital economy to spot unusual transaction patterns and possible fraudulent activities. This chapter learning objectives:

1. *Creating a network graph*: You'll learn to construct a network graph which serves as a visual representation of financial transactions among various accounts. Each node in this graph represents an account, and the edges symbolize transactions between accounts.
2. *Identifying fraudulent behavior*: You'll learn to use social network analysis techniques to identify potential patterns of fraudulent behavior. For instance, accounts known as *money mules*, which are often used to transfer fraudulently obtained money, might display unique transaction patterns that can be detected.

A. Al Aqqad, *Fraud Analytics in Action*
https://doi.org/10.1007/978-3-032-16023-2_18

3. *Data visualization techniques*: This chapter will guide you on how to visualize the graph with different colors representing each account type, making it easier to detect potential fraud visually.
4. *Understanding and using assortativity*: The chapter introduces the concept of assortativity in network graphs, which measures the correlation between connected nodes. This measure can provide insights about the homophily in your network based on the account type and can play a vital role in fraud detection.
5. *Working with real datasets*: You'll work with real-world datasets **transfers.csv** and **account_info.csv** that contain detailed information about financial transactions and account specifics, respectively.
6. *In-depth code analysis and application*: Step-by-step code analysis and its implementation are provided to understand each phase of the network analysis, from loading data, graph creation, adding node attributes, computing assortativity, defining a color map, to finally plotting the graph.

These topics will help you understand how social network analysis can discover financial fraud. This chapter's network analysis skills can be used in many fields.

Practical Example: Exploring Fraud Through Network Visualization and Homophily

Money mules are individuals who allow their bank accounts to be used by criminals to launder illicit proceeds. Identifying these accounts is crucial for disrupting money laundering operations. In this hands-on example, we use Python's networkx and pandas libraries to analyze transactional networks and assess the probability of an account acting as a money mule.

Objective: To identify potential money mule accounts using known indicators and evaluate the likelihood of involvement using *graph topology metrics* (specifically the degree ratio in subgraphs).

Techniques Covered:

- Constructing a transaction graph.
- Assigning account type as node attributes.
- Applying color mapping for better visual detection.

- Calculating assortativity coefficient to evaluate homophily in the fraud network.

The data for this example comes from two CSV files:

1. *transfers.csv:* This dataset contains financial transaction data, including the originator, beneficiary, amount transferred, time, beneficiary nation, and payment channel.
2. *account_info.csv:* Includes account IDs, *isMoneyMule* status (True/False), and account type.

The analysis involves the following steps:

1. Loading the necessary Python libraries for data handling, network analysis, and visualization.
2. Reading the transaction and account information datasets into pandas dataframes.
3. Creating a network graph from the transactions data, with nodes representing accounts and edges representing transactions.
4. Mapping account types to specific colors to visualize the different types of accounts in the network graph.
5. Drawing the network graph with labels and node colors representing the type of accounts.

Visualizing the transaction network might reveal odd trends that may suggest fraud. Money mules may have more transactions or move money to select accounts. These patterns help organizations detect and prevent fraud.

Practical Example Coding

In social network analysis, each node often represents an entity (e.g., an account) and may hold attributes such as type, status, or risk level. In our dataset, the account_info dataframe contains the type of each account—such as individual, business, or suspicious.

This example explores the concept of homophily, which in sociology refers to the tendency of similar entities to connect. In fraud networks, homophily may manifest as fraudsters transacting primarily with other fraudsters, while legitimate accounts interact more with similar lawful entities. The degree of this similarity can vary depending on business context, network structure, and fraud typology.

To evaluate homophily, we assign the type attribute to each node in the graph using the networkx method G.nodes[node]['attribute'] = value. Once the account types are mapped, we compute the attribute assortativity coefficient using NetworkX's built-in function. Since type is a categorical variable, the coefficient provides a meaningful measure of how strongly nodes of the same type are connected across the network.

This analysis will help us quantify whether suspicious account types are clustering—potentially forming fraud rings—or are randomly dispersed within the broader transaction network (See Fig. 18.1).

Accessing the Interactive Lab

The full interactive notebook and datasets for this chapter are available on GitHub.

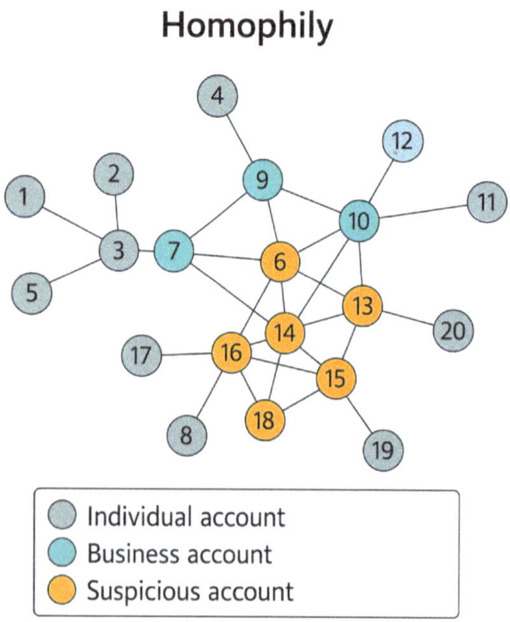

Fig. 18.1 Homophily in Fraud Networks (Categorical Node Assortativity Analysis): A graph visualization of a social network highlighting homophily. Nodes are categorized by type: individual accounts (gray), business accounts (blue), and suspicious accounts (orange). Suspicious nodes appear clustered, visually suggesting a fraud ring. The image supports analysis of categorical assortativity in fraud detection

Readers can explore all code examples, graphs, and analytical outputs directly through the nbviewer platform for correct rendering:

View online: https://nbviewer.org/github/Hands-On-Fraud-Analytics/Chapter-18-Social-Network-Analysis-Practical-Examples

Step 1: Importing necessary libraries*:* This code imports necessary libraries for data manipulation, network analysis, and visualization.

```
# Step 1: Import required libraries
import pandas as pd
import networkx as nx
import matplotlib.pyplot as plt
```

Step 2: Loading the data: These two lines load the transfers and account information from csv files into pandas DataFrame.

```
# Step 2: Load datasets
transfers = pd.read_csv('transfers.csv')          # Includes originator,
beneficiary, amount, etc.
account_info = pd.read_csv('account_info.csv')    # Includes id,
isMoneyMule, type
```

Step 3: Creating a network (graph): Here, a graph is created from the transfers data. This graph is undirected (nx.Graph()), and additional attributes ("amount," "time," "benef_country," "payment_channel") for the edges are included.

```
# Step 3: Create a graph from the transfer data
G = nx.from_pandas_edgelist(
    transfers,
    source='originator',
    target='beneficiary',
    edge_attr=True,
    create_using=nx.Graph()  # Undirected graph to study homophily
)
```

Step 4: Adding node attribute*:* These lines of code assign the 'type' from the 'account_info' DataFrame to the nodes in the network graph G as an attribute named 'account_type.'

```
# Step 4: Add account type attribute to nodes
account_types = account_info.set_index('id').to_dict()['type']
nx.set_node_attributes(G, account_types, 'account_type')
```

Step 5: Map account types to integers for assortativity calculation.

```
# Step 5: Map account types to integers for assortativity calculation
# Example: type 1 → 1, type 2 → 2, type 3 → 3
type_set = set(account_types.values())
type_mapping = {v: i+1 for i, v in enumerate(type_set)}
integer_type_attributes = {node: type_mapping.get(account_types[node], 0)
for node in G.nodes if node in account_types}
nx.set_node_attributes(G, integer_type_attributes, 'account_type_int')
```

Step 6: Computing assortativity: This step calculates the assortativity for node attributes. This measures the correlation between connected nodes in the network.

```
# Step 6: Calculate assortativity coefficient (homophily measure)
assortativity = nx.attribute_assortativity_coefficient(G,
'account_type_int')
print(f"Assortativity based on account_type: {assortativity:.2f}")
```

Step 7: Defining a color map and adding color attribute to nodes: Here, a color map is defined for the different account types. The "color" attribute is then added to each node in the graph G, based on its 'account_type'.

```
# Step 7: Define a color map for account types
color_palette = {1: 'grey', 2: 'lightblue', 3: 'darkorange'}  # Customize
based on your actual types
node_colors = []
for node in G.nodes():
    node_type = account_types.get(node)
    color = color_palette.get(node_type, 'lightgrey')  # Default color if
unknown
    node_colors.append(color)
```

Step 8: Draw the network graph.

```
# Step 8: Draw the network graph
plt.figure(figsize=(12, 8))
pos = nx.spring_layout(G, seed=42)
nx.draw(G, pos, node_color=node_colors, with_labels=True, node_size=400,
font_size=8)
plt.title("Transaction Network Colored by Account Type")
plt.axis('off')
plt.tight_layout()
plt.show()
```

This degree ratio quantifies how tightly connected the target account is to known money mule nodes. A higher ratio suggests stronger interaction within the fraud ring and could be flagged for further investigation. This method is especially valuable when you have partial labels or known suspects, and you want to extend suspicion to connected accounts. To add more context to your specific dataset, the color mapping is applied as follows (Fig. 18.2):

- Type 1 represents individual accounts.
- Type 2 represents business accounts.
- Type 3 represents suspicious accounts, which might be involved in fraudulent activities.

Now, the color mapping becomes:

- 'grey' represents individual accounts.
- 'lightblue' represents business accounts.
- 'darkorange' represents suspicious accounts (potentially fraudulent).

Based on the code provided, here are the observations that could be made (Fig. 18.3):

Practical Example: Money Mule Detection Using Subgraphs and Degree Ratios

Money mules are individuals who allow their bank accounts to be used by criminals to launder the proceeds of their illicit activities. Identifying money mule accounts in financial networks is crucial to prevent money laundering. In this analysis, we're going to use Python's networkx and pandas' libraries to investigate financial transactions and identify potential money mule accounts.

Objectives: To identify potential money mule accounts based on known indicators and assess the probability of an account being involved in fraud using graph topology metrics.

Techniques Covered:

- Adding is*MoneyMule* as a Boolean node attribute.

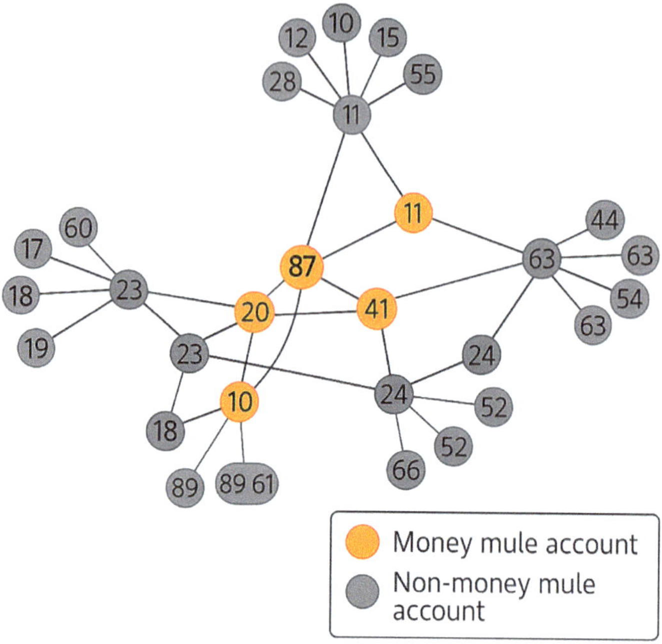

Fig. 18.2 Degree Ratio Analysis in Money Mule Detection Networks: A network graph showing accounts as nodes, with orange nodes labeled as known money mules and gray nodes as regular accounts. Edges represent transactions. Several central orange nodes are densely connected to others, suggesting fraud ring behavior. This image supports degree-ratio-based identification of suspicious nodes in financial fraud analysis

- Visualizing mule accounts distinctly (e.g., in orange).
- Building a subgraph of high-risk accounts.
- Computing a degree ratio to estimate money mule involvement probability.

Dataset: The analysis requires two datasets:

1. Transfers data: This dataset contains information about the financial transfers, specifically the originator and the beneficiary of each transaction.

Top Connected Accounts

Top 5 by In-Degree
(receive most transactions)

Account	In-Degree
187	5
120	5
163	3
141	3
164	3

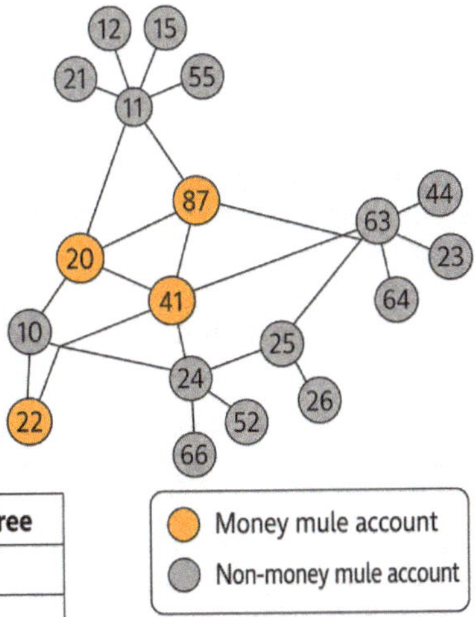

↑ Top 5 by Out-Degree
(send most transactions)

Account	Out-Degree
128	8
123	8
124	7
144	7
140	6

Flag accounts **187** and **120** for deeper review - they receive from many sources.

Audit senders **128**, **123**, and **124** - they push funds across the network.

Fig. 18.3 A graph showing a transaction network with nodes representing accounts, and edges representing transactions. Tables beside the graph list top accounts by in-degree (receiving funds) and out-degree (sending funds). Orange nodes are flagged as money mules. The diagram emphasizes accounts with high transaction volume as key points for fraud investigation, with in-degree and out-degree counts supporting suspicion prioritization

2. Account info data: This dataset contains information about each account, including the account id, whether it is a money mule account, and the account type.

Steps:

1. Load the "transfers" and "account_info" data.

2. Create a network graph based on the transfers data using networkx.
3. Add node attributes to the network graph based on the account info data.
4. Create a color map for the nodes based on whether they are identified as money mule accounts.
5. Plot the network graph with the color map.
6. Identify and print the IDs of money mule accounts.
7. Create a subgraph containing a specific account and all identified money mule accounts.
8. Compute the money mule probability of the specific account based on its interactions with identified money mule accounts.

The money mule accounts are identified and visualized on the network graph. The degree ratio (computed as the degree of the specific account in the subgraph divided by its degree in the full graph) gives an estimate of the probability that the specific account is involved in money mule activities. Higher degree ratios indicate a higher likelihood of money mule activity. This analysis can help financial institutions identify potential money mule accounts and take appropriate preventive actions (Fig. 18.4).

Step 1: Import necessary libraries: The script begins by importing required Python libraries. NetworkX for network analysis, pandas for data handling and matplotlib for plotting.

```
# Step 1: Import required libraries
import pandas as pd
import networkx as nx
import matplotlib.pyplot as plt
```

Step 2: Load the data: It then defines the ‘account_info_data’ and ‘transfer_info_data’. These data sets contain information about the accounts and transfers respectively.

```
# Step 2: Load the datasets
account_info = pd.read_csv('account_info.csv')
transfer_info = pd.read_csv('transfers.csv')
```

Step 3: Set index for account data: These datasets are converted to pandas DataFrames.

Top Connected Accounts

↑ **Top 5 by In-Degree**
(receive most transactions)

Account	In-Degree
I87	5
I20	5
I63	3
I41	3
I64	3

↓ **Top 5 by Out-Degree**
(send most transactions)

Account	Out-Degree
I28	8
I23	8
I24	7
I44	7
I40	6

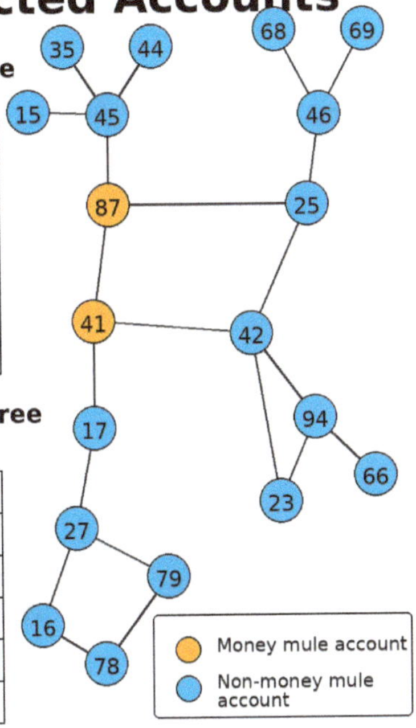

Flag accounts **I87** and **I20** for deeper review – they receive from many sources.

Audit senders **I28**, **I23**, and **I24** – they push funds across the network.

Fig. 18.4 Top Connected Accounts Based on Transaction Direction (In-Degree and Out-Degree): A network graph showing nodes (accounts) connected by directed transactions. Orange nodes are money mule accounts and blue nodes are non-money mule accounts. Two tables identify top 5 accounts by in-degree (receivers) and out-degree (senders). The diagram highlights accounts I69 and I44 as high in-degree nodes, and accounts I69, I77, and I93 as high out-degree nodes. These accounts are flagged for investigation due to abnormal transaction activity patterns, useful for detecting fraud rings and money laundering behaviors

```
# Step 3: Set 'id' as index for easy referencing
account_info.set_index('id', inplace=True)
```

Step 4: CBuild the network graph from transfer data: The ‘isMoneyMule’ column of the ‘account_info’ DataFrame is mapped to boolean values.

```
# Step 4: Build the network graph
G = nx.from_pandas_edgelist(transfer_info, source='originator',
target='beneficiary', create_using=nx.Graph())
```

Step 5: Add ‘isMoneyMule’ attribute to nodes: The “id” column is set as the index for the “account_info” DataFrame.

```
# Step 5: Add the 'isMoneyMule' attribute to nodes
for index, row in account_info.iterrows():
    if index in G:
        G.nodes[index]['isMoneyMule'] = row['isMoneyMule']
```

Step 6: Create color mapping based on mule status: It creates a Graph using NetworkX from the ‘transfer_info’ DataFrame, using ‘originator’ and ‘beneficiary’ as the nodes.

```
# Step 6: Create color mapping based on mule status
color_map = []
for node in G:
    if G.nodes[node].get('isMoneyMule', False):
        color_map.append('darkorange')
    else:
        color_map.append('lightblue')
```

Step 7: Plot the network graph: It then adds the ‘isMoneyMule’ attribute to the nodes in the graph.

This attribute indicates whether the account is a money mule or not.

```
# Step 7: Plot the graph
nx.draw(G, node_color=color_map, with_labels=True)
plt.show()
```

Step 8: Print IDs of money mule accounts: It creates a color map for the nodes, where money mule nodes are colored ‘darkorange’ and non-money mule nodes are colored ‘slateblue’.

```
# Step 8: Print IDs of money mule accounts# Step 8: Print IDs of money
mule accounts
print("Identified Money Mules:", account_info[account_info['isMoneyMule']
== True].index.tolist())
```

Step 9: Create a subgraph of target account and known money mules: It plots the graph using the created color map.

```
# Step 9: Create a subgraph of a target account and known money mules
target_node = "I41"
mules = ["I47", "I87", "I20"]
nodes = [target_node] + mules
subnet = G.subgraph(nodes)
```

Step 10: Calculate and print degree ratio for the target account: It prints the ids of the money mule accounts.

```
# Step 10: Calculate and print degree ratio for the target account
degree_ratio = subnet.degree(target_node) / G.degree(target_node)
print(f"Degree Ratio for {target_node}: {degree_ratio:.2f}")
```

Summary

As we conclude this chapter, we reflect on the insights gained in deploying social network analysis for fraud detection in financial transactions. The reader has traversed the pathway of setting up a network graph using Python, visualizing these complex relationships, and exploring the underlying patterns that signal fraudulent behaviors.

In this chapter, we started by discussing the importance of network graphs and how they act as visual representations of financial transactions. The creation of the graph was facilitated using the Python NetworkX library, a powerful tool for managing and visualizing large, complex networks.

We explored the essence of identifying patterns within the network that indicate fraudulent activities. We learned that this is often exhibited by accounts known as money mules, which show unique transaction patterns.

Data visualization was another key learning area. We employed different colors to represent account types in our graph, creating a visual aid that helps to quickly and effectively identify potential fraud.

We introduced the concept of assortativity, a measure in network analysis that highlights the correlation between connected nodes. This concept provided a new lens to view our network and detect fraud, identifying how similar or different the connected accounts are.

We worked hands-on with real-world datasets transfers.csv and account_info.csv, providing a practical approach to understanding how social network analysis applies to real-world financial transactions. The step-by-step code analysis demystified the process, from loading data, creating a graph, adding node attributes, calculating assortativity, and finally plotting the graph.

This journey through the world of social network analysis and fraud detection sets the stage for the next exciting part of our book—incorporating text data in fraud analysis. As we proceed to the next part, we delve deeper into the realm of data science, merging the textual aspect into our data analysis toolkit. We will explore the importance of text mining, text cleaning and preparation, and eventually move on to topic modeling for fraud detection, continuing to explore this fascinating and impactful world of fraud detection.

PART VI

Text Data in Fraud Analysis

Fraud leaves words. Emails, customer complaints, claim descriptions, chat logs, and social media posts contain some of the richest fraud signals available—yet they arrive in unstructured form, invisible to the numerical models that dominate fraud analytics. Text data does not fit neatly into a spreadsheet column, but it often contains precisely the language patterns, deceptive framing, and thematic fingerprints that betray fraudulent intent. Analysing it requires a different set of tools and a different way of thinking about what evidence looks like. Part VI introduces those tools through a single, focused chapter. Chapter 19 covers the full text analytics pipeline for fraud detection, from raw data ingestion and preprocessing through to topic modelling and fraudster identification. It examines text mining techniques, the transformation of unstructured language into analysable form, and the construction of dictionaries and corpora. At its core is Latent Dirichlet Allocation (LDA), the topic modelling approach used to surface hidden thematic patterns across large collections of text, enabling analysts to flag suspicious communications and trace fraudulent actors through the topics they write about. The chapter is grounded in a practical example using the Enron email dataset, one of the most well-known real-world fraud cases in which written communications proved central to uncovering deception. Part VI completes the book's analytical journey—from structured transactions to the unstructured human language where fraud so often hides in plain sight.

CHAPTER 19

Fraudulent Patterns: Unveiling Deception Through Text Analysis and Topic Modeling

As we navigate the intricate world of fraud detection, it's crucial to understand that fraudsters often leave their trails in more than just transactional data. They might attempt to disguise their activities in the veil of text data such as emails, transaction descriptions, or other forms of written communication. Unraveling the secrets hidden within this text data has become an essential part of modern fraud detection strategies. This is where our exploration takes us in this chapter—into the techniques and applications of *text mining* and machine learning to identify and prevent fraudulent activities.

Our journey starts with "Understanding and Cleaning Data for Fraud Detection." Here, we delve into the essential preprocessing tasks for *text mining*. Techniques such as *tokenization*, *stopword removal*, *lemmatization*, and *stemming* are presented as essential steps in the transformation of raw, unstructured text into clean, structured data that's ready for analysis.

A. Al Aqqad, *Fraud Analytics in Action*
https://doi.org/10.1007/978-3-032-16023-2_19

Next, in "Text Mining to Detect Fraud," we provide a hands-on approach to text mining using the Enron emails dataset. Practical tasks such as removing stopwords and punctuation, and transforming text using *lemmatization* and *stemming* techniques are explored. This section aims to ensure that we have clean data that's primed for *topic modeling* and subsequent fraud detection analysis.

"Topic Modeling for Fraud Detection" is where we unlock the power of *Latent Dirichlet Allocation (LDA)*. LDA is a technique for identifying abstract topics within text data that could be indicators of potential fraud. The process of implementing LDA is covered in its entirety, from data cleaning to dictionary creation, and corpus building. We also aim to deepen your understanding of LDA model outputs and how to visualize these associations for improved comprehension.

Finally, in "Flagging Fraud Using Topics," we learn how to apply the results of our LDA models for fraud detection. We scrutinize the prevalence of suspicious words within topics, compare topic frequencies in fraudulent and non-fraudulent cases, and learn how to flag potential fraudulent behavior. The emphasis is placed on the significance of visualizing topics for enhanced interpretation and the process of assigning these topics back to the original data.

Throughout this chapter, the immense power of text mining in detecting fraudulent activities will become increasingly evident. Furthermore, you will witness the pivotal role of machine learning, particularly *topic modeling*, in enhancing the robustness and efficiency of fraud detection. Prepare for an enlightening journey into the world of text data in fraud analysis.

Using Text Data in Fraud Analysis

Text data is frequently used in fraud studies and can reveal information that is helpful in identifying fraudulent activities. Numerous sources, including emails exchanged between businesses and their clients, internal communications, descriptions of transactions, notes on client accounts, insurance claims, and even taped phone conversations, can provide this information. In order to overcome the challenges of fraud detection, it is essential to comprehend how to handle and assess text data.

Incorporating text data in fraud analysis is an essential aspect of the process, as it often provides valuable insights that can help detect fraudulent activities. Textual data can be found in various sources such as emails between clients and the company, internal company communications, transaction descriptions, notes added by client service teams, insurance claim details, and even recorded phone calls. Utilizing text mining techniques, analysts can employ word searches to flag data containing specific terms, perform sentiment analysis to assess the positivity or negativity of a text, compare sentiment in fraudulent texts against normal text, conduct topic analysis and count word frequency to identify common themes and occurrences of specific words, and analyze text style to pinpoint texts with similar styles to known fraudulent data.

For example, if you need to flag client transactions mentioning a particular gambling company that has recently garnered negative attention, a simple word search across transactions and client emails can quickly identify any mentions of the company. These results can then be used as a filter, a standalone flag, or an additional feature in your machine learning model, all achievable with just a few lines of code. To further refine the analysis, you can use pandas functions to work with text data within a pandas Series or DataFrame, filtering on multiple words or phrases and creating flags for data containing these words.

Effectively integrating and analyzing text data can enhance your fraud detection capabilities, improving the accuracy of your models and enabling more effective identification of potential fraudulent activities. Additionally, staying up-to-date with the latest advancements in text mining techniques and incorporating them into your fraud analysis workflow can lead to even better results in identifying and preventing fraud.

Practical Example: Unveiling Hidden Patterns in Enron Emails

Enron's corporate scandal, which involved fraudulent financial reporting practices, led to one of the most significant bankruptcy cases in American history. By analyzing the Enron email dataset, we aim to uncover potential fraud indicators by identifying specific keywords and topics.

Objective: Our goal is to employ Natural Language Processing (NLP) techniques to detect suspicious emails and flag potentially fraudulent activities within the Enron email dataset.

Dataset: The dataset used is the Enron email dataset, which contains cleaned and pre-processed email content.

Steps:

1. Load the Enron email dataset into a pandas DataFrame.
2. Filter the DataFrame to pinpoint emails with specific keywords.
3. Compile a list of search terms to filter emails containing multiple keywords.
4. Establish a flag variable for emails matching the search terms.
5. Remove stopwords and punctuations and lemmatize the email text.
6. Apply Latent Dirichlet Allocation (LDA) to identify email topics.
7. Compute dominant topics and their probabilities for each email.
8. Create a flag for emails strongly associated with a specific topic.

Analysis: By carrying out the aforementioned processes, we may analyze the email dataset to find suspicious emails that may be connected to fraudulent activity. In order to identify the emails that match the search keywords, we first filter the dataset using specified search phrases and construct a flag variable. The email text is then preprocessed by having stopwords, punctuation, and word lemmatization removed. We determine the prominent subjects in the dataset using LDA and estimate their probabilities for every email. Finally, we develop a flag for emails that are strongly related to a particular subject and may be signs of fraud.

This approach can help in the initial screening of emails for potentially fraudulent activities. The flagged emails can then be further investigated or used as features in a machine learning model for fraud detection.

Based on the analysis done, we can make the following observations:

1. Particular terms like "enron stock," "sell stock," "stock bonus," and "sell enron stock" may be a sign of possible fraud. These keywords were used to flag emails for additional examination or as characteristics in a fraud detection algorithm.
2. Lemmatizing the words and deleting stopwords from the email text can help reduce noise and ensure that only pertinent information is

retained. Thus, the topic modeling procedure becomes more precise and efficient.

3. Different email subjects could be found using the Latent Dirichlet Allocation (LDA) model. This is helpful for deciphering the emails' context and seeing any potential fraudulent activity-related tendencies.
4. We can detect emails that are strongly related with a particular topic, which may be a sign of fraud, by examining the prominent themes and their probabilities for each email. These emails may be marked for additional examination or used as characteristics in a machine learning fraud detection model.

In summary, understanding the underlying subjects and spotting suspicious emails are two things that the analysis of the Enron email collection can assist with. The emails that have been reported can be looked into more thoroughly or used as features in a fraud detection model. It's crucial to remember that this strategy is predicated on the notion that the chosen phrases and themes are connected to fraudulent operations. To validate these results and raise the efficiency of the fraud detection process, more research and domain knowledge are needed.

Fraud Detection in Enron Emails: Word Search with Dataframes
In this exercise, we will work with a dataset containing emails from Enron employees. The Enron scandal is a well-known case of corporate fraud, where employees hid the company's deteriorating financial position, leading to an artificially high stock price. When the truth was revealed, Enron's stock value plummeted, leaving investors with significant losses. Your goal is to find all emails that mention specific phrases, such as "sell Enron stock."

By employing string operations on DataFrames, we can efficiently search through unstructured email data and generate flags based on the presence of certain words. The Enron email dataset has been loaded into a DataFrame called "df," and you can use it to identify potentially suspicious terms. Feel free to examine "df" in the Console before proceeding.

Instructions:

- Inspect the head of "df" in the Console and search for any emails mentioning "sell Enron stock."
- Identify the data in "df" that corresponds to the condition established earlier.

In this exercise, we'll practice using string operations on DataFrames to look for emails in the 'clean_content' column of the DataFrame df that contain certain words like "sell enron stock." To check the head of df on the console, issue the following command:

```
import pandas as pd

# load Enron email dataset
enron_df = pd.read_csv('enron_emails_clean.csv')

enron_df

# Find all cleaned emails that contain 'sell enron stock'
mask = enron_df['clean_content'].str.contains('sell enron stock', na=False
)

# Select the data from df using the mask
print(enron_df[mask])
```

Simply searching for particular string values in a dataframe, allows you to see that it is possible to incorporate textual data into your model or analysis. Your fraud detection model may employ this word search as an additional flag or as a feature. Let's now see how to filter the data using a variety of search terms (Fig. 19.1).

Fraud Detection in Enron Emails: Using List of Terms

We frequently favor searching for multiple terms over just one. We might create a comprehensive "fraud dictionary" with terms that would denote questionable clients or commercial dealings. Fraud analysts typically have an idea of what should be in such a lexicon. This exercise will flag multiple phrases, and the experiment that follows will create a new flag variable from it. The outputs of our machine learning model can either have this "flag" applied directly as a feature or with another filter on top. Let's first apply a set of terms to our data to filter it. Email DataFrame that has been cleaned up is once more available as df.

```
                                          Message-ID                       From  \
154  <6336501.1075841154311.JavaMail.evans@thyme>  ('sarah.palmer@enron.com')

                            To                 Date  \
154  ('sarah.palmer@enron.com')  2002-02-01 14:53:35

                                             content  \
154  \nJoint Venture: A 1997 Enron Meeting Belies O...

                                       clean_content
154  joint venture enron meeting belies officers cl...
```

Fig. 19.1 Sample email record from the Enron dataset (keyword klagging step): This figure displays a sample email record from the Enron email dataset. It includes metadata such as the message ID, sender and recipient email addresses, and timestamp. The email content field shows the subject and body of the message, while the clean_content field contains the preprocessed text stripped of formatting and punctuation. This cleaned version is typically used for keyword searches, NLP preprocessing, and topic modeling in fraud detection workflows

Instructions:

- Create a list of search terms, including 'enron stock', 'sell stock', 'stock bonus', and 'sell enron stock'.
- Combine the string terms in the search conditions.
- Filter data based on emails that match the list defined in searchfor.

```
# Create a list of terms to search for
searchfor = ['enron stock', 'sell stock', 'stock bonus', 'sell enron stock
']

# Filter cleaned emails on searchfor list and select from df
filtered_emails = enron_df[enron_df['clean_content'].str.contains('|'.join
(searchfor), na=False)]
print(filtered_emails)
```

The terms to search for are created in a list named \searchfor' by this code. The DataFrame df is then filtered based on whether any of these terms appear in the 'clean_content' column. The search terms are all combined into a string using the '|'.join (searchfor) method, which will be utilized in the str.contains() function to match any of the supplied terms. The na=False argument makes sure that rows with blank values are not taken into account. The filtered emails are printed off at the end (Fig. 19.2).

	message_id	from	content	
0	63485098.1875	1b/E365d440466	addfedbaddk@investoolscow±0f trust edi...	
1	63485098.1875	JavaHall1evans	addfeeddackS0invxxoblc4.evans0t6yme ...	
2	63485098.1875	JavaHall2.evans	josephl@chchase..com Rrowa.red By edt...	
3	63485098.1875	awatson@enron	Jeff.Love@enron.com PLEASE READ THIS.	
...	...	...	...	...
1	1151	a@venrq@enron	Investoolis Advisory Free Digest of trust edi ...	
2	1151	jalearygevans@	——Forwarded by Rlichard B Sanders/HOU/ECT ...	
3	1151	josciopn@com	—— 2022-01-17 13:52 To, Recu 3 will be Danned ...	
4	1151	banders@gaol	PLEASE READ THIS IMPORTANT INFORMATION CONC...	

314 rows < 6 columns)

To this...

	message_id	from	clean_content
0	63485098.1875	javestoollsadslvs	investools advisory free digest of trust edit ...
1	63485098.1875	addfeedbackk@	i am writing to let you know I will be banned ...
2	63485098.1876	rdardb.evans@thy	I am writing to let you know will be banded a ..
3	63485098.1876	awatson@enron.	blanca milosevilch12 santa clara avenuemilel..
4	63485098.1876	jadnalLavxco.com	denvero pleasse pay emodo moening denun..
5	63485098.1876	telicime.y.ehowers	emenge consient dengeny account in jandrem
6	63485098.1809	steven.j kean.com	recommend update faving dnyeng unyytamai

314 rows < 6 columns) Index: object

Fig. 19.2 Preprocessing Enron email data for fraud detection analysis: This figure shows a transformation of raw Enron email records into a cleaned version for natural language processing. The top table presents the original dataset with noisy email addresses and partially garbled content. The bottom table, labeled "To this...," displays the cleaned version where the from field has been normalized and the clean_content column holds simplified, readable text. This preprocessing step is essential for keyword extraction, topic modeling, and machine learning in fraud detection

Fraud Detection in Enron Emails: Creating a Flag

In this exercise, we'll make a flag variable that, if any of the relevant search terms are present in the emails, will be set to 1; else, it will be set to 0. The searchfor list is the one established in the last exercise, and we may carry on working with the DataFrame df containing the emails.

Instructions:

1. Use a numpy where condition to flag "1" where the cleaned email contains words on the searchfor list and 0 otherwise.
2. Join the words on the searchfor list with an "or" indicator.
3. Count the values of the newly created flag variable.

```
import numpy as np

# Create flag variable where the emails match the searchfor terms
enron_df['flag'] = np.where((enron_df['clean_content'].str.contains('|'.jo
in(searchfor), na=False) == True), 1, 0)

# Count the values of the flag variable
count = enron_df['flag'].value_counts()
print(count)
```

```
0    1776
1     314
Name: flag, dtype: int64
```

Text Mining Techniques for Fraud Detection

Preparing your text data Before working with text data for tasks like word search, topic modeling, sentiment analysis, or text style analysis, it is crucial to clean and preprocess the data. There are four key steps to follow:

- Tokenization: Split the text into sentences and words, convert everything to lowercase, and remove punctuation.
- Stopword removal: Eliminate stopwords as they can interfere with your analysis. You can use available dictionaries for this purpose.
- Lemmatization: Convert words to their base form, such as changing third-person words to first-person and transforming verbs into their present tense. This helps in combining similar words.
- Stemming: Reduce words to their root form (e.g., "walking" and "walked" are reduced to "walk").

Transforming Raw Text Data

Following these four steps, you can transform messy, unstructured text data into a clean, structured format (Fig. 19.3).

Text Data After Preprocessing

After preprocessing, your text data will be a clean and structured list of words per DataFrame row.

Data preprocessing—Part 1

In order to actually clean your data, start with tokenization by breaking up words into smaller strings using the nltk word tokenizer. Regular expressions are used with rstrip to remove whitespace and convert all text to lowercase. Next, eliminate stopwords and punctuation using the English stopwords list provided by nltk. Join is used to add a space between each word after a loop through the words you want to maintain.

Go from this...

	headline_text	index
0	aba decides against community broadcasting licenc.	0
1	act fire witnesses must be aware of defamisma	1
2	a-g calls for infrastructur protect, summit	3
3	air nz staff in aussie strike for payrls	4
4	air nz strike to affect australian travellers	5

To this...

	To st	index
0	[decid, communiti, broadcast, lic	1
1	[wit, awar, defam]	2
2	[call, infrastructur, protect, summit	3
3	[staff, aust, strike, rise, rise	4
4	[strike, affect, australian, travel	5
6	[ambiti, oslon, win, trial, jump]	6
7	[antic, delight, record, break, barca	7
8	[aussi, qualificc, saut, wright, match]	8
9	[station, arrest, secury, council, iraq]	

Name: headline_text, dtype: object

Fig. 19.3 Text mormalization and tokenization for NLP modeling: The figure illustrates a text preprocessing transformation process commonly used in NLP. The top portion labeled "Go from this..." shows raw news headlines containing typos, abbreviations, and grammatical inconsistencies. The bottom portion labeled "To this..." displays the same text after preprocessing, including lower-casing, tokenization, and stemming. Words are reduced to their base forms (e.g., "decides" becomes "decid," "broadcasting" becomes "broadcast") and stored as clean token lists for each document. This transformation is critical for improving machine learning model performance in text classification or topic modeling tasks

```
# 1. Tokenization
from nltk.tokenize import word_tokenize
text = df['email_body'].apply(lambda row:
word_tokenize(row.lower().strip()))

# 2. Remove all stopwords and punctuation
from nltk.corpus import stopwords
import string

stop_words = set(stopwords.words('english'))
text_cleaned = text.apply(lambda words: [
    word for word in words
    if word not in stop_words and word not in string.punctuation and not
word.isdigit()
])
```

Data preprocessing—Part 2

Next, lemmatize words using nltk's WordNetLemmatizer, looping over the words and separating them with spaces. For stemming, use nltk's PorterStemmer. After these steps, your text data should be clean, consisting of lists of cleaned words for each row in your DataFrame (Fig. 19.4).

```
# 3. Lemmatization
from nltk.stem import WordNetLemmatizer
lemmatizer = WordNetLemmatizer()
text_lemmatized = text_cleaned.apply(lambda words:
[lemmatizer.lemmatize(word) for word in words])

# 4. Stemming
from nltk.stem import PorterStemmer
stemmer = PorterStemmer()
text_stemmed = text_lemmatized.apply(lambda words: [stemmer.stem(word) for
word in words])
```

Removing Stopwords

The Enron emails will be cleaned in the practices that follow so that the data is ready to be used in a topic model. We will study various techniques to effectively clean text because it can be difficult to do so. The dataframe, df, that contains the emails is accessible. We must first specify the list of stopwords and punctuation that will be eliminated from the text data in the upcoming experiment. Let's try it out.

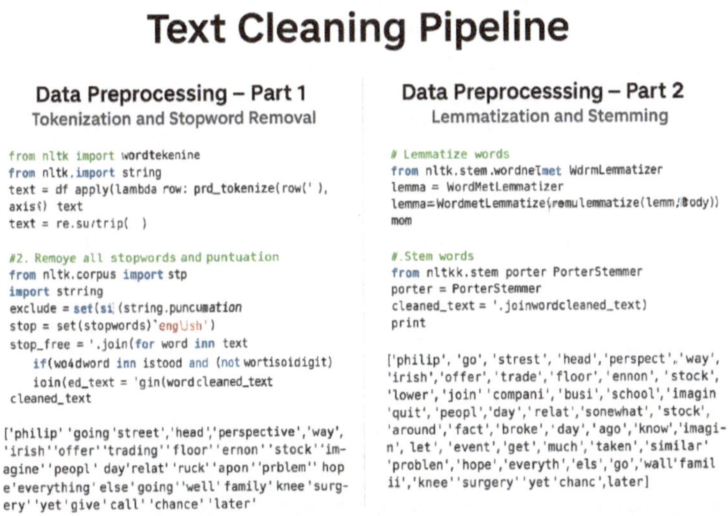

Fig. 19.4 Text cleaning pipeline: from raw emails to tokenized and cleaned text: This figure shows a two-part data preprocessing pipeline using Python and the NLTK library. Part 1 includes tokenization and removal of stopwords and punctuation. Part 2 continues with lemmatization using WordNetLemmatizer and stemming using PorterStemmer. The result is a structured list of meaningful, cleaned words per row for downstream analysis

Instructions:

- Import the stopwords from nltk. Define "english" words to use as stopwords under the variable stop. Get the punctuation set from the string package and assign it to exclude.

```
import nltk
nltk.download('stopwords')

# Import nltk packages and string
from nltk.corpus import stopwords
import string

# Define stopwords to exclude
stop = set(stopwords.words('english'))
stop.update(("to","cc","subject","http","from","sent", "ect", "u", "fwd",
"www", "com"))

# Define punctuations to exclude and lemmatizer
exclude = set(string.punctuation)
```

Cleaning Text Data

The Enron emails in the dataframe df can be cleaned up using the stopwords and punctuation that we established earlier. The terms "stop" and "exclude" are accessible for lists that contain stopwords and punctuation. Before we have cleansed the data, there are still a few procedures to complete, including "lemmatization" of words and verb stemming. The lemmatization and verb stemming for the email data have already been completed for you in this exercise.

Instructions:

- Use the previously defined variables "stop" and "exclude" to complete the cleaning function:
- First, strip the words from whitespaces using "rstrip"
- Exclude stopwords and punctuations
- Finally, lemmatize the words and assign them to the variable "normalized"

```
# Import the lemmatizer from nltk
from nltk.stem.wordnet import WordNetLemmatizer
lemma = WordNetLemmatizer()

# Define word cleaning function
def clean(text, stop):
    text = text.rstrip()
    # Remove stopwords
    stop_free = " ".join([word for word in text.lower().split() if ((word
not in stop) and (not word.isdigit()))])
    # Remove punctuations
    punc_free = ''.join(word for word in stop_free if word not in exclude)
    # Lemmatize all words
    normalized = " ".join(lemma.lemmatize(word) for word in punc_free.spli
t())
    return normalized
```

Next, to apply the clean(text, stop) function on each line of text data in your DataFrame, you can use the following code:

```
import nltk
nltk.download('wordnet')

# Import the lemmatizer from nltk
from nltk.stem.wordnet import WordNetLemmatizer
lemma = WordNetLemmatizer()

# Define word cleaning function
def clean(text, stop):
    if isinstance(text, str):  # Check if the text is a string
        text = text.rstrip()
        stop_free = " ".join([i for i in text.lower().split() if((i not in
 stop) and (not i.isdigit()))])
        punc_free = ''.join(i for i in stop_free if i not in exclude)
        normalized = " ".join(lemma.lemmatize(i) for i in punc_free.split(
))
```

```
        return normalized
    else:
        return ""  # Return an empty string if the text is not a string


text_clean = []
for text in enron_df['clean_content']:
    text_clean.append(clean(text, stop).split())
print(text_clean)


# Clean the emails in df and print results
text_clean = []
for text in enron_df['clean_content']:
    text_clean.append(clean(text, stop).split())
print(text_clean)
```

```
[nltk_data] Downloading package wordnet to /root/nltk_data...
[nltk_data]   Package wordnet is already up-to-date!
IOPub data rate exceeded.
The notebook server will temporarily stop sending output
to the client in order to avoid crashing it.
To change this limit, set the config variable
`--NotebookApp.iopub_data_rate_limit`.

Current values:
NotebookApp.iopub_data_rate_limit=1000000.0 (bytes/sec)
NotebookApp.rate_limit_window=3.0 (secs)
```

Now that we have cleaned our data entirely with the necessary steps, including splitting the text into words, removing stopwords and punctuations, and lemmatizing your words. We are now ready to run a topic model on this data. In the following exercises we are going to explore how to do that.

Topic Modeling for Fraud Detection

For finding fraud in text data, topic modeling is a potent tool. By looking at the frequency of particular phrases, it enables you to identify abstract subjects that are present in a collection of texts. Topic modeling groups words that are related to the same topic, much like clustering does. Identifying the most prevalent themes in known fraud instances allows you to compare them to unreported cases if you have text data from those cases.

You can assess which issues seem to indicate fraudulent behavior and call for additional inquiry even without labeled data.

Latent Dirichlet Allocation (LDA): Latent Dirichlet Allocation (LDA) is a widely used topic modeling technique. It generates a "topic per document" model and a "words per topic" model, known as Dirichlet distributions. Implementing LDA involves cleaning your data, creating a dictionary of word frequencies, and building a corpus of word counts for each document (Fig. 19.5).

Understanding LDA Output: The two primary outputs of the LDA model are the probabilistic associations between each document and each

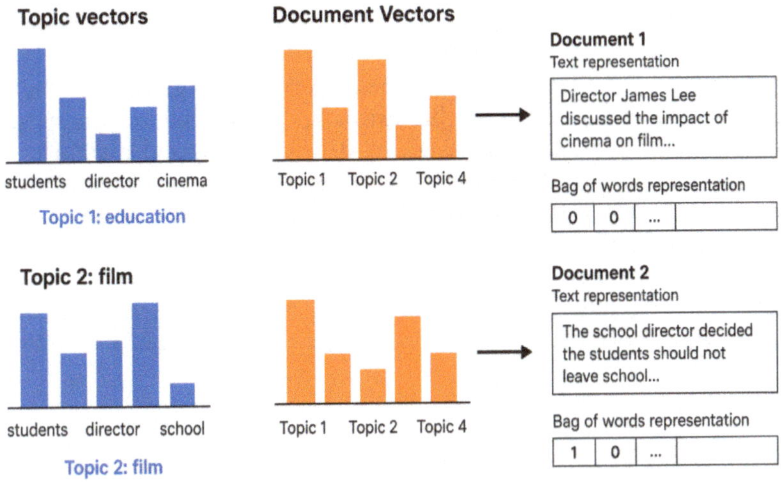

Fig. 19.5 Topic modeling and document representation using topic vectors: This diagram illustrates how topic modeling transforms documents into topic vectors. It shows two example topics: Topic 1 (education) and Topic 2 (film), each represented by bar charts of word relevance such as "students," "director," and "cinema." Document 1 and Document 2 are shown with their associated text content and corresponding topic distributions. Document 1 has a higher weight on Topic 2 (film), while Document 2 aligns more with Topic 1 (education). Both documents are also mapped to sparse bag-of-words representations. This visualization demonstrates how documents are represented in terms of underlying topic distributions for natural language processing tasks like clustering or classification

subject and the associations between each word in the dataset and the various themes. As seen in the figure on the right, you may visualize these associations between documents and topics. For more in-depth details on LDA, refer to the Gensim documentation at at https://radimrehurek.com/gensim/

Bag of Words: Dictionary and Corpus: Start by importing the corpora function from gensim in order to create an LDA model. Use the dictionary function in corpora to create a dictionary from the cleaned text data (such as cleaned emails). The word frequencies for each word in the dataset are included in this dictionary. Remove outlier noise by removing words that appear in less than five emails and keeping only the 50,000 most common words. Then, using the doc2bow function to transform the text data into a bag-of-words format, generate a corpus with word counts for each email (Fig. 19.6).

Running LDA with Gensim: You are prepared to use gensim to execute the LDA model after cleaning the text data, creating the dictionary, and building the corpus. Give the LDA model the corpus and dictionary as input. You'll need to decide on the number of topics in advance, much like with K-means clustering, even if you don't yet know what those topics are. The associated terms for each topic and the topic scores for each email are included in the generated LDA model. To get the top words from the subjects, use the print_topics function. You can print the themes and their top keywords once the model has run to get a rough idea of the findings (Fig. 19.7).

Create Dictionary and Corpus

To execute an LDA topic model, you must first establish your dictionary and corpus, as they are essential inputs for the model. You will continue working with the cleaned text data from previous exercises. This means that "text_clean" is already available for further processing, and you will use it to create both your dictionary and corpus.

Please note that this exercise might take longer to complete than usual.

Instructions:

- To Import the "gensim" package and "corpora" from "gensim" separately.

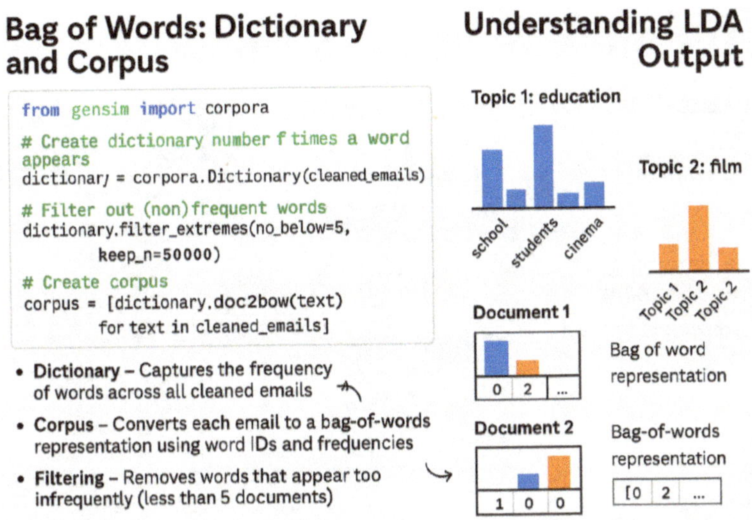

Fig. 19.6 Bag of words construction and topic modeling with LDA: This image illustrates the process of generating a bag-of-words representation and interpreting LDA (Latent Dirichlet Allocation) output. On the left, Python code using the Gensim library shows how to create a dictionary from cleaned email text, filter out infrequent words (less than 5 occurrences), and build a corpus. Below the code, key terms are explained: dictionary captures word frequencies, corpus converts text into bag-of-words format, and filtering removes rare terms. On the right, bar charts show the output of two discovered topics: Topic 1 (education) and Topic 2 (film), with word distributions like "school," "students," and "cinema." Two example documents are visualized using topic vectors and bag-of-words representations, highlighting how documents are mapped to topic probabilities and word frequency vectors for downstream analysis

- Create your dictionary by applying the appropriate function on the cleaned data, "text_clean."
- Construct the corpus by executing "doc2bow" on each piece of text within "text_clean."
- Display your results to examine the structure of the dictionary and corpus (Fig. 19.8).

Three example topics are shown

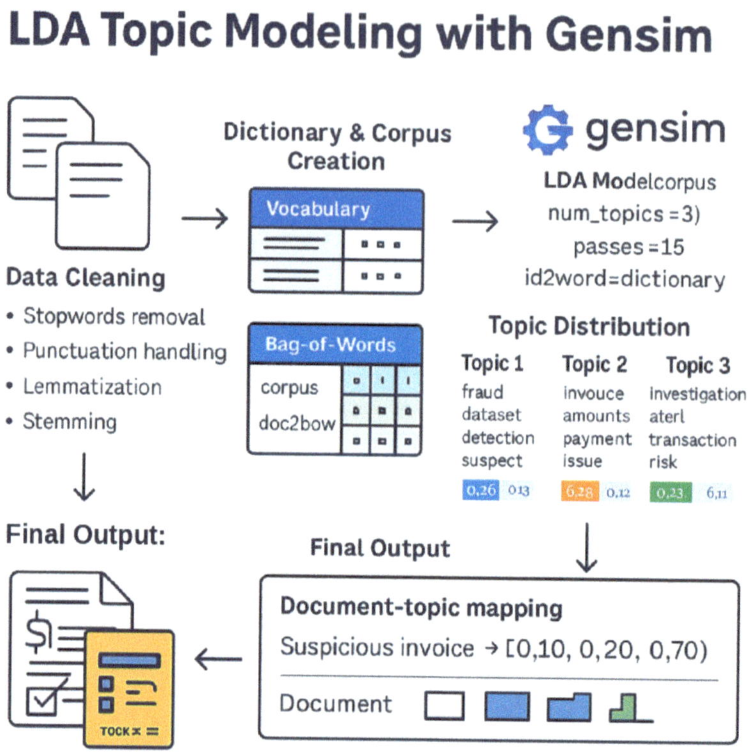

Fig. 19.7 LDA topic modeling workflow using Gensim: This infographic illustrates the complete pipeline for Latent Dirichlet Allocation (LDA) topic modeling using the Gensim library. The process begins with data cleaning steps such as stopwords removal, punctuation handling, lemmatization, and stemming. Cleaned text is then used to create a dictionary (vocabulary) and a bag-of-words corpus using corpora.Dictionary and doc2bow. The LDA model is defined with 3 topics using parameters like num_topics=3 and passes=15. Output includes topic distributions, showing top keywords associated with each topic (e.g., Topic 1: "fraud," "dataset," "detection"), and document-topic mappings, such as a suspicious invoice represented by a vector [0.10, 0.20, 0.70]. The visual highlights how each document is expressed as a mixture of topics, supporting fraud detection via unsupervised learning

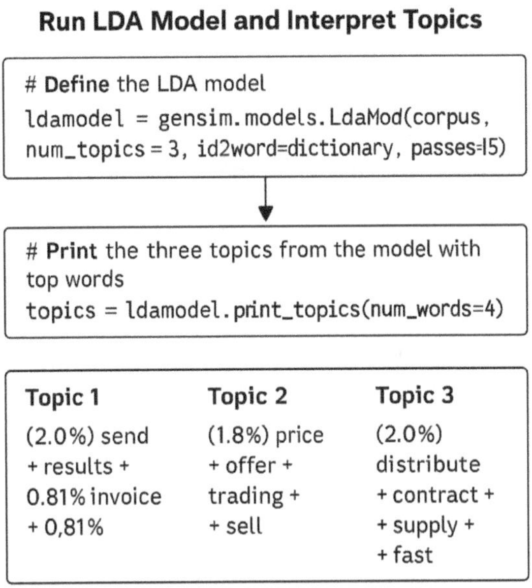

Fig. 19.8 Executing the LDA model and extracting key topics: This diagram outlines the process of running a Latent Dirichlet Allocation (LDA) model using Gensim and interpreting its topics. The first step shows the code to define the LDA model with parameters num_topics=3, id2word=dictionary, and passes=15. The next step demonstrates how to extract and display the top words from each topic using ldamodel.print_topics (num_words=4).

- Topic 1 emphasizes words like "send," "results," and "invoice" (with 2.0% and 0.81% probabilities).
- Topic 2 includes "price," "offer," "trading," and "sell."
- Topic 3 highlights "distribute," "contract," "supply," and "fast."

This visual helps interpret the semantic themes captured by the LDA model from unstructured text data.

Constructing the LDA Model

Now that the dictionary and corpus have been prepared, it is time to build the LDA model. This will help us recognize the subjects covered in the Enron emails. We may quickly explore the themes by printing the words associated with them, and see if any distinct topics emerge. Remember that the topic model calculation could take some time. Let's attempt it right away!

Instructions:

- Create the LDA model from gensim models by providing the corpus and dictionary.
- Extract the 5 topics using the print_topics function on the model results and select the top 5 words.

```
# Define the LDA model with 20 passes
ldamodel = gensim.models.ldamodel.LdaModel(corpus, num_topics=5, id2word=d
ictionary, passes=20)


# Save the topics and top 5 words
topics = ldamodel.print_topics(num_words=5)


# Print the results
for topic in topics:
    print(topic)
```

```
(0, '0.039*"image" + 0.038*"td" + 0.026*"net" + 0.025*"money" + 0.024*"tr"')
(1, '0.012*"message" + 0.010*"original" + 0.008*"enron" + 0.008*"e" + 0.007*"please"')
(2, '0.081*"enron" + 0.023*"hou" + 0.012*"development" + 0.011*"corp" + 0.009*"pm"')
(3, '0.019*"enron" + 0.011*"company" + 0.006*"stock" + 0.005*"energy" + 0.005*"new"')
(4, '0.011*"bakernet" + 0.009*"pm" + 0.007*"mailto" + 0.006*"outage" + 0.006*"e"')
```

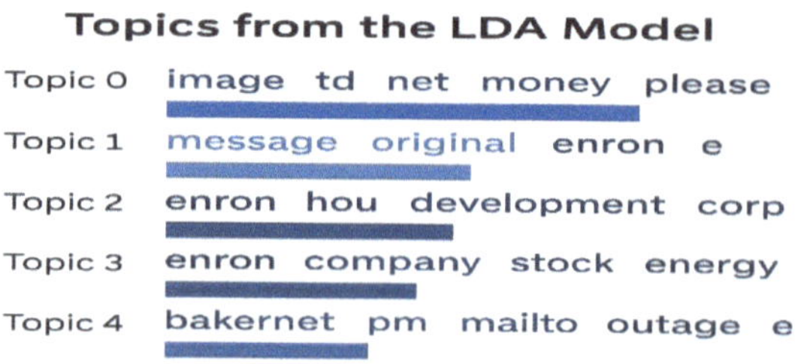

By increasing the number of passes, the model will have more opportunities to refine the topics and the associated words. Keep in mind that increasing the number of passes will also increase the computation time.

Flagging Fraud Using Topics

In this section, we will learn how to utilize the results of our LDA model for detecting fraud.

Applying LDA model results for fraud detection: Without labels, we may start by looking at the prevalence of shady words inside themes and figuring out whether the topics appear to depict dishonest behavior. A suspect subject for the Enron email data may be conversations about stock bonuses, stock sales, the price of Enron's stock, or references to accounting or bad financials. It helps to have some prior knowledge of the fraudulent activity in order to spot suspect themes. If the fraudulent topic is noticeable, you can flag all instances with a high probability for that topic. If we have prior fraud cases, you might run a topic model on just the fraud text as well as the non-fraud text, compare the results, and determine whether the subject frequencies in fraud and non-fraud cases are comparable. Finally, we may see if some themes have higher chance scores for fraud cases. If so, you can run a topic model on fresh data and immediately set a flag for instances that do well on those particular topics (Fig. 19.9).

Visualizing topics for better understanding: It can be difficult to interpret abstract themes, thus we need powerful visualization tools to go further and comprehend the underlying topics. Although it only functions with Jupyter notebooks, the pyLDAvis module for gensim offers a great visualization tool. After building our model, we may produce a thorough visualization using just two lines of code. We can easily display the outcomes by feeding the model, corpus, and lexicon into the pyLDAvis package (Fig. 19.10).

Examining topic differences: The interactive display looks like this, with each bubble on the left side denoting a different subject. The topic is

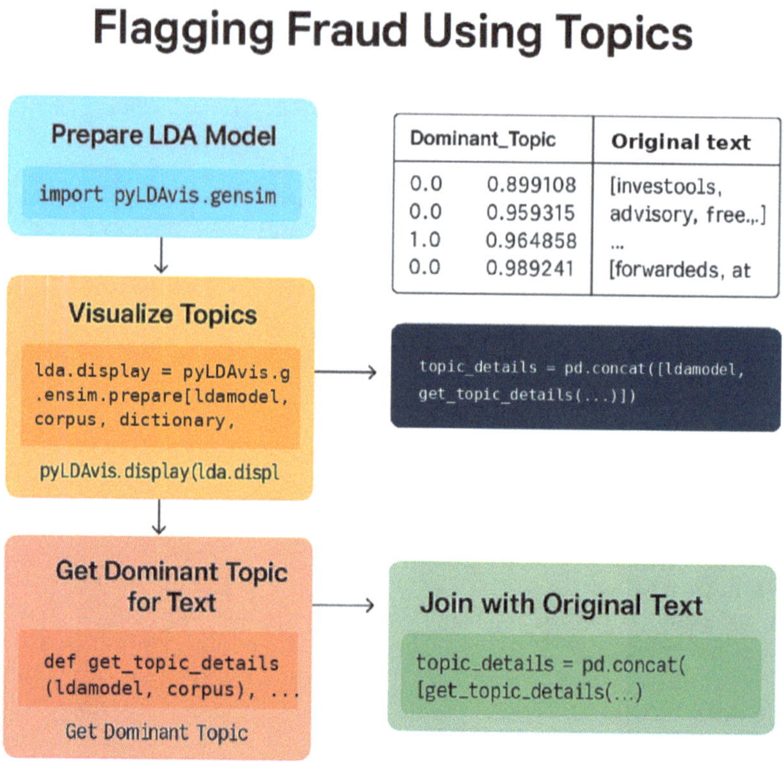

Fig. 19.9 Flagging fraud using topics with LDA and pyLDAvis: This flowchart demonstrates how to flag potential fraud in text data using topic modeling. The process starts with preparing the LDA model using the pyLDAvis.gensim module. Next, topics are visualized using pyLDAvis.display, which reveals dominant topics within the text corpus. A function named get_topic_details extracts the dominant topic for each document. These topics are then joined with the original text to highlight suspicious content based on topic distribution. A sample table shows dominant topic probabilities and corresponding text snippets. This technique helps link topic patterns with potentially fraudulent communications

```
import pyLDAvis.gensim

lda_display = pyLDAvis.gensim.prepare(ldamodel, corpus,
                      dictionary, sort_topics=False)

pyLDAvis.display(lda_display)
```

Fig. 19.10 Flagging fraud using topics with LDA and pyLDAvis: Visualizing LDA topics with pyLDAvis: Python code demonstrating how to visualize topics from a Latent Dirichlet Allocation (LDA) model using the pyLDAvis.gensim module. The script imports the pyLDAvis.gensim library, prepares the LDA visualization with the prepare() function by passing the ldamodel, corpus, and dictionary, and sets sort_topics=False to retain the original topic order. The visualization is then displayed using pyLDAvis.display(lda_display), allowing interactive topic exploration and interpretation in a Jupyter notebook or web-based interface

more well-liked when the bubble is larger. Clicking on a topic in the right panel will display the specifics for that topic along with a list of the key terms that make up that topic. Large, non-overlapping bubbles dispersed over the chart suggest a good topic model. A model with too many subjects will have many overlaps or little bubbles clustered together in one area. In our case, subjects two and three barely overlap, which might indicate that we have too many topics.

Assigning topics to our original data: A useful application of topic modeling is to identify the topic of a given text. Find the topic number in the text that contributes the most percentage-wise to accomplish this. The get_topic_details function compiles this data into a clear table, despite the fact that it is not a simple task.

Assigning topics to your original data:

Combining the original text data with the output of the get_topic_details function is how the function is used. Each row will contain the dominating topic number, the likelihood score for that topic, and the original text data (Figs. 19.11, 19.12 and 19.13).

```
def get_topic_details(ldamodel, corpus):
    topic_details_df = pd.DataFrame()
    for i, row in enumerate(ldamodel[corpus]):
        row = sorted(row, key=lambda x: (x[1]), reverse=True)
        for j, (topic_num, prop_topic) in enumerate(row):
            if j == 0:  # => dominant topic
                wp = ldamodel.show_topic(topic_num)
                topic_details_df = topic_details_df.append(pd.Series([topic_num, prop_topic]),
                                                           ignore_index=True)
    topic_details_df.columns = ['Dominant_Topic', '% Score']
    return topic_details_df
```

Fig. 19.11 Get dominant topic from LDA output: Python code snippet defining the get_topic_details() function to extract the dominant topic and its percentage score from each document in a corpus using a trained LDA model. The function iterates through topic distributions, selects the top topic based on probability, and stores the results in a DataFrame with columns Dominant_Topic and % Score

```
contents = pd.DataFrame({'Original text':text_clean})
topic_details = pd.concat([get_topic_details(ldamodel,
                           corpus), contents], axis=1)
topic_details.head()
```

Fig. 19.12 Join dominant topic with cleaned email content: Python code using pandas to merge topic modeling results with the original cleaned text. A DataFrame named contents holds the preprocessed text, which is concatenated with the dominant topic details returned by the get_topic_details() function to form a unified dataset, stored in topic_details

Dominant_Topic		% Score	Original text
0.0	0.989108	0.989108	[inveštootools, advisory, free,]
0.0	0.959315	0.995315	[forwarraded, richard, b, ...]
1.0	0.964588	0.964588	[hey, wearing, t, target, purple,..]
0.0	0.989241	0.989241	[leslie, milosevic, santa, clara, ...]

Fig. 19.13 Dominant topic assignments per email: A data table displaying the output of an LDA topic modeling process, showing each document's most dominant topic along with its percentage score. The columns include Dominant_Topic, % Score, and the Original text tokens. For example, the first email is strongly associated with Topic 0 with a score of 0.989, and its content includes words like "investools" and "advisory." This helps in identifying which emails are closely linked to particular themes for further fraud analysis

Finding Fraudsters Based on Topic

In this exercise, the focus will be on connecting the topic model results to the initial data. It has been determined that any information related to topic 3 should be flagged. However, accomplishing this task can be quite challenging. The function get_topic_details(), which takes the inputs ldamodel and corpus, will be provided. This function extracts the topic details for each line of text. The results can then be added back to the original data using this function. For a deeper understanding of working with the model results, which is beyond the scope of this chapter, it is highly recommended to consult a relevant article on the subject.

The dictionary and corpus are available, along with the cleaned text data (text_clean) and the model results (ldamodel). The get_topic_details() function has also been defined.

Instructions:

- Print and analyze the get_topic_details() function results by inputting your LDA model results and corpus.
- Concatenate the results of the previously defined function get_topic_details() column by column to the original text data stored in contents and check the results.
- Create a flag using the np.where() function to mark any content with a 1 that has subject 3 as a dominating topic, and a 0 otherwise.

1. Import the panda's library.

```
import pandas as pd
```

2. Define the **get_topic_details_modified** function. This function takes an LDA model and a corpus as input and returns a DataFrame containing dominant topics, topic probabilities, and topic keywords.

```
def get_topic_details_modified(ldamodel, corpus):
    topic_details_df = pd.DataFrame()

    for i, row in enumerate(ldamodel[corpus]):
        row = sorted(row, key=lambda x: (x[1]), reverse=True)
        for j, (topic_num, prop_topic) in enumerate(row):
            if j == 0:  # => dominant topic
                wp = ldamodel.show_topic(topic_num)
                topic_keywords = ", ".join([word for word, prop in wp])
                topic_details_df = pd.concat([topic_details_df, pd.DataFra
me([[int(topic_num), round(prop_topic, 4), topic_keywords]])], ignore_inde
x=True)

    topic_details_df.columns = ['Dominant_Topic', '% Score', 'Topic_Keywor
ds']

    return(topic_details_df)
```

3. Run the **get_topic_details_modified** function and print the results.

```
# Run get_topic_details_modified function and check the results
print(get_topic_details_modified(ldamodel, corpus))
```

4. Calculate the dominant topics using the alternative approach, and add the original text to the topic details in a DataFrame.

```
# Calculate dominant topics using the alternative approach
dominant_topics = []

for doc_topics in ldamodel[corpus]:
    dominant_topic = max(doc_topics, key=lambda x: x[1])
    dominant_topics.append(dominant_topic)

# Create a DataFrame with the dominant topics and probabilities
topic_details = pd.DataFrame(dominant_topics, columns=['Dominant Topic', '
Probability'])

# Add original text to topic details in a DataFrame
contents = pd.DataFrame({'Original text': text_clean})
topic_details = pd.concat([topic_details, contents], axis=1)

print(topic_details.head())
```

5. Add original text to topic details in a dataframe and Create flag for text

Dominant_Topic	% Score	Topic_Keywords	Original text	flag
0	0.446	forwarded, richard, hou, millstonevittie	Forwarded richar...	0
0	0.9754	hey, wearing, target, purple, exactly	Hey wearing target	0
3	0.6979	investor, enron, update, advantees, sduck	Enron update update hich	1
0	0.9364	uly, yesterday, stock, pm, future	Have worth discussing	0

The goal of this code is to use a Latent Dirichlet Allocation (LDA) model to analyze a corpus of text documents (in this example, the Enron email dataset). LDA is a generative probabilistic model that aids in the identification of underlying topics in a corpus. It can be used to uncover the primary themes in a huge collection of documents, allowing for better information interpretation, organization, and retrieval.

The code runs over the input data, trains an LDA model, and then extracts the prominent topics from each document in the dataset. For easy understanding and analysis, the dominating themes, topic probabilities, topic keywords, and original texts are integrated into a DataFrame.

Conclusions:

1. In the Enron email dataset, the LDA model correctly detected topics.
2. The dominating topic, likelihood, and keywords for each document have been extracted and integrated in a DataFrame with the original text.
3. The DataFrame aids comprehension of the dataset's major subjects and can be utilized for further research or visualization.
4. A flag has been added to the DataFrame to identify the papers that are most closely related to subject 3. This might be useful for filtering or selecting specific papers based on their relationship to a specific topic.
5. You can acquire insights into the primary themes and issues mentioned in the Enron email dataset by analyzing the topic keywords and studying the prevalent topics for each document.

Overall, the code demonstrates how LDA can be used to analyze a large collection of text documents, helping you uncover underlying topics and understand the structure of the dataset.

Lab Summary: Enron Email Topic Modeling for Fraud Detection

Lab Title: Enron Fraud Detection Using LDA Topic Modeling.

Objective: Apply Latent Dirichlet Allocation (LDA) to the Enron email dataset to identify potentially fraudulent topics in communications and flag suspicious messages based on their dominant topic.

Key Concepts Applied:

- Text data preprocessing (tokenization, stopword removal, stemming, lemmatization)
- Bag-of-Words model and dictionary/corpus construction
- Gensim's LDA for unsupervised topic modeling
- Fraud risk flagging using dominant topic assignment

Dataset Used: Enron Email Dataset

Source: Kaggle (Dataset ID: wcukierski/enron-email-dataset).

Tools & Technologies:

- Python, NLTK, Gensim, Pandas, NumPy
- Google Colab for live execution
- pyLDAvis for topic visualization

Outcome: By completing this lab, readers will:

- Understand how to preprocess unstructured email data
- Train an LDA model to uncover hidden topics
- Interpret model output and link it to fraud indicators
- Generate a structured fraud flag for further investigation

Notebook File Name: enron_fraud_topic_modeling_lda.ipynb.

Location: This lab is accessible via the companion GitHub repository

Summary

In this chapter, we've taken a deep dive into the techniques and applications of text mining and machine learning for fraud detection. Beginning with the critical process of data preprocessing, we've learned about the important tasks such as tokenization, stopword removal, lemmatization, and stemming. By doing these, we have understood how to convert raw, unstructured text into clean, structured data that's ready for analysis.

Moving forward, we utilized the Enron emails dataset to practically apply these cleaning tasks. By removing stopwords and punctuation, and transforming the text using lemmatization and stemming techniques, we created data that's prepared for advanced processes like topic modeling and fraud detection analysis.

Then, we discovered the power of Latent Dirichlet Allocation (LDA) for identifying potential fraud indications through abstract topics in text data. From data cleaning to dictionary creation, and corpus building, we've gone through the entire process of implementing LDA, and also focused on understanding its outputs and visualizing these associations for better comprehension.

Lastly, we applied the results of our LDA models to detect fraud, examined the prevalence of suspicious words within topics, compared topic frequencies in fraudulent and non-fraudulent cases, and flagged potential fraudulent behavior. The chapter concluded by underlining the importance of visualizing topics for improved interpretation and assigning these topics back to the original data.

Kolibri 360 GmbH
Ferdinand-Jühlke-Straße 7
99095 Erfurt, Deutschland
produktsicherheit@kolibri360.de